GOOGLE CLASSROOM
MADE EASY

Online Learning For Everyone

By James Bernstein

Copyright © 2020 by James Bernstein. All rights reserved.

All rights reserved. This book or any portion thereof
may not be reproduced or used in any manner whatsoever
without the express written permission of the publisher
except for the use of brief quotations in a book review.

Printed in the United States of America

Bernstein, James
Google Classroom Made Easy
Part of the Computers Made Easy series

For more information on reproducing sections of this book or sales of this book,
go to www.madeeasybookseries.com

Contents

Introduction 5

Chapter 1 – What is Google Classroom? 6
    Intended Users 6
    G-suite for Education 7
    Google Classroom Interface 9

Chapter 2 – Accessing Google Classroom 12
    Signing Up for a Google Account 12
    Signing into Google Classroom 13
    Teacher vs. Student Views 15

Chapter 3 – Creating a Class 20
    Adding a Class 20
    Class Settings 23
    Customizing the Look of Your Class 26
    Copying a Class 29
    Adding Students to Your Class 33
    Removing Students and Leaving Classes 39
    Inviting Other Teachers to Your Class 42
    Classroom Guardians 43
    Organizing Your Class Cards 45
    Archiving and Deleting Classes 46

Chapter 4 – Running Your Classes 51
    Stream Tab 51
    Stream Tab Attachments 58
    Adding Assignments, Materials and Quizzes Using the Classwork Tab 62
    Topics 81

    People Tab 86

    To Review and To-do Sections 89

    Class Drive Folder 95

Chapter 5 – Grading 99

    Grades Tab 99

    Grading and Returning Assignments 101

    Grade Categories 110

    Grade Calculation 113

    Giving Feedback Within Assignments 117

    Rubrics 120

Chapter 6 – Google Drive and Google Docs 130

    Google Drive 130

    Google Docs 146

Chapter 7 – Additional Features 226

    Classroom Calendars 226

    Using Google Meet For Your Classes 230

    Transferring Ownership of a Classroom 232

    Reusing Assignments and Posts 236

    Using Google Classroom on Your Mobile Devices 239

    Notification Settings 242

    Originality Reports 245

    Comment Bank 247

    Mote Google Chrome Web Browser Extension 250

What's Next? 255

About the Author 257

Introduction

In today's changing environment we need to be able to adapt and change along with it in order to still be able to get the things done that we need to. This applies to both our work, home and learning environments and if we need to spend all of our time figuring out how to do our work then we will never get any of it done.

When it comes to online learning, it's important to have a system that is easy to use yet can utilize all of the functionality of a real life in person classroom such as assigning tasks to students, having interactive live meetings and testing them on what they have learned. Plus of course you also need a way to grade your students based on their performance.

Google Classroom has been around for some time now and is always being improved upon to make it easier to use and more capable as an online teaching and learning tool. With Classroom you can host various classes with specific students in each class and also have the same students in multiple classes. You can also prepare lesson plans, assignments, quizzes and other material specific to each one of your classes or share the content between some or all of your classes.

The goal of this book is to get you up and running with Google Classroom and show you how to create your classes, add students, distribute your learning materials and grade your student's performance. I will also show you how to join and participate in a class from a student's point of view so you can see how each side works. You will see that there are several ways to accomplish many of the typical tasks you will be performing so you will be able to find the way that works the best for you, or use several methods!

The way you use Google Classroom will most likely vary from the way other teachers or students use it so it is a good idea to know the ins and outs of how it works so you can get your work done no matter where you are within the application. Once you get the hang of Classroom you will find that it's not nearly as difficult as it might appear at the begging. So on that note, let's start the learning process!

Chapter 1 – What is Google Classroom?

If you are reading this book then you are either a Google Classroom user who wants to learn more about the application or a future Classroom user who will soon be using the application to teach their classes or at least supplement their classes with an online curriculum.

Classroom can be used to run an entire class or group of classes for all of you students in one place. It's easy to keep things organized by creating specific classes for all of your subjects and you can even have multiple classes per subject if that is what you normally do in your physical classroom.

Once you have your classrooms created you can add the students you want to attend by inviting them via email or sending them a classroom code that they can enter into their Classroom page and they will then be a student in your class.

As for class materials and assignments you can do things such as upload documents and other files directly to your class so that all of your students can then use for their studies. Or you can take advantage of Google Drive to store all of your class related files and even use Google Docs to create your study and test materials.

If you do need to have some live interactions with your students you can use Google Meet which is an online video conferencing service that allows you to host video calls and share your screen with your participants. It is very similar to the popular Zoom video conferencing service.

Google Classroom does not have to be used exclusively as an online teaching tool but can be used as an additional tool to help your students learn and get their work done while they are at home. For example, you can have your regular in person class and then give your students assignments and quizzes that they can complete online using their Classroom account. The main thing to remember about Google Classroom is that it is not just a teaching tool for teachers but also a learning tool for students.

Intended Users
Even though Google Classroom can be used by anyone with a Google account it is still geared more towards traditional teachers with typical style classrooms that use an assignment and grading type system. You can test your students with

Chapter 1 – What is Google Classroom?

question and answer style quizzes, multiple choice test and also essay style assignments.

The majority of Google Classroom users are in elementary or high school but that doesn't mean that it can't be used for college level courses and of course it is obviously being used at colleges around the world. But once you start using Classroom you will see how it fits better for pre-college level classes.

One great feature of Classroom is the ability to have multiple teachers participate in one class or even have the parents of your students get involved by allowing them to receive information about a student's courses and work once they are invited by the teacher. This way they can keep an eye on their children and see what they are working on and how they are doing.

G-suite for Education

If you are new to Google or don't know about the various types of accounts you can have then it might be a good idea to get yourself familiar with them if you plan on hosting classes using Google Classroom.

Most people who have a Google account have the free type which provides you with many apps and features that you can use to do things such as send emails, plan your activities on your calendar, store your files in the cloud and have access to a multitude of online productivity applications.

If you are interested in learning about all the Google products you can use for free then check out my book titled **Google Apps Made Easy**.
https://www.amazon.com/dp/1798114992

If you need more than what the free Google account has to offer (which most people don't) then you can sign up for a *G-suite* account which offers additional features such as customized email address domain (@customname), additional online storage capabilities, 24/7 phone and email support, extra security features and so on. These accounts are geared more towards businesses and offer a centralized administrator that manages all of the accounts associated within the organization.

Chapter 1 – What is Google Classroom?

Then we have the G-suite for Education account which is used by schools so that they can centralize their teachers and students and offers more control over what their students are allowed to do and how they do it. Plus it allows you to use your school's email address domain for your Classroom accounts rather than having to use a Gmail email address for teachers and students. So if you use **jsmith@school.edu** for your email address and your students use **timmy@school.edu** for their school email addresses you will be able to use these accounts with Google Classroom rather than your **jsmith@gmail.com** address.

G-suite for Education also offers additional features such as enhanced security for your data, advanced Google Meet features, extra reporting capabilities, email summaries of student work for guardians, advanced mobile management and much more.

In order to use G-suite for Education, your school (according to Google) must have a not-for-profit status or be a government recognized, formally accredited educational institution delivering nationally or internationally approved certifications at primary, secondary, or third level. It's very easy to apply for a G-suite for Education account and you can do so online. It should take about a week to get your approval results.

If you are not part of a school system or if your school doesn't meet the requirements above, that doesn't mean you can't use Google Classroom to host your own classes. In fact, you can even mix and match your teacher and student account types as shown in the table below.

Chapter 1 – What is Google Classroom?

If a student uses Classroom with...	And the primary teacher uses Classroom with...	Can the student join the class?
G Suite for Education or Nonprofits	G Suite for Education or Nonprofits	Yes, if class settings in both organizations allow it.
G Suite Basic, Business, or Enterprise	G Suite Basic, Business, or Enterprise	Yes, if class settings in both organizations allow it.
G Suite for Education or Nonprofits	G Suite Basic, Business, or Enterprise, or a personal Google Account	No
G Suite Basic, Business, or Enterprise	G Suite for Education or Nonprofits or a personal Google Account	No
Personal Google Account	G Suite for Education or G Suite Basic, Business, or Enterprise	Yes, if the G Suite organization allows it.
Personal Google Account	Personal Google Account	Yes

Google Classroom Interface

Even though I will be going into detail about all of the components used in Google Classroom, I just wanted to start by giving you a quick bird's eye view of the main interface so you will be a little more familiar with it before you start your own classroom configuration.

If you are a teacher, you will have four main sections for each class, and they are Stream, Classwork, People and Grades and they will be shown above your classroom banner image as seen in figure 1.1.

Chapter 1 – What is Google Classroom?

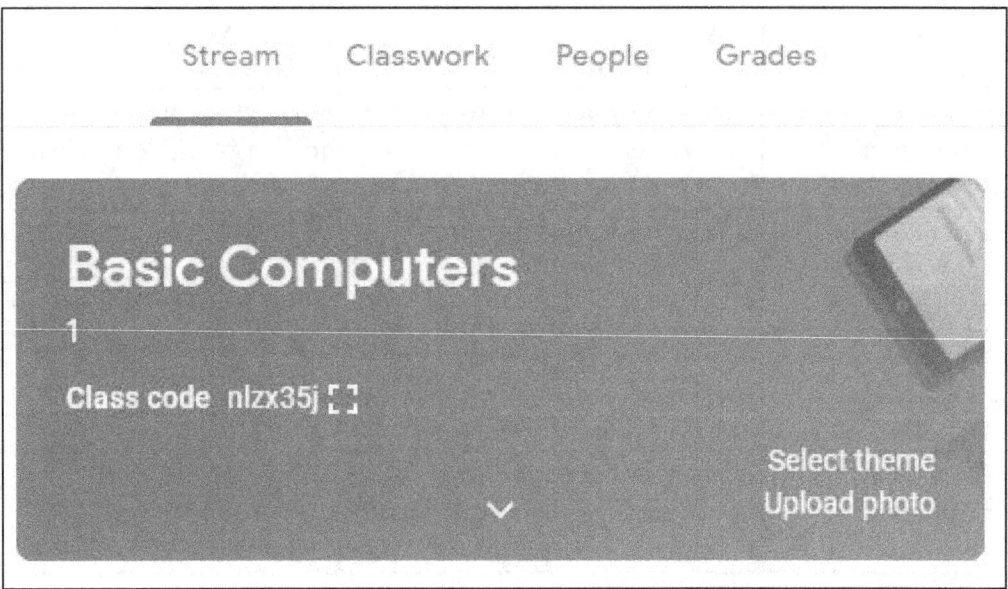

Figure 1.1

Since I will be going over these in detail later I will just give you a quick summary of what each section is for.

- **Stream** – This area contains a feed of activity for your class such as announcements, upcoming assignments and materials such as website links and YouTube videos.
- **Classwork** – Here you will see what assignments and quizzes you have coming up as well as their due dates.

- **People** – The People are is where you can see a listing of all of your students and teachers, and you can do things such as email them or remove them from the class from here.

- **Grades** – Once you start grading assignments and quizzes you can see how your students are doing overall from this section.

Your students will have the Stream, Classwork and People sections within their interface but not the Grades section for obvious reasons!

At the top left of your classroom page you will see three vertical bars next to the class name that you can click on to get more information about that class and other Classroom settings such as your class calendar and items that need to be reviewed such as assignments. You will most likely want to check out the *Settings* section at some point, but I will get to that later.

Chapter 1 – What is Google Classroom?

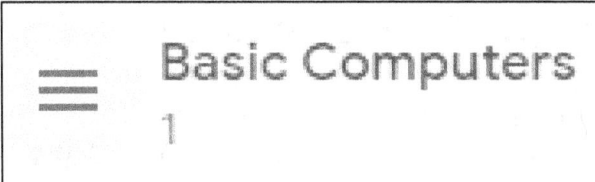

Figure 1.2

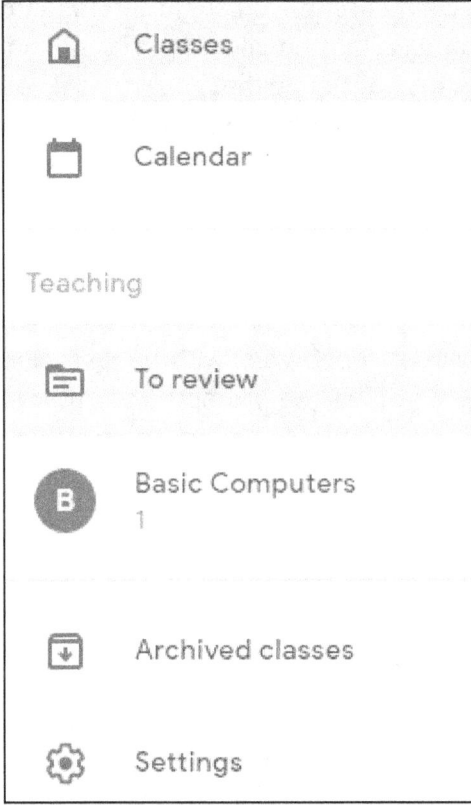

Figure 1.3

As you go through this book you will see that Google Classroom is not very complicated yet there is still a lot to it and there are many ways to customize it to make it work its best for you.

Chapter 2 – Accessing Google Classroom

Getting to your Google Classroom is as simple as navigating to the Classroom website and signing in with the appropriate account. Keep in mind that the account you need to sign in with will be the one that you plan to use Classroom with and is the one that has been configured for you by your G-suite administrator assuming you are a G-suite or G-suite for Education user. If you are just a standard Google user with a free account then you can use that email address to sign in, but you will not have all of the Classroom features available that you would if you were using an Education account. So if you are not one of the administrators of your company or school then you will need to reach out to them to get your account setup for Google Classroom.

Signing Up for a Google Account
If you are planning on just using a free account to login and don't have one then it's very easy to sign up for one. To begin, simply open your web browser and navigate to **https://accounts.google.com/** and you will be prompted to enter in your account details such as name, desired email address and a password to go along with your new account.

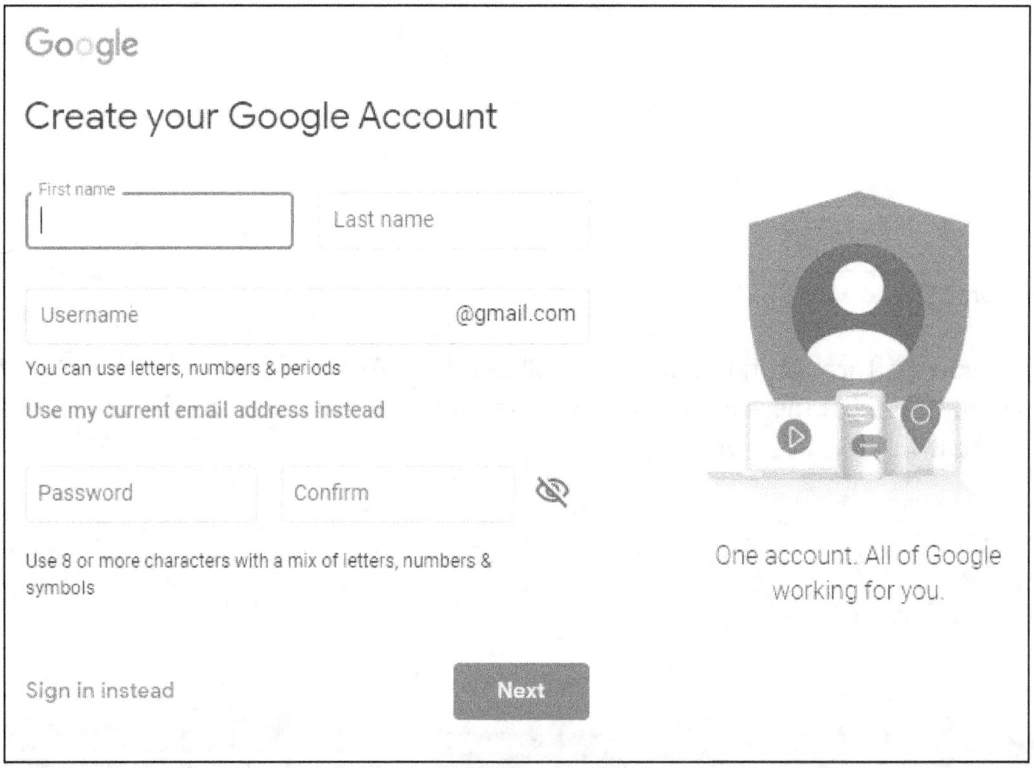

Figure 2.1

Chapter 2 – Accessing Google Classroom

Simply enter your first and last name and choose a username, which will also be used for your Gmail email account ending in *@gmail.com*. If the username has already been taken, then you will be prompted to enter a new one. Notice that there is an option that says *Use my current email address instead*. This can be used if you do not want a Gmail email address, but still want to create a Google account with your current email address.

Then you will need to come up with a password that has 8 or more characters and uses letters, numbers, and symbols (such as **!** or **#** for example) and click on *Next*.

After that, you will need to enter your phone number so Google can verify it is really you. It will send you a six digit number via text message that you will have to enter in the next step. Doing this will also tie your phone number to your Google account, which comes in handy for things like password recovery if you forget your password. If you don't have a smartphone you can have Google call you with the code instead of texting it.

Next, you enter a recovery email address (which can also be used for password recovery), as well as your birth date information. The birth date information is used because some Google services have age requirements. The gender information it asks for is optional and is not shown to other Google users. You can also edit your Google account later if you wish to change or add anything.

If you *don't* want your number to be used at all, simply click on *Skip,* and you will be brought to the *Privacy and Terms* agreement, which you can read if you like. To continue, you will need to click on the *I agree* button. Finally, after clicking on *I agree,* your account will be created, and you will be logged in automatically. If you are on the Google home page, then you will see your first initial up in the right hand corner. You can go into your settings and edit your profile and add a picture if you like.

Signing into Google Classroom
Whether you have a G-suite account or a free Google account, the process for signing into your Classroom account will be the same. If you go to the Google home page and are signed in to your Google account, you will see many of your Google apps listed when you click on the 6 squares (referred to as the waffle) next to your profile letter or picture as seen in figure 2.2. If you don't see the letter of your first name or profile picture but rather see a button that says Sign in, that means you are not logged into your Google account.

Chapter 2 – Accessing Google Classroom

If you don't see the icon for Classroom then you will have to scroll down in the list to find it and then you can click on it from there.

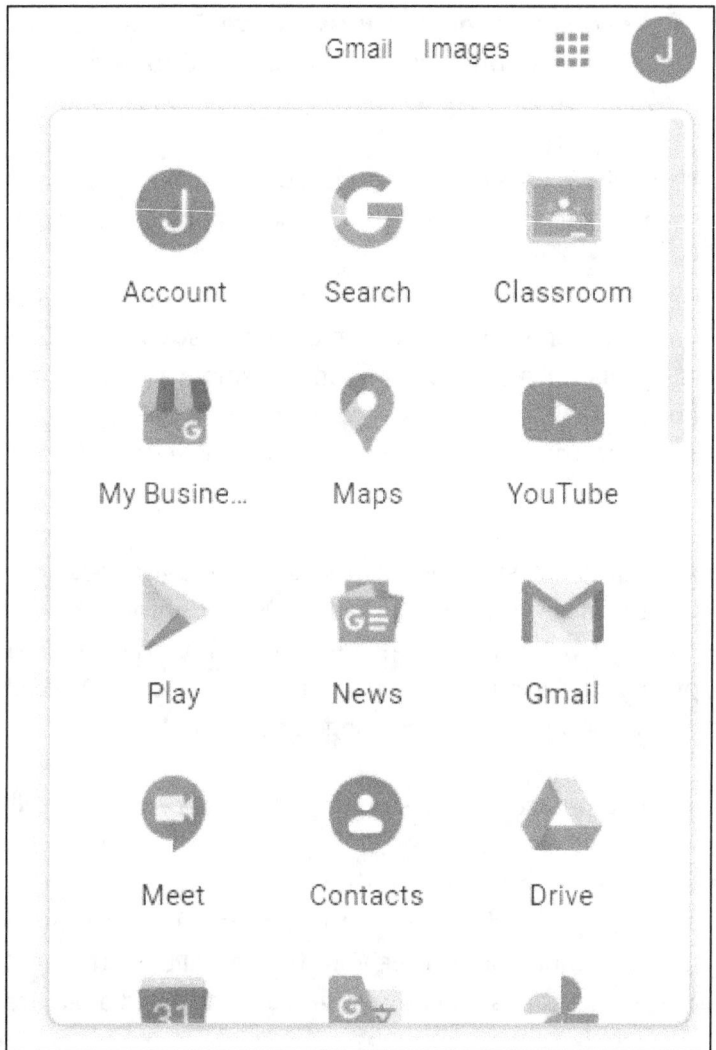

Figure 2.2

 One you are logged into your Google account you can click on the waffle icons and drag and drop any of them to place them in any order you like. Then every time you log in, they will remain in the same order… or at least the should!

14

Chapter 2 – Accessing Google Classroom

Another way to get to your Classroom account is to type in **classroom.google.com** into your web browser and if you are logged into your Google account it will bring you right into the Classroom interface. You can also bookmark the Classroom site for easy access.

Teacher vs. Student Views
One great thing about Google Classroom is that the teacher and student interface looks very similar making it easy for you to know what your students are looking at and it also allows you to help them navigate their classes easier since your screen will look the same as theirs.

Of course you as a teacher will have some items on your screen that your students will not. Figure 2.3 shows the *Stream* tab in the teacher's view of a class while figure 2.4 shows the same class but from the student's view. The items that are different in the teacher view are highlighted with boxes around them and include the settings gear icon, the Grades tab, the class code and the option to upload a class theme or change the photo. All of these items will be discussed in more detail later in the book.

Chapter 2 – Accessing Google Classroom

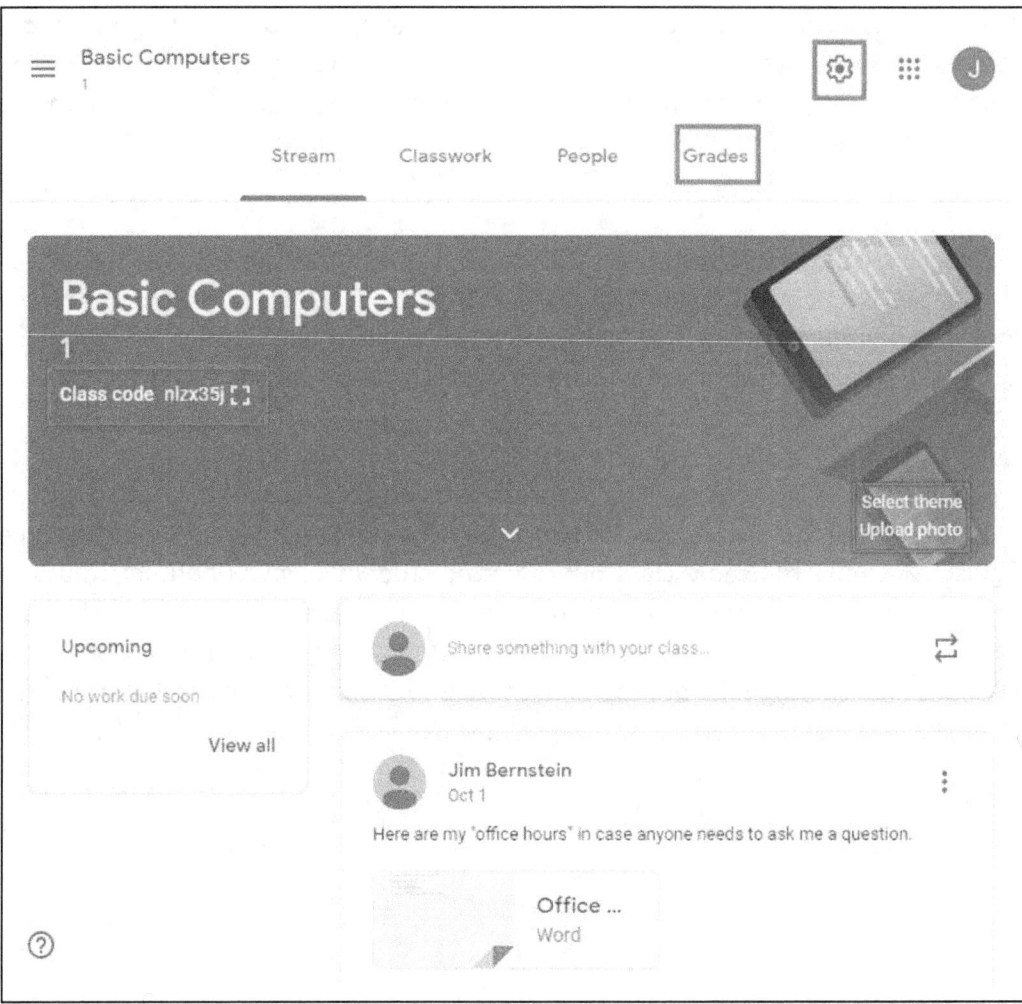
Figure 2.3

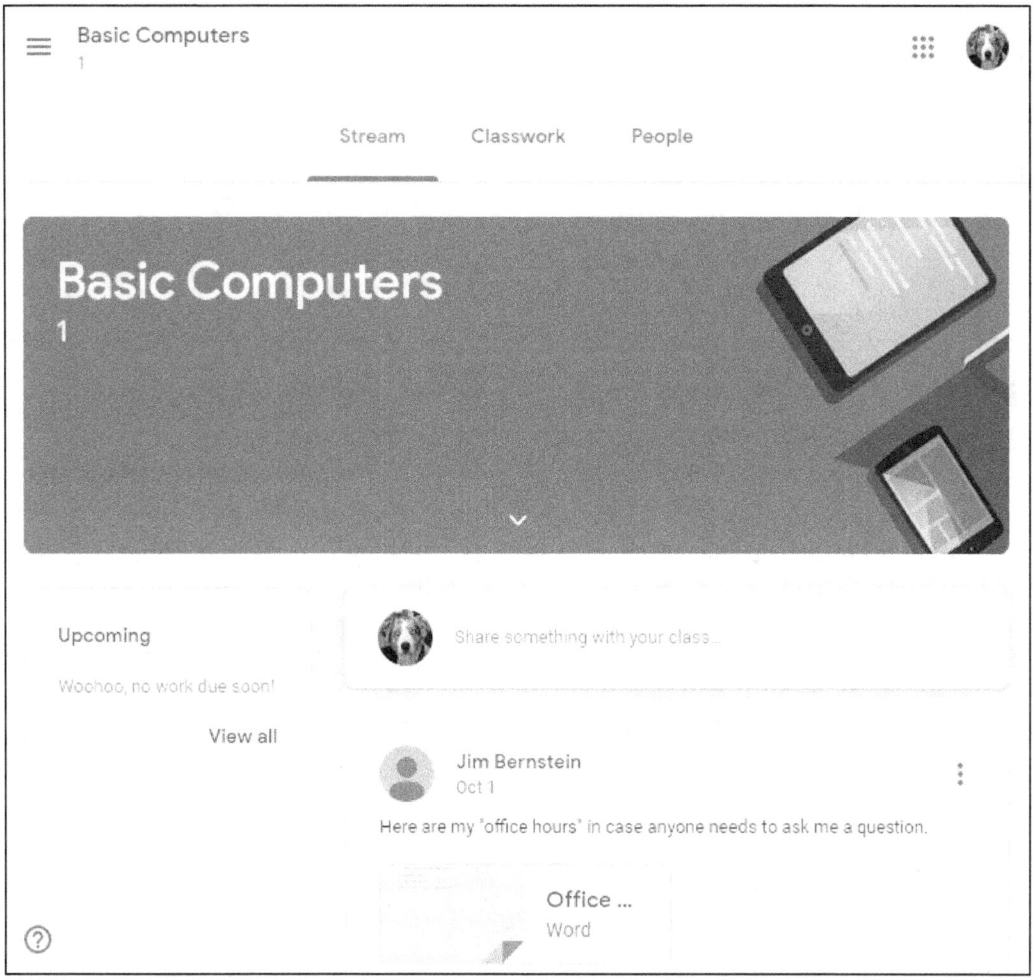

Chapter 2 – Accessing Google Classroom

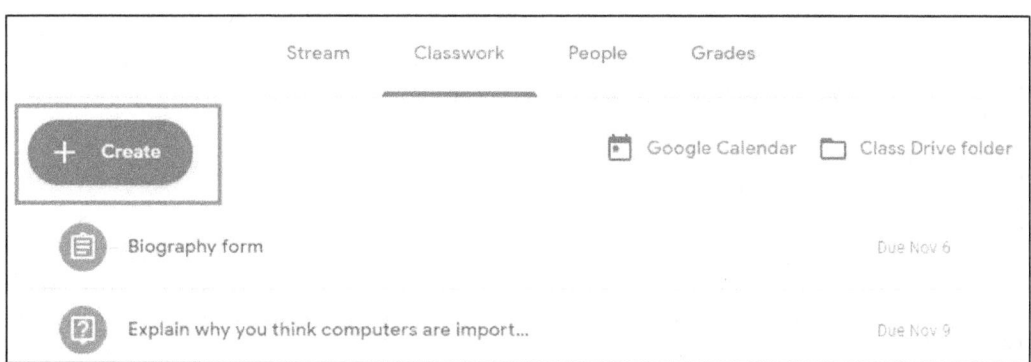

Figure 2.4

The only real difference in the *Classwork* tab is that the teacher will have a *Create* button and will see all of the assignments and the students will have a *View your work* link and only see the work that has been assigned to them.

Figure 2.5

Chapter 2 – Accessing Google Classroom

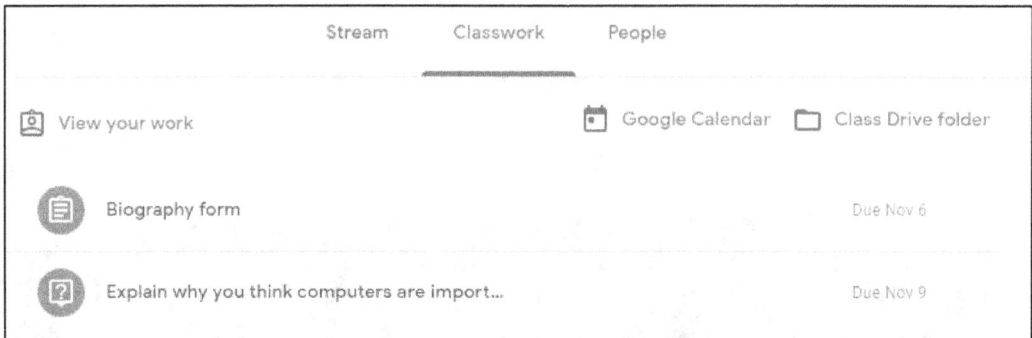

Figure 2.6

As for the *People* tab, the teacher view will show all of the teachers and all of the students enrolled in that class as well as an *Actions* dropdown where they can do things such as email, mute or remove students. They will also have the *add teachers* and *add students' button* as well as the email student choice they have by clicking on the three vertical dots next to their name.

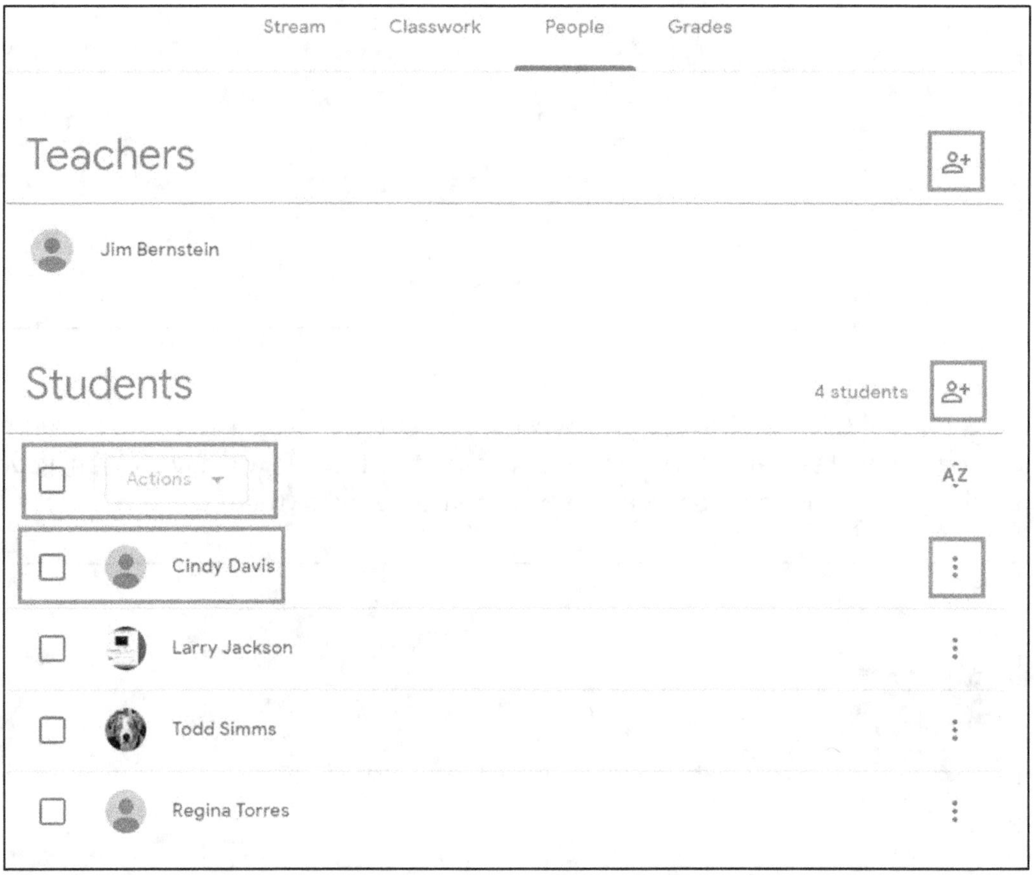

Figure 2.7

Chapter 2 – Accessing Google Classroom

The students will see the teacher and other students enrolled in the class, but the student will not see their own name listed here.

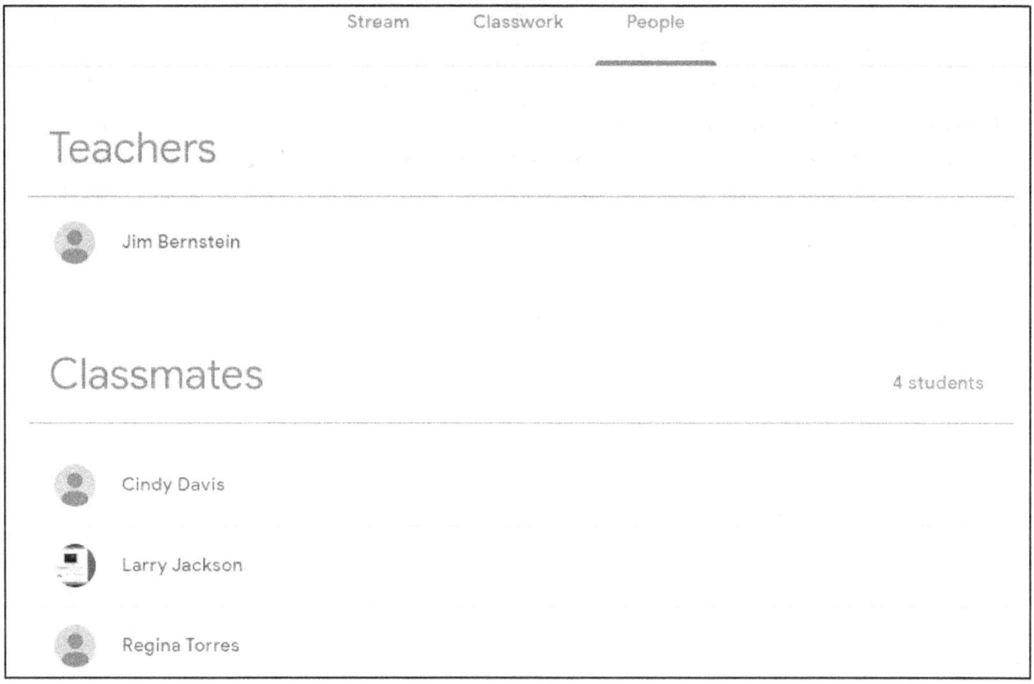

| Stream | Classwork | People |

Teachers

- Jim Bernstein

Classmates   4 students

- Cindy Davis
- Larry Jackson
- Regina Torres

Figure 2.8

I recommend you create a student account for your classes so you can see what your students will see to make sure everything looks correct to ensure there is no confusion with what your students see. Depending on how your Classroom environment is configured, you might have to contact your school administrator to have another account set up for you as a student to do this.

Chapter 3 – Creating a Class

Now that you have your Google Classroom account setup, it's time to start adding your classes so your students will have something to join so they can start working on their assignments. I recommend planning out your classes in advance before creating them in Classroom so you have a game plan and don't end up with classes you don't need or a bunch of changes you will need to make to get things configured correctly.

Adding a Class
Once you know your class subjects you can start adding your classes\classrooms and get them configured the way you like before inviting your students to join your classes. Just make sure you give yourself enough time to get them set up, so you aren't scrambling at the last minute trying to get things done in time for when school officially starts.

When you first log into Classroom you will essentially have a blank page and you will need to click on the + next to your profile icon and choose *Create class* to add a new class.

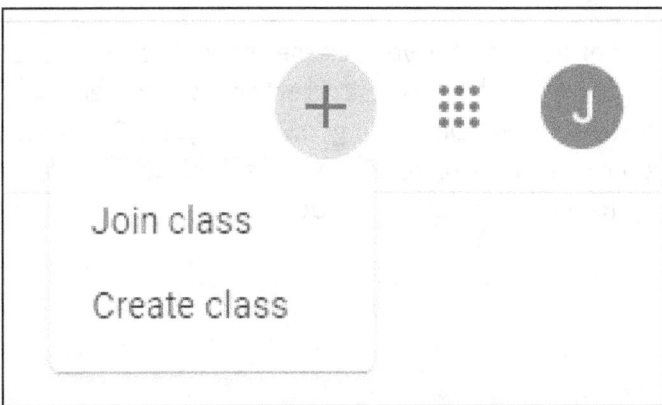

Figure 3.1

Next you will need to enter in the class name and if you like you can enter in the information for the other areas as well (figure 3.2). The *Section* area is where you can add a number or name to break up different levels of the same class. The *Subject* area is where you will enter the area of study related to the class. There are some built in subjects that will appear as you start typing if you would like to choose one of them. Finally you can use the *Room* area to enter the location of

Chapter 3 – Creating a Class

the class. After you have entered in all of this information simply click on the *Create* button to have your class created.

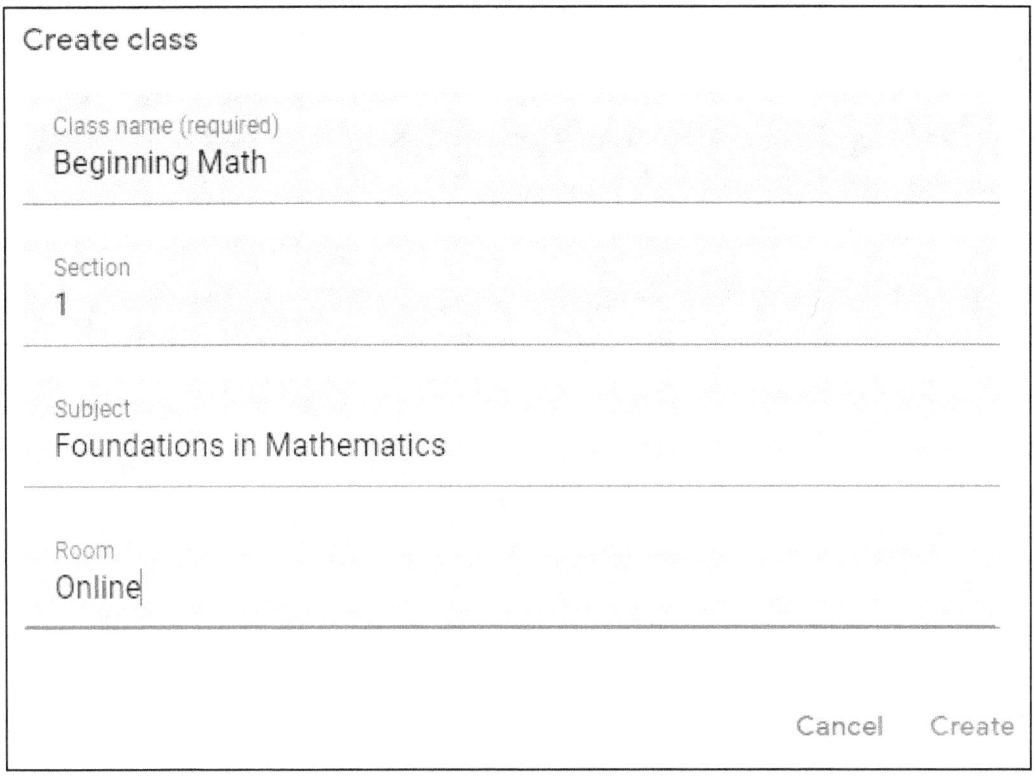

Create class

Class name (required)
Beginning Math

Section
1

Subject
Foundations in Mathematics

Room
Online

Cancel   Create

Figure 3.2

You will then be brought into your new classroom where you can then start adding classwork, customizing the look of your class and eventually adding students.

Chapter 3 – Creating a Class

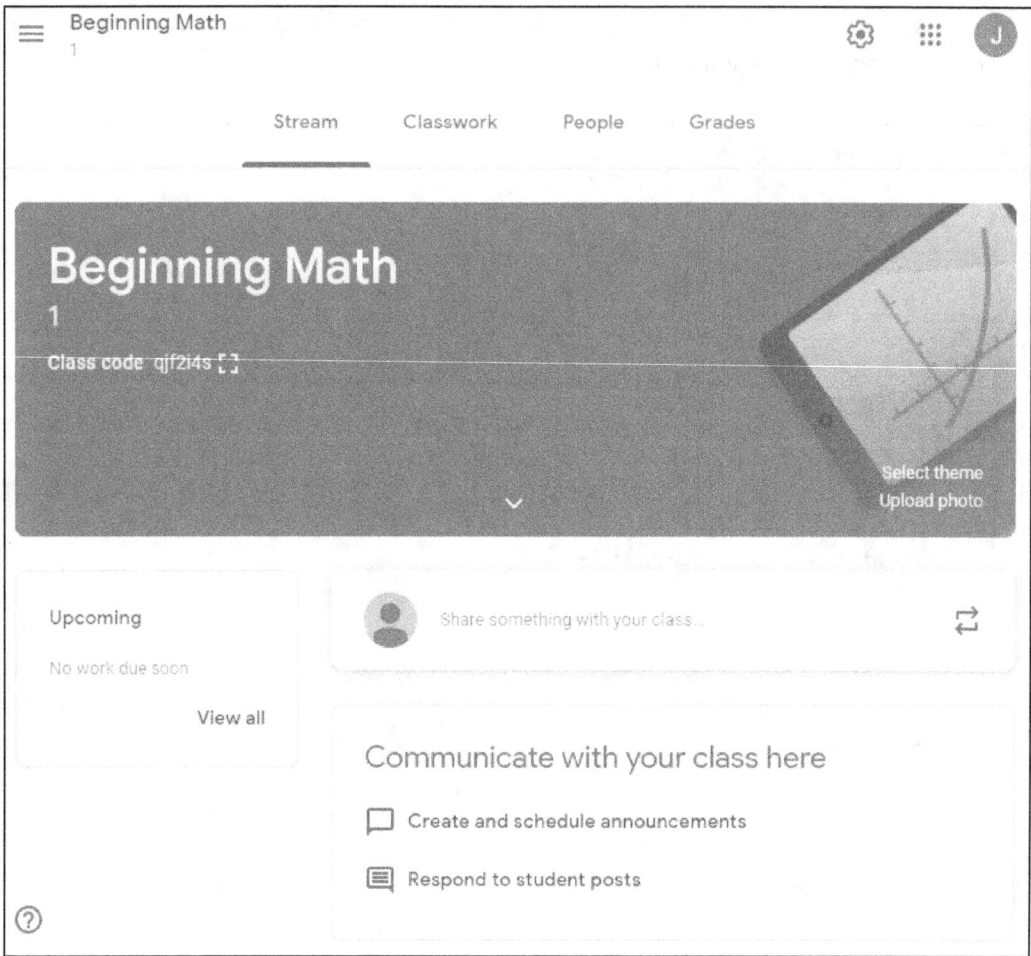

Figure 3.3

If you click on the three horizontal bars in the upper left hand corner and then on *Classes* you will be brought back to your main Classroom screen where you will then see all of your configured classrooms.

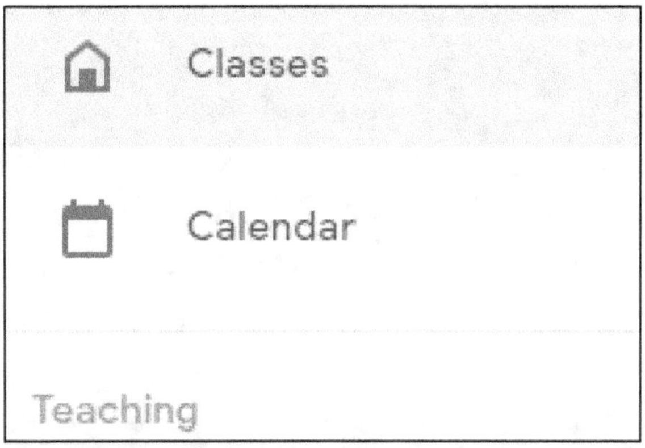

Figure 3.4

Chapter 3 – Creating a Class

Now you will see what are known as class *Cards* which is just a name for the classroom icons you will have for each class. You can then click on any of these cards to go into that specific classroom. Figure 3.5 shows that I only have two class cards meaning I only have two classrooms configured.

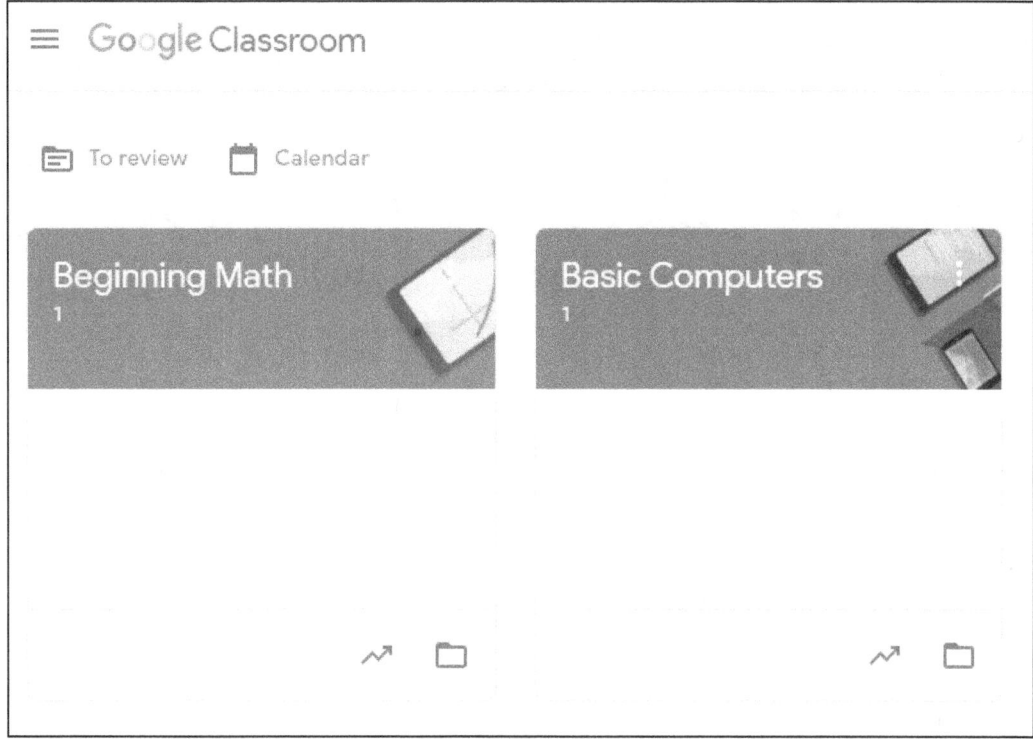

Figure 3.5

Class Settings
Once you get your initial class configured you will most likely want to go into the settings for that class and do some tweaking to fine tune the way it's configured. To get to the settings for a particular class you will need to be in that class and then click on the gear icon located at the top right of the screen by your profile image.

The class settings are broken down into three sections that you can then configure to your liking.

Class Details
This area shows pretty much the same settings as when you first created the class such as the name subject but also has a section to add a class description.

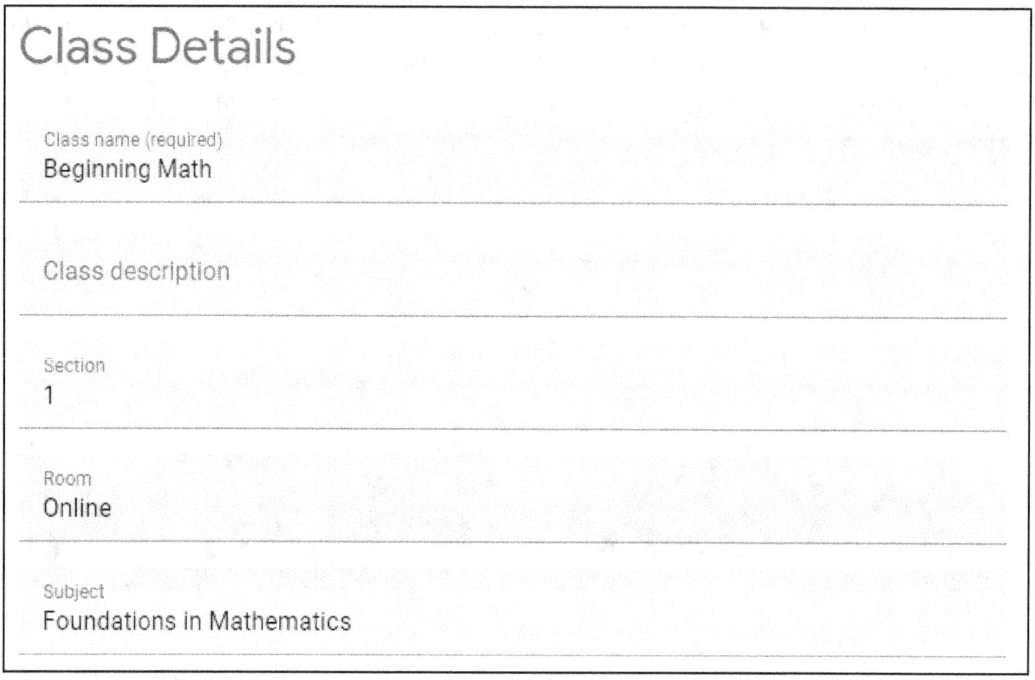

Chapter 3 – Creating a Class

> **Class Details**
>
> Class name (required)
> Beginning Math
>
> Class description
>
> Section
> 1
>
> Room
> Online
>
> Subject
> Foundations in Mathematics

Figure 3.6

General
Here is where you can manage your invite codes (discussed later in this chapter) and also decide what is shown on your class stream in regards to comments and notifications. And if you would like your deleted items to be shown for other teachers, you can enable this here.

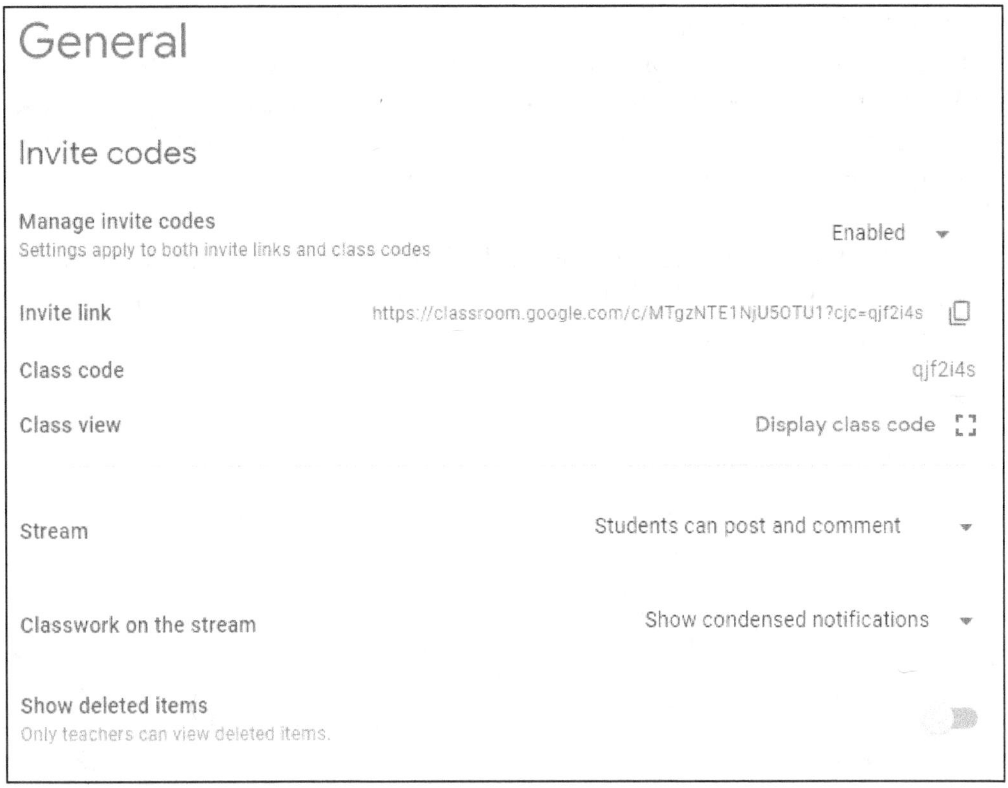

Chapter 3 – Creating a Class

General

Invite codes

Manage invite codes Settings apply to both invite links and class codes	Enabled ▼
Invite link	https://classroom.google.com/c/MTgzNTE1NjU5OTU1?cjc=qjf2i4s
Class code	qjf2i4s
Class view	Display class code
Stream	Students can post and comment ▼
Classwork on the stream	Show condensed notifications ▼
Show deleted items Only teachers can view deleted items.	

Figure 3.7

Grading
Since there is a good chance you will grade some of your classes differently than others, you can come to this section to change the overall grade calculation, add grade categories and also determine whether or not your students will see their overall grade. Grades will be discussed in more detail in Chapter 5.

Grading

Grade calculation

Overall grade calculation Choose a grading system. Learn more	No overall grade ▼
Show overall grade to students	

Grade categories

Add grade category

Figure 3.8

Chapter 3 – Creating a Class

Customizing the Look of Your Class
When you create a class, Google Classroom will add a background image for that class based on the subject matter of that class. But there is a chance that the image won't quite fit the look you are going for and you are able to change this image if you want to find something else that has a better fit.

There are two ways to go about changing the look of your class. The first way is to change the theme of the class by clicking on *Select theme* from the lower right hand corner of the class image.

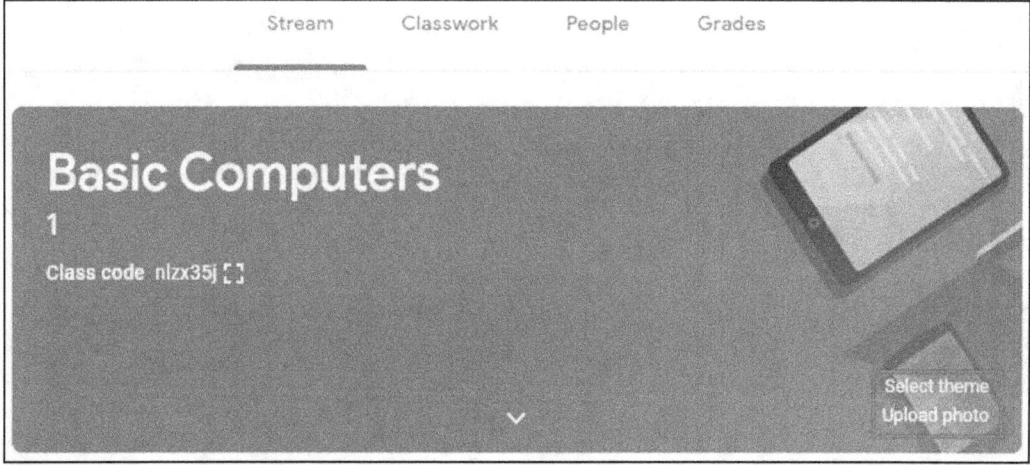
Figure 3.9

This will allow you to choose one of the built in themes based on the categories that Classroom provides as shown in figure 3.10.

Chapter 3 – Creating a Class

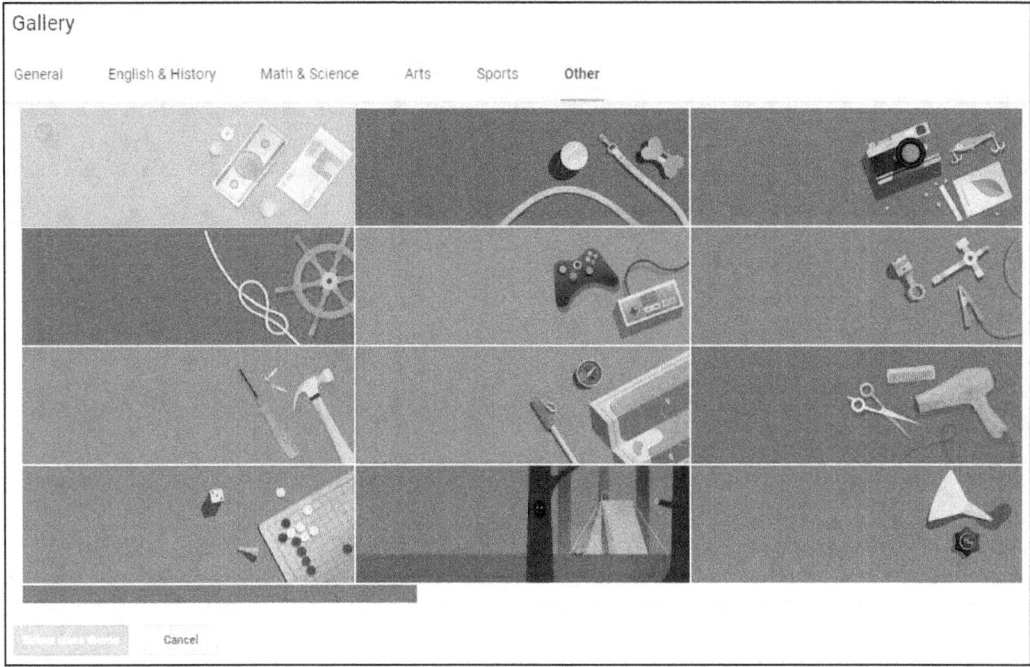

Figure 3.10

If you can't find a theme that works for you then you also have the ability to upload your own photo by clicking on Upload photo and then browsing your computer for a photo that you have saved on your drive. Keep in mind that this photo needs to be at least 800x200 pixels in size otherwise you won't be able to use it.

Once you upload your photo you will need to crop it to fit the dimensions of the class card, so it fits properly as seen in figure 3.11.

Chapter 3 – Creating a Class

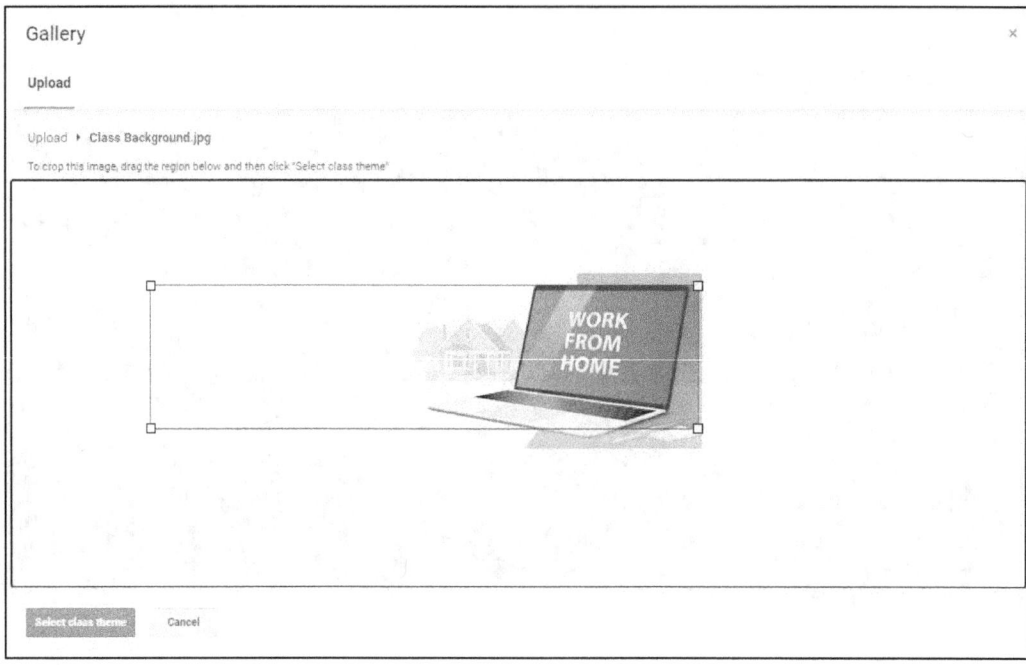

Figure 3.11

Once you have everything looking the way you like you can click on the *Select class theme* button to have your picture applied to your class card. One thing you will notice is that the image will have a tint applied to it which will make it a little darker than the original so it's a good idea to use a picture with bright colors, so it doesn't get washed out.

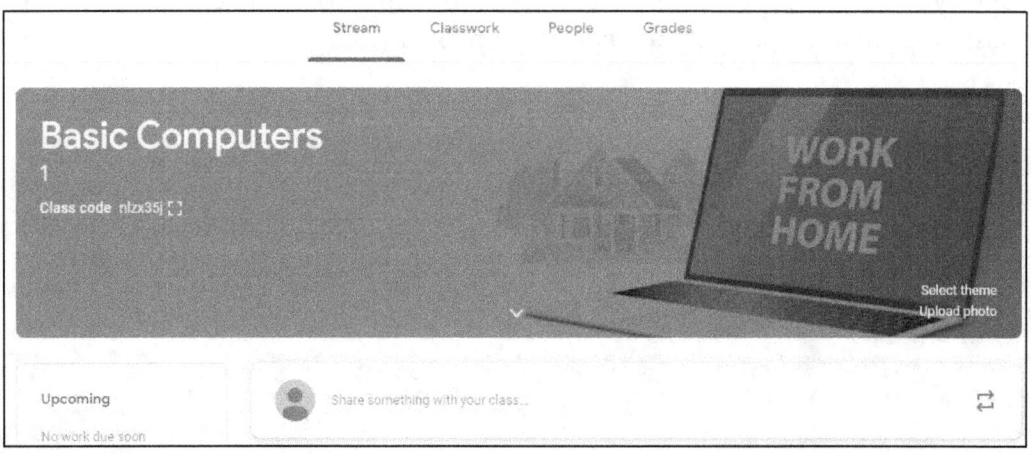

Figure 3.12

Copying a Class

If you plan on having a lot of similar classes or maybe even the same class with different students then it might be a good idea to make copies of your classes rather than recreate them each time. Then after you copy the class you can tweak it with any changes that need to be made.

When you copy a class, any assignments and questions you have created will be saved as drafts which you can then make active if you want to use them with your new class. Other things that will get copied with your class include:

- Title
- Section
- Description
- Course subject
- Topics
- Classwork
- Your grading system

Items that won't get copied with your class include:

- Teacher announcements
- Deleted classwork items
- Students and co-teachers
- Student posts
- Attachments that you don't have permission to copy
- Google Sites files
- Custom class theme images

To copy a class all you need to do is go to your list of classes and click the three vertical dots on the class card and choose the Copy option as seen in figure 3.13.

Chapter 3 – Creating a Class

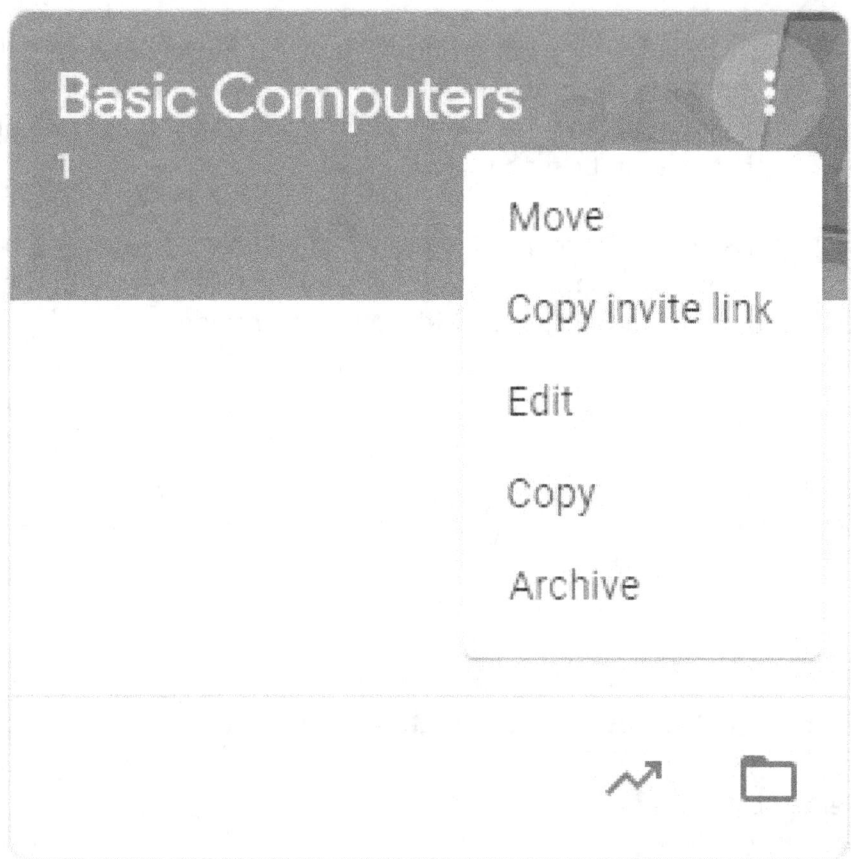

Figure 3.13

The name and detail information will automatically be taken from your existing class and you can edit them or leave it as is. The room information will not be copied over though.

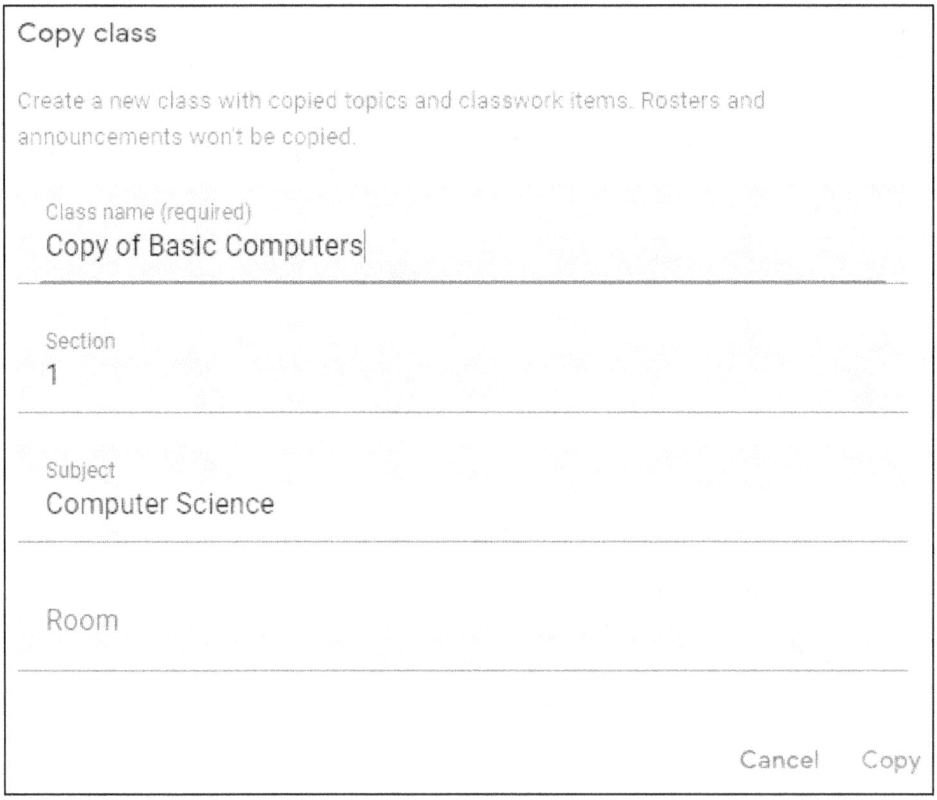

Chapter 3 – Creating a Class

![Copy class dialog]

Copy class

Create a new class with copied topics and classwork items. Rosters and announcements won't be copied.

Class name (required)
Copy of Basic Computers

Section
1

Subject
Computer Science

Room

Cancel   Copy

Figure 3.14

I will leave things as is and click on *Copy* to start the copy process which might take a few minutes depending on how much information you have in your class. Then when I go back to my class list I will see my newly copied class along with my others.

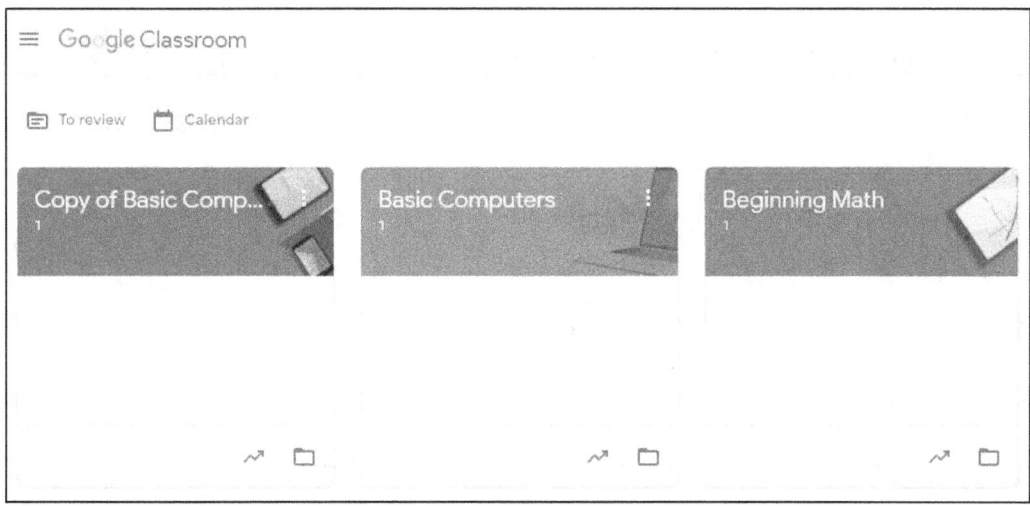

Figure 3.15

31

Chapter 3 – Creating a Class

When I go into the *Classwork* section of my copied class I can see that my assignments are in *draft* status and if I click on the three vertical dots that will appear when I click on draft and then click on Edit I will be able to take this assignment out of draft status by clicking on the *Assign* button as seen in figure 3.17.

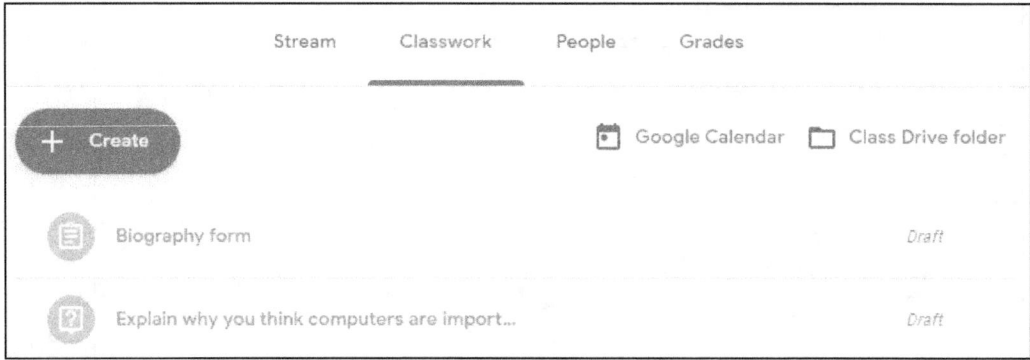

Figure 3.16

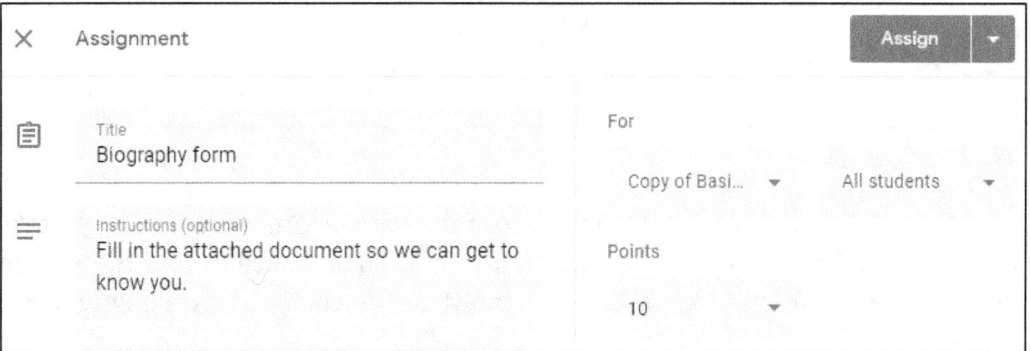

Figure 3.17

As you can see, this assignment is now live and not in draft status anymore.

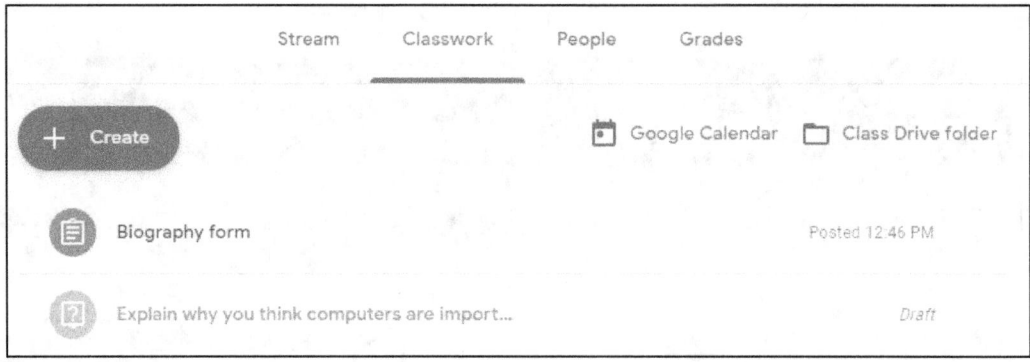

Figure 3.18

32

Chapter 3 – Creating a Class

Remember that when you copy a class you will need to add students to your new class since the copy process will not copy them over. You can add students to a copied class the same way you would add them to a new class.

Adding Students to Your Class

Now that you have a class ready to go, it's time to add some students otherwise you will have a pretty uneventful teaching experience! There are several ways to add or invite students to your class and the way you will do this is up to you, or it's possible your school may have a required procedure that you will need to follow to do this. Regardless, I will show you the methods you can take to invite students to your class.

When you go to the People tab in your new class you will see that there are no students enrolled in the class. You can then click on the *Invite* button or click on the + icon to the right of the word Students to start the process and either one of these choices will take you to the same place as seen in figure 3.20.

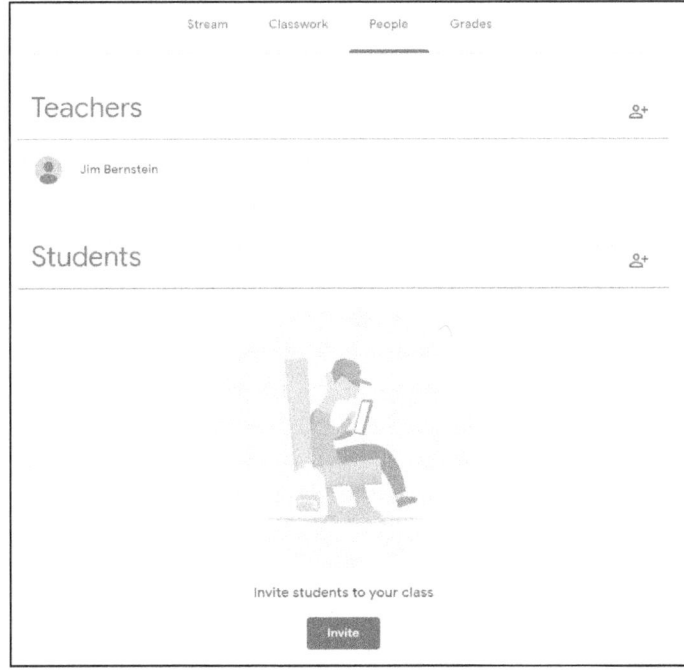

Figure 3.19

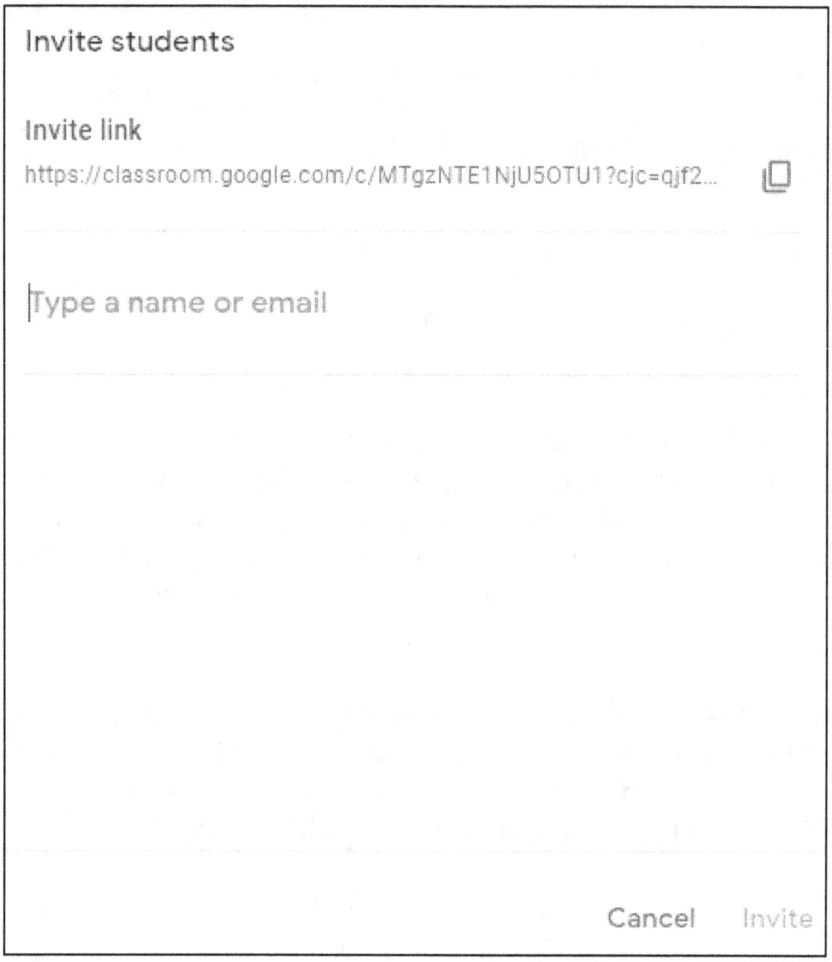

Chapter 3 – Creating a Class

Invite students
Invite link
https://classroom.google.com/c/MTgzNTE1NjU5OTU1?cjc=qjf2...
Type a name or email
Cancel   Invite

Figure 3.20

If you were to type in the student's email address or name (for school accounts) and then click on Invite it would send them an email invitation that would look similar to figure 3.21. From there the student can click on the Join button to join your class.

Chapter 3 – Creating a Class

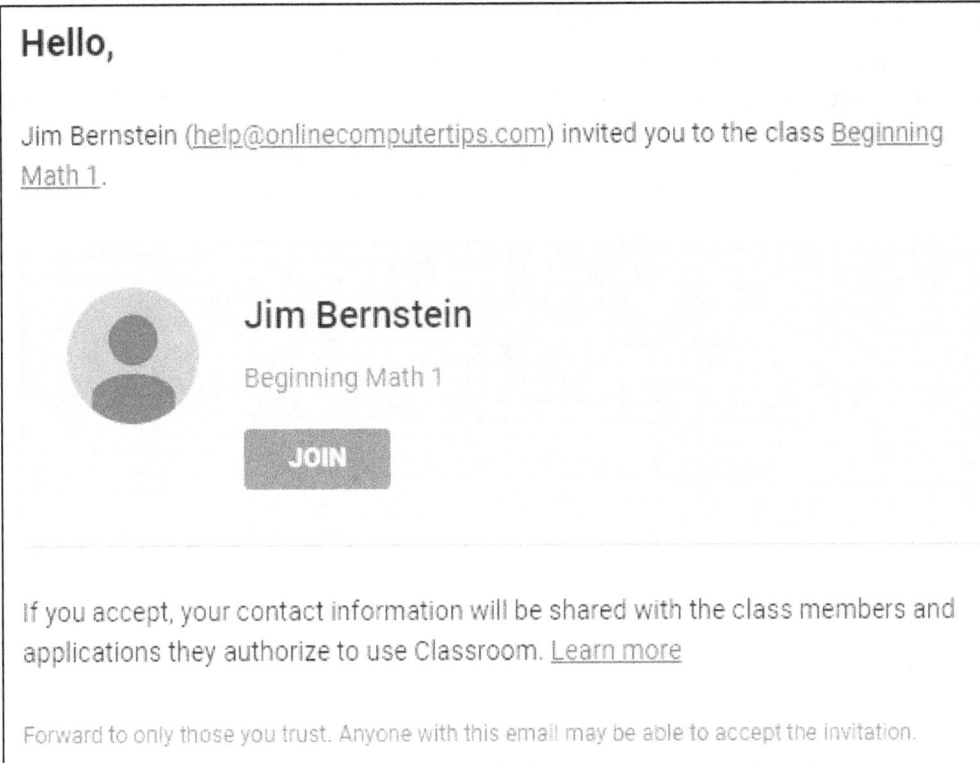

Figure 3.21

Once you invite a student this way you will see that they now show up in your student list with a status of invited.

Figure 3.22

Chapter 3 – Creating a Class

You can also copy the invite link as shown in figure 3.20 and then paste it into an email or instant message etc. and when the student clicks on the link they will be taken to a page where they will have the option to join your class by clicking on the *Join class* button.

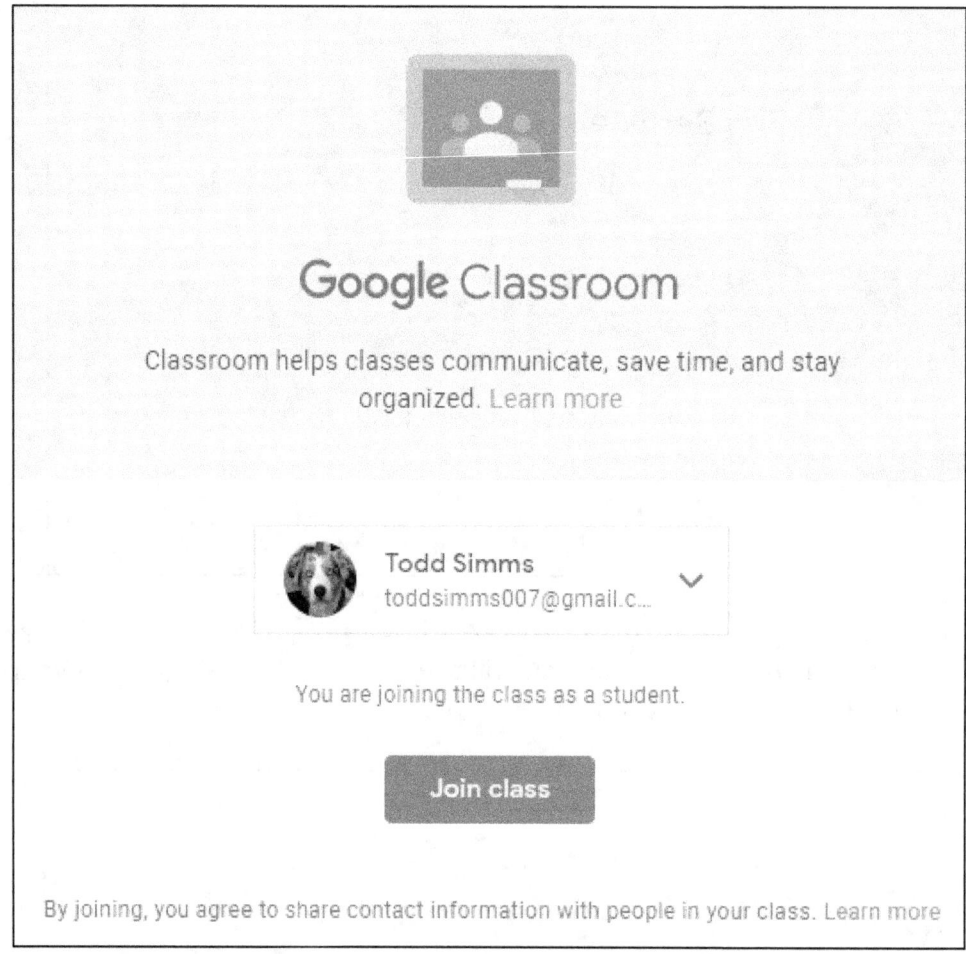

Figure 3.23

Another common way to invite students to your class is to send them the class code which can be found on the class card in your main classroom area (figure 3.24). If you click on the class code it will then be enlarged, making it easier to copy (and read) and then you can send this code to your students via email etc.

Chapter 3 – Creating a Class

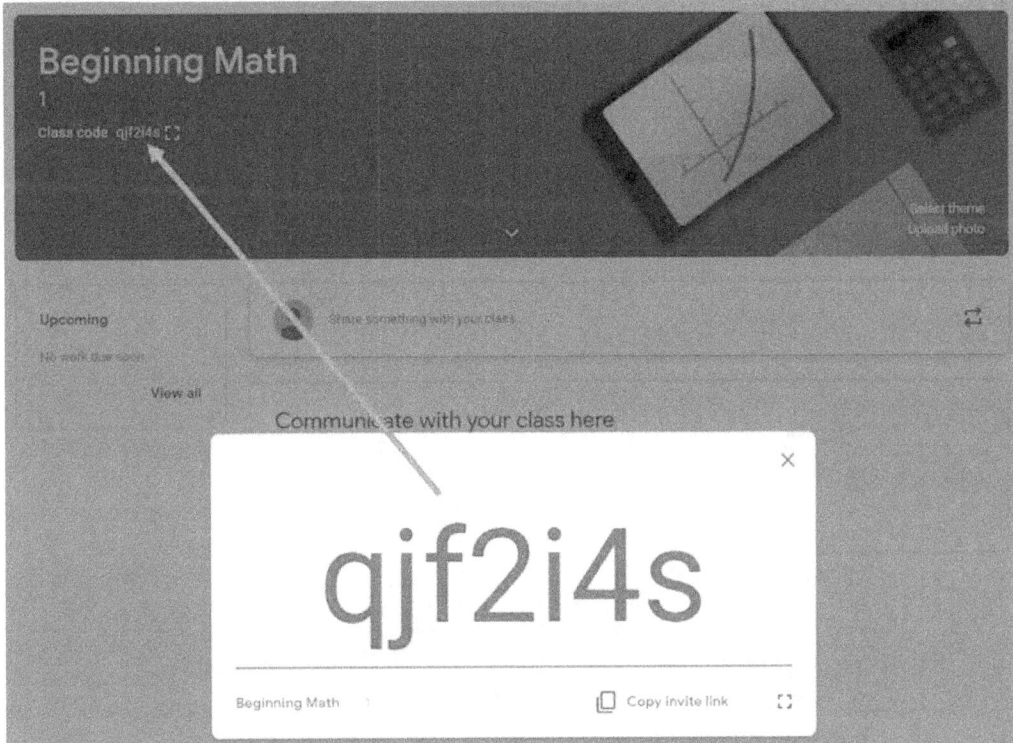

Figure 3.24

Once the student has your class code then can then go to their classroom environment and click on the + sign next to their profile picture and choose *Join class*.

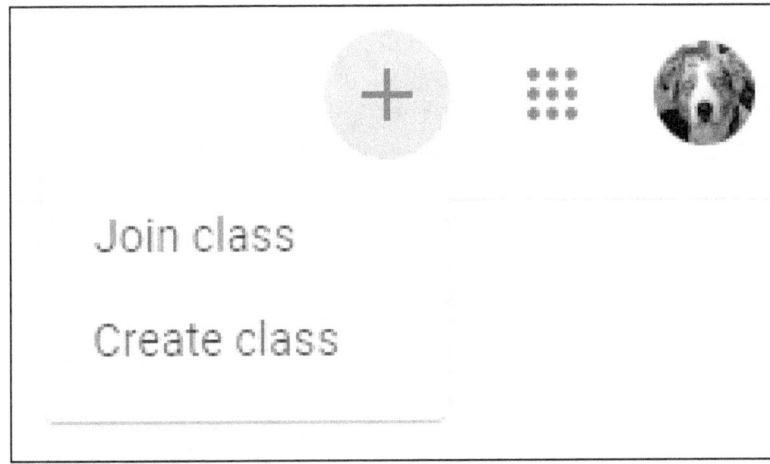

Figure 3.25

Then they would paste or type in the code they received from you and click on the *Join* button to join your class.

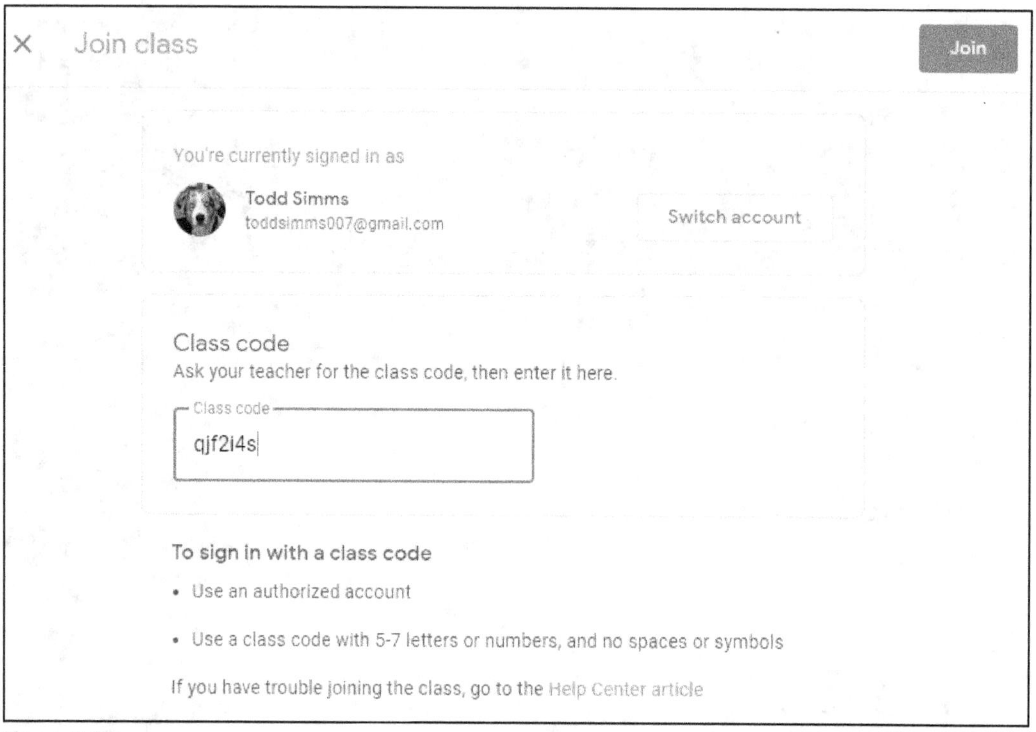

Chapter 3 – Creating a Class

Figure 3.26

After the student joins, they will show up in your People tab as a student.

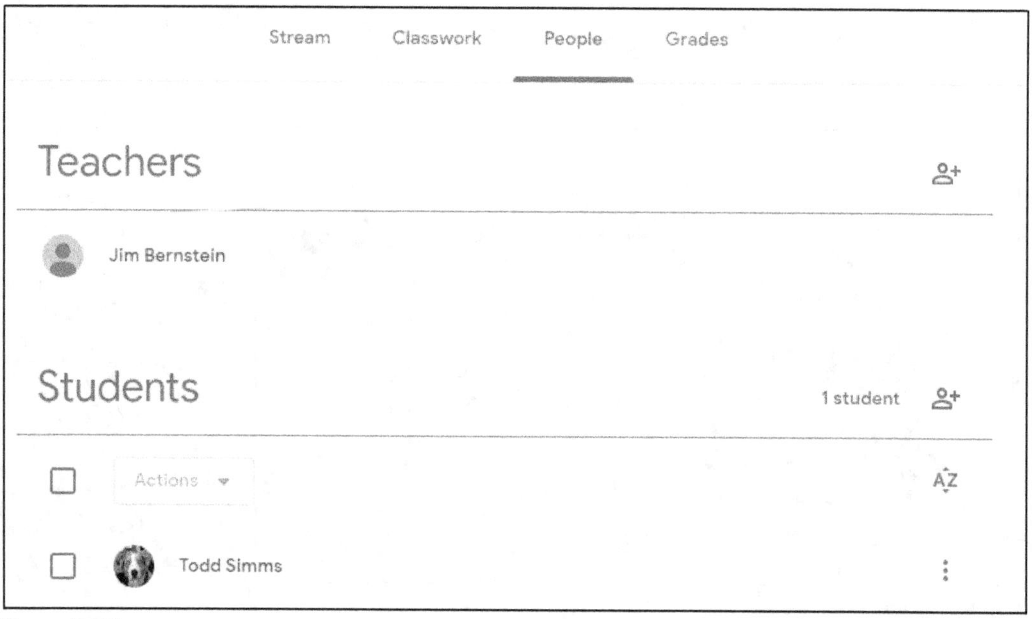

Figure 3.27

Chapter 3 – Creating a Class

If you come across a situation where your class code has been compromised or given out to people that shouldn't have it then it's easy to reset the code so nobody else can use it to join your class.

To do so you will need to go into that class and then click the Settings gear icon to go into your classroom settings. From there you will go to the *General* section and where it says *Manage invite codes* you can either reset the code or disable it altogether.

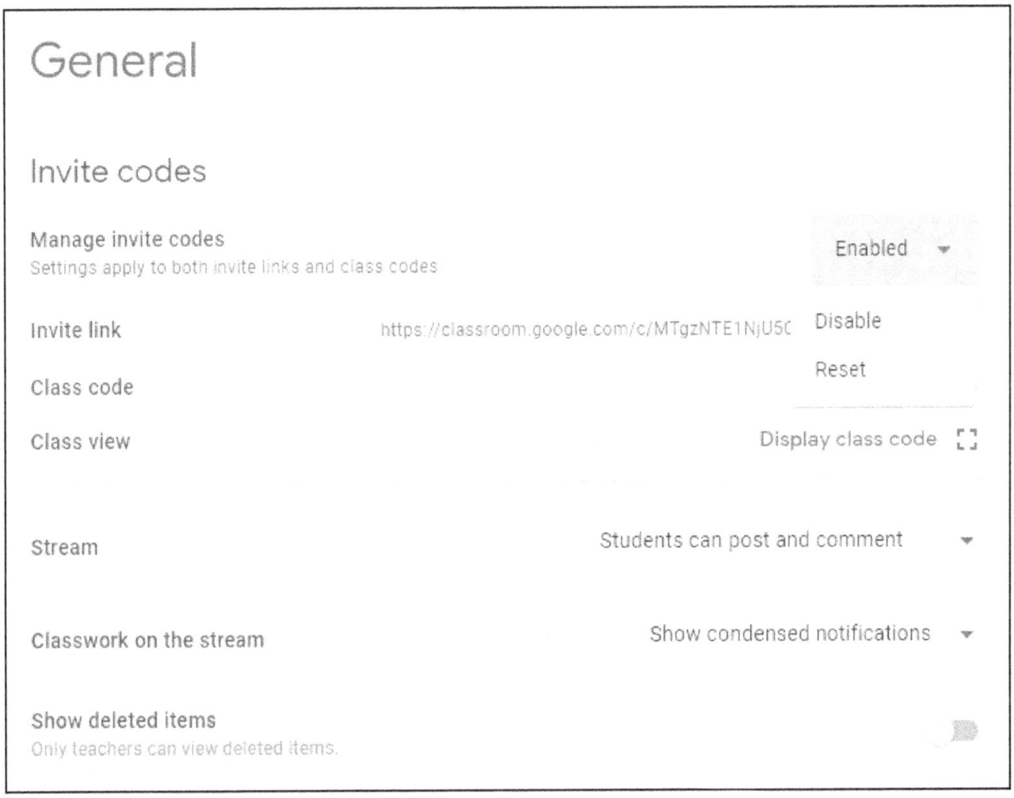

Figure 3.28

Removing Students and Leaving Classes
As you probably know, students will come and go, and you usually don't end up with the same number of students in the enrollment period as you do once your class is up and running. And you probably also know that mistakes happen, and students occasionally get assigned to the wrong classes or simply change their mind and decide they don't want to take a certain class.

Chapter 3 – Creating a Class

This is why it's important to know how to remove a student from your class in case it becomes necessary and also to know how a student can remove themself from a class if needed.

To remove a student from a class you will need to go to that class and then to the *People* tab. From there you would check the box next to the name or names of the students you wish to remove. Then from the *Actions* menu choose *Remove*.

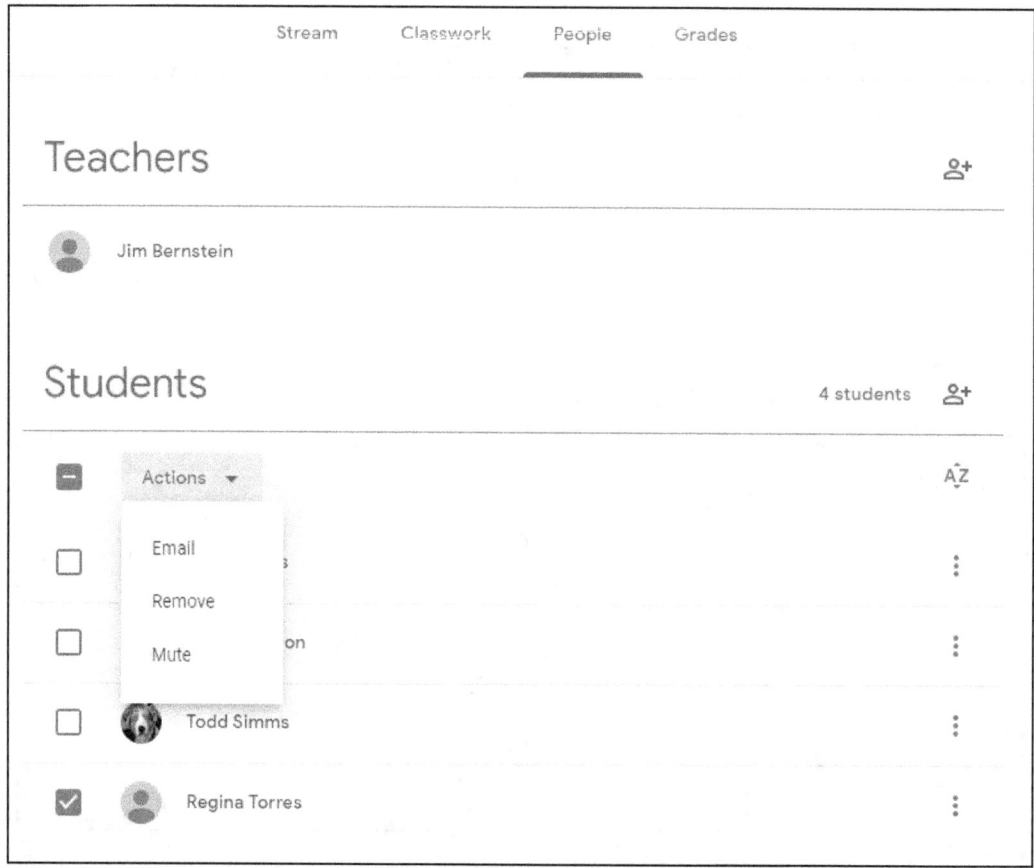

Figure 3.29

If you are a student that wants to remove themself from a particular class then this is very easy to do. Simply go to your class list and find the class that you would like to remove yourself from. Next, you will click on the three vertical dots and then choose Unenroll (figure 3.30).

Chapter 3 – Creating a Class

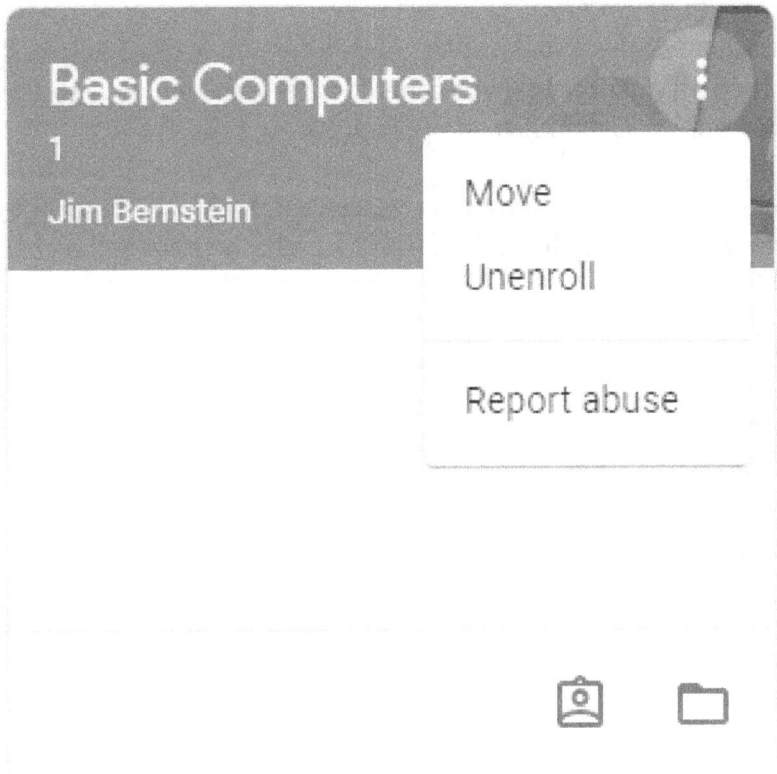

Figure 3.30

You will then see a message telling you that any files you have for that class folder in Google Drive (discussed in Chapter 6) will remain intact in case you wish to go back to them later. Once you click on *Unenroll* you will then be removed from the class and it won't show up in your class list section anymore.

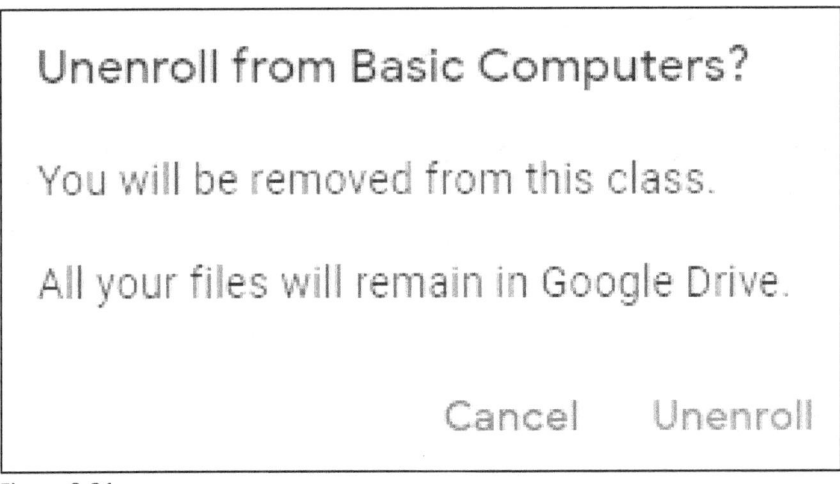

Figure 3.31

Chapter 3 – Creating a Class

Inviting Other Teachers to Your Class
If you are sharing teaching duties with another teacher or simply need help with your teaching work then it's possible to invite other teachers (co-teachers) to your class so they can then lend you a hand when needed.

The process for inviting teachers to your class is the same as it is for inviting students but this time you will click the add teacher + icon to the right of *Teachers* in the *People* tab.

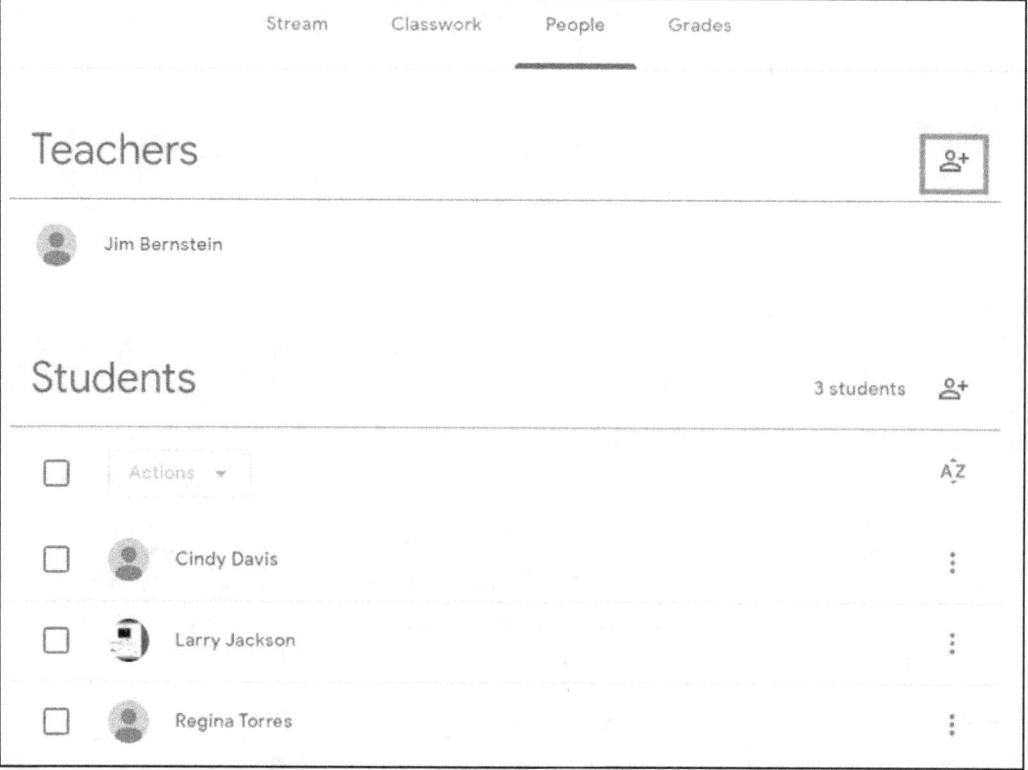
Figure 3.32

Then you will type in the name or email address of the teacher you wish to invite and then click on *Invite*.

Chapter 3 – Creating a Class

Figure 3.33

When the teacher accepts your invitation they will be added to your Teachers list under the People tab and will be able to perform the same tasks that you can.

Classroom Guardians
Classroom has a neat feature where you can invite parents (guardians) to your classes so they can be informed as to how their kids are doing in your class. Guardians are not members of the student's class and must be invited using their email address. This feature is only available for classrooms set up with a G-suite account so if you don't have the option to invite a guardian then this is why.

Guardians cannot see their child's Stream, Classwork, People, or Grades pages, but rather will get an email summary of their child's work. Such as missing and upcoming work as well as class activities.

The process to invite a guardian is the same as inviting a student or co-teacher and you will click on the student's name under the People tab and then click on *Invite guardians*. Then you will enter in their email address or multiple email addresses and the invitation will be sent out.

Chapter 3 – Creating a Class

Once a guardian accepts the invitation they will receive summaries for every class that student is enrolled in assuming the class summaries are enabled for the class. The guardian email summaries option is disabled by default, but you can enable it from the class settings in the General section.

Figure 3.34 shows an example of a guardian summary for Todd showing his past due (missed) work and also his work that is going to be due in the next week from all the classes he is enrolled in that have the summaries enabled.

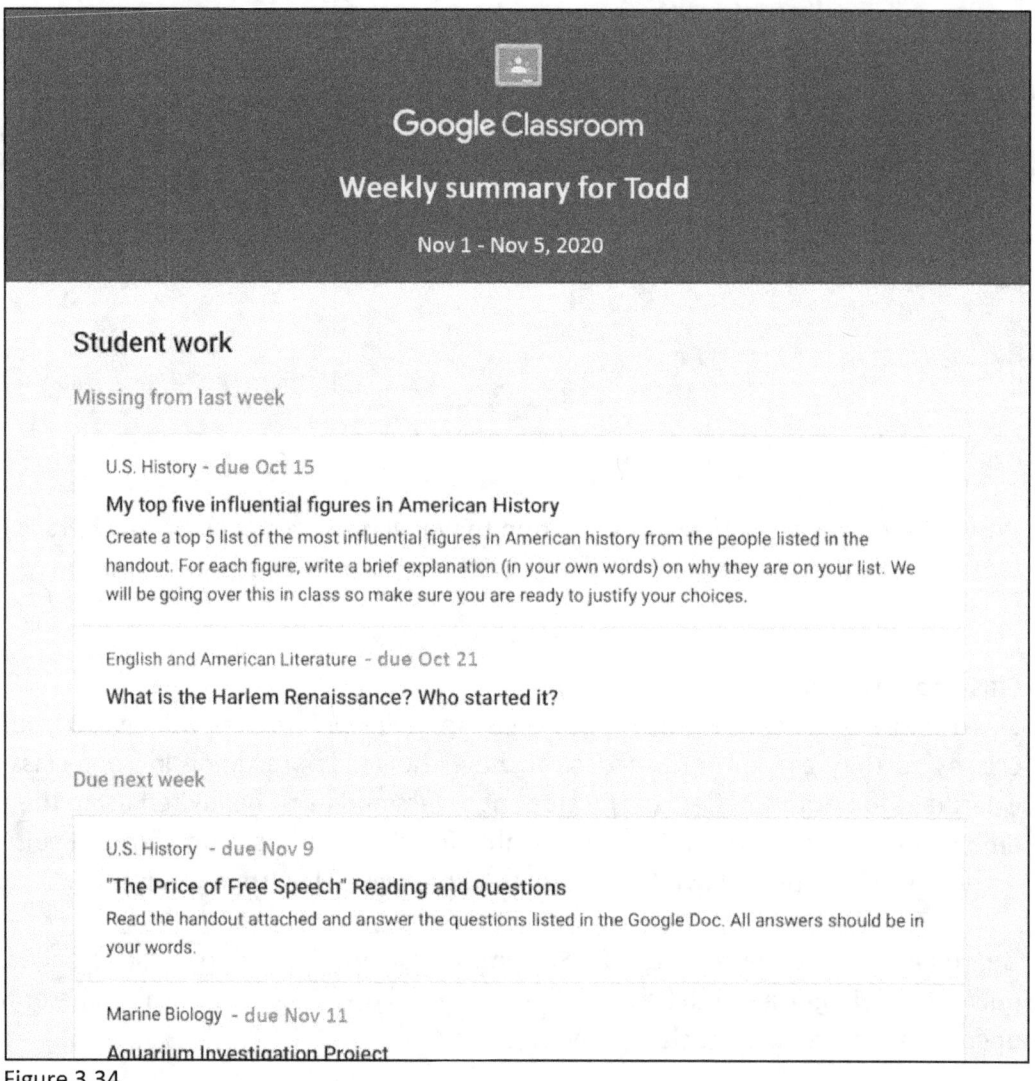

Figure 3.34

Chapter 3 – Creating a Class

Organizing Your Class Cards

If you plan on having a lot of different classes in your Classroom environment then things might start to look a little cluttered as you add more classes. I added a few more classes to my "school" as you can see in figure 3.35 and they are not really in any particular order which might make things harder to keep track of.

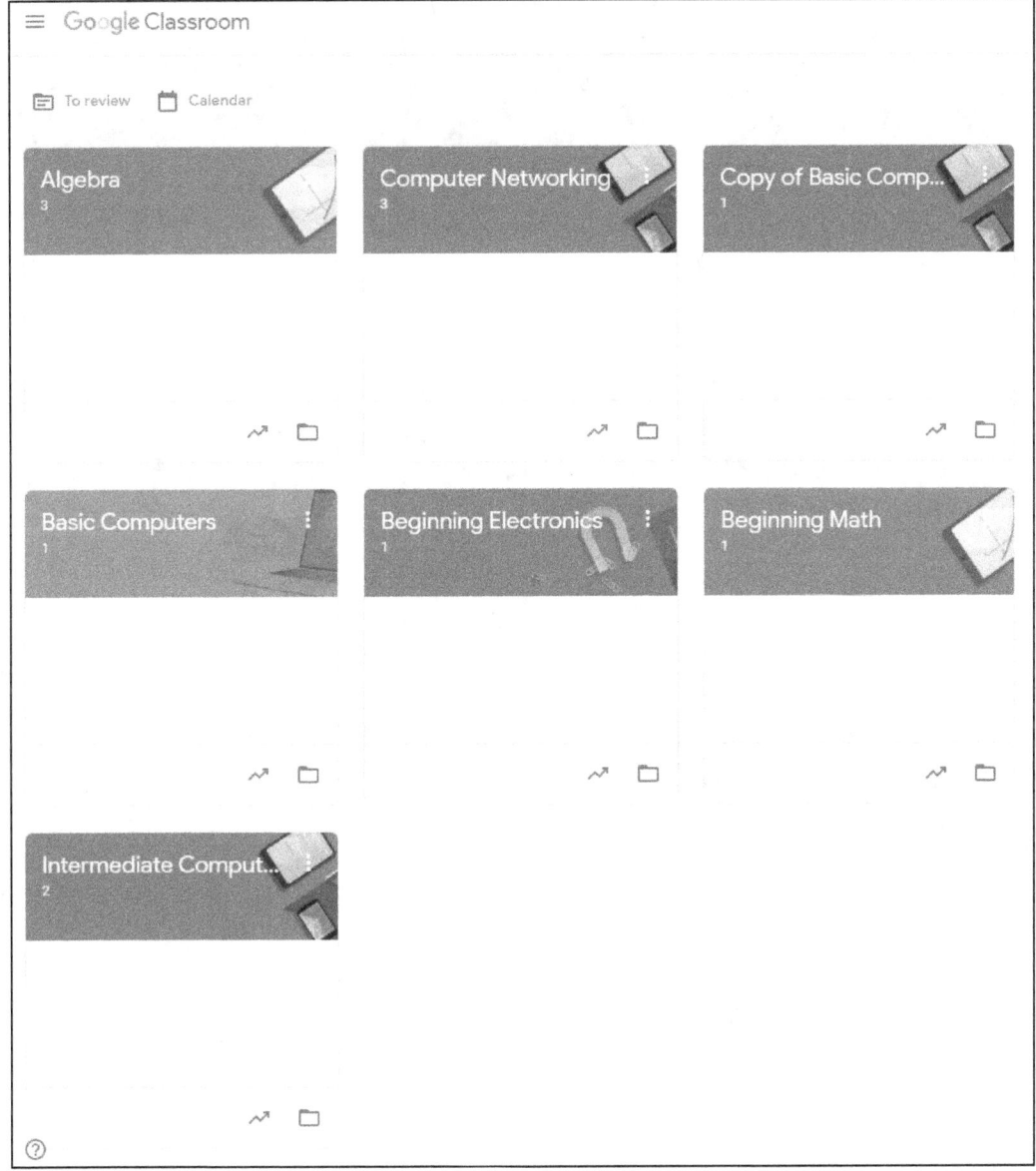

Figure 3.35

To organize my classes, all I need to do is drag and drop them in the order that works best for me. So what I did was organize the subjects together and then ordered them by the level of the classes. As you can see in figure 3.36 I have my

Chapter 3 – Creating a Class

math classes first and then my computer classes in level order (1-3) and then finally my standalone electronics class.

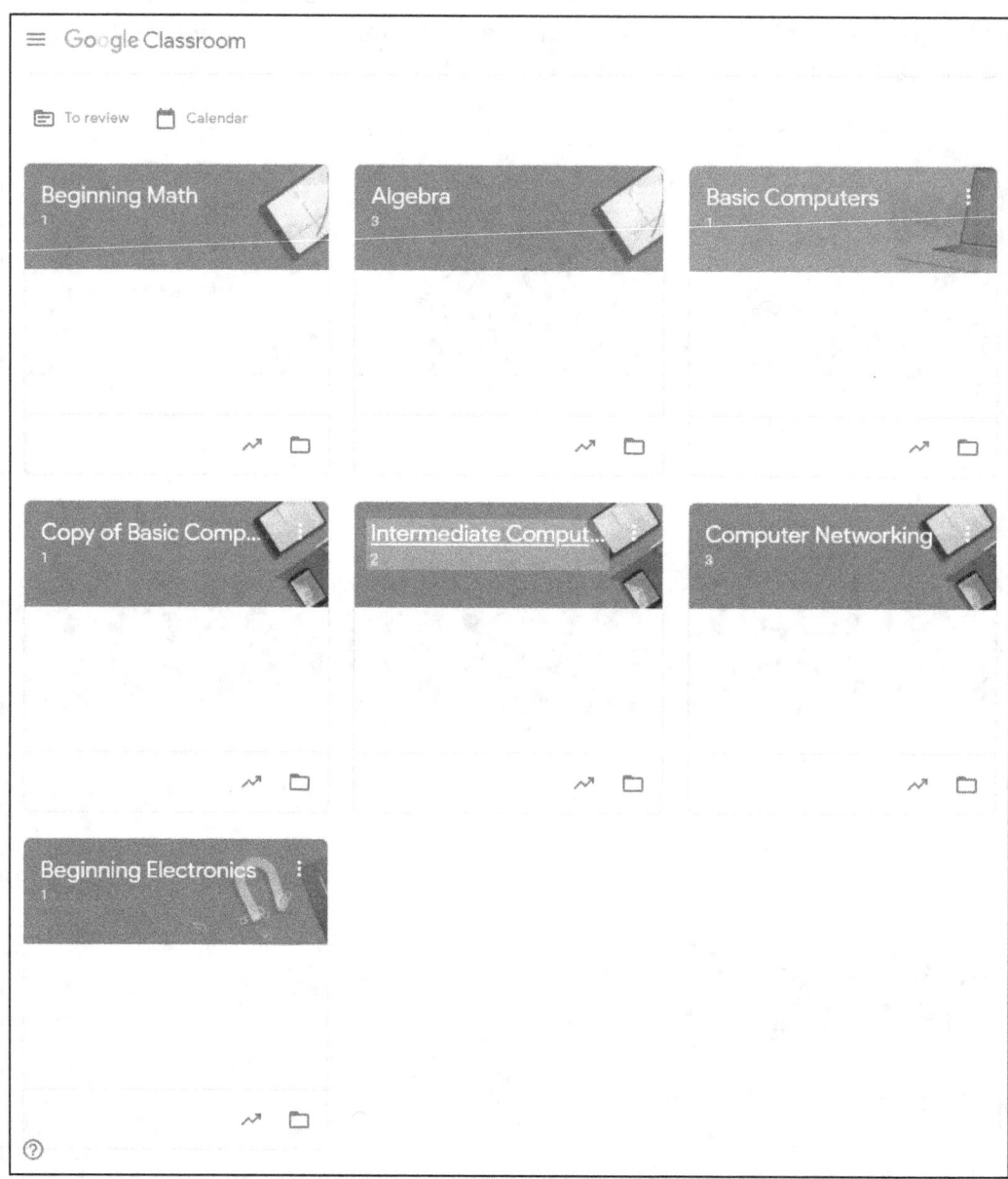

Figure 3.36

Archiving and Deleting Classes
If you use Google Classroom for an extended period of time you will most likely come across a situation where you have classes that you don't need any more and are simply taking up space in your main classroom area.

Chapter 3 – Creating a Class

Fortunately, there is a way to clear out these unneeded classrooms to make room for new classrooms or just make your environment a little more organized. To do this you can either archive or delete any classes that you don't need anymore. But there is one catch that you need to be aware of and that is in order to delete a class it will have to be archived first.

To archive a class you will need to go to your class card and click on the three vertical dots and choose *Archive* from the choices that appear.

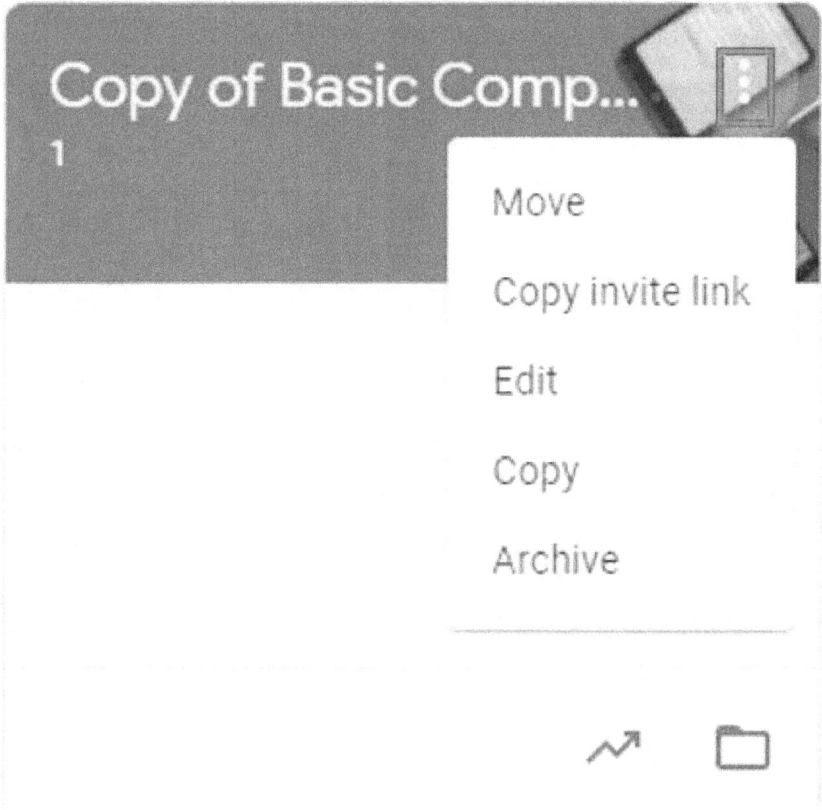

Figure 3.37

You will then see a message telling you that when you archive a class that it can't be modified unless it's restored first and that also any class files you have in Google Drive will remain intact in case you need them.

47

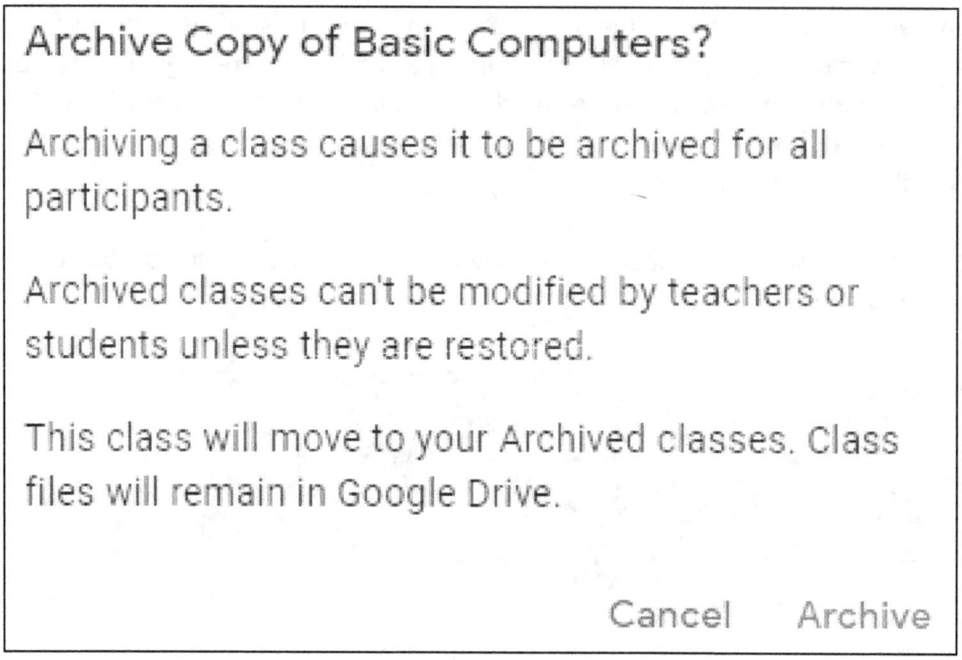

Chapter 3 – Creating a Class

> **Archive Copy of Basic Computers?**
>
> Archiving a class causes it to be archived for all participants.
>
> Archived classes can't be modified by teachers or students unless they are restored.
>
> This class will move to your Archived classes. Class files will remain in Google Drive.
>
> Cancel   Archive

Figure 3.38

Once you click on *Archive* the class will then be removed from your main classroom area.

To see your archived classes you will need to click on the three horizontal lines at the top left of the screen and then click on *Archived classes* as seen in figure 3.39.

Chapter 3 – Creating a Class

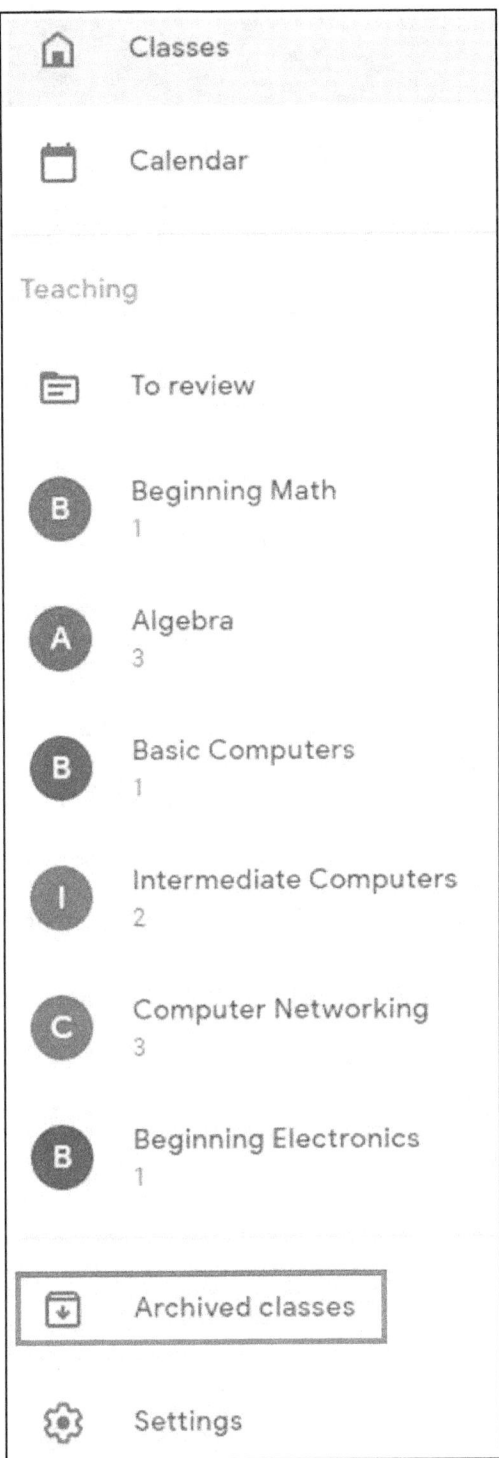

Figure 3.39

You can tell that a class is archived because the graphic for that class will have lines going through it.

Chapter 3 – Creating a Class

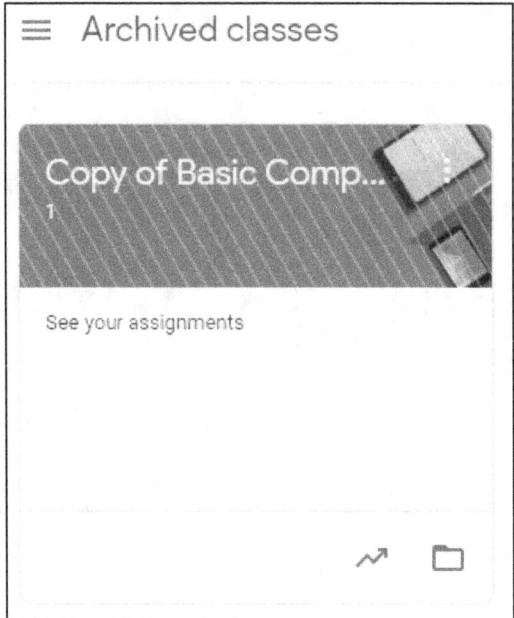

Figure 3.40

Even though a class is archived, you can still look at the assignments for that class by clicking on *See your assignments*. You can also see the grades for the class by clicking the arrow icon at the bottom left as well as see the class files by clicking on the folder icon.

To restore the class and remove it from your archive simply click the three vertical dots again and choose *Restore*.

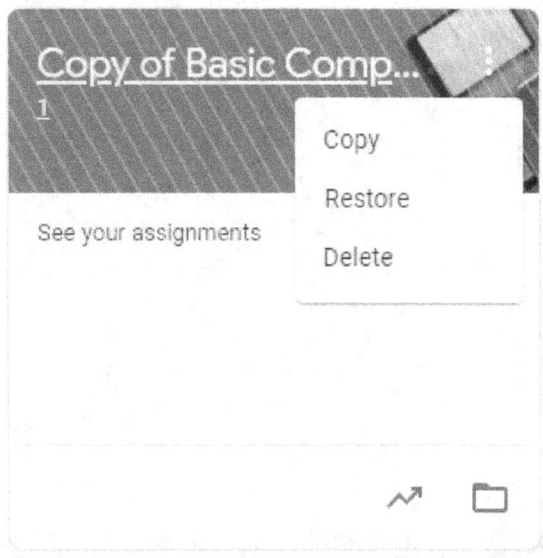

Figure 3.41

Chapter 4 – Running Your Classes

Now that you have your initial class setup complete, it's time to start adding some content to your classes so your students have some things to work on. Of course you will be adding things like assignments and quizzes as your classes progress, but you might also want to add some additional informational materials for your students, so they have something to see when they first join your class.

In this chapter I will be covering the concepts you will need to know in order to add various types of items to your classrooms and will also be discussing methods you can use to manage your classrooms (and students) once class is in session.

Stream Tab
As a teacher (or a student) you know that there is a lot of information that goes along with teaching a class and not all of it relates to assignments or tests. This is where the Stream tab comes into play within your classroom. The Stream tab is where you can post things such as announcements, links, YouTube videos, informational documents and so on.

Figure 4.1 shows the Stream tab for my Basic Computers class and as you can see I added things such as my office hours and the class syllabus. When you post class assignments they will also show up in your stream, so think of it as a place to see everything that is going on within a class. Think of it as being similar to a feed you would have on a social media site such as Facebook.

As you can see, if you have a lot going on in your class things can get a little cluttered so keep that in mind when making posts. I will show you how you can keep your Stream tab a little cleaner in a bit.

Chapter 4 – Running Your Classes

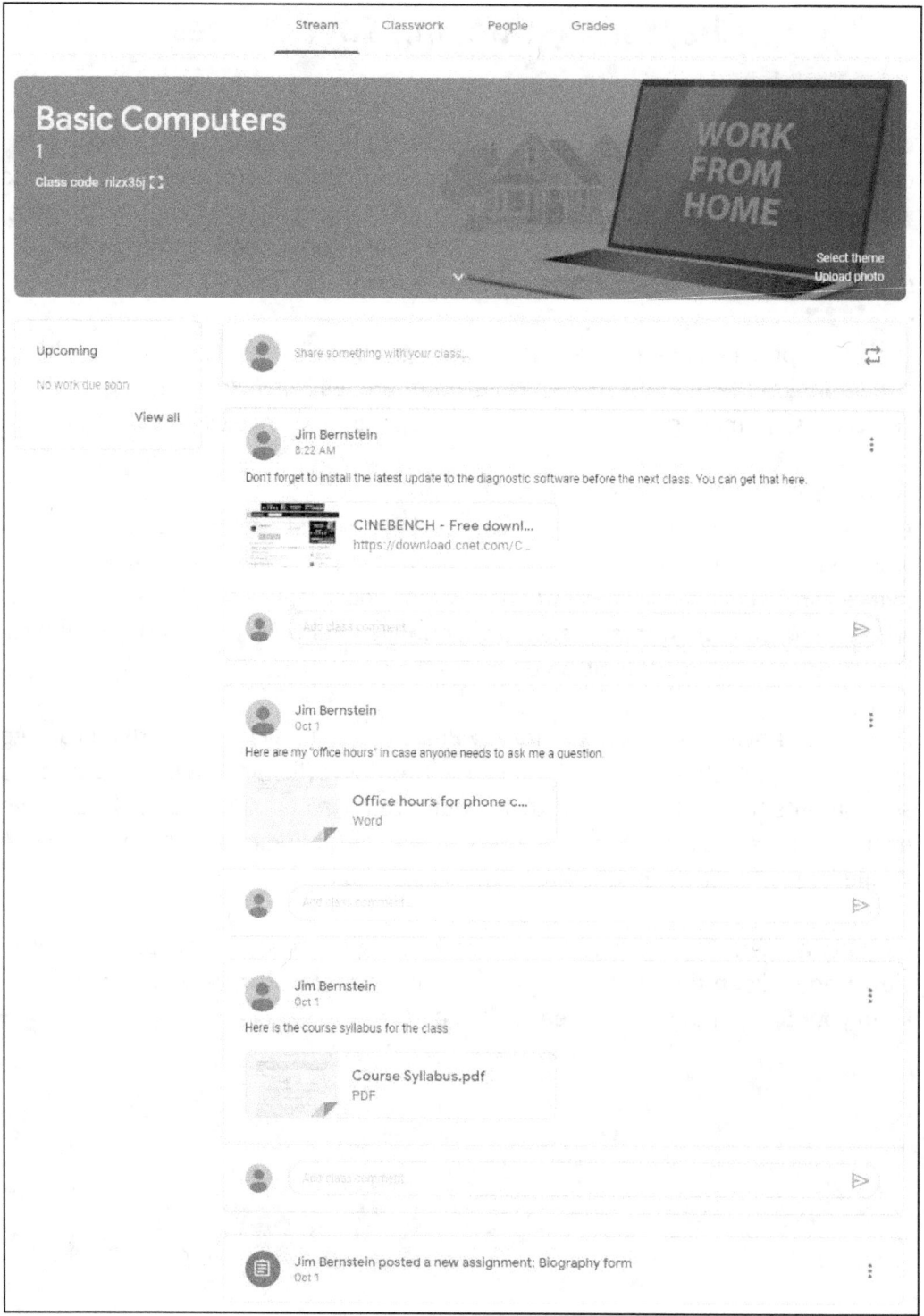

Figure 4.1

Chapter 4 – Running Your Classes

To make a post in the Stream tab, all you need to do is click on the link at the top that says *Share something with your class*. Then you can type in your message or announcement and if you would like to add a file, link or video, you can do so by clicking on the *Add* button and choosing the type of attachment you would like to add. I will be going over what each one of these choices will do in the next section

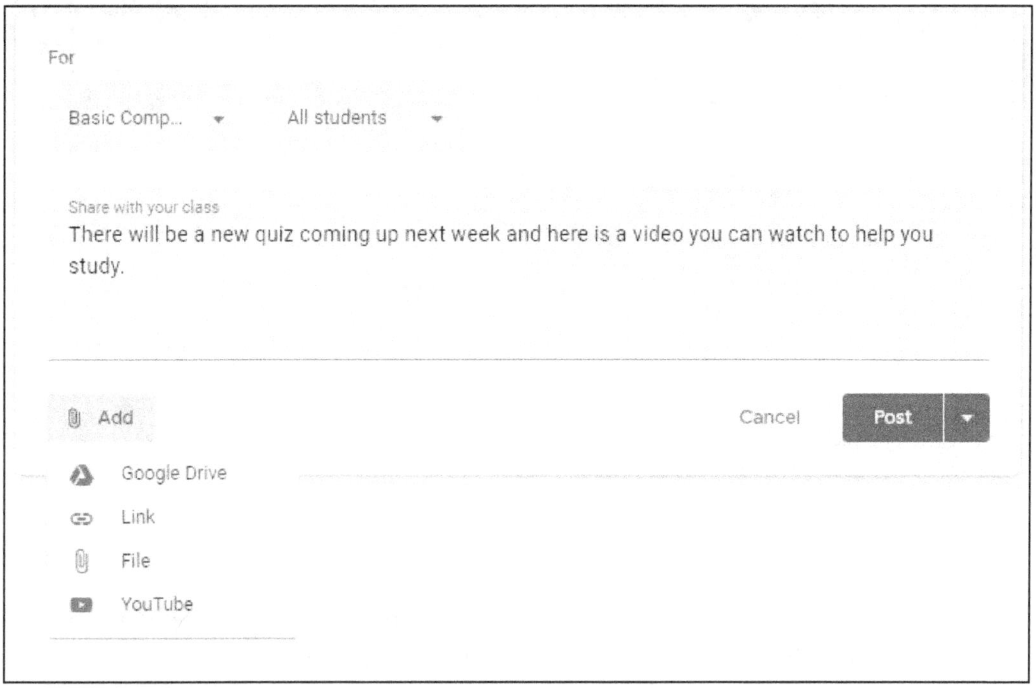

Figure 4.2

For my post I will add a link to a YouTube video so my students can watch it to help their studies. Then at the top I can leave the default of *All students* which means that everyone in my class will see my post, or I can choose which students should be able to see it in their stream. If I would like to make this post in a different classroom than the one I am in, I can change it at the top left.

When I have everything looking the way I like I can either click on the *Post* button to have it posted immediately to my Stream or I can click the down arrow next to the Post button and choose one of the other options. These options include the ability to schedule when your message will be posted, or you can save it as a draft and continue working on it later.

Chapter 4 – Running Your Classes

Figure 4.3 shows my Stream tab with the latest post shown at the top of the page.

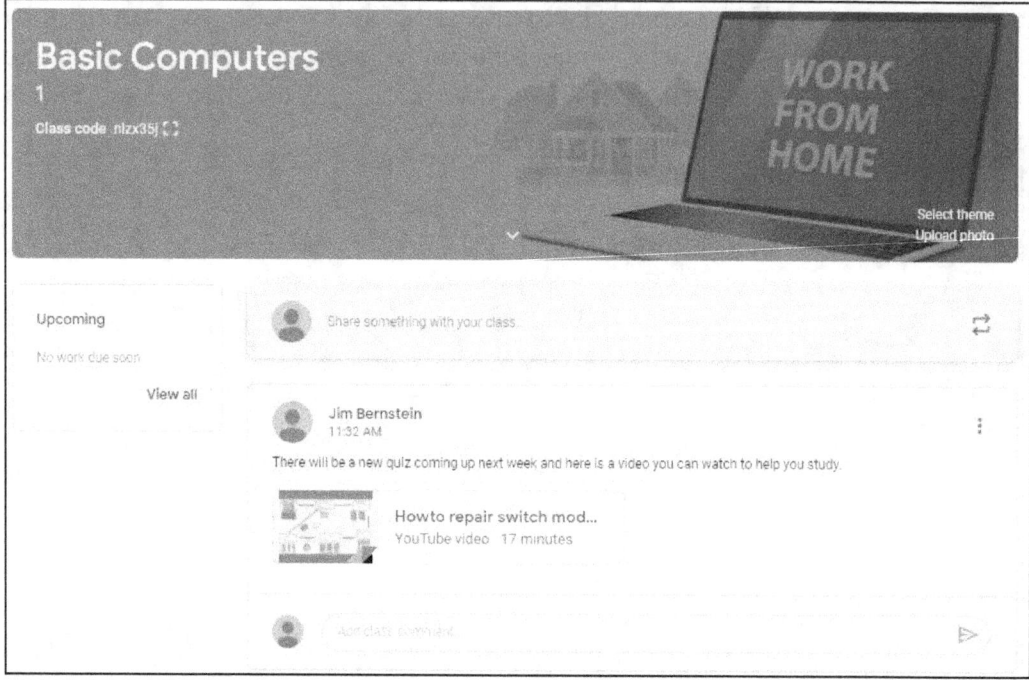

Figure 4.3

If I need to make any changes to my post then I can click on the three vertical dots in the upper right hand corner and choose to edit the post, delete the post or copy a link that I can then email or message to someone that will take them directly to this post assuming they are in the class.

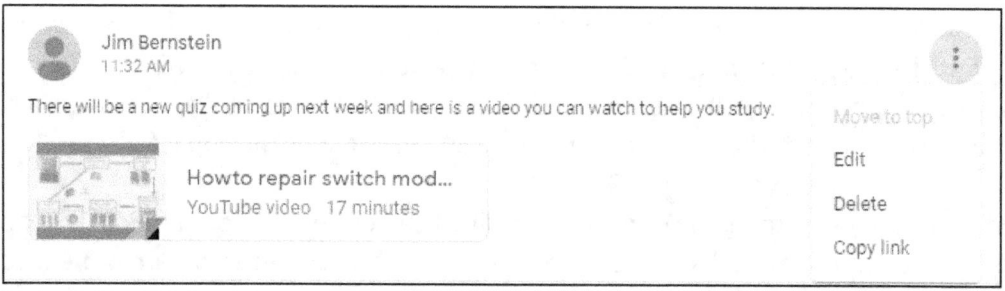

Figure 4.4

There is also an option that says *Move to top* and this can be used to move your post to the top of the stream, so it shows first in the listings. If it's already at the top of the list then this option will be greyed out.

Chapter 4 – Running Your Classes

When you students log into your class they will be able to see everything that you post and they can make comments on your post if you allow it (figure 4.5 & 4.6), and this is enabled by default. They can also make their own posts which will be seen by you and your other students by default.

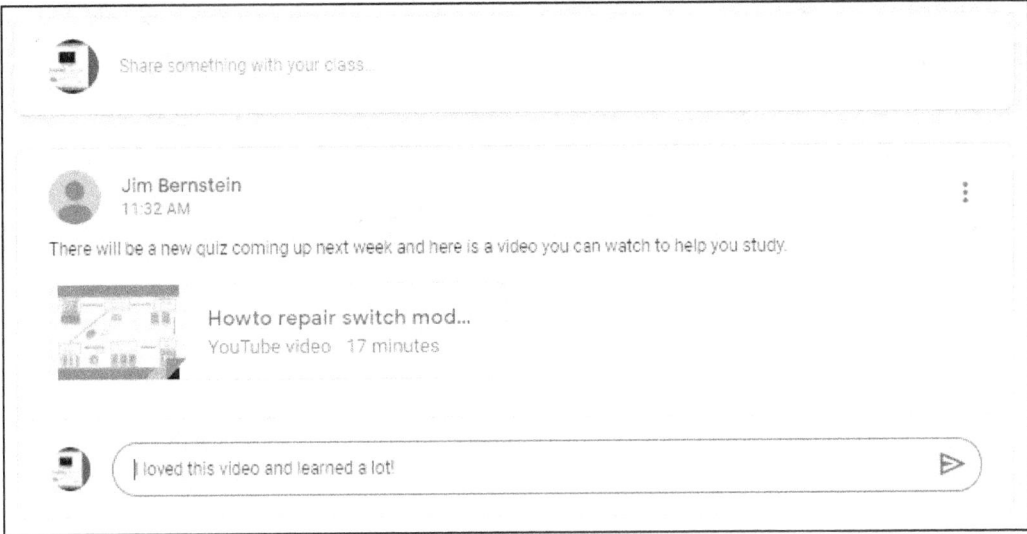

Figure 4.5

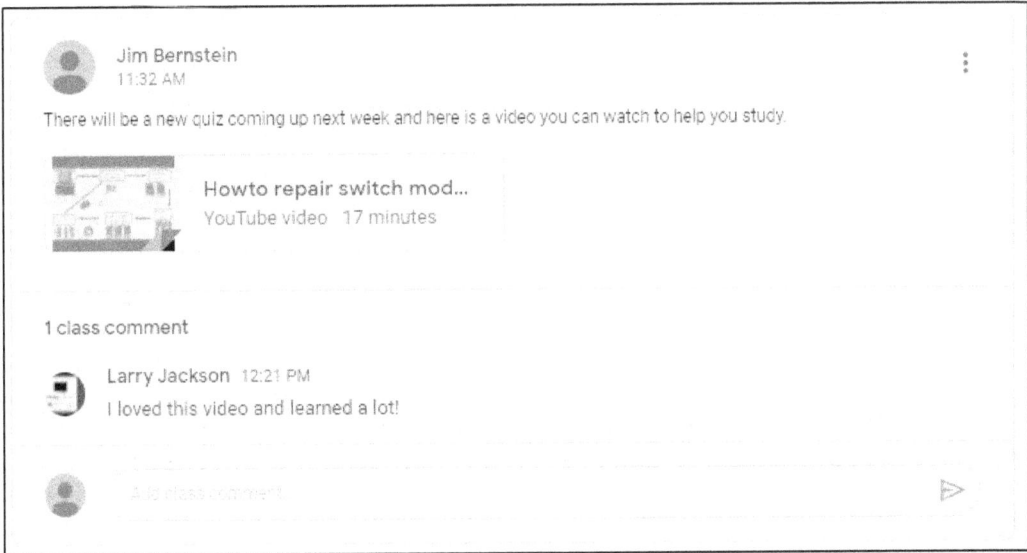

Figure 4.6

When someone makes a post in your class stream, you will receive an email letting you know who made the post and what they said as seen in figure 4.7.

Chapter 4 – Running Your Classes

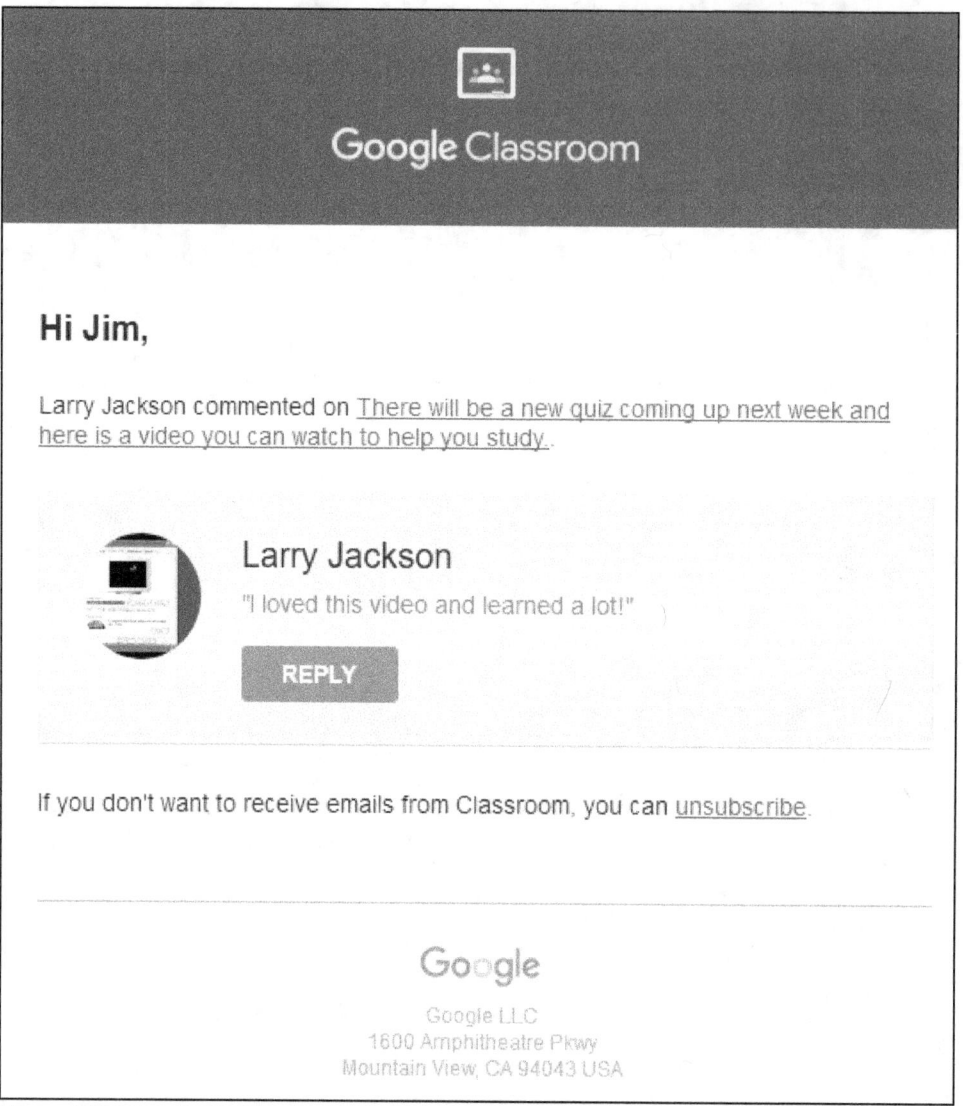

Figure 4.7

If you find that your Stream is getting too cluttered or your students are posting comments that don't apply to the class or are inappropriate then you can go into the class settings and change your Stream options from the General section (figure 4.8).

Under the *Stream* settings you have the option to allow students to create new posts and comment on other posts or you can change to where students can only comment on existing posts and not create new ones. Or if that is still too much for you then you can change it so only teachers can post and comment.

Chapter 4 – Running Your Classes

 If you have some announcements, links, documents or so on that you have posted in your stream that you don't want to be there anymore then you can remove them by clicking on the three vertical dots on the post and then on *Delete*.

Figure 4.8

Under the *Classwork on the stream* section you can have your stream show only condensed notifications, or you can expand it to have attachments and details shown. Or you can hide classwork notifications altogether. Keep in mind that these options apply only to your classwork and not to other posts.

One last thing I want to mention from the Stream tab is the *Upcoming* section (figure 4.9) on the left side of the page under your class graphic. Here you will see items that are coming due so you can keep track of things you need to make sure to address before they are past due. Both you and your students will have an Upcoming section in their stream, so everyone knows what items are going to be due soon.

Chapter 4 – Running Your Classes

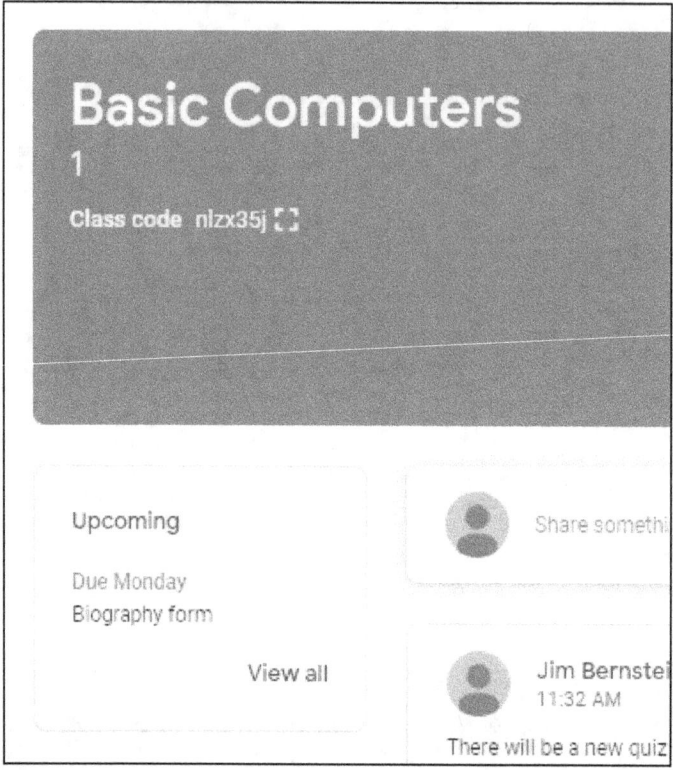
Figure 4.9

Stream Tab Attachments
As you might have noticed, when you click on the *Add* button you have several options to choose from when it comes to attachments and each one has its own purpose.

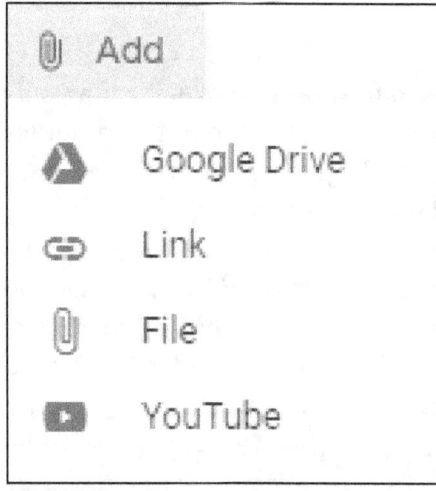
Figure 4.10

Chapter 4 – Running Your Classes

Google Drive
Google Drive is Google's online "cloud" storage platform where you can save your files online and access them anywhere that you have an internet connection. It's a great way to backup important files and also to share them with others you collaborate with.

When you click on Google Drive you will be brought to the Drive account that you are logged into which should be your teacher account. From there you can go to *My Drive* to see a listing of all of your files or you can click on *Recent* to see files that you have recently saved to your Google Drive. Then all you need to do is select the file you want to attach and click on *Insert*. You can also select more than one file to add to your Stream if you wish. Google Drive will be discussed in more detail in Chapter 6.

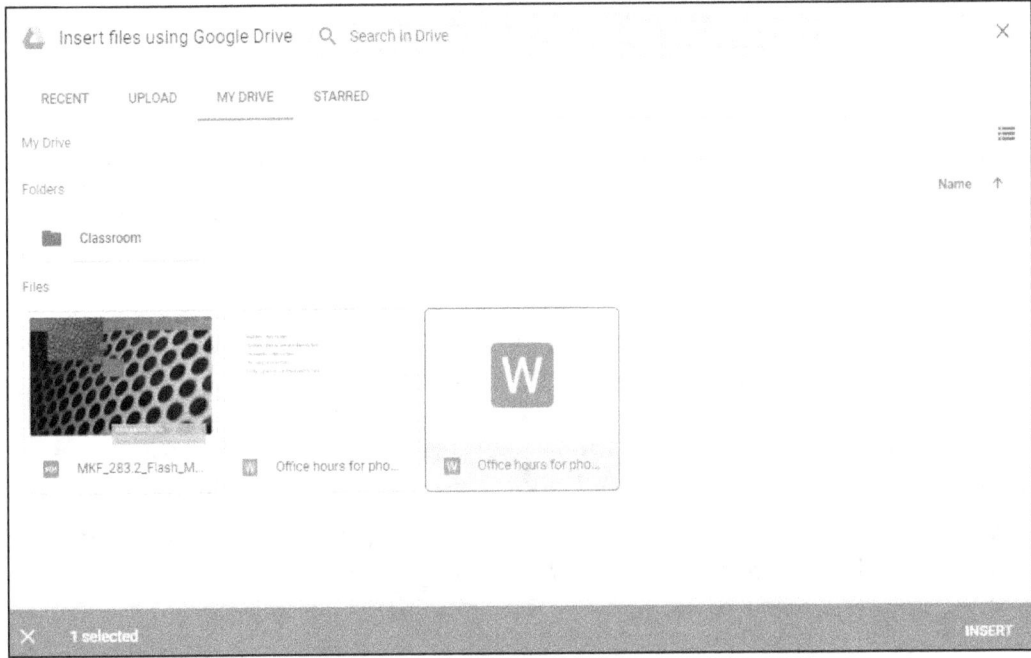

Figure 4.11

If you would like to learn more about Google Drive and other online cloud storage solutions then check out my book titled **Cloud Storage Made Easy**.
https://www.amazon.com/dp/1730838359

Chapter 4 – Running Your Classes

Link

Links are used to add clickable website link that a student can click on to bring them to a particular website for web pages related to their classwork. All you need to do is type in the website address or better yet, copy and paste it from your web browser and then click on *Add link*.

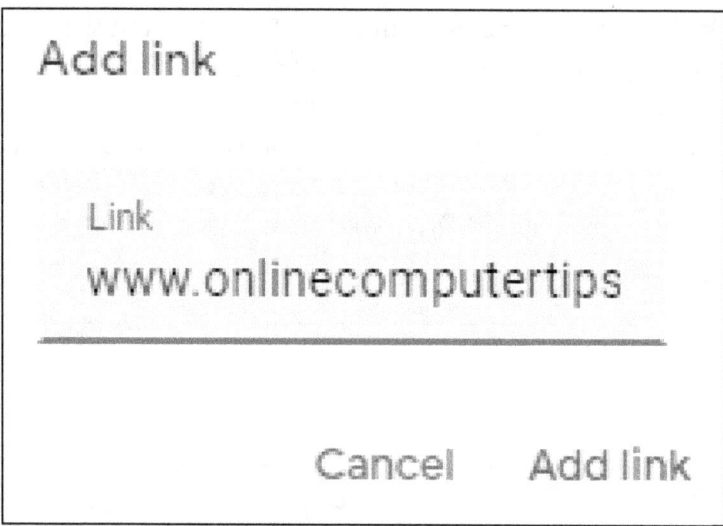

Figure 4.12

File

The File options is similar to the Google Drive option except here you are attaching a file from your local computer rather than your online Drive account. When you click on File it will look the same as when you click on Google Drive but to attach a file from your computer's hard drive you will need to click on *Upload* and then click the *Browse* button to navigate to the location where the file is stored on your computer. You can also drag and drop a file from your computer\desktop right into this window to have it uploaded to your classroom.

Chapter 4 – Running Your Classes

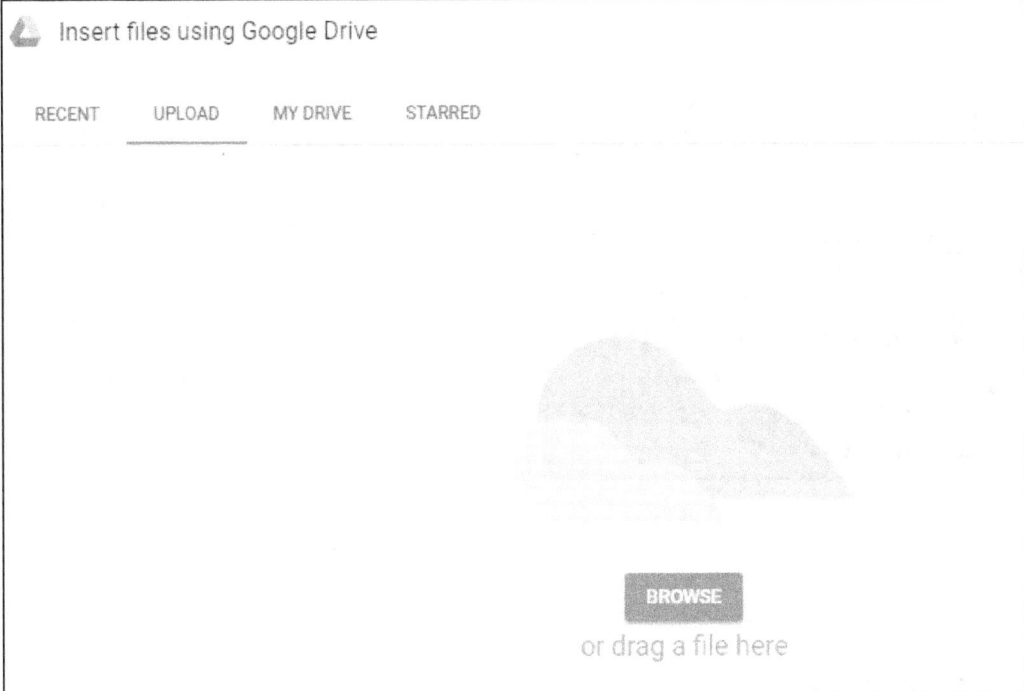

Figure 4.13

YouTube
Since Google owns YouTube, it makes sense that they would want to integrate it into Google Classroom so your students can take advantage of the educational videos that are available on YouTube. And yes there are actually videos on YouTube that are not a waste of time!

To attach a YouTube video you can either search for the type of video you want or paste a URL (Universal Resource Locator) which is just a fancy term for website address. Once you find the video you like or paste in its address all you need to do is click on the *Add* button and it will appear in your Stream and your students can watch it just by clicking on it.

Chapter 4 – Running Your Classes

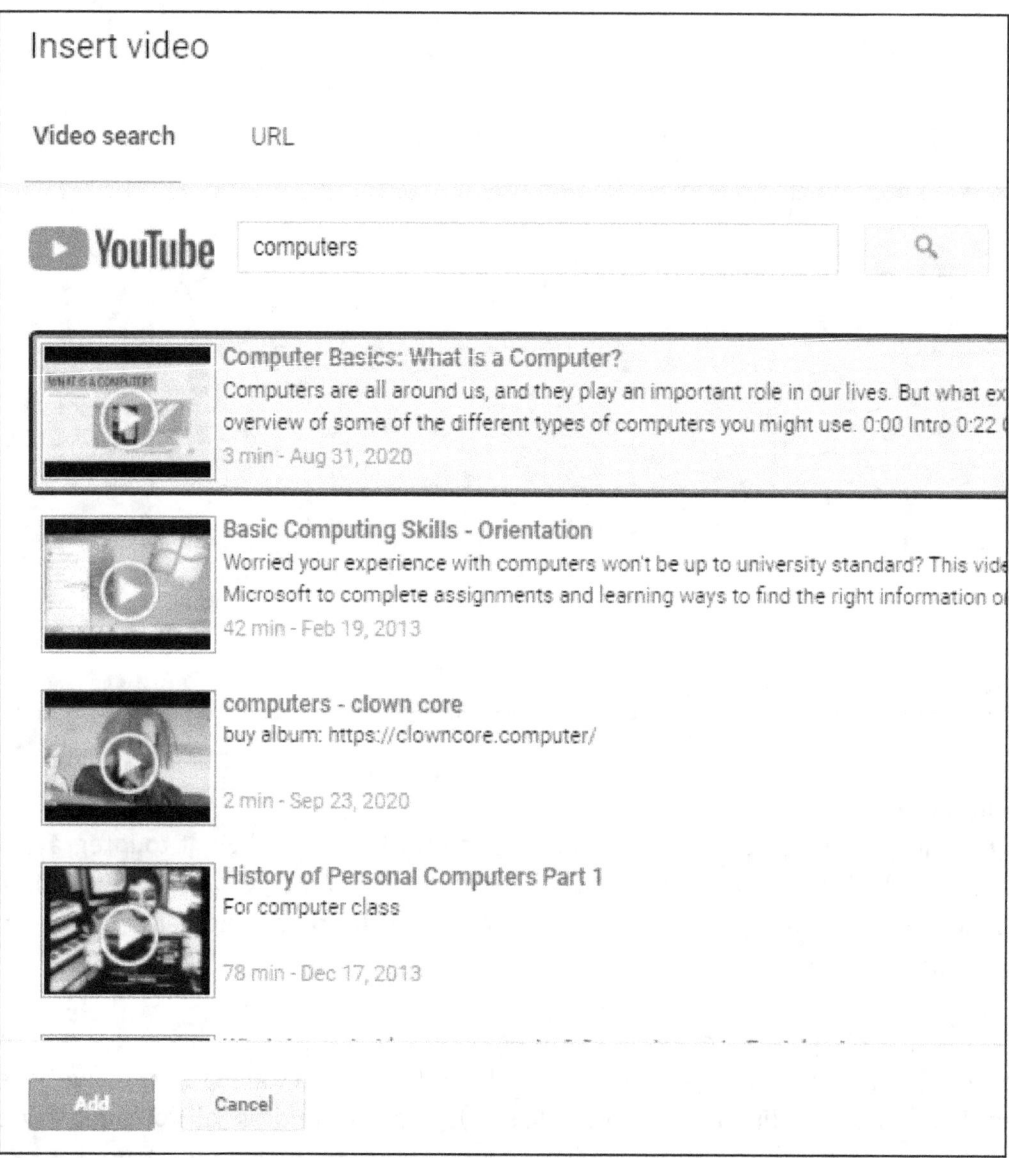

Figure 4.14

Adding Assignments, Materials and Quizzes Using the Classwork Tab

One of the most important tabs in your class is the Classroom tab because this is where all of your assignments and quizzes etc. will be kept and where your students will be going to see their work.

The first time you go to your Classwork tab it will be empty, but in my case I have some work listed in mine as shown in figure 4.15. The icons next to each item will tell you the type of item that you have posted, and you will get used to these icons

Chapter 4 – Running Your Classes

over time and will soon know what each type is when looking at your Classwork tab. As you can see, I have a quiz, resource (Flash Memory Guide), Assignment (Biography form) and question.

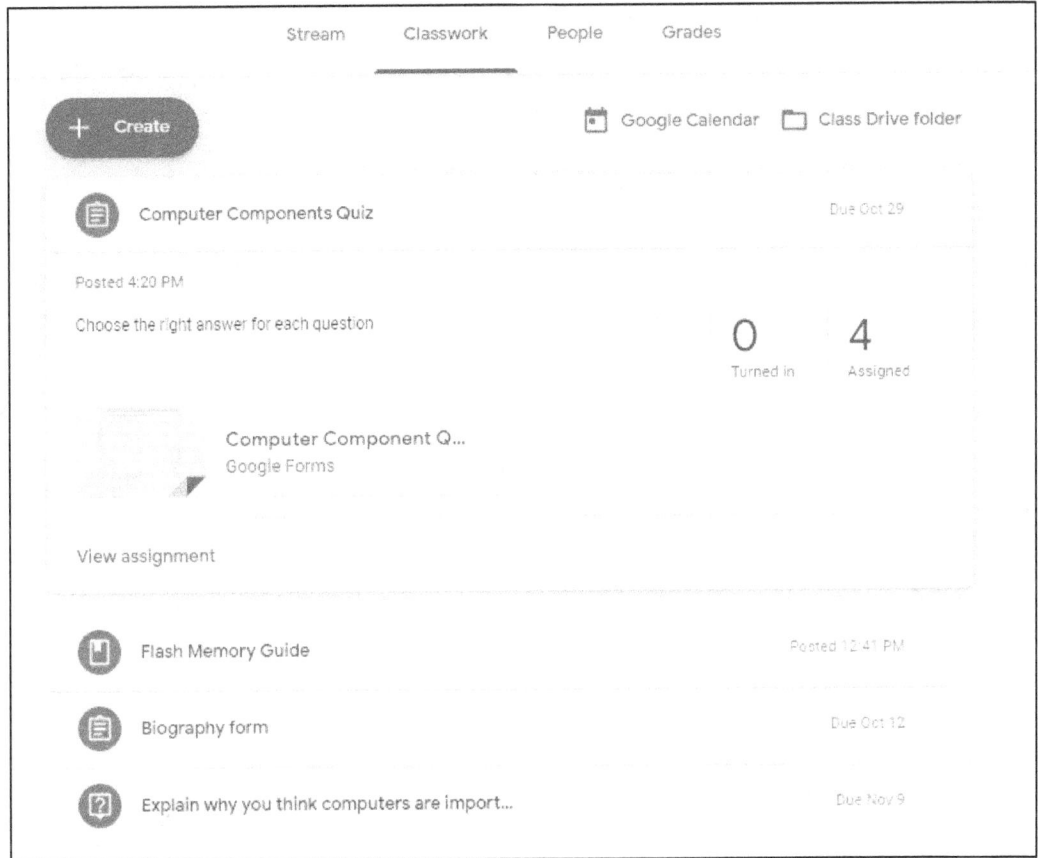

Figure 4.15

The *Create* button is what you will use to add new classwork for your students and when you click on it, you will have many different choices as to what kind of work you want to assign.

Chapter 4 – Running Your Classes

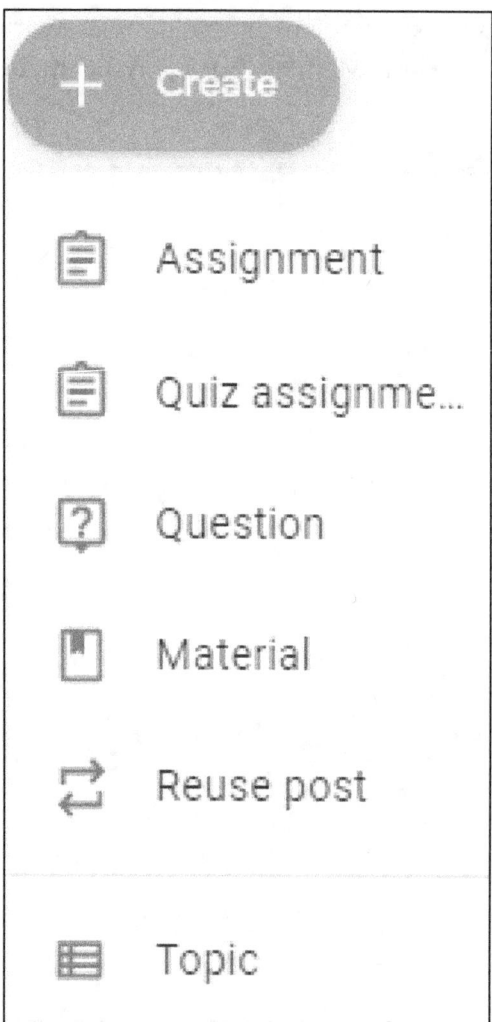

Figure 4.16

When you create an assignment, quiz, question or study material, your students will receive an email letting them know that there is something new in their classroom so they can go take a look and start working on it (figure 4.17). In fact, they can even go right to that assignment etc. directly from the email by clicking on the *Open* button.

Chapter 4 – Running Your Classes

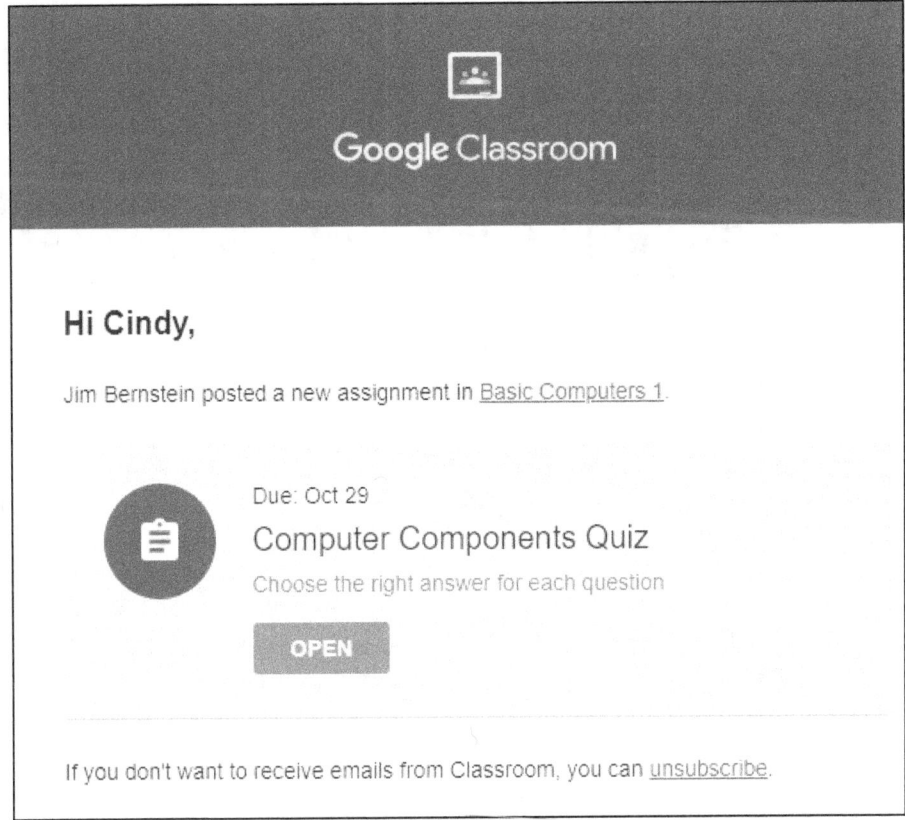

Figure 4.17

Now I would like to take a little time to go over each one of these items that you can create for your class.

Assignment
If you just want to create your own type of assignment that is not a typical quiz with predefined questions and answers then you can do so from here. Of course you can still ask questions on an assignment but here you have a little more freedom to give your students some detail as to what you would like them to accomplish.

Figure 4.18 shows the choices that you have when creating an assignment. You can give it a title and also optional instructions if needed. The *For* section will allow you to change what class it is for and also let you select which students will receive this assignment if you don't want to stick with the default choice of all students.

Points are used as a grade and you can assign as many points as you like to this assignment or you can leave it as ungraded. Then you can set a due date, so your students know when they need to complete the assignment. Topics are used to

Chapter 4 – Running Your Classes

separate out your classwork into categories and I will be going over this a little later in this chapter. *Rubrics* are a special type of grading method which will be discussed in Chapter 5.

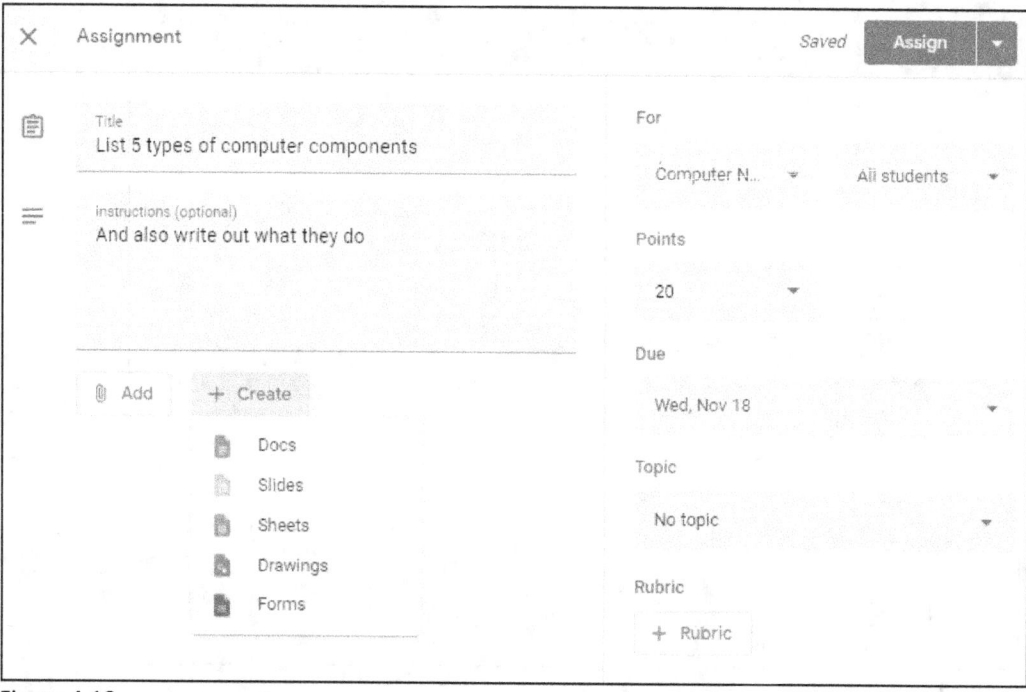

Figure 4.18

The *Add* button will give you the same Google Drive, Link, File and YouTube options that I previously discussed. The *Create* button will allow you to create a Google Document and have it saved to your class Google Drive and also attach it to your assignment. Google Docs will be discussed in Chapter 6, but they are basically various types of files such as documents, spreadsheets and presentations that you can use for your classes. I will choose a Doc file which is similar to a Microsoft Word file for this assignment.

Then I will type in the information I want my students to use for their assignment and also change the title of the document from the default of *Untitled Document* to *List 5 types of computer components*.

Chapter 4 – Running Your Classes

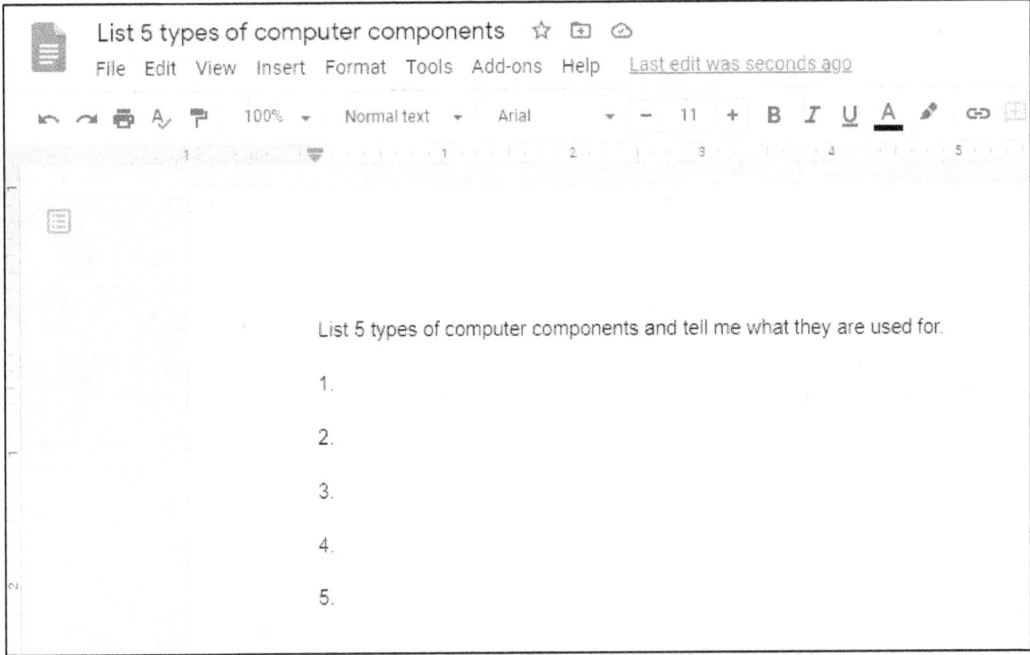

Figure 4.19

Now when I go back to my assignment I will see my new Google Doc attached at the bottom. One important thing you should do is choose the option for *Make a copy for each student* so that way each student in your class will be able to do their own work on their own document.

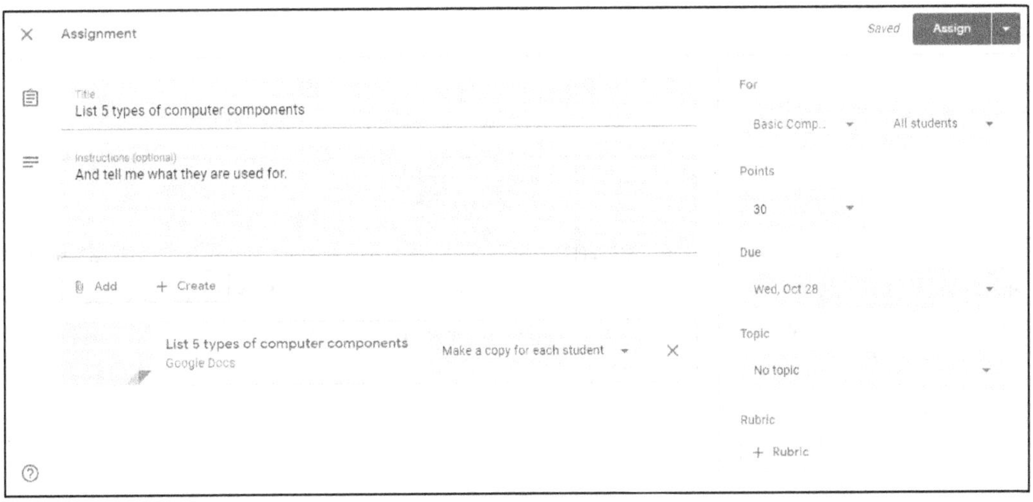

Figure 4.20

Chapter 4 – Running Your Classes

You might notice that your Google document name doesn't update after you create your document and go back to the assignment. To fix this simply refresh the web page to have it update. You can press the F5 key for Windows users and Command + R for Mac users.

Once everything looks good you will need to click on the *Assign* button to have the assignment pushed out to your students. You can also schedule the assignment if you don't want it to go out right away or save it as a draft to work on later.

When the student clicks on the assignment they will be able to open the document from the top right corner of the screen to add their answers and then click on the *Turn in* button to send it back to be graded. They can also click the *Add or create* button to create additional documents to go with the assignment if needed.

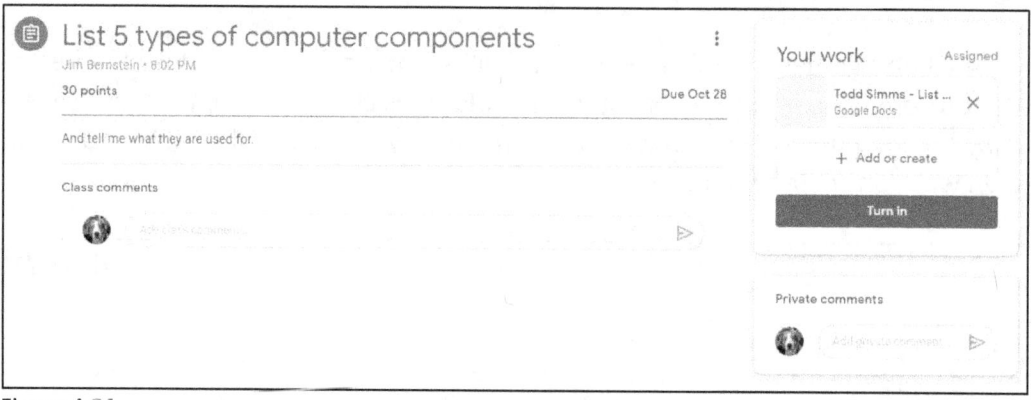
Figure 4.21

Take a look at the title of the document in figure 4.22 and you will see that it has automatically been renamed so the student's name is at the beginning. This is because I told Classroom to make a copy for each student.

Chapter 4 – Running Your Classes

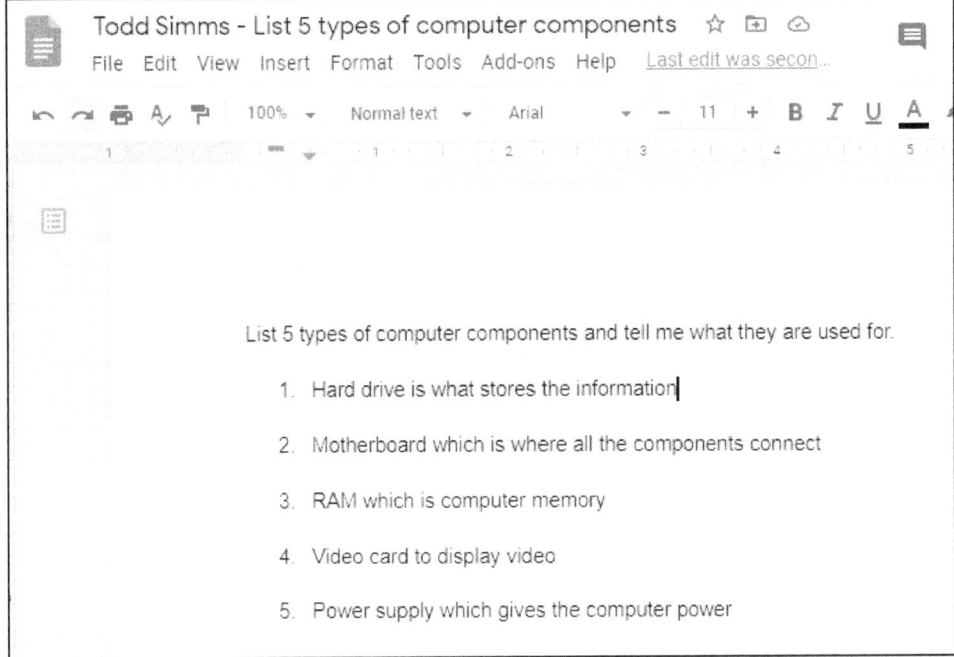

Figure 4.22

If you look back at figure 4.21 you will see that there is a button that says *Turn in* and the student can click on this button to have their assignment and the corresponding document turned in to the teacher for grading. When they click this button they will be asked to confirm that they want to turn in their work, and they can click on *Turn in* again.

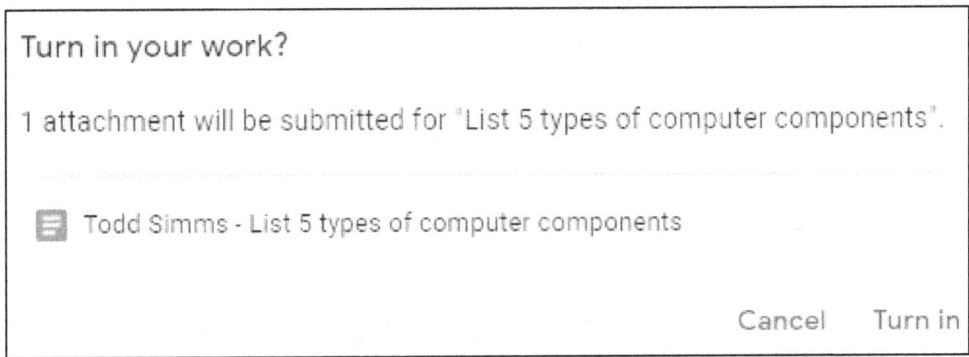

Figure 4.23

If the student decides that they need to make a change then they can click on the *Unsumbit* button to have the work be active again so they can make changes before the due date. You can disable this feature if you don't want them to have this option.

Chapter 4 – Running Your Classes

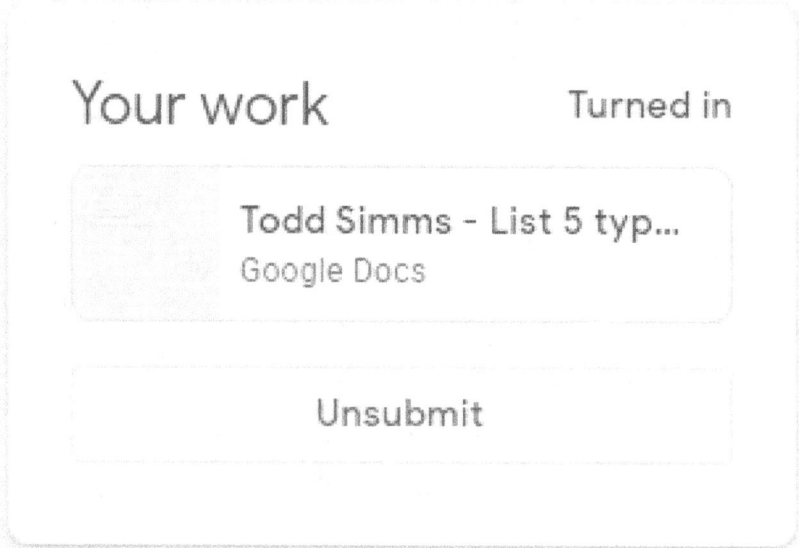

Figure 4.24

Now if the student goes back to the Classroom tab and clicks on the *View your work* link they will be able to see all of their classwork and their status.

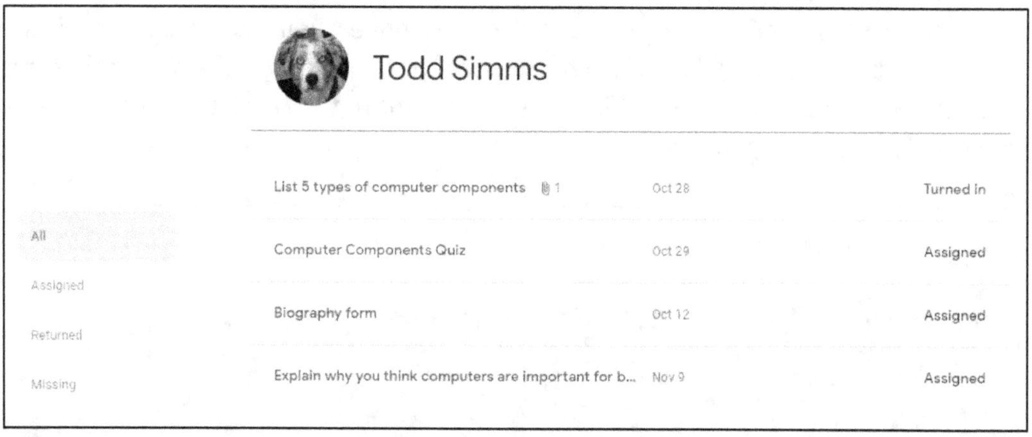

Figure 4.25

As the teacher you can also go back to the Classwork tab and click on a particular assignment and see how many people it has been assigned to and how many of them have turned it in.

Chapter 4 – Running Your Classes

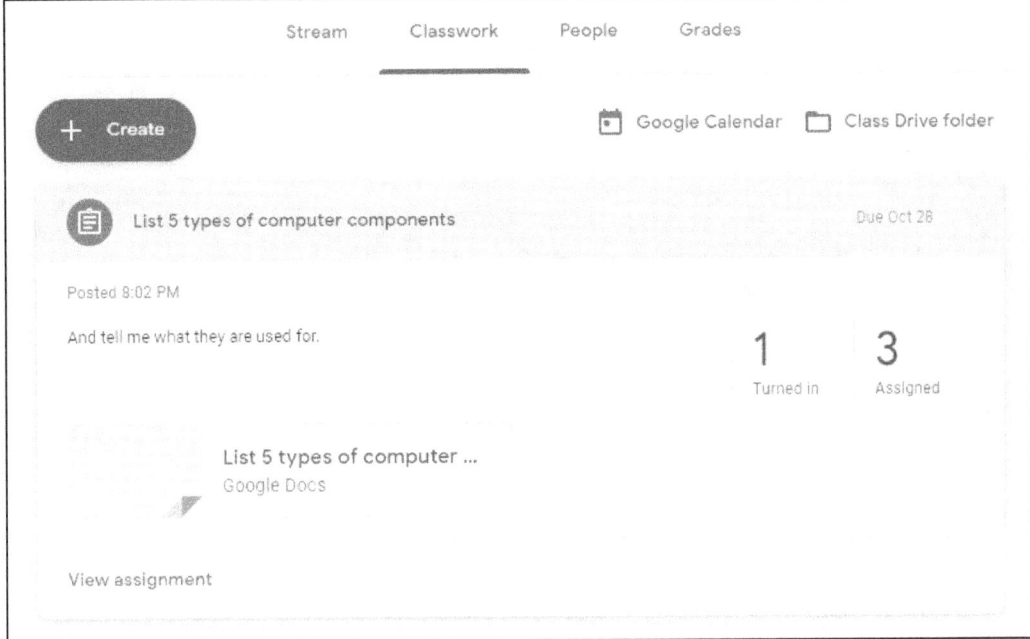

Figure 4.26

Quiz Assignment
A Quiz Assignment is similar to a regular assignment except that you will use an online Google Form to create a quiz that will then be attached to the assignment and the students will use this form to take their test.

Using a Google Form is similar to using a Google Doc like I did in the last section except there is a little more to creating a question and answer form than there is a basic document.

Immediately after you click on Quiz Assignment, Classroom will create a blank form and attach it to your assignment as seen in figure 4.27. You will still have all of the other options title, grading, due date and so on.

Chapter 4 – Running Your Classes

Figure 4.27

You can then click on the Blank Quiz to have it opened up so you can then edit it and add your questions.

Figure 4.28

72

Chapter 4 – Running Your Classes

When editing your quiz you can have it configured as a multiple choice, short answer, paragraph or you can use other types of responses. For my example I will be using a multiple choice configuration.

To begin I will type in the first question on the top line and then type in the first multiple choice answer where it says *Option 1*. I can then click on *Add Option* to add a second answer choice for my question and so on until I have all my choices. Then I will click on *Answer key* and select the correct answer, mark the question as required and assign it a value of 5 points. Finally I will click on the *Done* button.

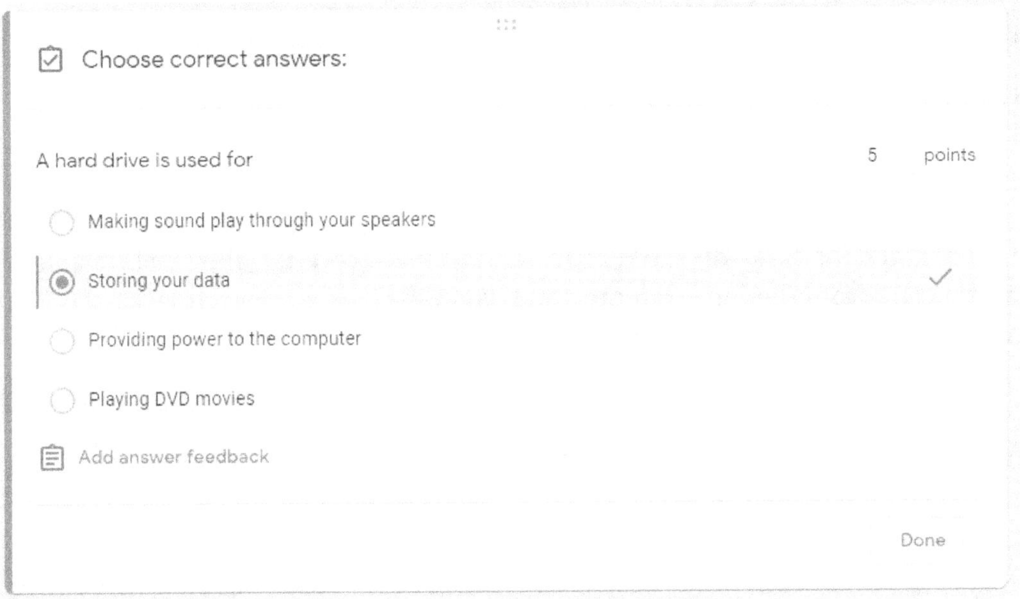

☑ Choose correct answers:

A hard drive is used for   5   points

○ Making sound play through your speakers

◉ Storing your data   ✓

○ Providing power to the computer

○ Playing DVD movies

▤ Add answer feedback

                                                                        Done

Figure 4.29

Then to add the next question I will simply click on the + sign at the bottom of the page as seen in figure 4.28 and repeat the process until I have all of my questions and answers ready to go. Next I will click on the title of the quiz to change the name of it from Blank Quiz to something more suited for my class. Figure 4.30 shows my configured quiz ready to go and all I need to do is click on *Assign* to have it pushed out to my students.

Chapter 4 – Running Your Classes

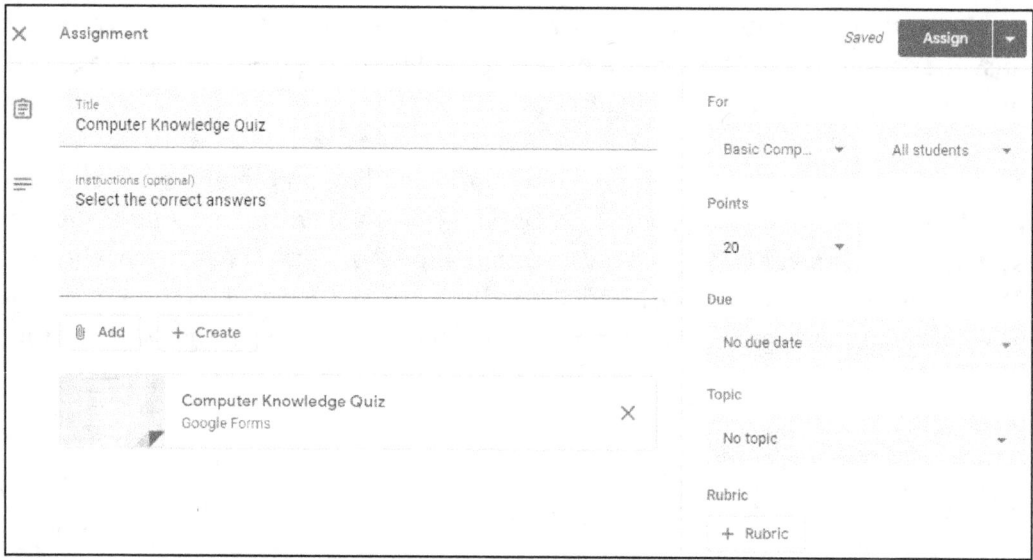

Figure 4.30

When a student clicks on the quiz from their Classwork tab they will be able to take it right from the form I created and when they are finished they can click on *Submit* to send the quiz back to be graded.

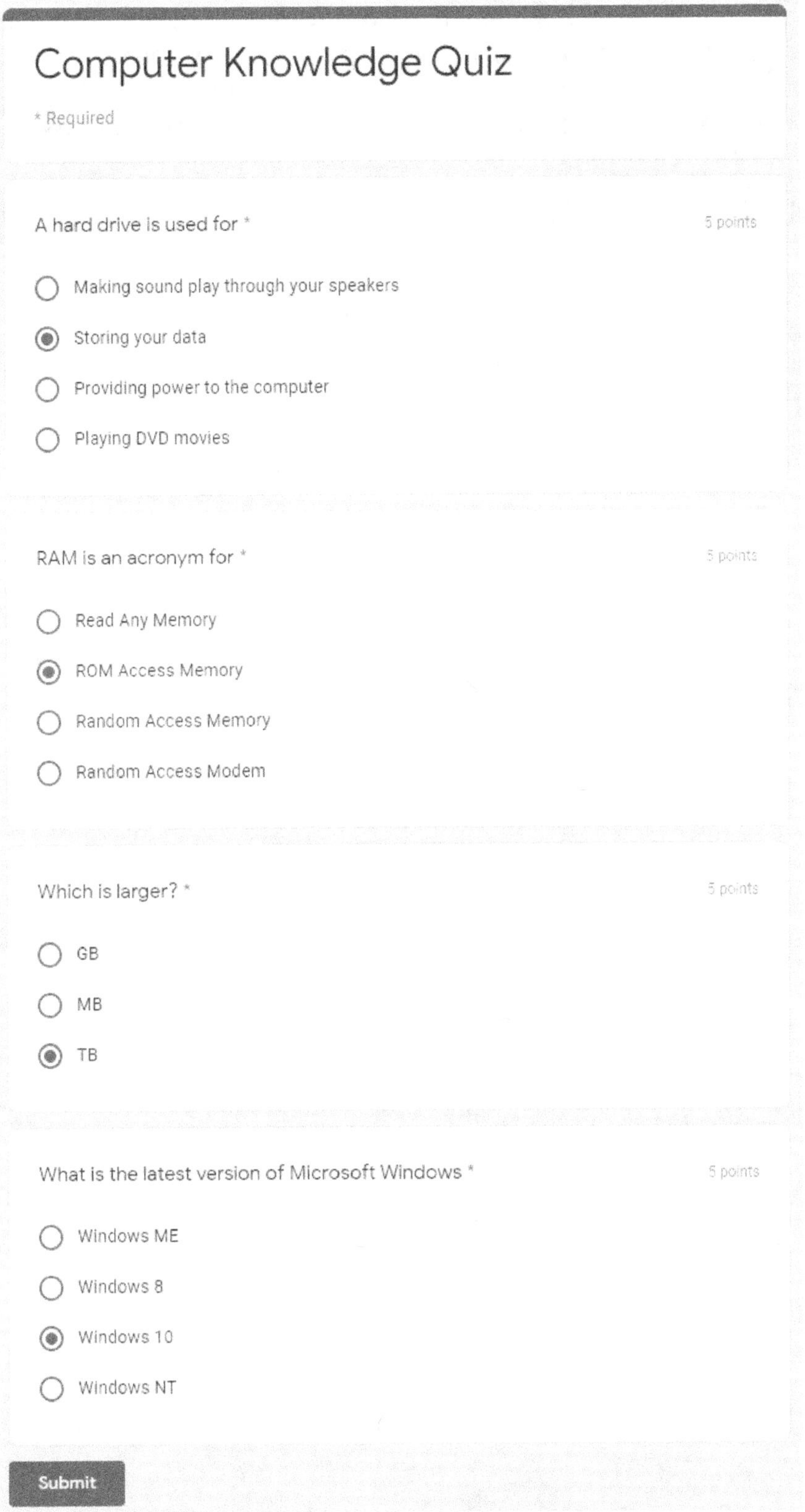

Chapter 4 – Running Your Classes

Computer Knowledge Quiz

* Required

A hard drive is used for *   5 points

○ Making sound play through your speakers
◉ Storing your data
○ Providing power to the computer
○ Playing DVD movies

RAM is an acronym for *   5 points

○ Read Any Memory
◉ ROM Access Memory
○ Random Access Memory
○ Random Access Modem

Which is larger? *   5 points

○ GB
○ MB
◉ TB

What is the latest version of Microsoft Windows *   5 points

○ Windows ME
○ Windows 8
◉ Windows 10
○ Windows NT

Submit

Figure 4.31

Chapter 4 – Running Your Classes

After they submit their answers they can see the results by clicking on *View score* or they can change their answers by clicking on *Submit another response*.

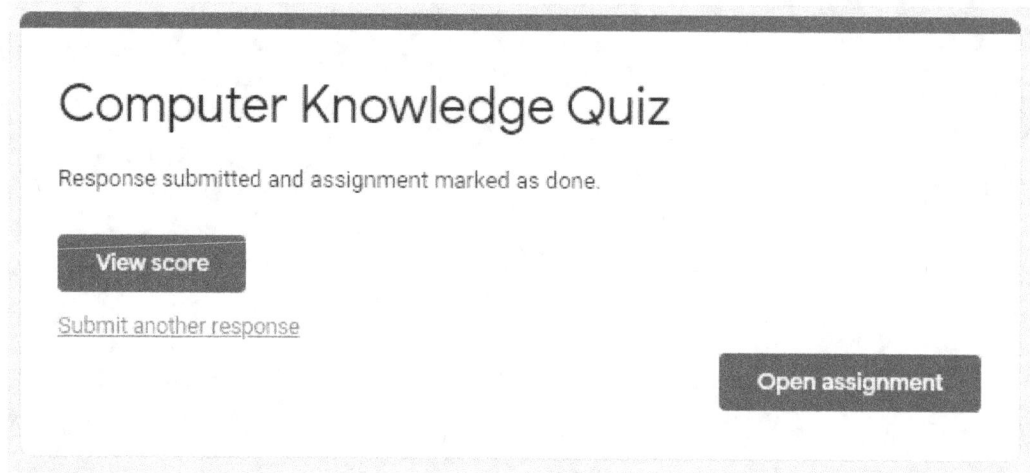

Figure 4.32

Figure 4.33 shows that Todd missed one of the questions, so he only got 15 out of 20 possible points.

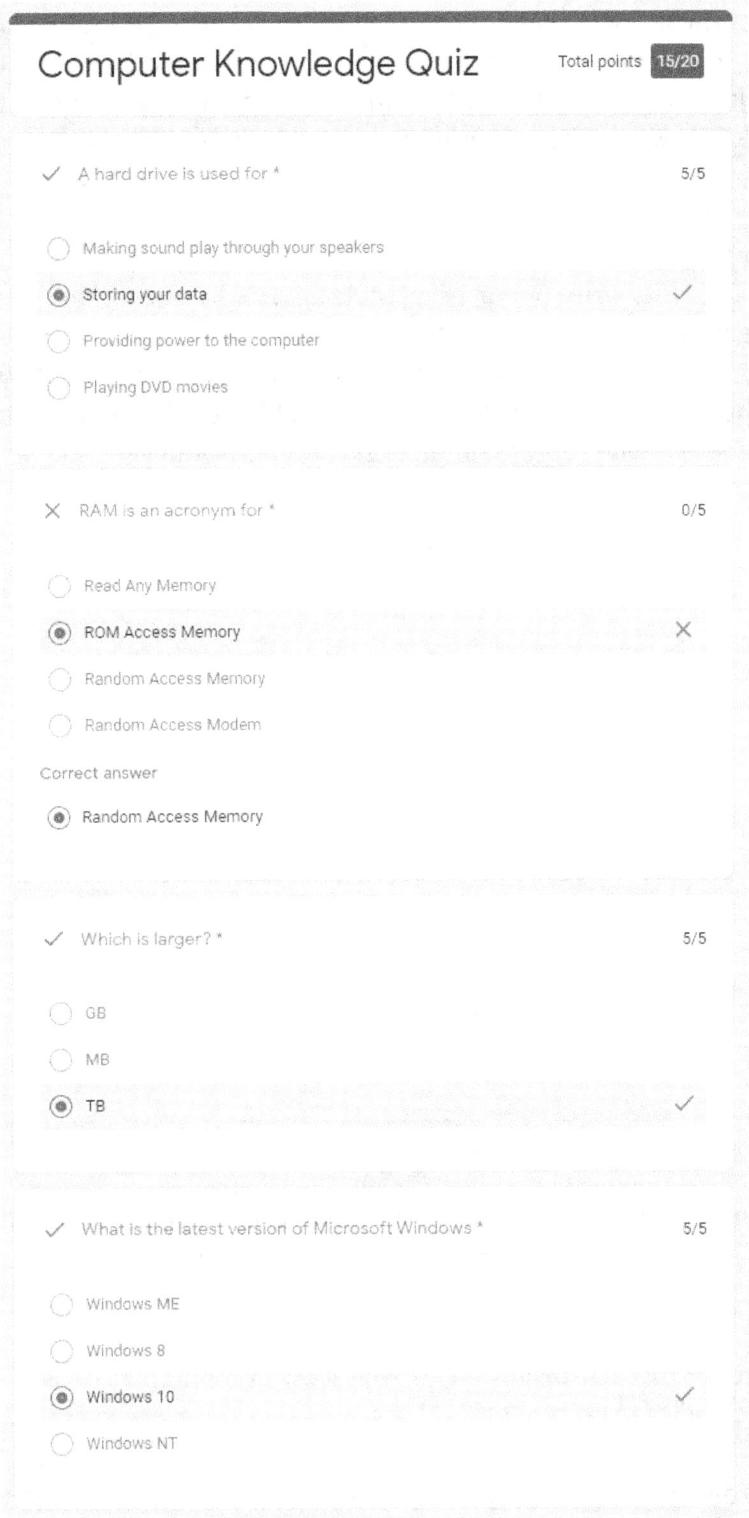

Chapter 4 – Running Your Classes

Computer Knowledge Quiz
Total points 15/20

✓ A hard drive is used for * — 5/5

○ Making sound play through your speakers
◉ Storing your data ✓
○ Providing power to the computer
○ Playing DVD movies

✗ RAM is an acronym for * — 0/5

○ Read Any Memory
◉ ROM Access Memory ✗
○ Random Access Memory
○ Random Access Modem

Correct answer
◉ Random Access Memory

✓ Which is larger? * — 5/5

○ GB
○ MB
◉ TB ✓

✓ What is the latest version of Microsoft Windows * — 5/5

○ Windows ME
○ Windows 8
◉ Windows 10 ✓
○ Windows NT

Figure 4.33

Chapter 4 – Running Your Classes

Google Forms is one of those tools that is simple yet very powerful and it would be impossible to give you a complete understanding of how it works without writing another book just on Forms itself so I recommend playing around with it by going to the Google Forms website rather than in your Classroom so you don't affect any of your assignments.

Question
If you prefer that your students write out an essay style answer to a question then you can choose to create a Question rather than an Assignment. If you choose *Short answer* as the type then there will be no answers to choose from and they can simply write out their answer and submit it. If you would like to provide them with a blank document to type out their answer on then you can add an attachment or create a new Google Document.

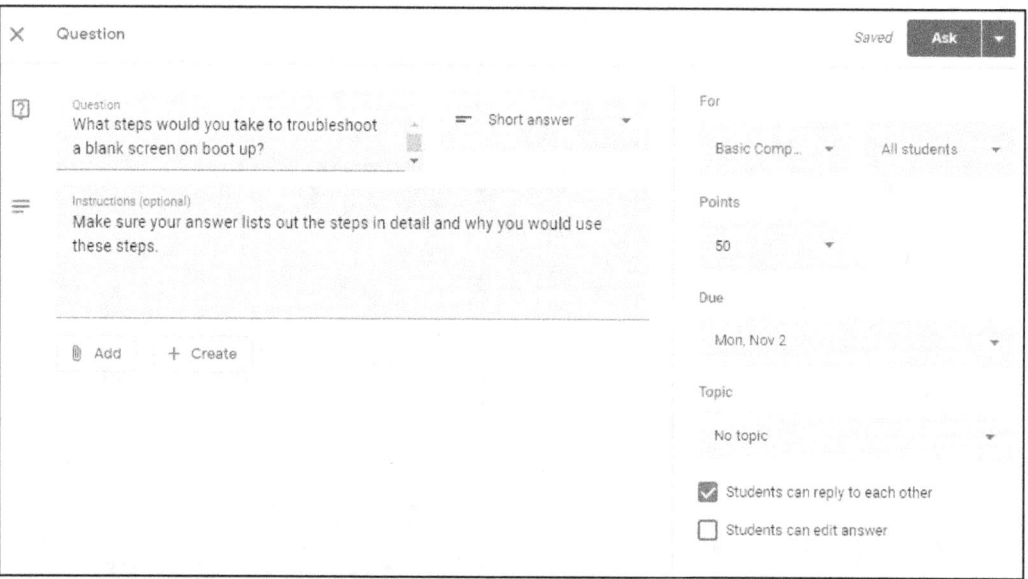

Figure 4.34

Questions have the same areas for points and due dates etc. but if you look at the bottom of figure 4.34 you will see that there are a couple of additional items you can check off.

- **Students can reply to each other** – This will allow students to see each other's answers and then comment on them

- **Students can edit answer** – This allows the student to go back and edit their work after they have turned it in to fix any mistakes before the due date.

Chapter 4 – Running Your Classes

When the student sees the question it will look like what you see in figure 4.35 and they would type in their answer at the top right where it says *Type your answer*.

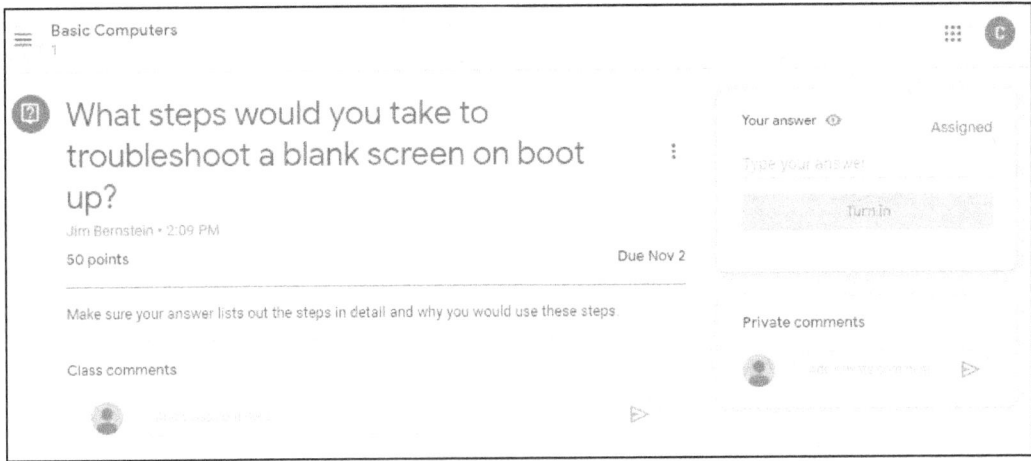

Figure 4.35

Once the student types in their answer and clicks on the Turn in button they will see a message as seen in figure 4.36 if the option to edit their work has not been enabled.

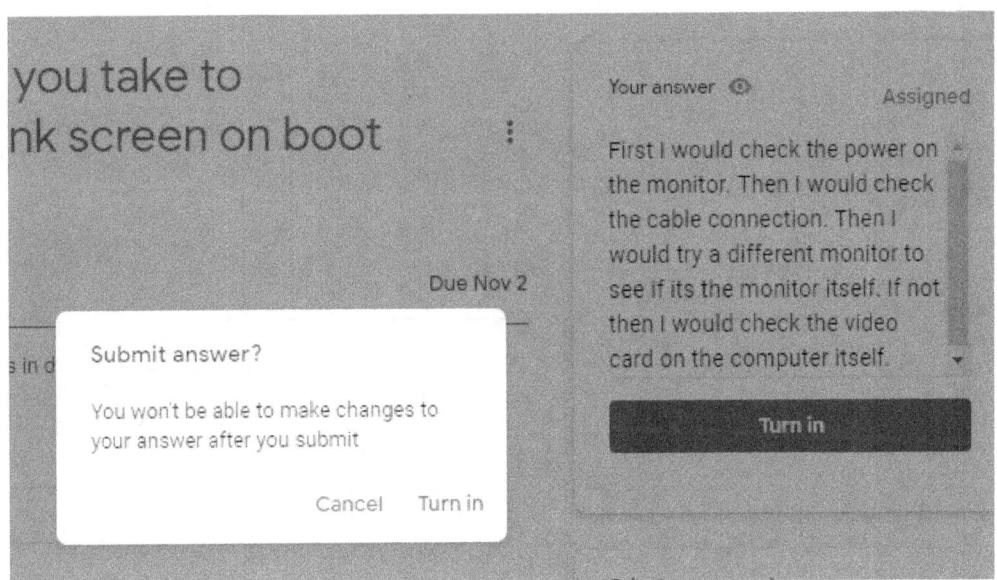

Figure 4.36

After a student turns in their answer they can go back into the question and click on See classmate answers (figure 4.37) to see how their fellow classmates answered the same question (figure 4.38).

Chapter 4 – Running Your Classes

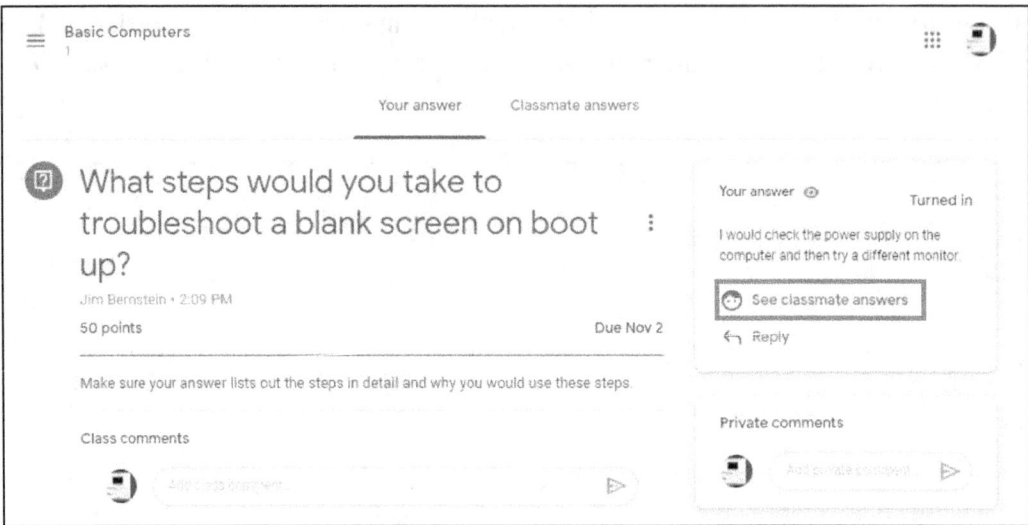

Figure 4.37

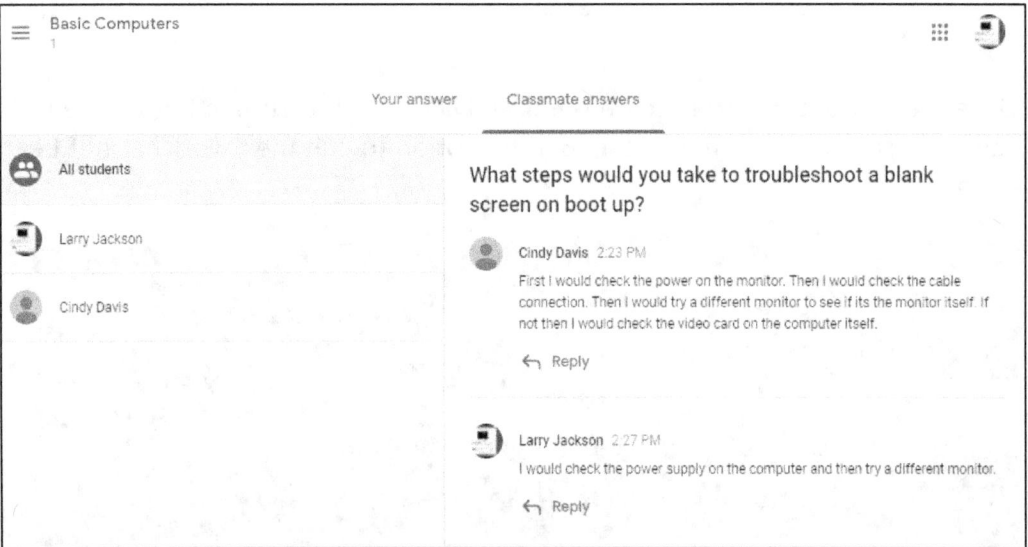

Figure 4.38

You might have noticed that there are a couple of spots to type comments in figure 4.37 and each one has a different purpose.

- **Class comments** – Any comments here can be seen by the teacher and any students in the class.

- **Private comments** – Comments made here will only be seen by the teacher or teachers.

Chapter 4 – Running Your Classes

Material

As a teacher, you know how important it is to have the right training materials to be able to give your students the information they need to learn the material in your class. When students are in a physical classroom setting they usually have their books with them as well as any handouts you might provide. Or maybe you show training videos on the projector in the classroom from time to time as well.

With Classroom you can still have the same types of learning materials, but your students will just go about obtaining them a different way when leaning at home. To add training material to a class you simply click on the *Create* button and choose *Material*.

From here you can do all of the same things that I have already discussed such as add a website link, YouTube video, attached file and even create new Google files on the spot and have them attached. Then this materials post will show up in the student's Classroom tab and they will also get an email notifying them of this new post.

Figure 4.39

Topics

You will most likely have a lot of assignments, materials and quizzes etc. in your Classwork tab and I guarantee it will get cluttered and difficult to manage very quickly. This is where topics can be used to help you organize all of your content into groups such as weekly work or by class sections etc.

Chapter 4 – Running Your Classes

You can create a topic from the Create button that you use to create assignments and quizzes etc. You can also create a topic as you are creating your classwork so you can have it organized on the spot rather than having to add your topic later.

To create a topic, click on the *Create* button while in the Classroom tab and then choose *Topic*. Then type in the name for your topic and then click the *Add* button.

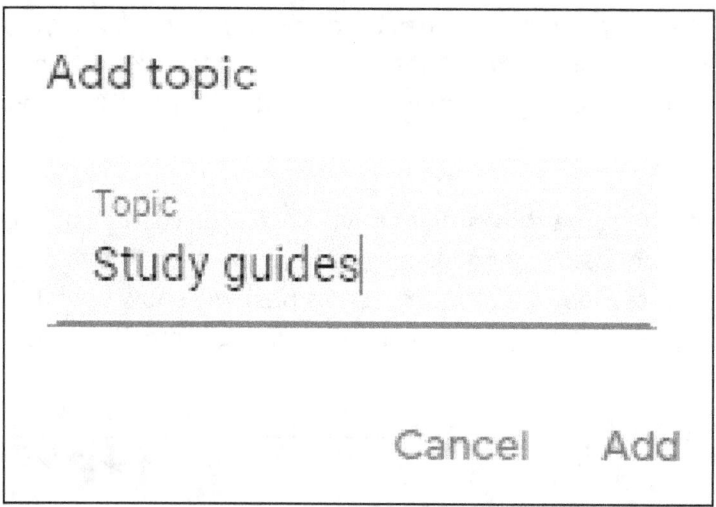

Figure 4.40

Now when I go back to my Classroom tab I will see my new Study guides topic at the bottom as well as on the left side of the screen under *All topics* (figure 4.41). I will now create some additional topics that I can use to help organize my classwork.

Chapter 4 – Running Your Classes

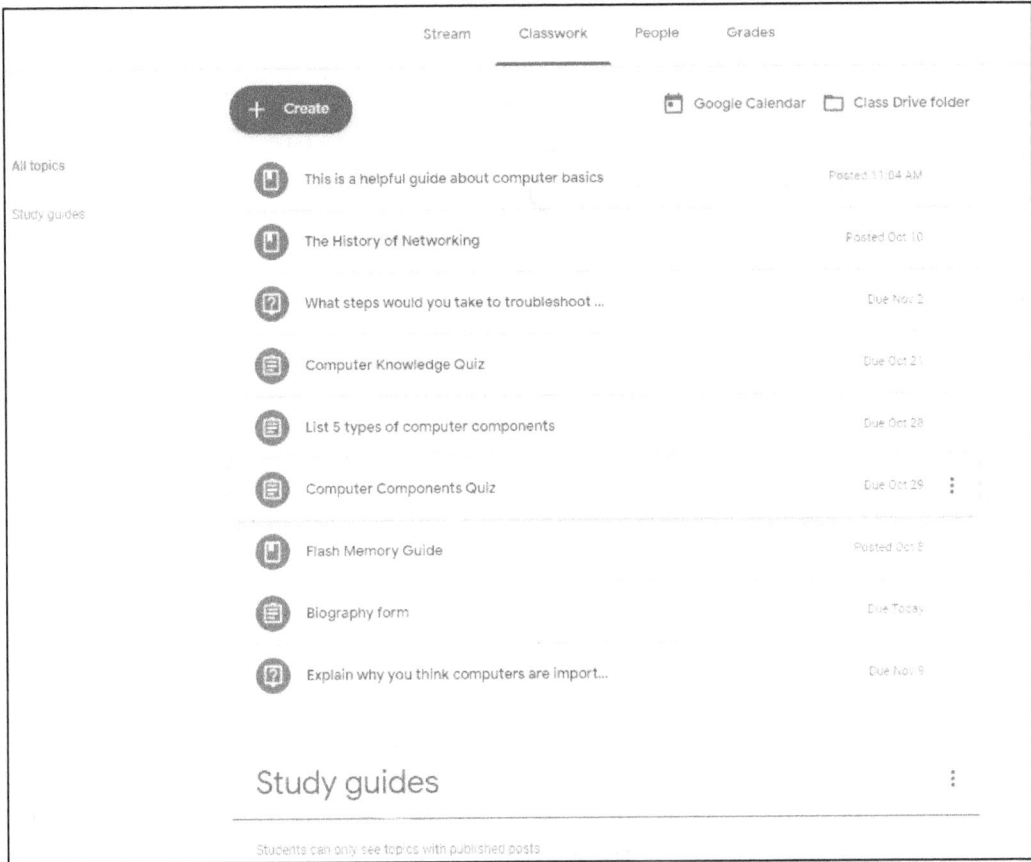

Figure 4.41

Once you create your topics you can simply drag and drop your assignments and quizzes into each topic section, or you can click the three vertical dots next to an assignment and choose Edit. From there you can then add that assignment to one of the topics you have created (figure 4.42).

Chapter 4 – Running Your Classes

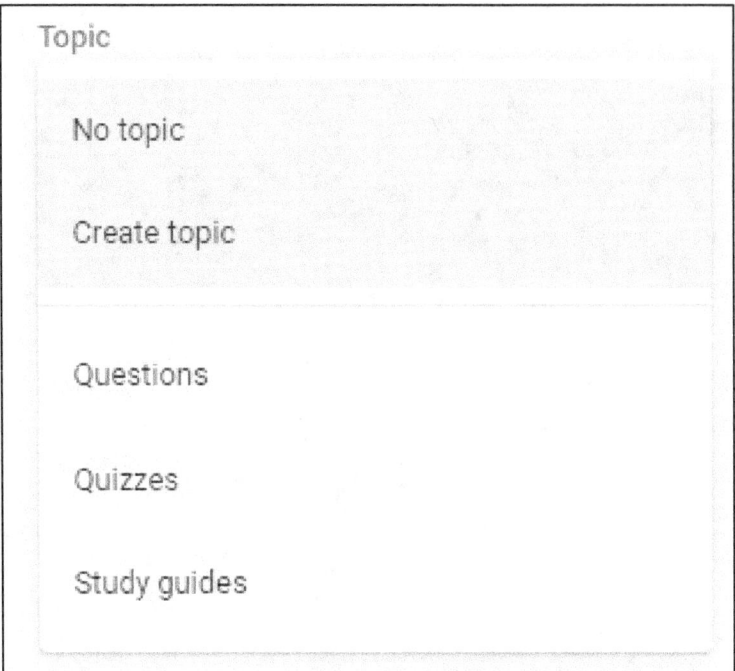

Figure 4.42

Figure 4.43 shows my Classwork tab after organizing everything into their respective topics. When your students go into their Classwork tab, they will see the same topics and have their assignments organized the same way, but they will not have the option to rearrange them into different topics.

If you click on a specific topic on the left side list then it will only show your work for that particular topic. This is a great way to narrow down your view, so you are only seeing what you need to see at the moment. You can also drag and drop your topics around the page to change their order.

 If you have more than ten items within one topic then you will see a *View More* button that you will need to click on in order to see your additional assignments and quizzes. You can always drag and drop your items around to have your favorites at the top.

Chapter 4 – Running Your Classes

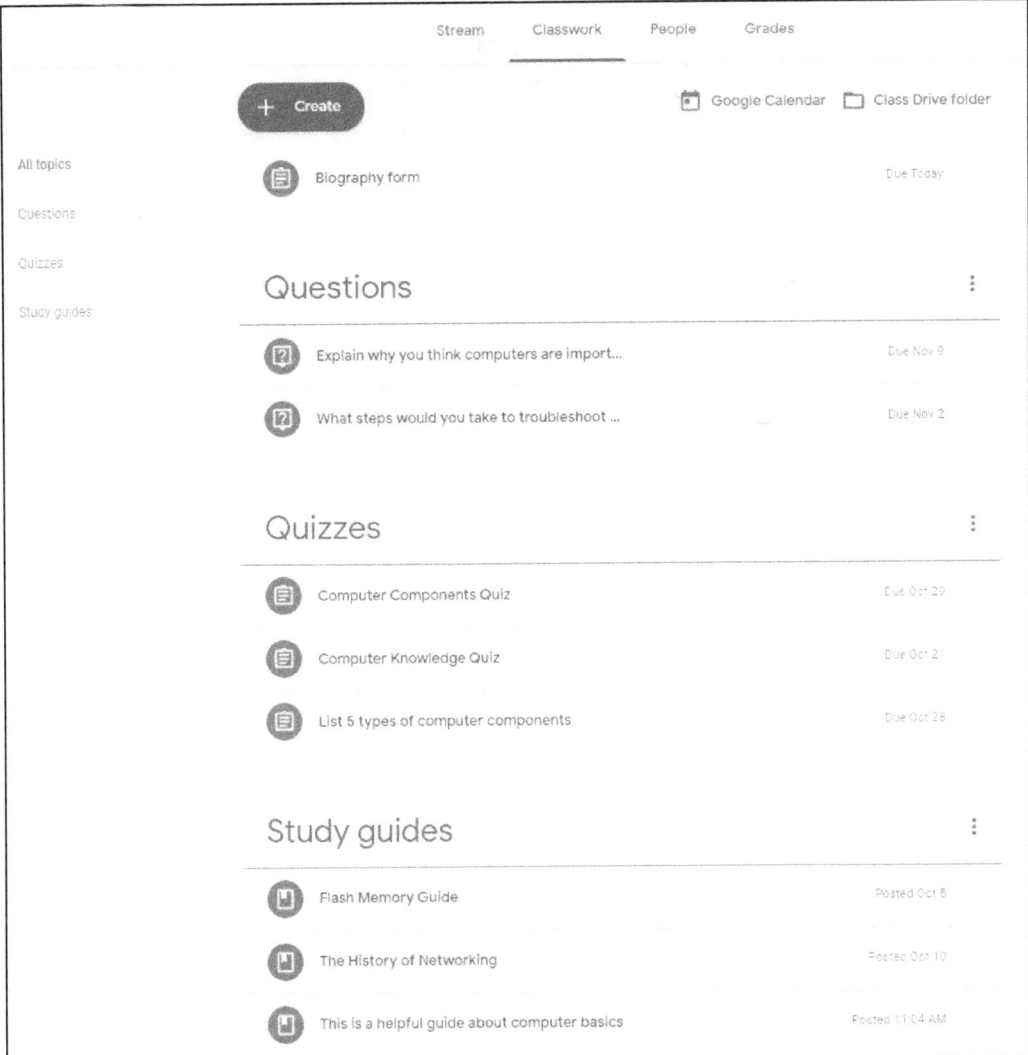

Figure 4.43

Another way to assign a topic to your student's work is to choose the topic while creating the assignment (figure 4.44). Then when you assign the work it will automatically be placed under the topic that you chose.

Chapter 4 – Running Your Classes

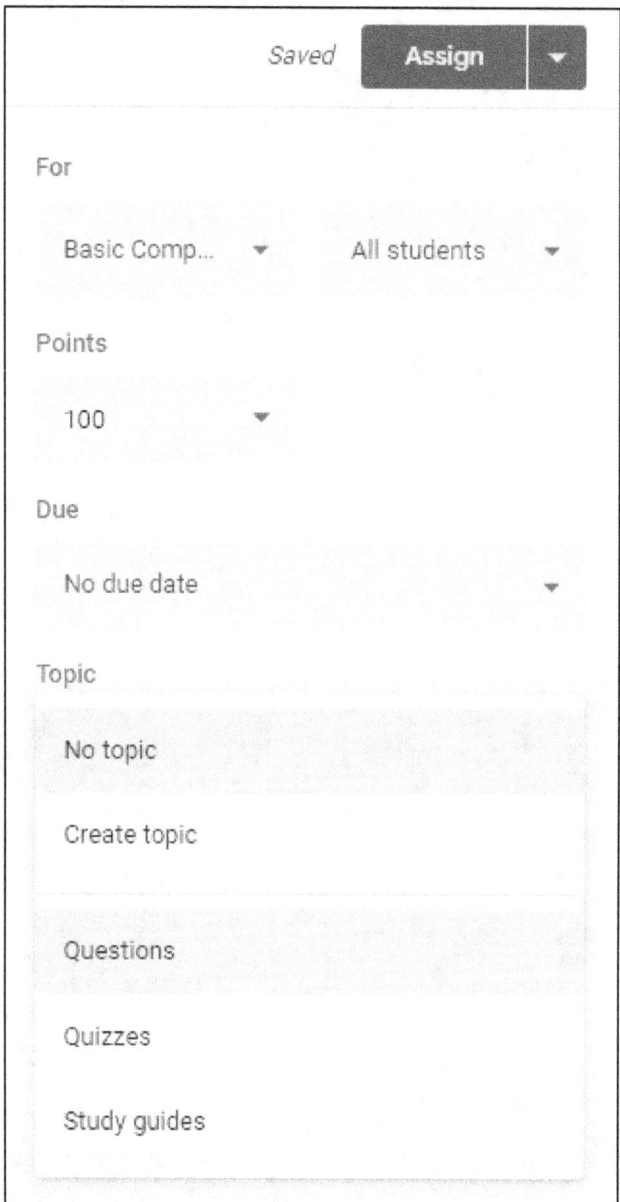

Figure 4.44

People Tab
When running a class, it's important to be able to keep track of all of your students so you know who is in what class and how to get in contact with your students when needed.

Chapter 4 – Running Your Classes

The People tab is fairly simple, and it will show you a listing of all the students in your class as well as the teacher (you) and any co-teachers you might have helping you out. From here you can also add additional students and teachers as needed.

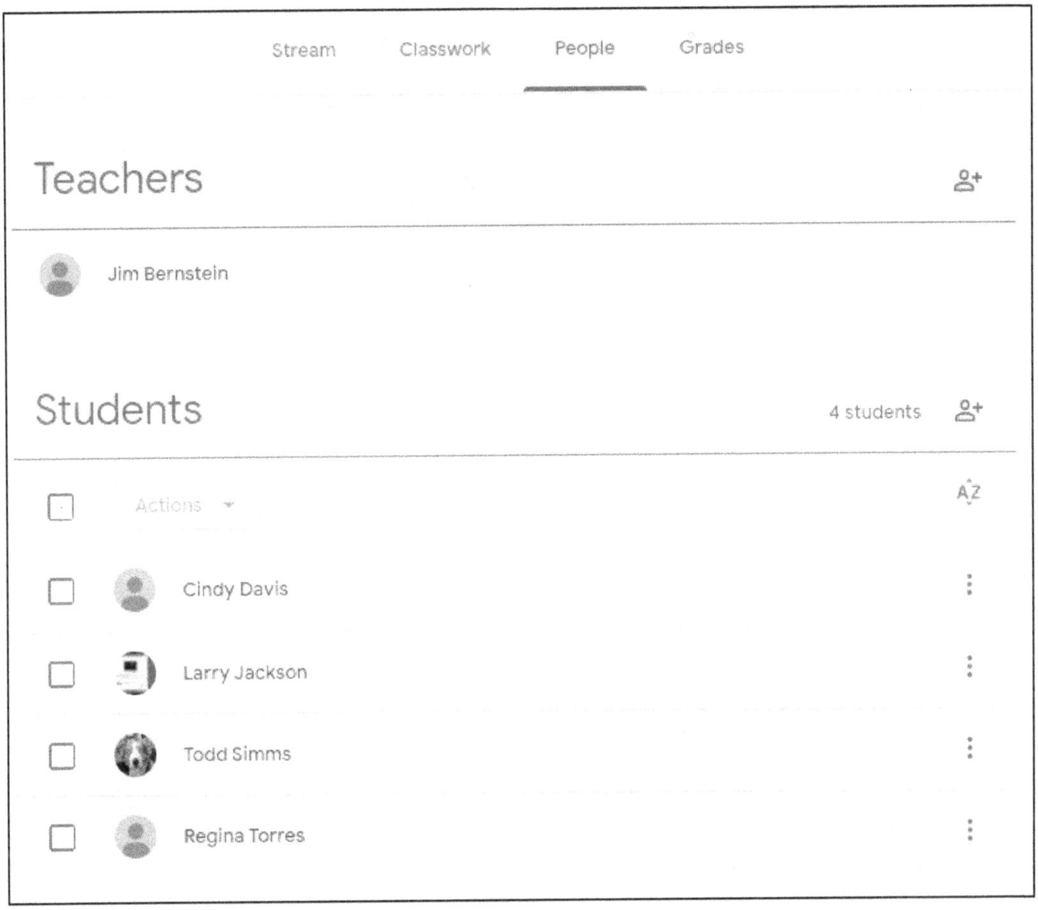

Figure 4.45

As I discussed in Chapter 3, to add a student or teacher you would click on the icon with the + symbol next to it and then you can type in their name or email address to invite them to your class. If you are using just a standard Google account and not a G-suite account then you will need to use their email address.

The *Actions* dropdown can be used to email, remove or mute a student or multiple students depending on how many of them you have selected using the checkbox next to their name.

Chapter 4 – Running Your Classes

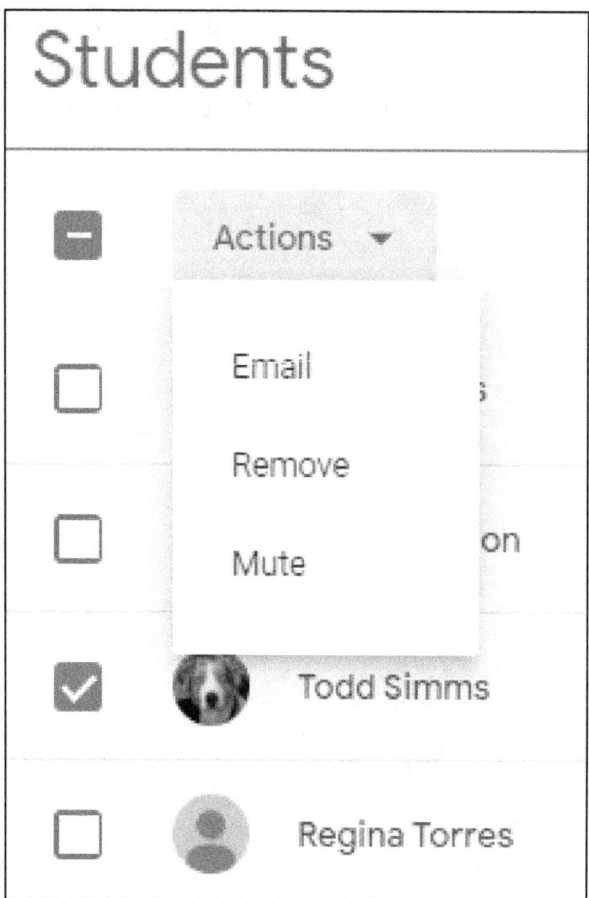

Figure 4.46

When you mute a student they won't be able to post or comment in the class stream but can still send private messages to the teacher. They also won't be able to reply to other student's work and other students won't see their turned in work until they are unmuted.

If you have a lot of students and would like to change how they are listed then you can click on the AZ button to have them sorted alphabetically starting from A or starting from Z.

Clicking on a particular student will bring you into their work summary where you can see their work and filter it based on all work, turned in, returned or missing.

Chapter 4 – Running Your Classes

	Todd Simms		
All	What steps would you take to troubleshoot a blank sc...	Oct 26	Assigned
Turned in	Computer Knowledge Quiz	Oct 21	15/20
Returned	List 5 types of computer components 1	Oct 28	Turned in
Missing	Computer Components Quiz	Oct 29	15/20 Not turned in
	Biography form	Today	Assigned
	Explain why you think computers are important for b...	Oct 21	Assigned

Figure 4.47

To Review and To-do Sections

Once you start adding things like assignments, quizzes and questions to your classes for your students to work on you might find that things will start to get a little overwhelming and hard to keep track of. Your students might also have the same issue if they have a lot of classes and assignments to work on.

Fortunately, Classroom has a place where both students and teachers can go to see what work they have coming up to help them manage their time and to ensure that the work gets turned in and graded on time.

If you are a teacher and wish to see how well your tasks are getting completed, you can click on the three horizontal lines at the top left of the screen and from there you will click on *To review*.

Chapter 4 – Running Your Classes

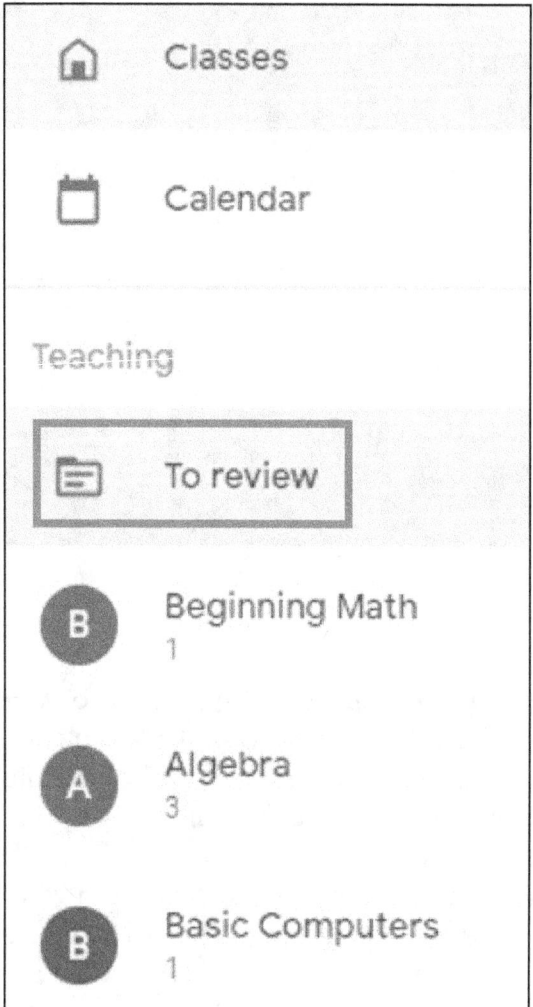

Figure 4.48

The To review section is divided up between work in progress with due dates and then other work with no due dates. As you can see in figure 4.49 I have one item with no due dates and six items pending that do have due dates. I can click on any of these items to be taken to the summary statistics for that assignment as seen in figure 4.50. From here I can view, grade and return the assignment if needed. I will be going over grading in Chapter 5.

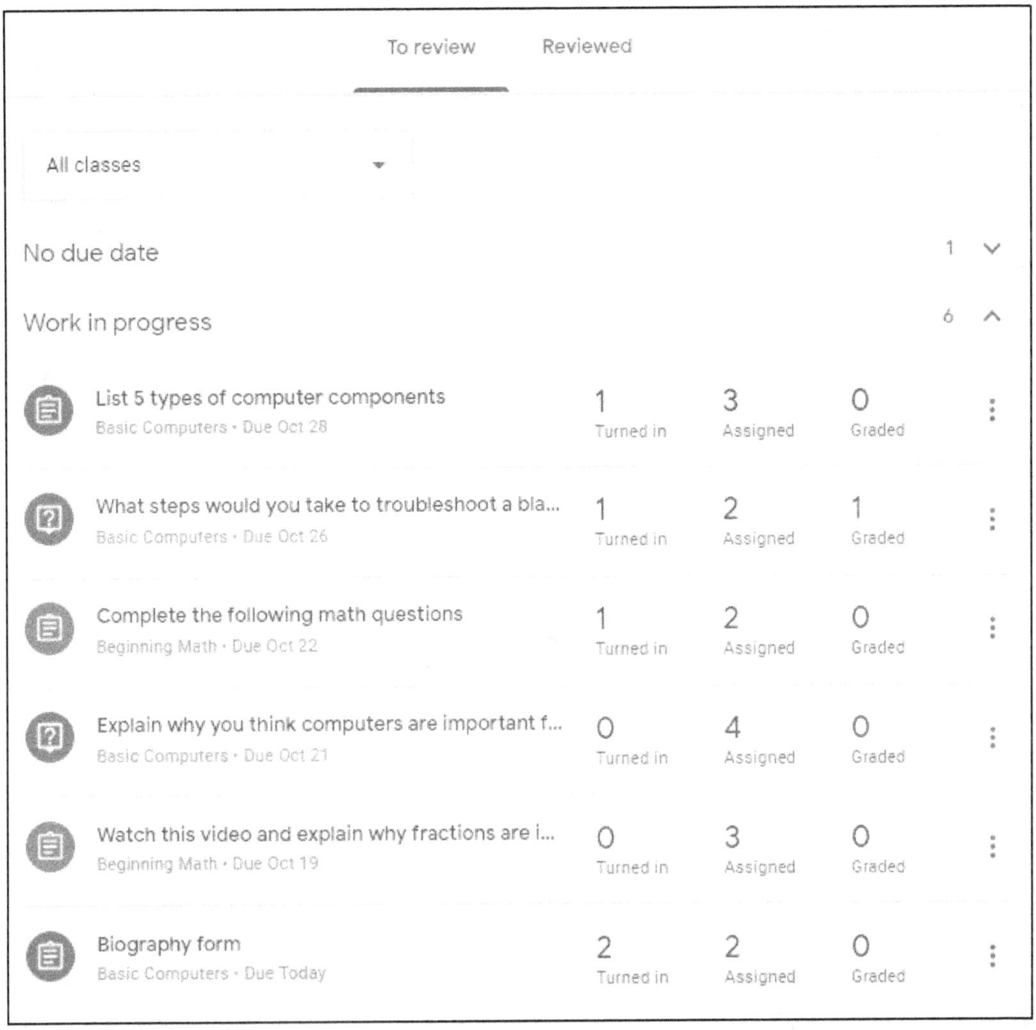

Chapter 4 – Running Your Classes

	To review	Reviewed			
All classes ▼					
No due date				1	˅
Work in progress				6	˄
List 5 types of computer components Basic Computers · Due Oct 28	1 Turned in	3 Assigned	0 Graded		⋮
What steps would you take to troubleshoot a bla... Basic Computers · Due Oct 26	1 Turned in	2 Assigned	1 Graded		⋮
Complete the following math questions Beginning Math · Due Oct 22	1 Turned in	2 Assigned	0 Graded		⋮
Explain why you think computers are important f... Basic Computers · Due Oct 21	0 Turned in	4 Assigned	0 Graded		⋮
Watch this video and explain why fractions are i... Beginning Math · Due Oct 19	0 Turned in	3 Assigned	0 Graded		⋮
Biography form Basic Computers · Due Today	2 Turned in	2 Assigned	0 Graded		⋮

Figure 4.49

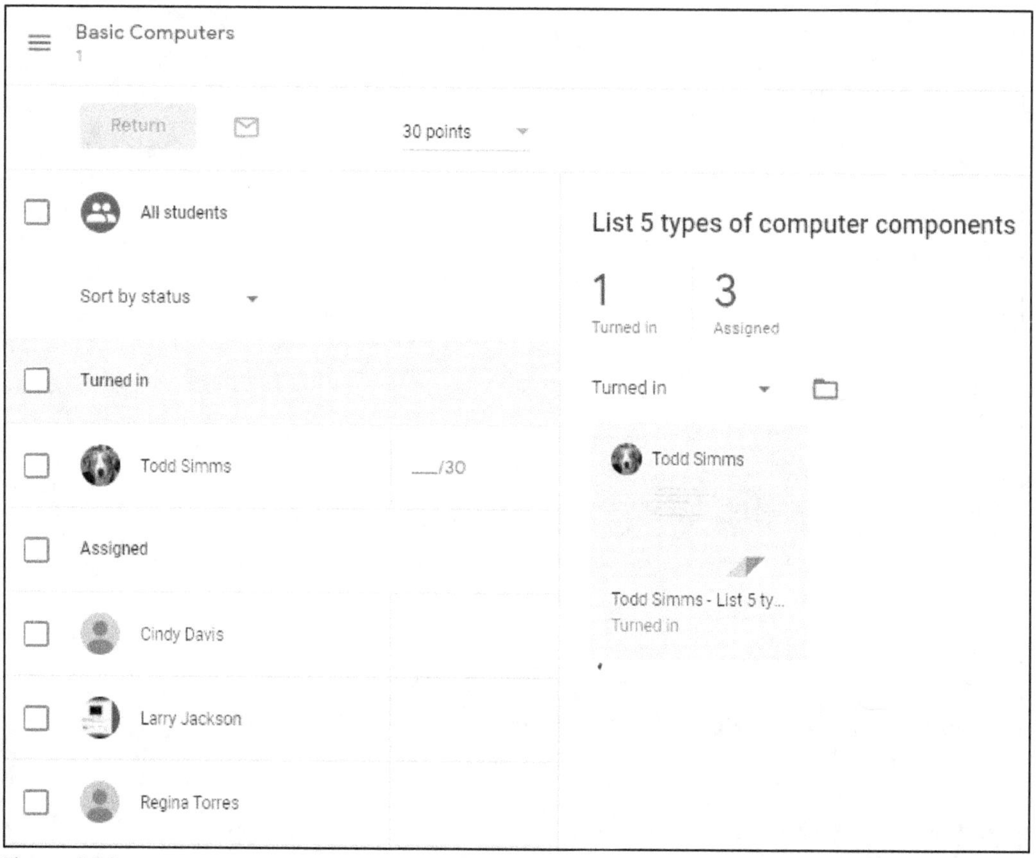

Chapter 4 – Running Your Classes

Figure 4.50

When you have reviewed, graded and returned an assignment you should then mark it as reviewed by clicking on the three vertical dots next to that assignment and then click on *Mark as reviewed*. After you do this it will then show up under the *Reviewed* tab as seen in figure 4.51. If you change your mind you can click on the three dots again from here and choose *Mark as not reviewed*.

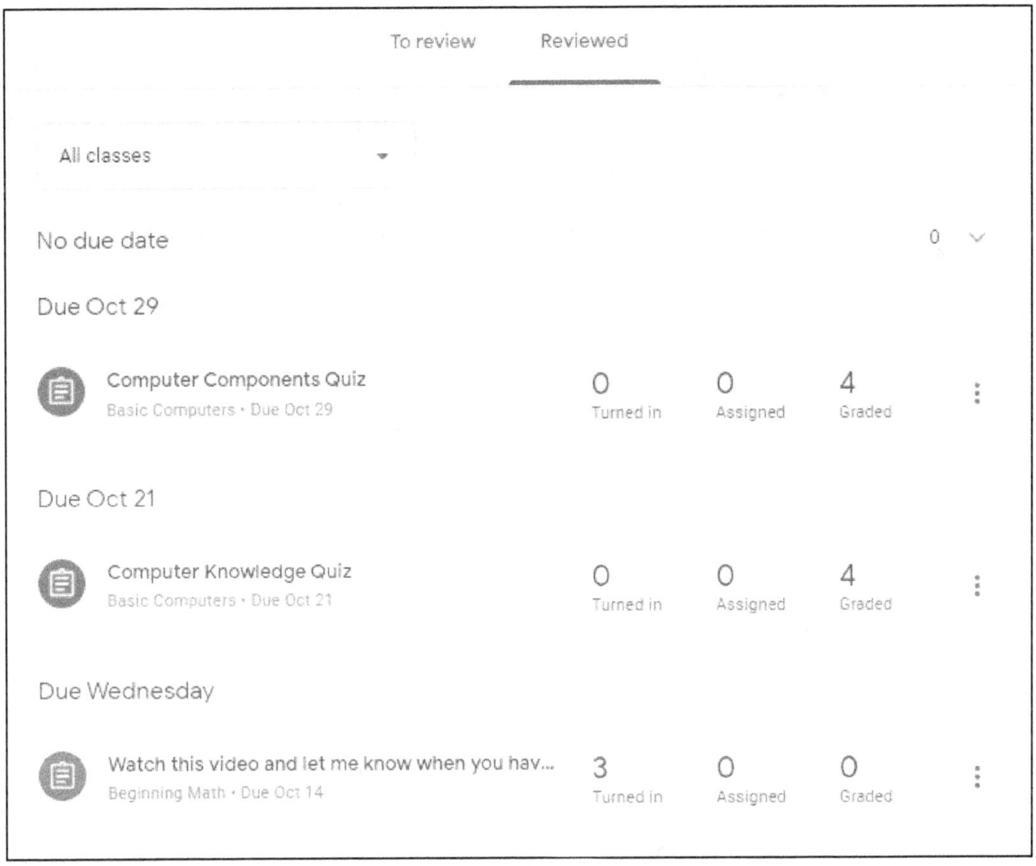

Chapter 4 – Running Your Classes

	To review	Reviewed			
All classes					
No due date					0
Due Oct 29					
Computer Components Quiz Basic Computers · Due Oct 29		0 Turned in	0 Assigned	4 Graded	
Due Oct 21					
Computer Knowledge Quiz Basic Computers · Due Oct 21		0 Turned in	0 Assigned	4 Graded	
Due Wednesday					
Watch this video and let me know when you hav... Beginning Math · Due Oct 14		3 Turned in	0 Assigned	0 Graded	

Figure 4.51

Your students will have a similar area that they can go to and see their upcoming work, so they don't miss out on anything that is due soon. From the same three vertical lines then will click on *To-do* which will take them to an area where they can see their work in progress as seen in figure 4.52.

Chapter 4 – Running Your Classes

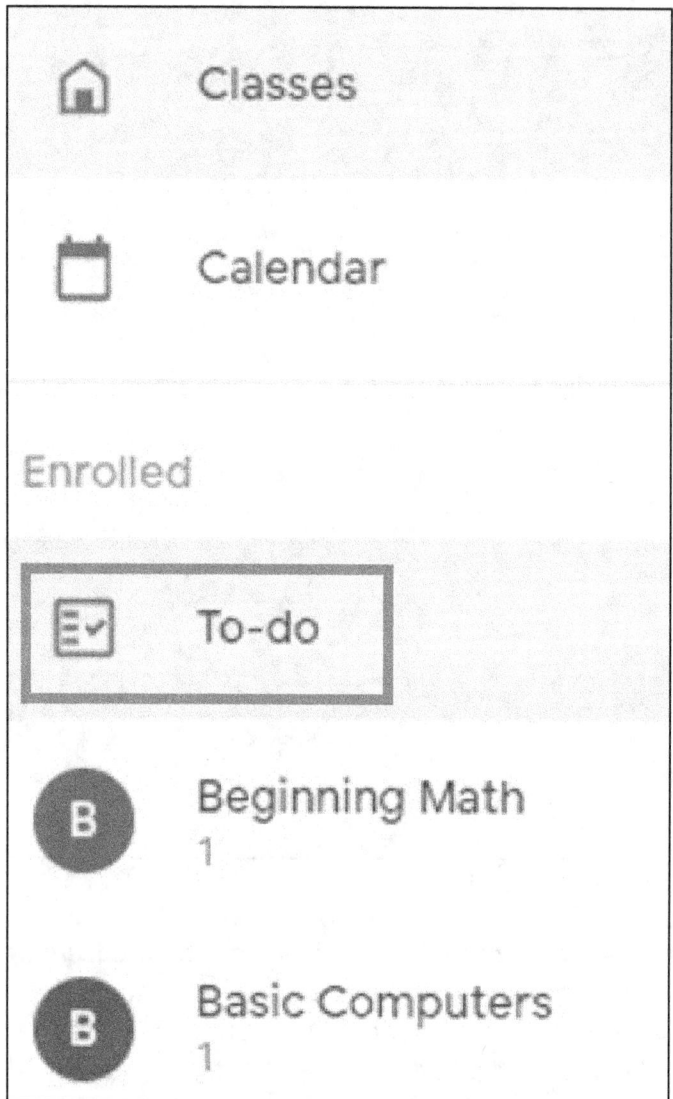

Figure 4.52

Chapter 4 – Running Your Classes

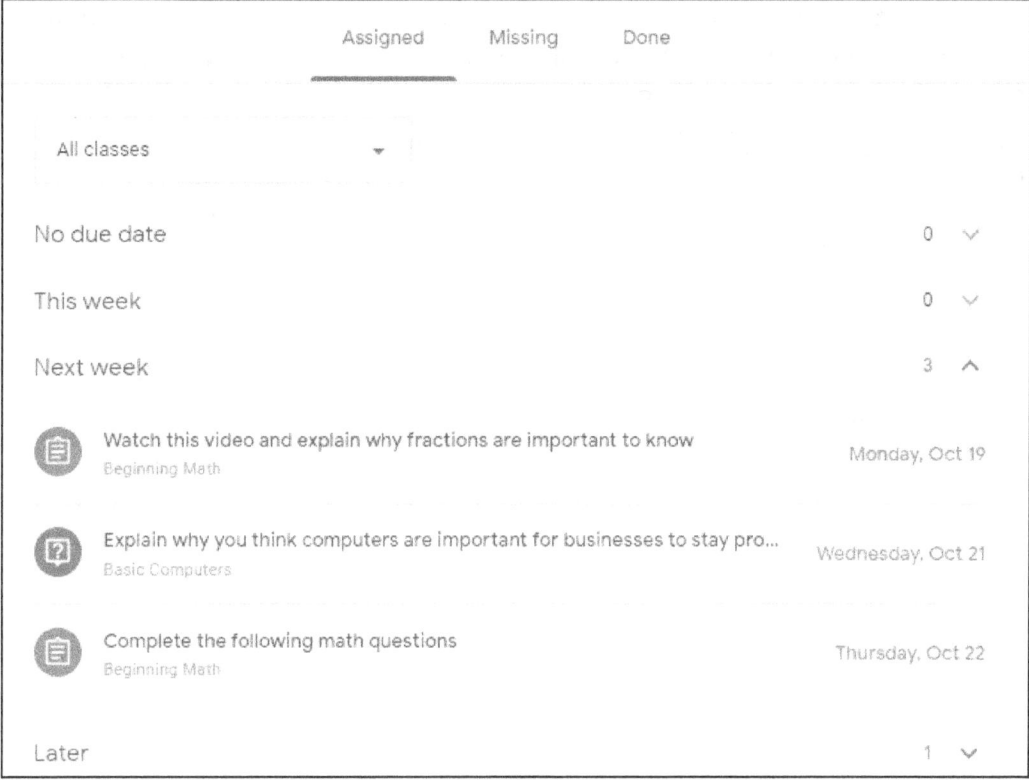

Figure 4.53

From here they can view the work that is assigned to them from all of their classes or they can select to see only the work from a particular class. This section is broken down into work that has no due date, work that is due this week, work that is due next week and work that is due later.

They can also click on the *Missing* tab to see any work that is past due as well as click on the *Done* tab to see work that they have completed.

Class Drive Folder
When you upload documents or create class files using Google Docs, these files will get uploaded to your Google Drive folder for that particular class, making them easy to find if you need to get to them later on. By keeping them online in your Drive, you can access them anywhere you have an internet connection. If you only kept them on your computer's hard drive and were not at your computer and needed a document/file then you would be out of luck.

Chapter 4 – Running Your Classes

You might have noticed that when you attach a file from your Google Drive to an assignment that you have a folder called *Classroom* listed in the My Drive section of your Drive.

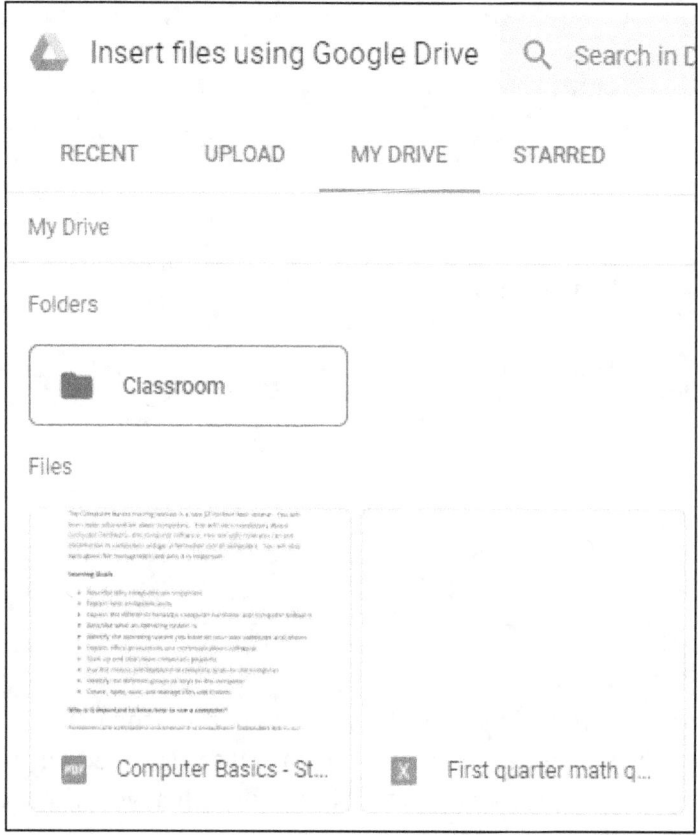

Figure 4.54

If you double click on the Classroom folder it will open up to show you all of the subfolders it has for your Classroom account. There will be one folder for each one of your classes and these folders will store the files associated with that class.

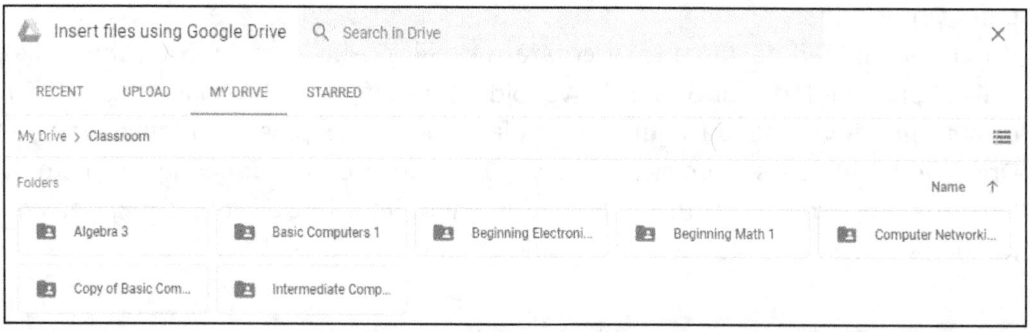

Figure 4.55

Chapter 4 – Running Your Classes

For example, If I were to double click on my Basic Computers folder I would see the files associated with that class (figure 4.56).

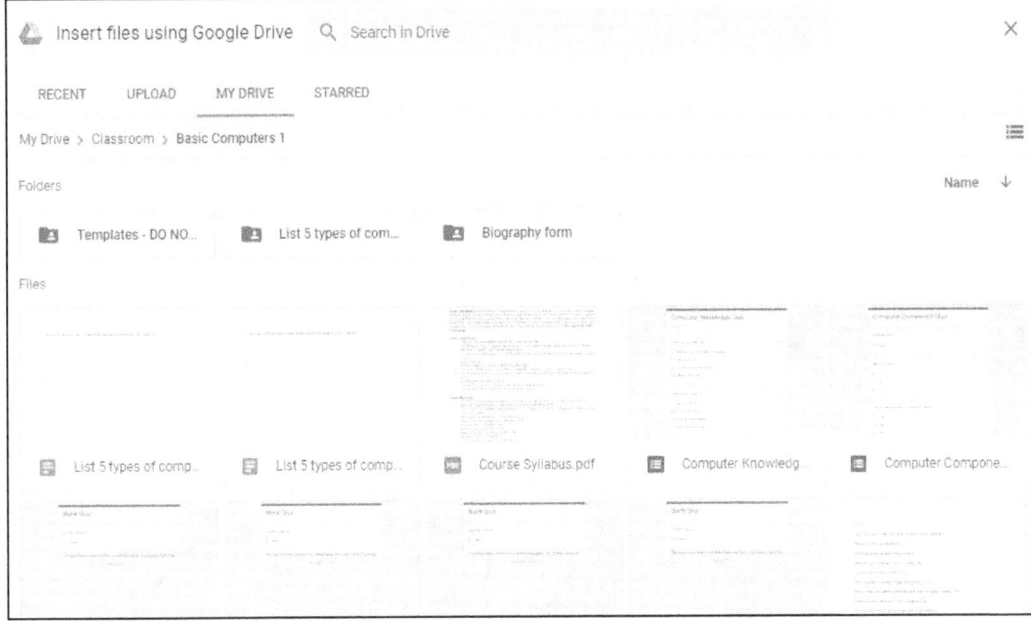

Figure 4.56

There are also folders within this classroom folder that are automatically created by Classroom as needed to organize certain files such as the responses to my Biography form assignment that were turned in by my students.

If you would like to see your Drive files for a certain class without having to go through the process of creating an assignment then you can go to the Classwork tab of that class and then click on *Class Drive folder* or click the folder icon on your class card.

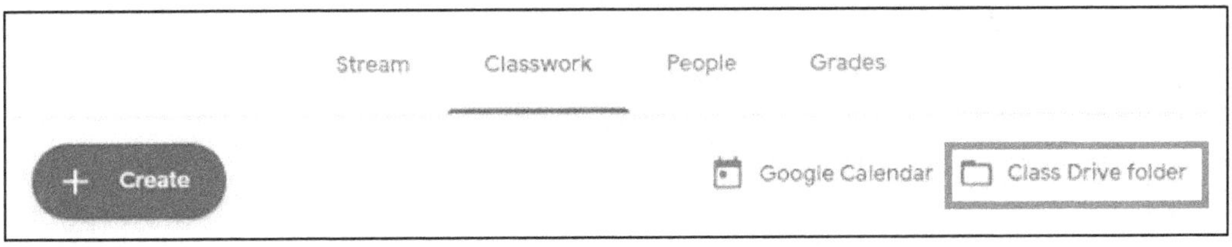

Figure 4.57

You can also go to your Google Apps next to your profile picture and click on the Drive icon to open the Google Drive folders for your account which will show you all of your files and folders.

Chapter 4 – Running Your Classes

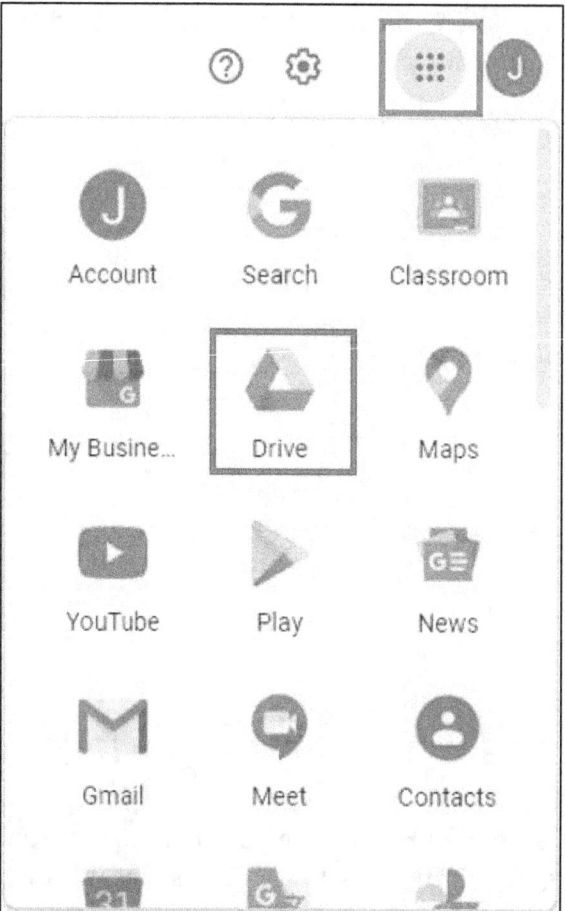
Figure 4.58

From here I can do things such as download my files to my hard drive, upload new files to my Google Drive or delete files I don't need anymore. I will be going into more detail on Google Drive in Chapter 6.

Chapter 5 – Grading

In order for your students and their parents to know how well they are doing in your classes; you will need to provide them with some type of report card or grades that will show their overall performance. Fortunately, Google Classroom has a built in grading system that you can use to grade their assignments and quizzes and then you can send them the results when you are finished.

The grading system in Classroom is not perfect and may be on the simple side for some teachers but it still offers an effective way for you to let your students know how well they are performing in your classes. There are also a few different ways to grade their work and I will be going over these methods in this chapter.

There are several ways to get to your student work so you can start the grading process so it's up to you to use the method that works the best for you, or you can use several methods once you get the hang of how things work.

Grades Tab
You most likely have noticed the Grades tab while working with your classes and assumed that this is where you will need to go to do your grading. Yes, this is one place you can go for the grading process but it's not the only way to get the job done.

To see the overall grades for a particular class you can click on the Grades tab while in that class to see your assignments and quizzes to find out who has turned them in and what grades you have given your students so far. If you have not graded any work then you won't see any grades like you do for some of my student's classwork shown in figure 5.1.

Chapter 5 – Grading

		Oct 26 What steps...	Oct 21 Computer Knowled...	Oct 28 List 5 types of...	Oct 29 Computer Compon...	Oct 12 Biography form	Oct 21 Explain why you...
Sort by last name		out of 50	out of 20	out of 30	out of 20	out of 10	out of 10
Class average		40	17.5		17.5		
Cindy Davis		40	15	__/30	0 Draft	__/10	__/10
Larry Jackson		__/50	20		20 Resubmitted	__/10	__/10
Todd Simms		__/50	15	__/30	15 Resubmitted	Missing	__/10
Regina Torres			20		0 Draft	Missing	__/10

Figure 5.1

If you would like to view a specific assignment before grading it then you can simply click on the assignment name at the top of the particular column to open it up and show a more detailed view of its status as seen in figure 5.2.

As you can see, two of my students have turned in the assignment (Larry & Todd) but I haven't graded them, one student still needs to turn in the assignment (Regina) and one other student has received a grade (Cindy).

At the top of the screen you can see that I can toggle between the question and the student's answers since this was a question and answer type assignment and you can also see that the point value for this assignment is 50. The __/50 means that I need to assign a point value grade to those students with 50 points being the highest score they can receive.

If I want to comment on my student's work I can type in a message where it says *Reply* under their answer and send them some feedback on why I gave them the grade I did.

Chapter 5 – Grading

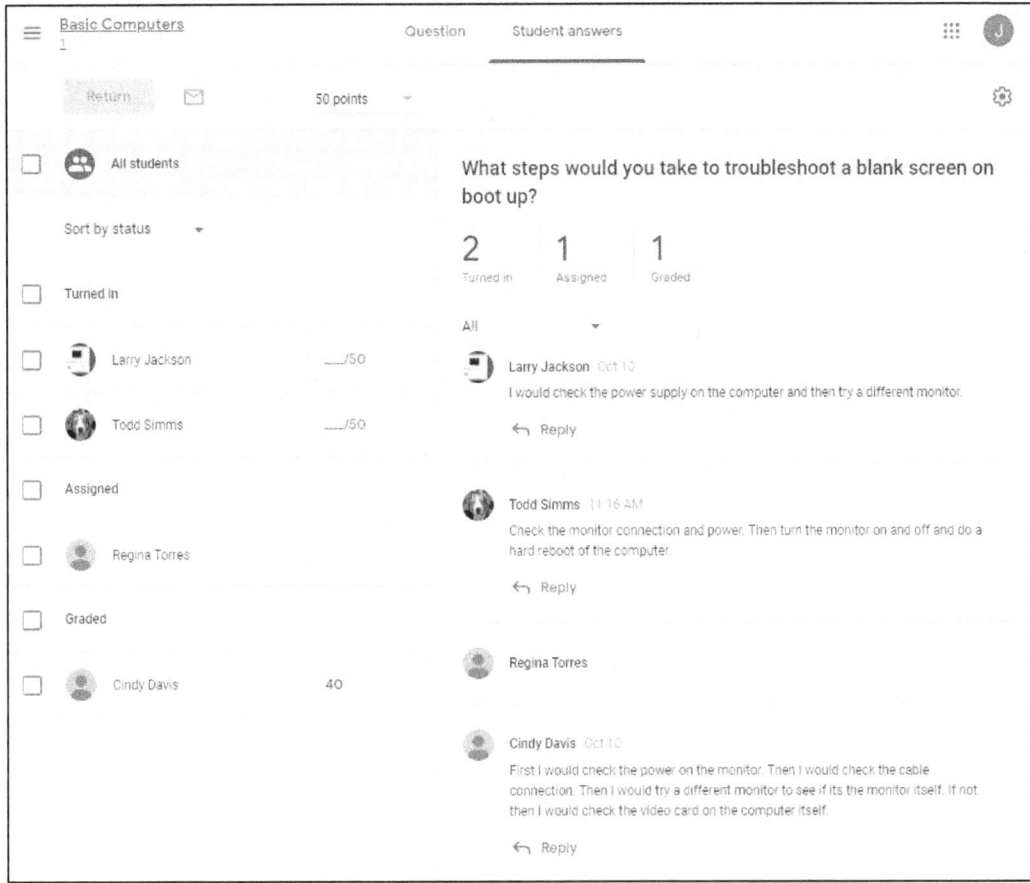

Figure 5.2

Grading and Returning Assignments

Once you find the assignment or quiz you would like to grade, it's very easy to assign a grade to the work and then send it back to the student. Figure 5.3 shows that I determined that Larry deserved 30 points out of 50 for his answer and I also typed in a comment as to why I gave him that score below his answer. Once I am done grading his work I can click on the *Return* button to have his grade and my comment sent back to him. Once I click Return I will have the opportunity to include a private comment to Larry before clicking on Return once again to have his grade sent back to him (figure 5.4).

Chapter 5 – Grading

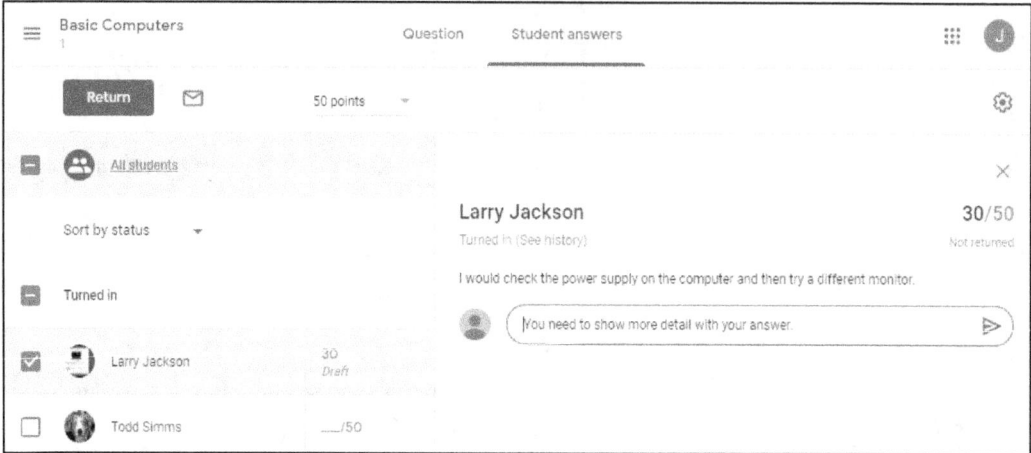

Figure 5.3

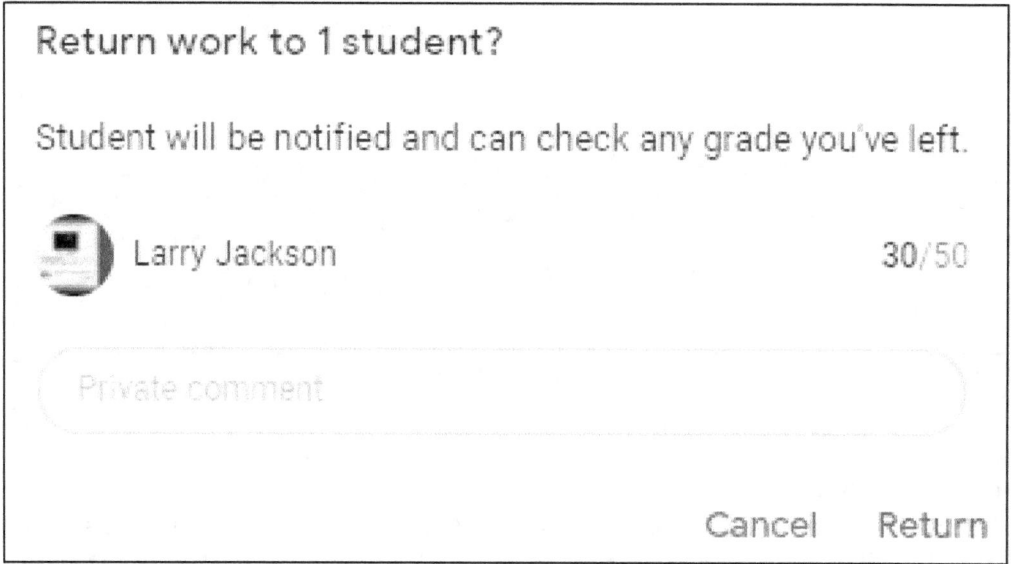

Figure 5.4

Now when I go back to the same assignment I will see that Larry is now listed under the Graded section along with the 30 point score that I just gave him.

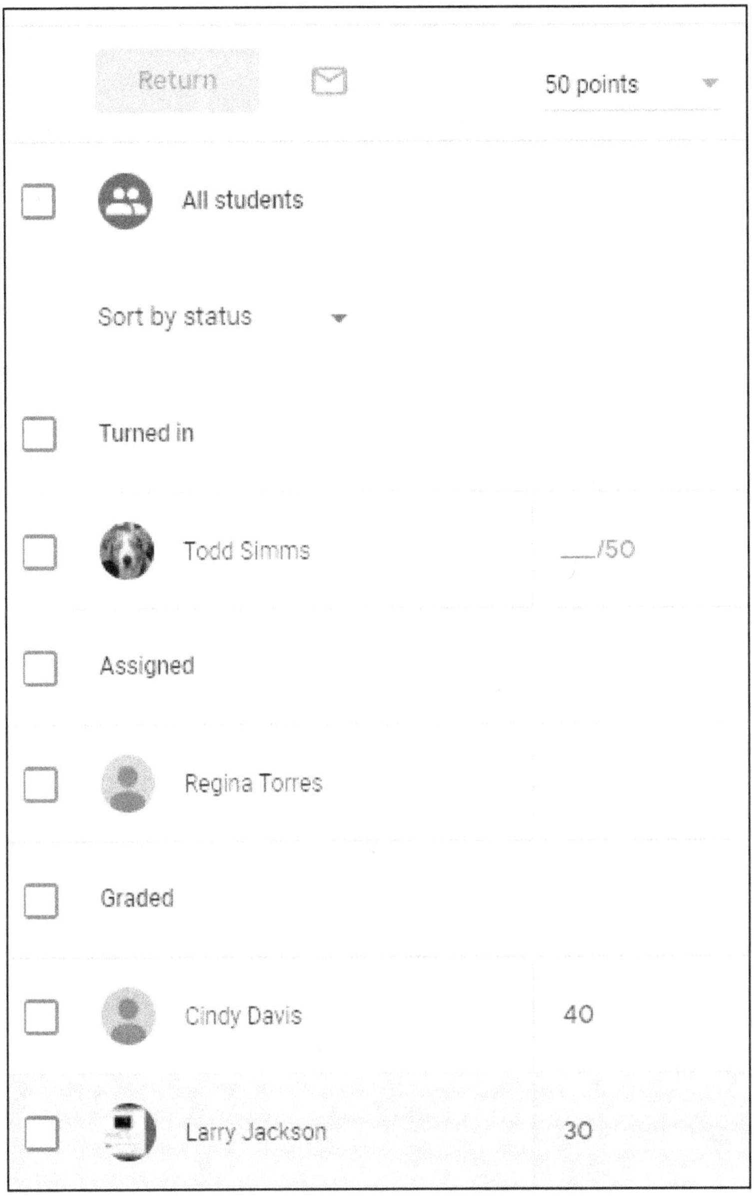

Chapter 5 – Grading

Figure 5.5

If Larry were to go back to the Classwork tab for this class he would now see that it now shows that the assignment has been graded.

Chapter 5 – Grading

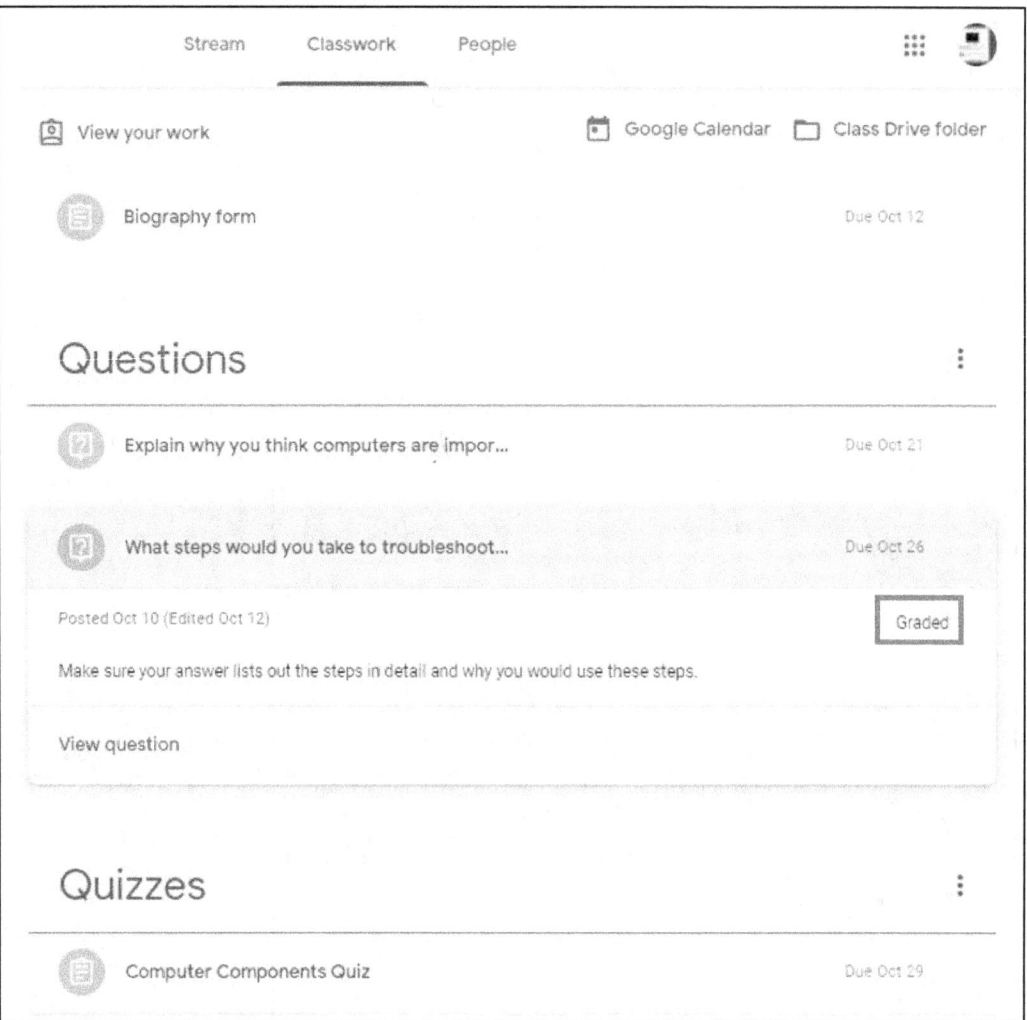

Figure 5.6

Then if he clicks on that assignment he will see the comment that I made about his work.

Chapter 5 – Grading

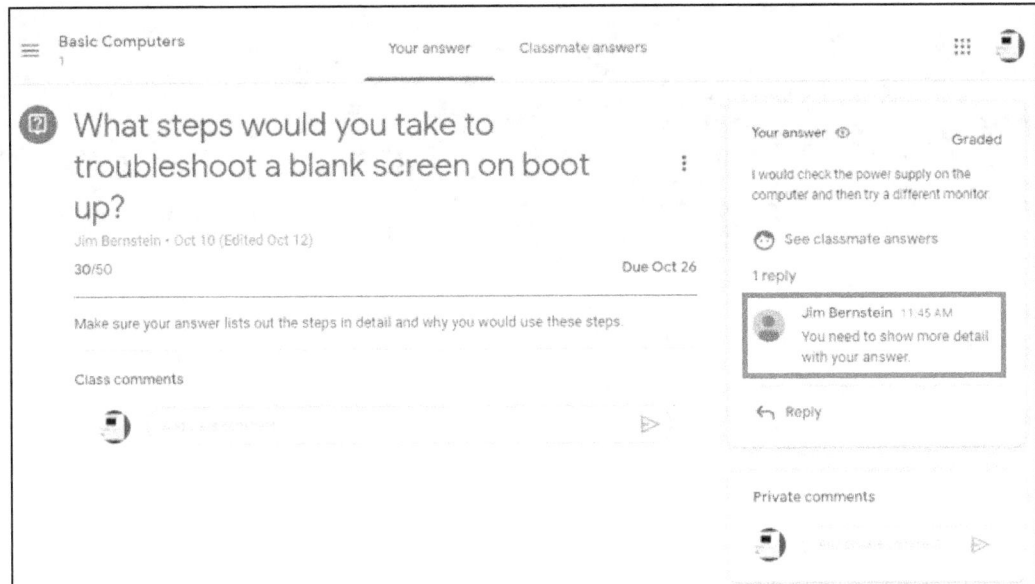

Figure 5.7

Larry will also receive an email informing him that his assignment has been graded and what his final score was. From here he can click on the *Open* button and be taken right to that assignment.

Chapter 5 – Grading

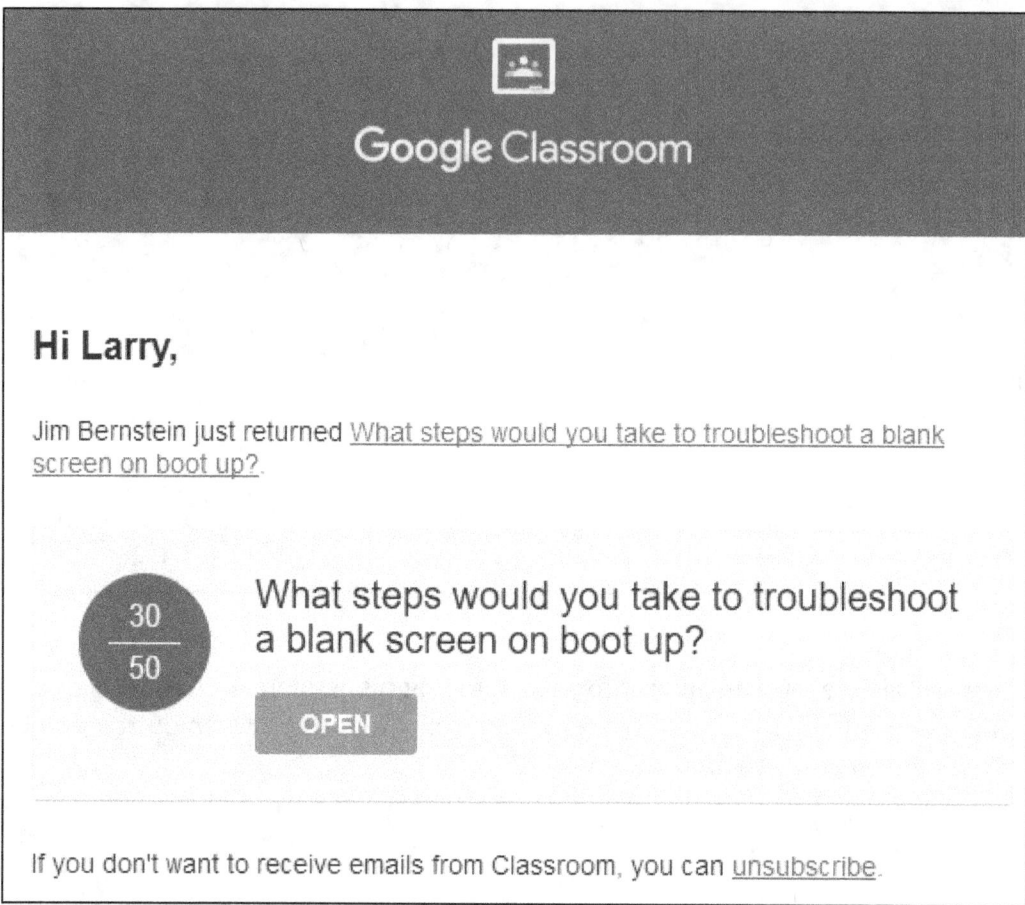

Figure 5.8

I also have the ability to grade a student's assignment quickly right from the Grades tab by typing in my grade, clicking on the three vertical dots and then choosing *Return* (figure 5.9). Or I can grade all of the student's assignments and then click on the three vertical dots at the top of the column for that assignment and choose *Return all* (figure 5.10).

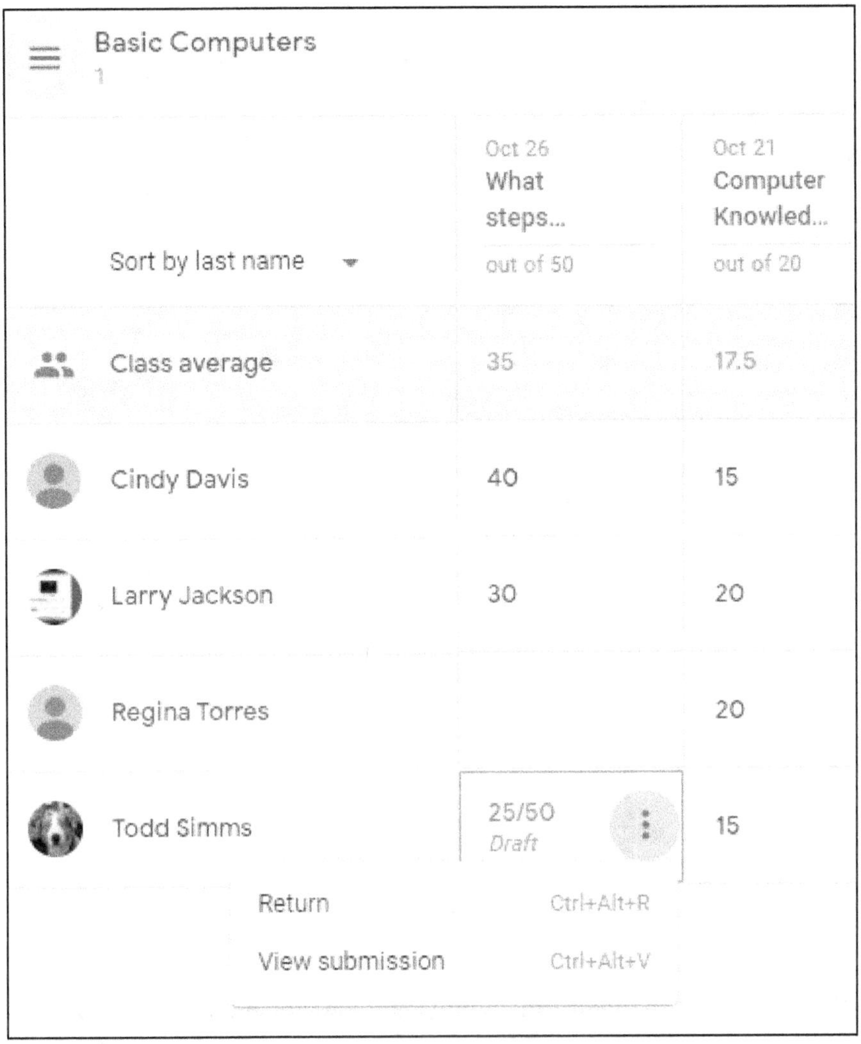

Chapter 5 – Grading

		Oct 26 What steps... out of 50	Oct 21 Computer Knowled... out of 20
	Sort by last name ▼		
👥	Class average	35	17.5
	Cindy Davis	40	15
	Larry Jackson	30	20
	Regina Torres		20
	Todd Simms	25/50 *Draft*	15
	Return		Ctrl+Alt+R
	View submission		Ctrl+Alt+V

Figure 5.9

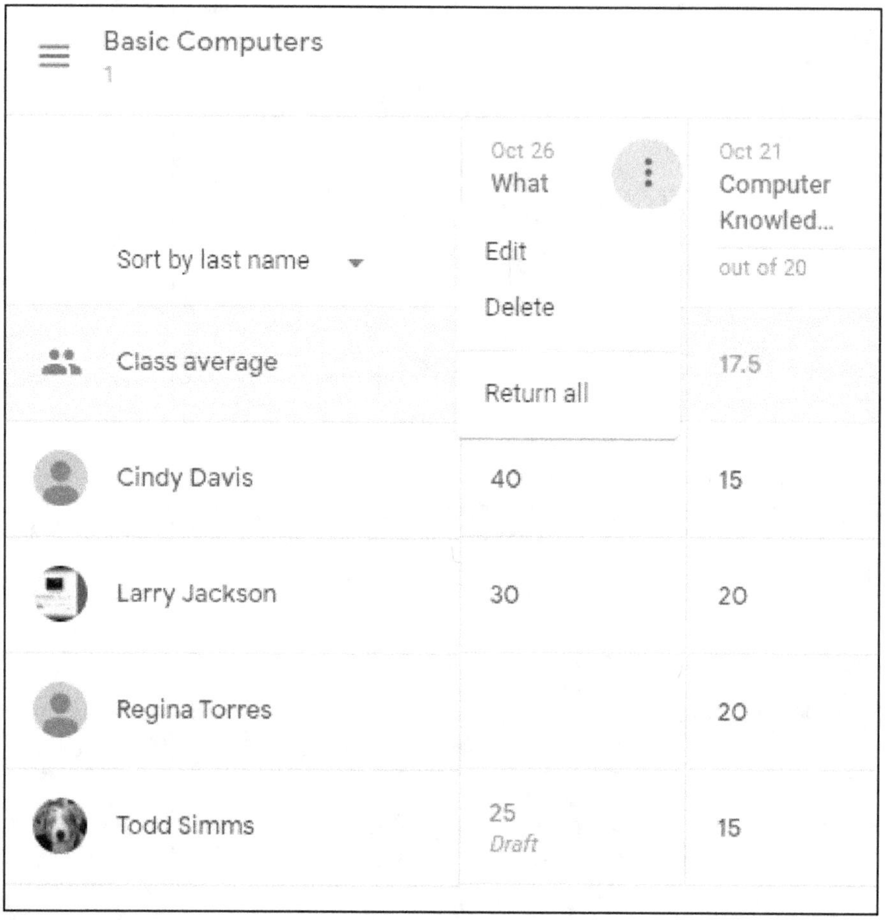

Chapter 5 – Grading

		Oct 26 What		Oct 21 Computer Knowled...
	Sort by last name ▼	Edit Delete	⋮	out of 20
👥	Class average	Return all		17.5
👤	Cindy Davis	40		15
👤	Larry Jackson	30		20
👤	Regina Torres			20
🐕	Todd Simms	25 *Draft*		15

Figure 5.10

There is more than one way to get your grading done besides going to the Grades tab. You can also get to your student's assignments for grading by going to the People tab, finding the student whose work you wish to grade and then you can click on their name to see all of their turned in, returned and missing work (figure 5.11).

From here you can simply click on the assignment or quiz you wish to grade and then click on *View details* to bring up that assignment for everyone who it was assigned to (figure 5.12). From there you can grade just that student's work or you can grade other student's work at the same time.

Chapter 5 – Grading

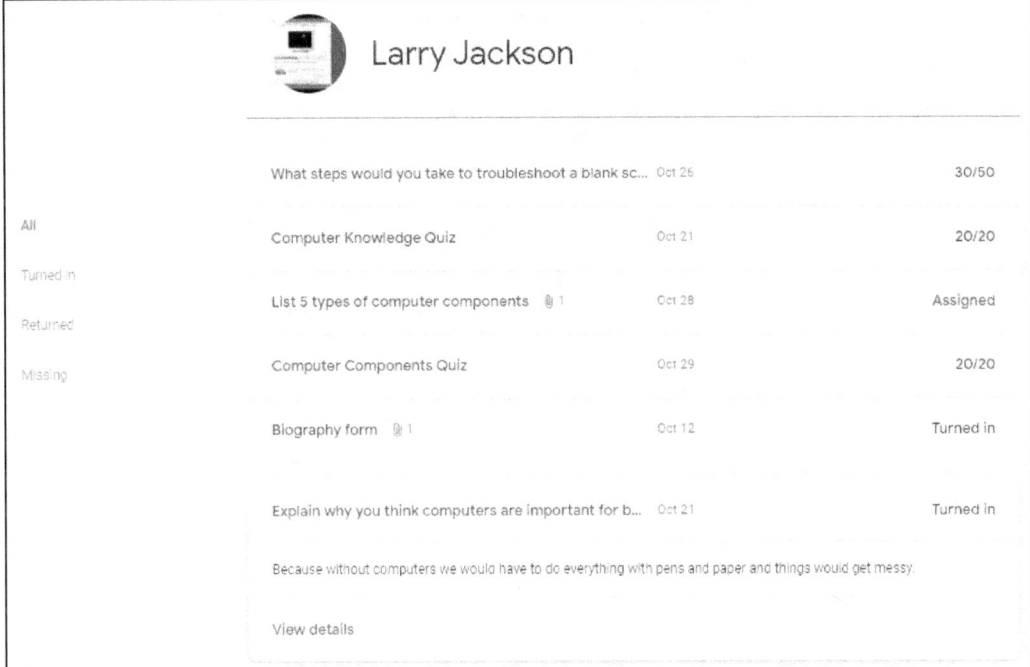

Figure 5.11

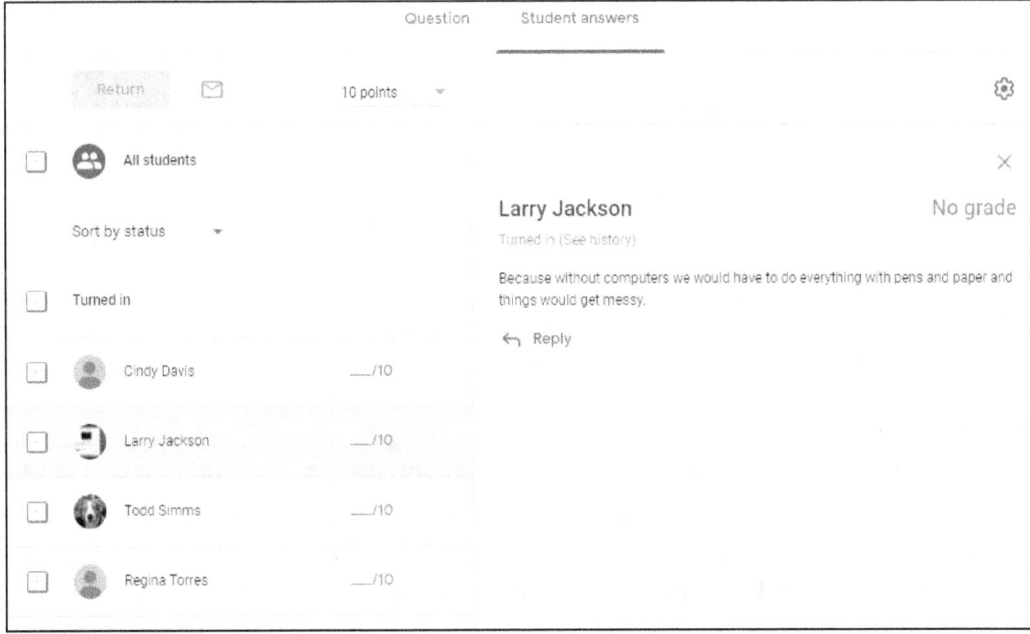

Figure 5.12

You can also get to the grading section from the *To review* area (figure 5.13) that I discussed in Chapter 4. Once you are there all you need to do is click on the

Chapter 5 – Grading

assignment you would like to grade, and you will be taken to the same grading page as seen in figure 5.12.

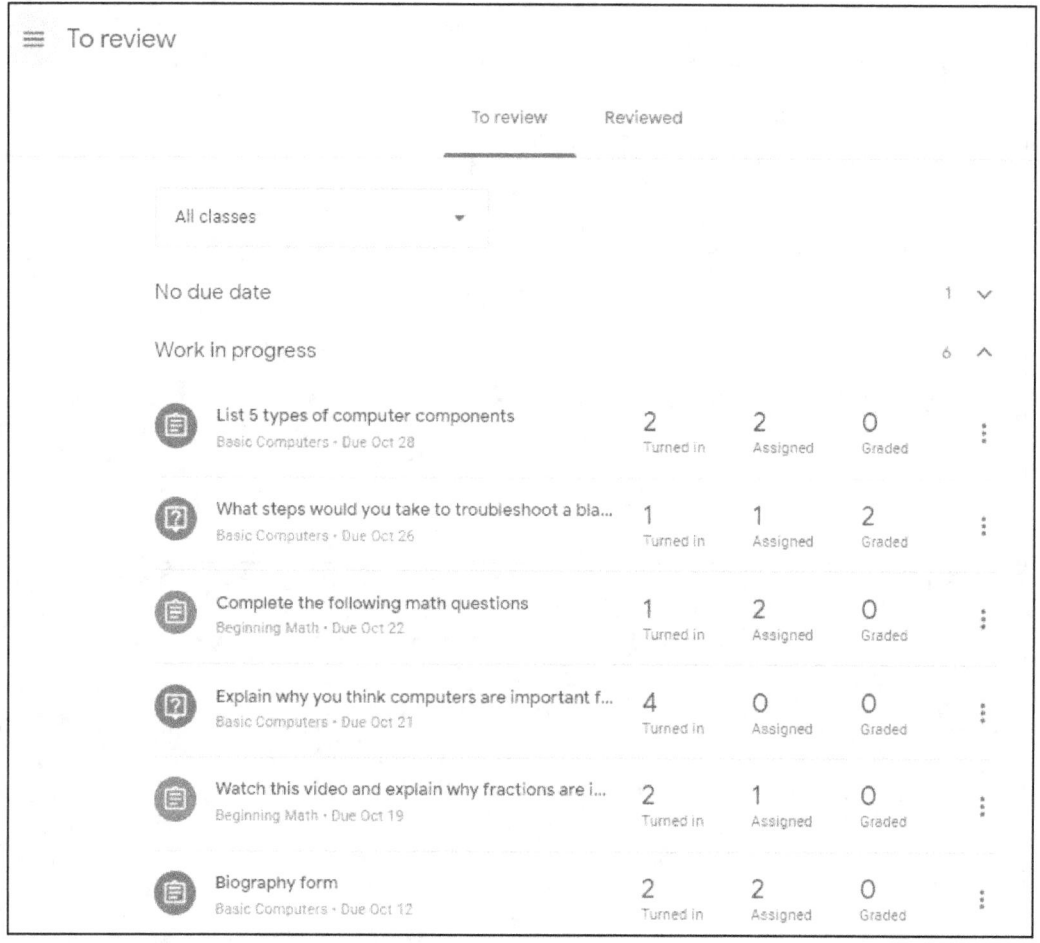

Figure 5.13

Grade Categories
If you have a lot of different types of work that you will be grading then you might want to create grade categories for these so that you can keep your grading system a little more organized. Grade categories are not required in order to grade your student's work, but they can come in handy to help you manage your grades.

By default there are no grade categories configured in Classroom so if you want to set some up you will need to go to the settings for that particular classroom since they are classroom independent, meaning that they only apply to the class you set them up in.

Chapter 5 – Grading

So in case you forgot how to get to a classroom's settings you will need to first go to that classroom and then click the Settings gear icon at the top right corner of the page.

From there you can scroll down to the Grading area and find the section labeled *Grade categories* and then click on *Add a grade category*.

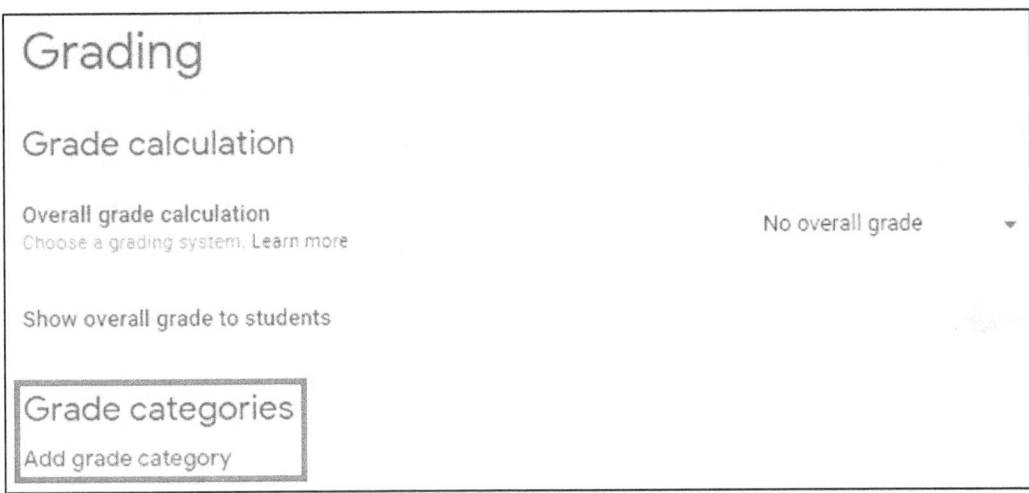
Figure 5.14

Next you will type in the grade categories that correspond with the type of work your students will be turning in and then assign a default point value to each type of work. So if you look at figure 5.15 you can see that I added four grade categories and assigned point values to each one of them. After you add your first grade category you can click on *Add grade category* to add an additional line to create another category.

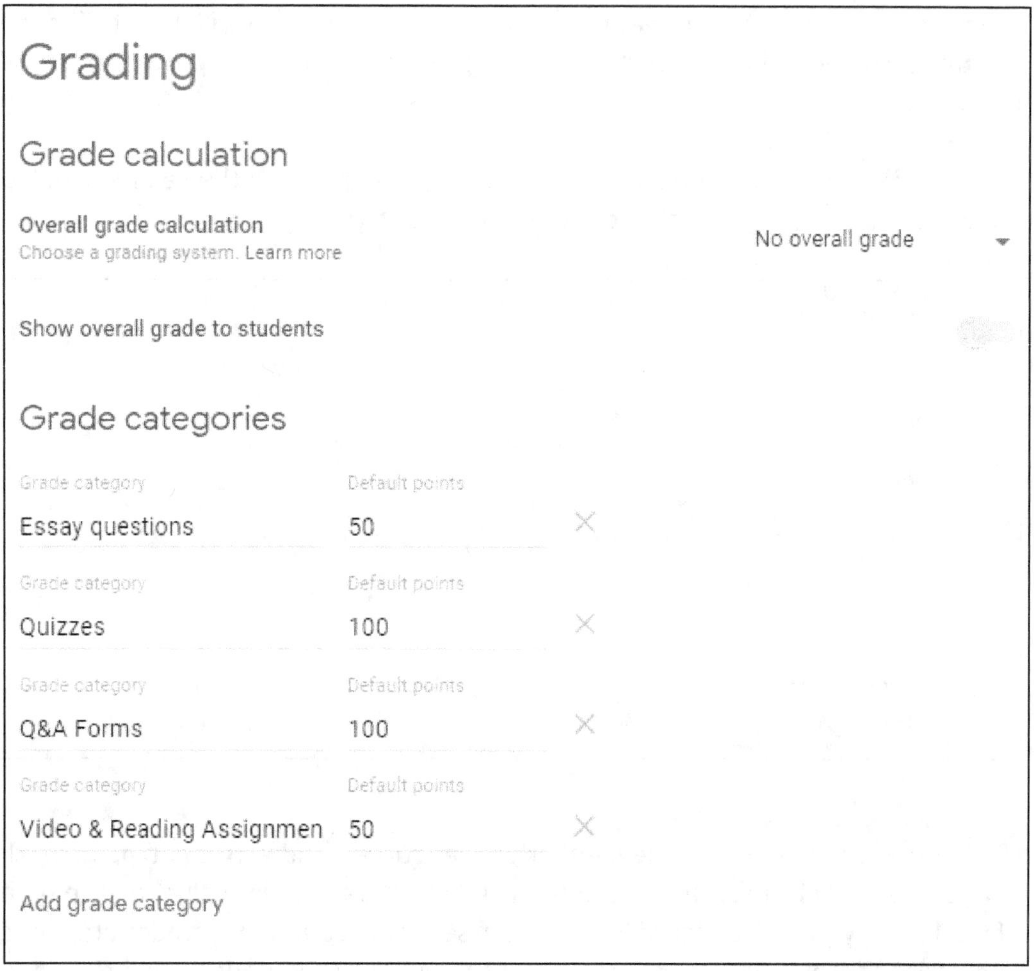

Chapter 5 – Grading

> ## Grading
>
> ### Grade calculation
>
> **Overall grade calculation**　　　　　　　　　　　　　　No overall grade ▼
> Choose a grading system. Learn more
>
> Show overall grade to students
>
> ### Grade categories
>
> | Grade category | Default points | |
> |---|---|---|
> | Essay questions | 50 | ✕ |
> | Quizzes | 100 | ✕ |
> | Q&A Forms | 100 | ✕ |
> | Video & Reading Assignmen | 50 | ✕ |
>
> Add grade category

Figure 5.15

When you are finished you will need to click on the *Save* button at the upper right corner of the page otherwise your categories will not be added.

Now if I were to edit a particular assignment or quiz I can now assign a grade category to it so I can keep things organized and have Classroom assign the point value that goes along with that category. When I create new classwork I can also use these grade categories to assign the work a category for grading purposes.

Chapter 5 – Grading

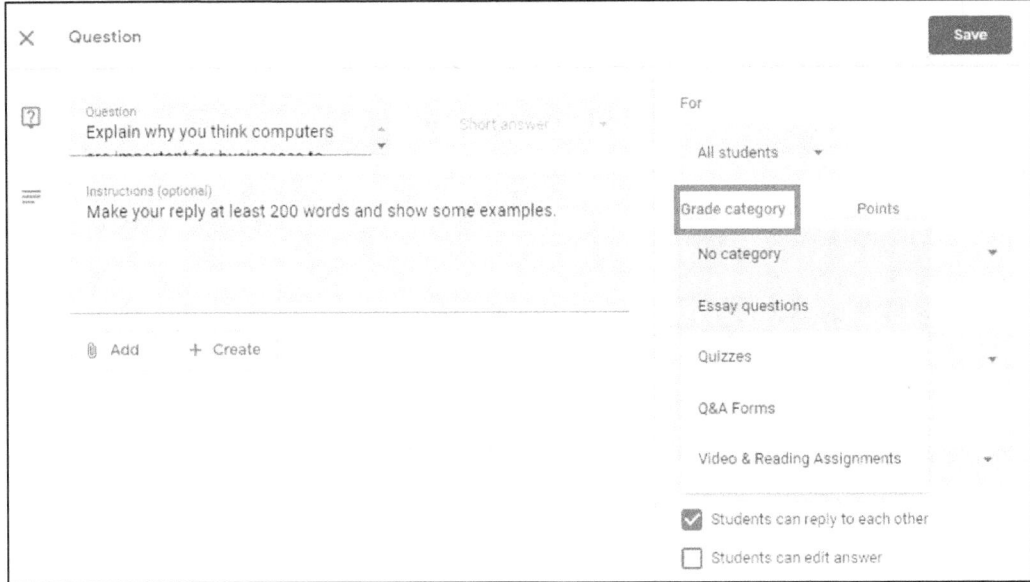

Figure 5.16

If you add a grade category to an assignment that already has a point value assigned to it then you will get a messing asking, "Are you sure you want to update the point value of this question?" This is because the new grade category point value will overwrite the existing point value for that work.

 If you create a new assignment or go to edit some existing classwork and don't see the Category section, this is because you have not setup any grade categories. Once you configure a grade category you will have the Category drop down option available.

Grade Calculation
If you would like to have your student overall grades calculated for you then you can try out one of the options under Grade calculation which can be found in the settings for your classroom. By default, the grade calculation feature is turned off (set to no overall grade).

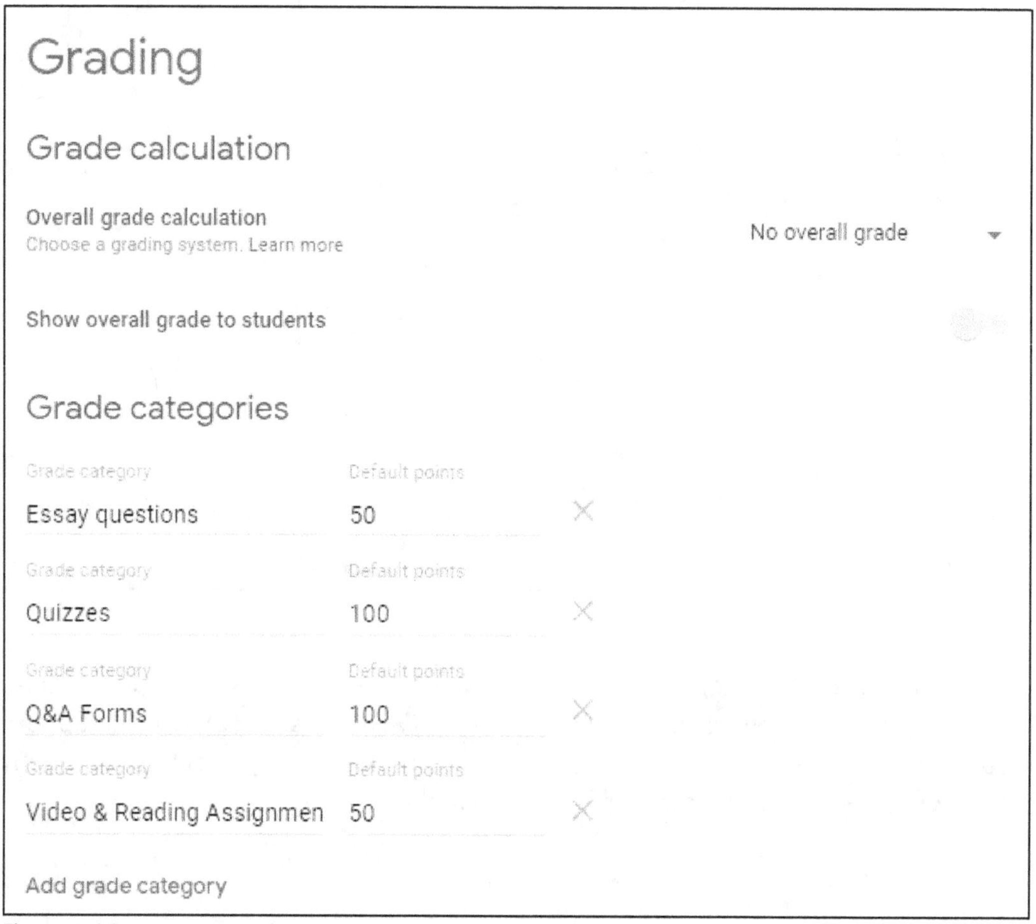

Chapter 5 – Grading

![Grading settings screenshot showing Grade calculation with "No overall grade" dropdown, and Grade categories: Essay questions (50), Quizzes (100), Q&A Forms (100), Video & Reading Assignmen (50), with Add grade category option]

Figure 5.17

If you wish to use the grade calculation feature then you have two options to choose from and these can be selected by clicking on the down arrow next to *No overall grade*.

Total Points
This grade calculation method will calculate a grade by dividing the total points a student has earned by the total points possible for the particular class. Going back to my grade categories as shown in 5.17, let's just say for the sake of simplicity I have the Essay questions and Quizzes categories with the Essay questions category having a maximum point value of 50 per essay and the Quizzes category having a maximum point value of 100 per quiz.

Chapter 5 – Grading

Now let's say that Todd scores a 30 out of 50 on an essay question and an 80 out of 100 on a quiz.

Essay 1 – 30/50
Quiz 1 – 80/100

If we add the total points possible for his overall class grade we get **150** by adding the 50 points maximum from the essay category and the 100 points maximum from the quiz category.

Now if we add Todd's 30 essay category points to his 80 quiz points we get a total of **110** points for the class.

Next we will take Todd's points/Total points possible to get his grade so:
110/150 = .73333 or about 73% which you can say is a C grade.

The good part is that if you use this grade calculation, Google Classroom will do the math for you, but you just need to make sure you have all of your maximum points configured and make sure that you enter the grades to keep things accurate.

Weighted by category
If you would like to grade your students based on your categories and then give them an overall grade for all of your categories then you can use the Weighted by category grade calculation.

When I choose the Weighted by category option it changes my grade categories to a percentage number where they will all need to add up to 100% (figure 5.18). So if you plan on using this type of grade calculation you might want to plan out all of your grade categories and their percentage of the overall grade beforehand.

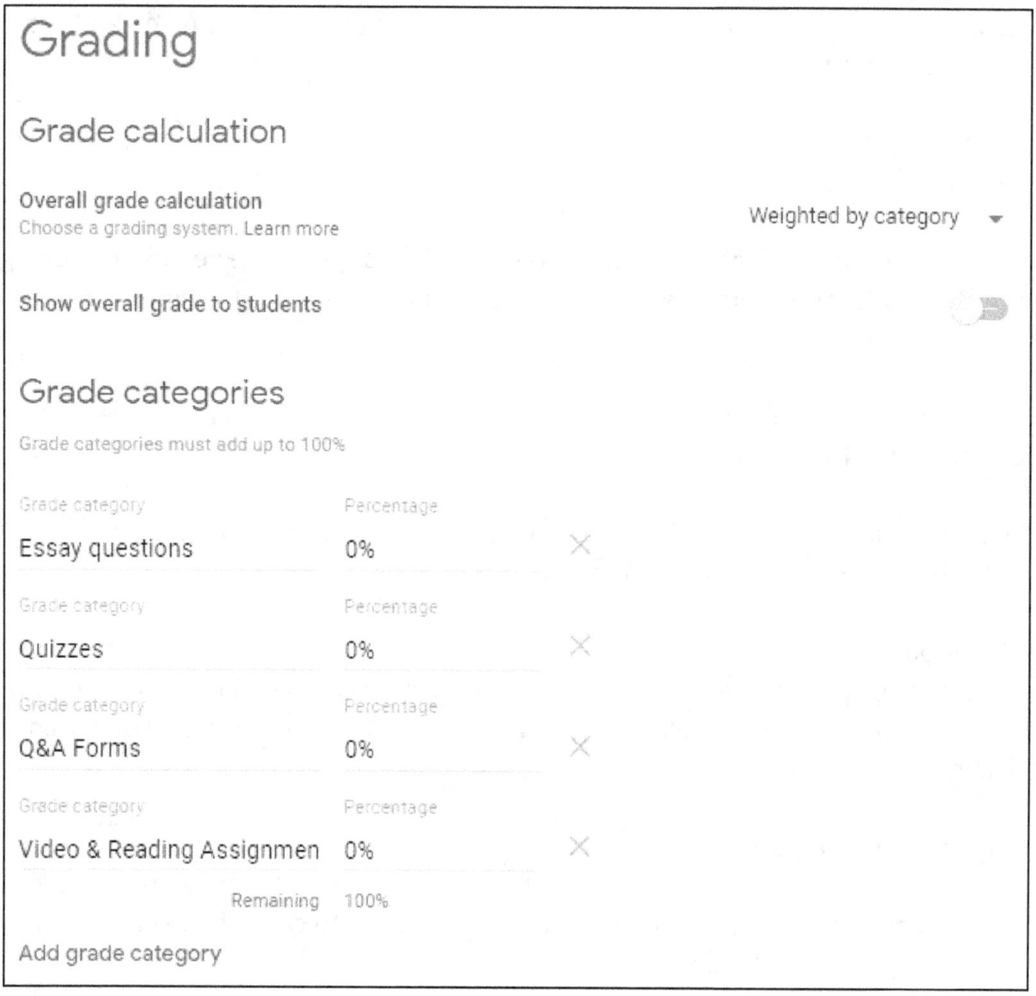

Grading

Grade calculation

Overall grade calculation
Choose a grading system. Learn more — Weighted by category

Show overall grade to students

Grade categories

Grade categories must add up to 100%

Grade category	Percentage	
Essay questions	0%	×
Quizzes	0%	×
Q&A Forms	0%	×
Video & Reading Assignmen	0%	×
Remaining	100%	

Add grade category

Figure 5.18

Going back to my two grade category example I will now add an additional essay question and quiz to my grade to show you a simplified version of how this works.

I have an essay category that is 40% of my total grade and a quiz category that is 60% of my total grade. I then have two essay assignments with each one having a maximum point value of 50 points and two quizzes with each one having a maximum value of 100 points.

Todd then gets a 30 out of 50 on one essay and a 50 out of 50 on the second essay. He also gets an 80 out of 100 on the first quiz and a 90 out of 100 on the second quiz.

Chapter 5 – Grading

Now I will take the percentages of the two quizzes, add them together and then divide it by 2 since there are 2 quizzes. 30/50 is a 60% score and 50/50 is a 100% score. When I do the math I come up with an 80% average score.

Todd also got an 80 out of 100 on the first quiz which is an 80% and then a 90 out of 100 on the second quiz which is a 90%. I then add up the 80 and 90 and divide it by 2 since there are 2 quizzes. When I do the math I come up with an 85% average score.

Since the essay category is 40% of the total grade I will need to multiply Todd's average score by .4 to get the category score which comes out to 32%. Then I will multiply Todd's average quiz score by .6 since the quiz category is 60% of the total grade to get 51%. Finally I will add the 32% to the 50% to get an overall grade of 83%. The table below shows the breakdown of this grade calculation.

Essay category: 40% of grade	Quiz category: 60% of grade	Overall grade out of 100%
Essay 1: 30/50	Quiz 1: 80/100	
Essay 2: 50/50	Quiz 2: 90/100	
• (60% + 100%) ÷ 2 = 80 avg. • 80 x .4 = 32	• (80% + 90%) ÷ 2 = 85 avg. • 85 x .6 = 51	
Category score = 32%	Category score = 51%	Overall grade: 32 + 51 = 83%

Giving Feedback Within Assignments
As you grade your student's work you will find that you might want to make some comments about why you gave them the grade you did or what they can do to improve their work. Or maybe you just want to tell them that they did an excellent job!

You have seen how you can make comments while grading student work from the grading area but if you are using Google Docs for your work then you can take it one step further and add comments to the actual work itself that your students can then see after you return it to them.

To give feedback you will need to open an assignment that contains a Google document and then open the copy of that document for the student you wish to give feedback for.

Chapter 5 – Grading

For example, figure 5.19 shows that I opened an assignment in my Basic Computers class and now I want to look at the work that Cindy Davis turned in and then give her some feedback if necessary. I would click on her document to open it up to see what she has done.

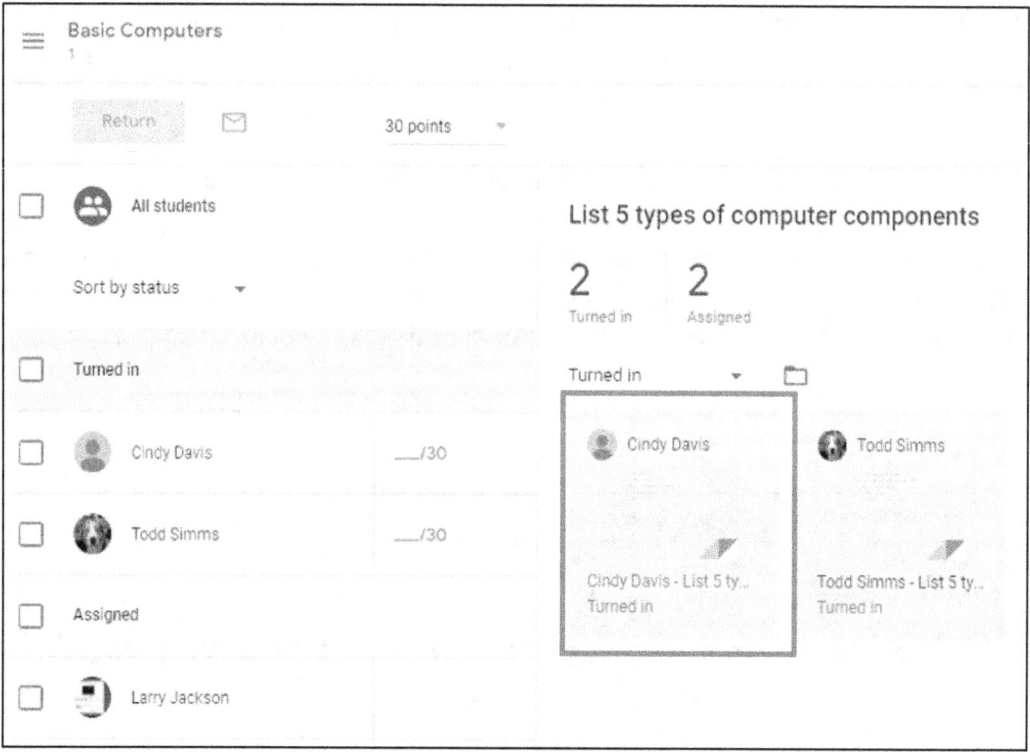

Figure 5.19

Next I will need to highlight the area of the document that I wish to comment on and then click on the *Add comment* button off to the right.

Chapter 5 – Grading

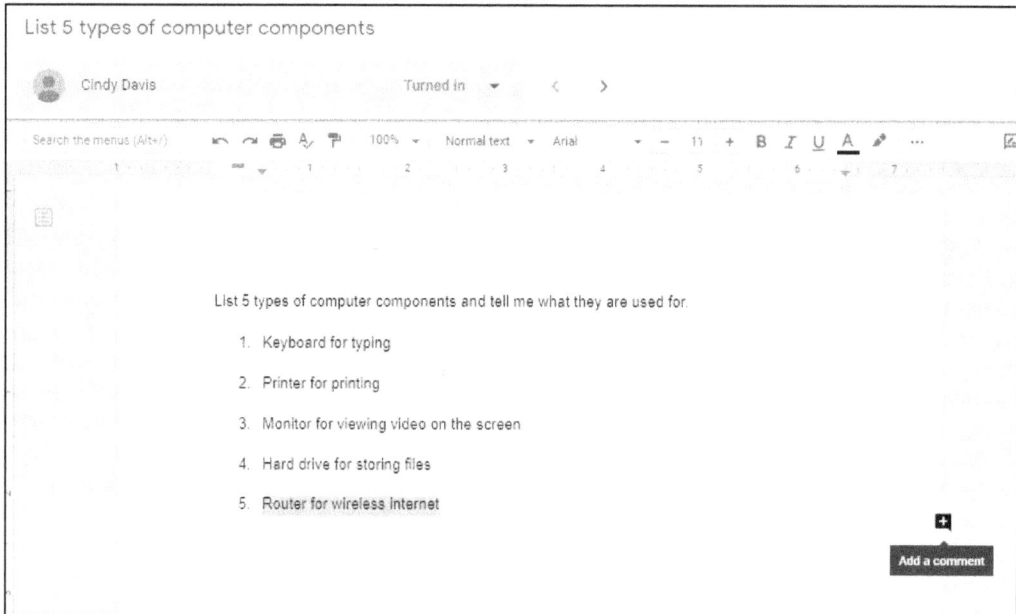

Figure 5.20

Now I can type in my feedback and click on the Comment button when I am finished.

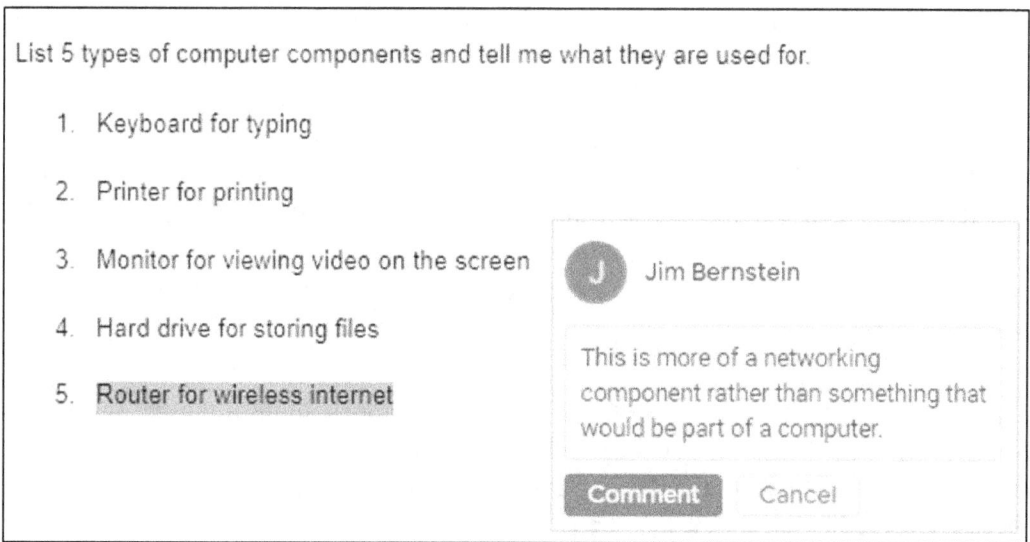

Figure 5.21

Now when Cindy goes back to look at her assignment she will see that the section that I had commented on is highlighted and if she hovers her mouse over it she will see my name indicating that I am the one who made the comment. She will also see the comment over at the right hand side of the page.

Chapter 5 – Grading

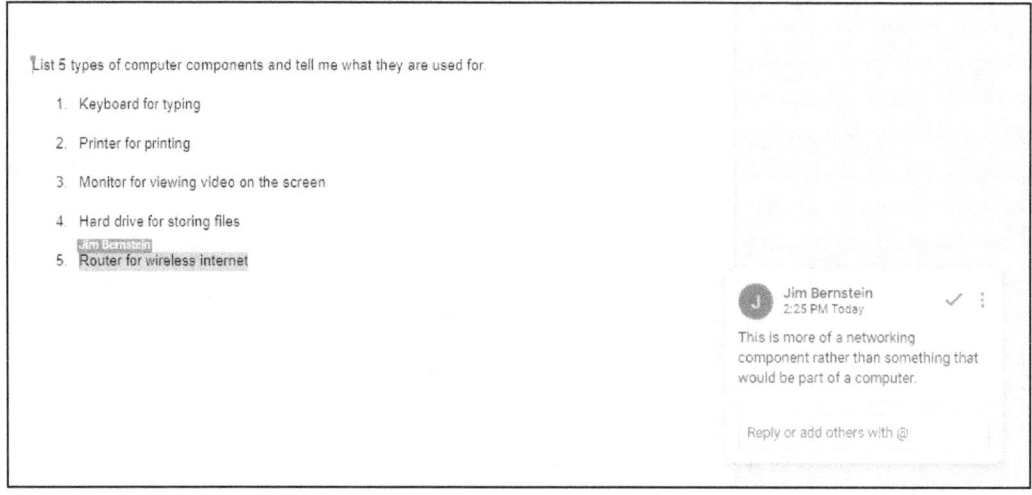

Figure 5.22

From here she can reply to my feedback if she chooses to do so by typing in the box underneath my comment.

Rubrics
The final topic I would like to discuss in regards to grading is the concept of rubrics which is actually one of the newer features of Google Classroom. Rubrics allow you to grade assignments based on points associated with certain criteria that you choose

Using this method allows you to break down the grading of your assignment into performance categories rather than give it one overall grade for the entire assignment. This allows you to fine tune how it's graded and also lets your students know how they will be graded so they can try and meet all of your criteria.

To create a rubric you can either do so from an existing assignment or when you create a new assignment which is the method I will be using for my example. You create the assignment just like you would any other assignment but for the grading you will need to choose the *Rubric* option at the bottom right of the page (figure 5.23). You can either create a new rubric, reuse a rubric you have already created, or import one from a Google Sheets spreadsheet file that you have or maybe that someone sent you to use. I will be creating a new rubric for this assignment.

Chapter 5 – Grading

If you are attaching any documents for this assignment you should set it where it makes a copy for each student so you will have a document for each one of your students.

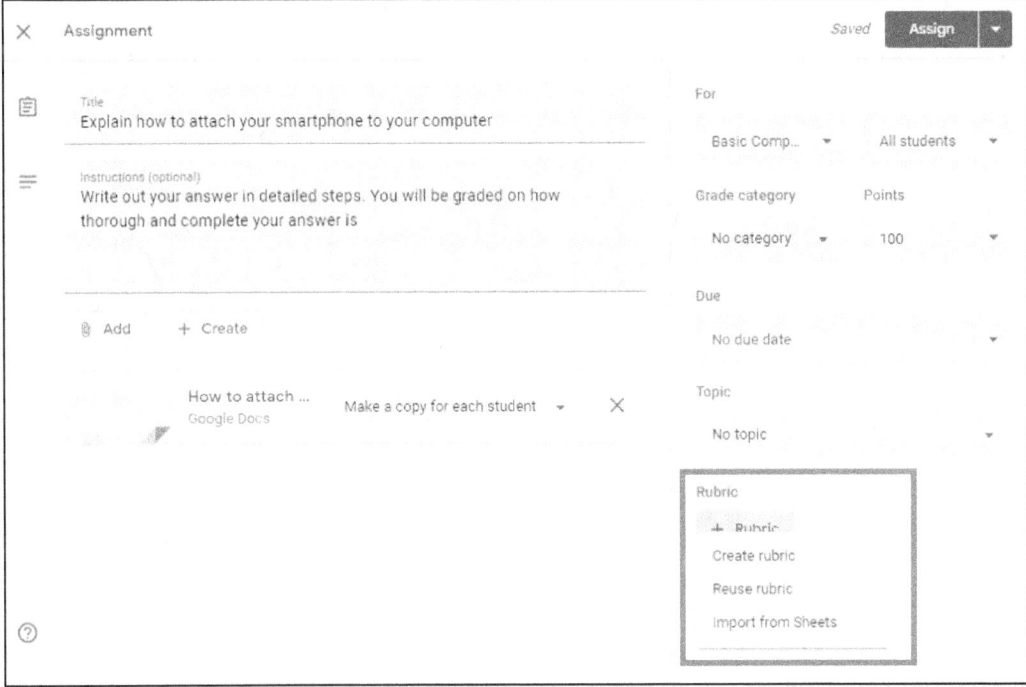

Figure 5.23

The first step in creating a rubric involves adding your first criterion and to give it a point value. I will by using completeness as my first criterion and making the highest point value my students can achieve be 10 points. Figure 5.24 shows that I have *Completeness* for the title and that I added an optional description for my criterion and gave this first level a point value of 10.

If I click the + symbol next to this entry and can add another level and then enter in my requirements and points values as seen in figure 5.25. As you can see, now I have four levels and each one has a different point value which decreases as the quality of the student work decreases.

Chapter 5 – Grading

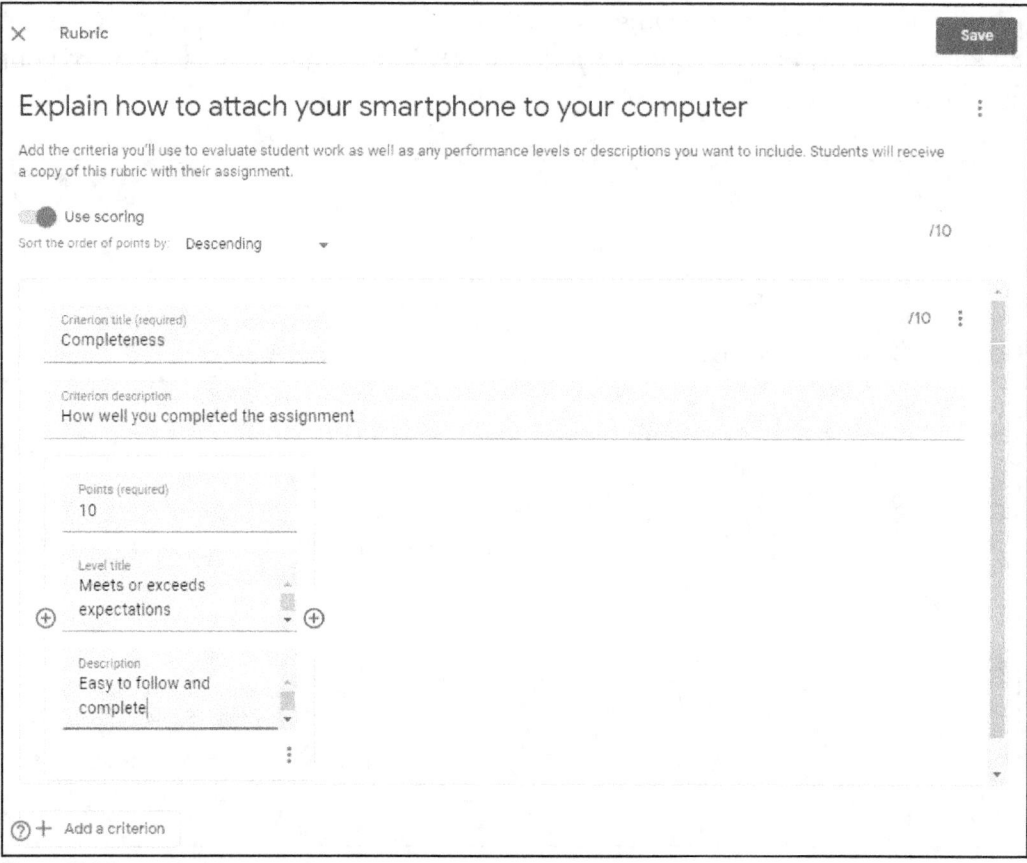

Figure 5.24

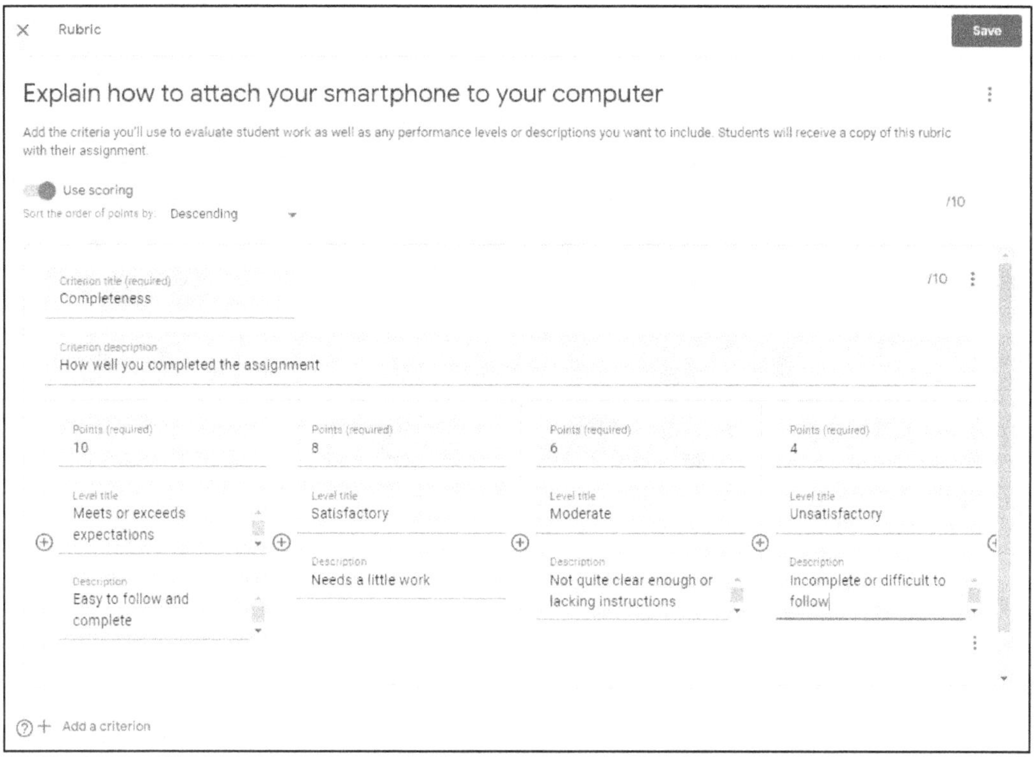

Chapter 5 – Grading

Figure 5.25

Next I will add my next performance criterion by clicking on the *+ Add criterion* button at the lower left side of the screen. I can also click the three vertical dots at the top of my first criterion and choose *Duplicate criterion* to have a copy made which I can then edit to suit my needs if that were to work faster for me. I can also use these options to delete a criterion or change their overall order for my rubric.

Chapter 5 – Grading

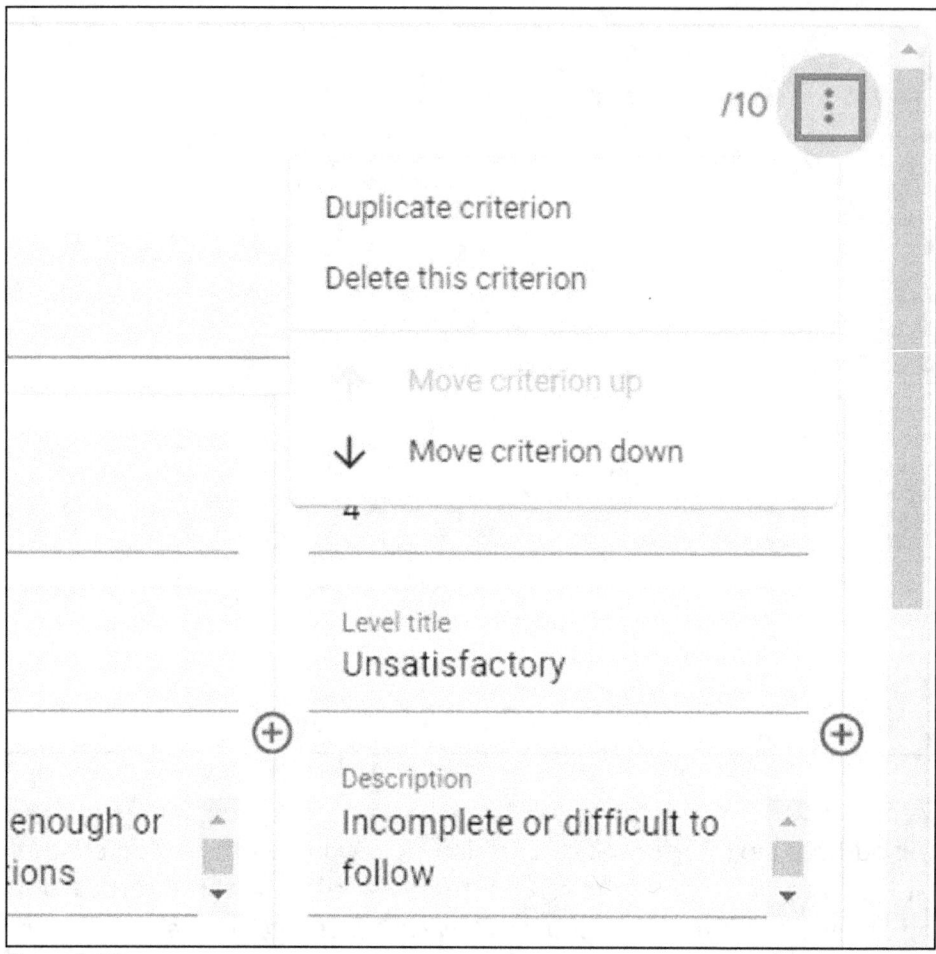

Figure 5.26

Now I will add another criterion called *Examples* where I will assign point values based on how well my students provided examples in their work. Once again the highest point value for this category is 10 points and after I create it you will see that the total point value changes to 20 (figure 5.27).

Chapter 5 – Grading

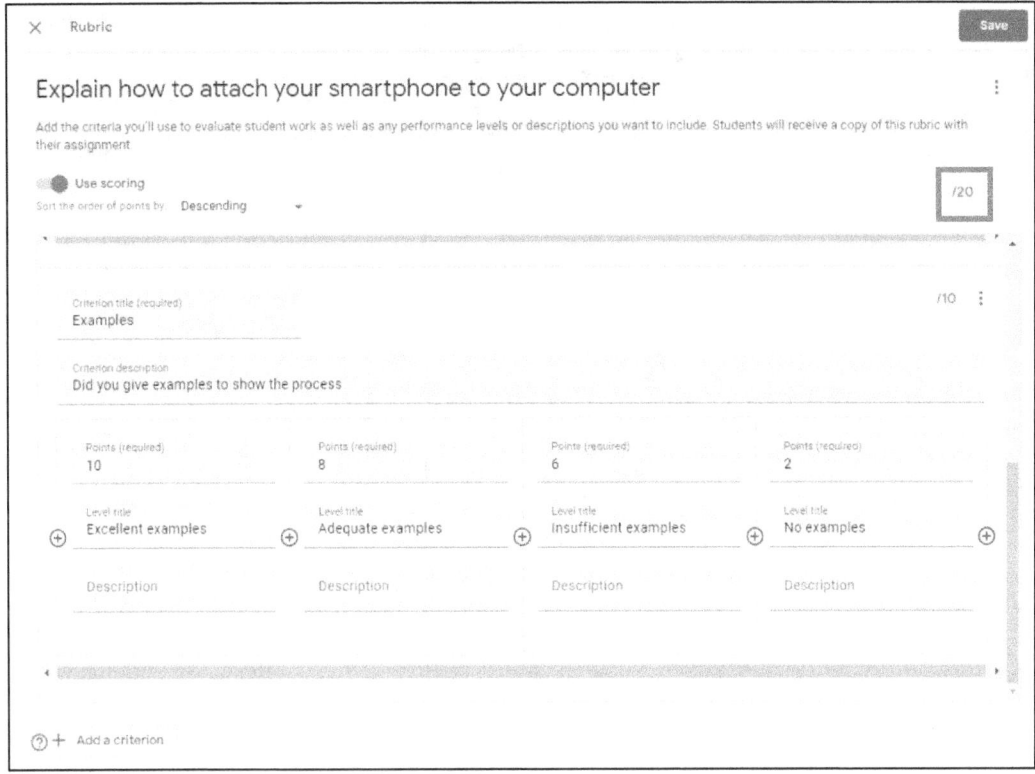

Figure 5.27

When I am finished adding all of my criteria I will need to click on the *Save* button and then the X to the left of Rubric which will then take me back to my assignment. Also be sure that the *Use scoring* option is enabled at the upper left otherwise you won't be able to assign points for any of your criteria.

One thing you will need to do is make sure that your total points for the assignment match your rubric points. As you can see in figure 5.28 mine do not so I will need to change this manually. Hopefully Google will make this automatic in the near future.

If I need to edit my rubric I can simply click on it from here as well to open it up and make my changes. Once everything is configured and looking good I will click on the *Assign* button to send it off to my students.

Chapter 5 – Grading

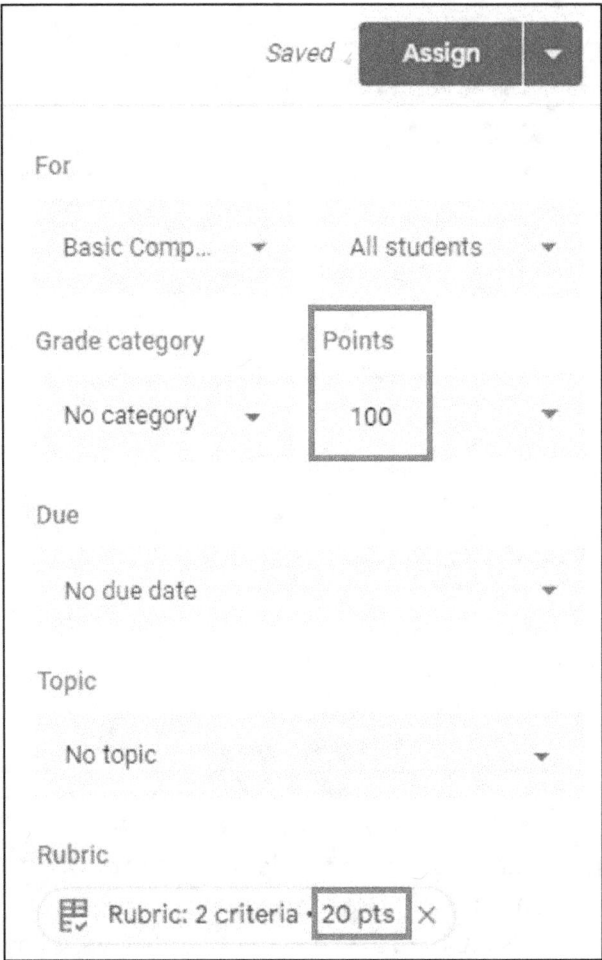

Figure 5.28

Now my students can view the assignment and will be able to see the rubric criteria so they will know how they will be graded (figure 5.29).

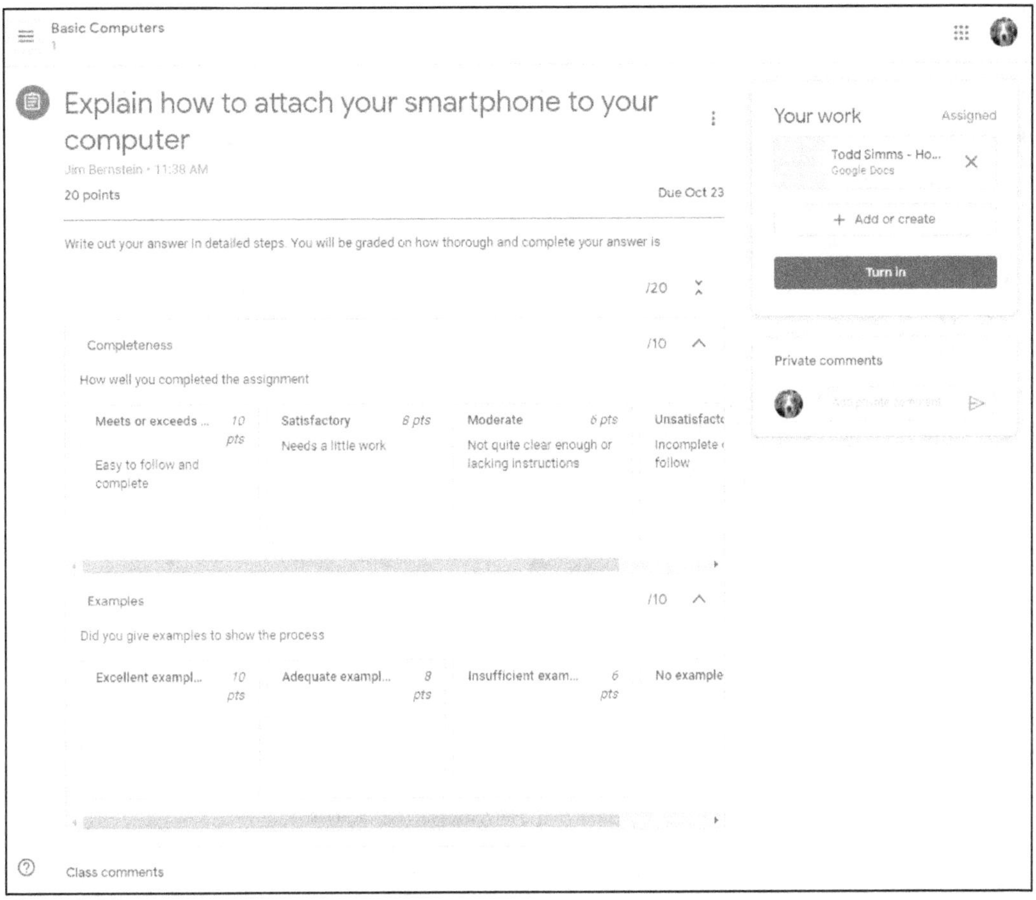

Chapter 5 – Grading

Figure 5.29

Figure 5.30 shows how the grading process works for an assignment with a rubric. As you can see, I am able to grade on each of my criteria to give a total grade which is shown at the upper right hand corner. So for this assignment, Todd received a 14 out of 20 possible points.

Chapter 5 – Grading

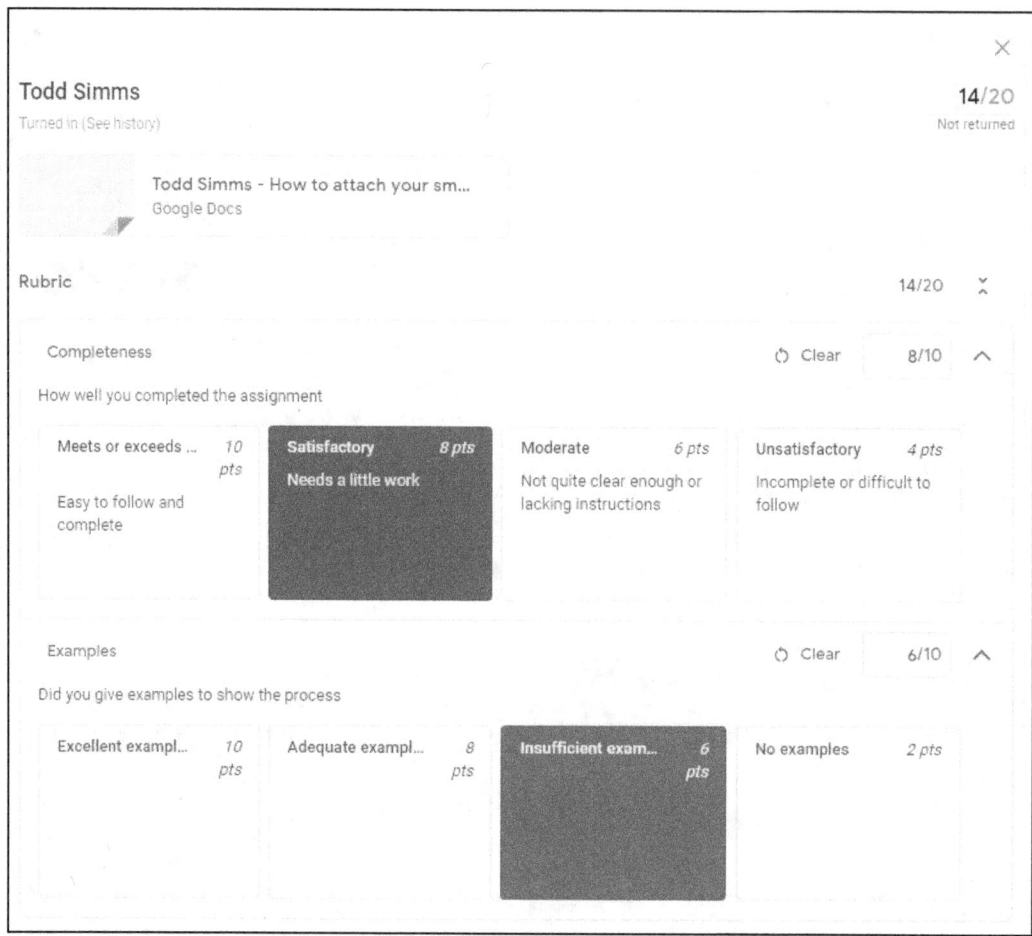

Figure 5.30

Now when Todd goes back to check on his grade he will see a similar looking screen as to what I saw when grading the assignment (figure 5.31). If he still has time before the due date and if I allow it, he can make some changes to his work and use the *Resubmit* button to send it back to me to see if he can improve his score.

Chapter 5 – Grading

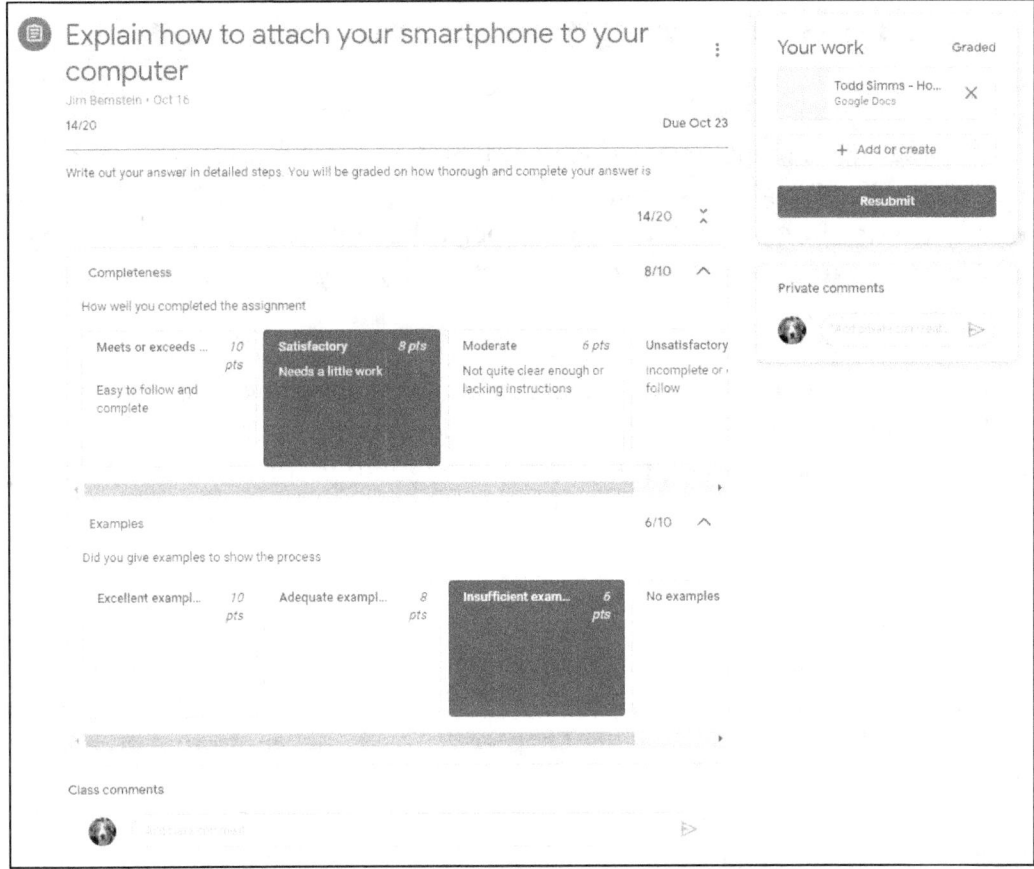

Figure 5.31

Chapter 6 – Google Drive and Google Docs

Since Google likes to integrate its apps with each other, it makes sense that they would do so for Google Classroom. If you have ever looked at the "waffle" icon by your profile picture (or letter) on the Google homepage or any other Google application page then you have seen just how many applications they have available for us to use.

By now you have noticed that you will be using Google Drive and Google Apps quite a bit during your teaching and your students will be using them as well for their assignments. In this chapter I will be going into more detail about Google Drive and Google Apps so you will have a better idea of what they do and what you can do with them.

Google Drive
If you already have a Google account or Gmail address, then you already have access to Google Drive. If not, then all you need to do is head over to Google and create an account as I discussed in Chapter 2. You can also use that address to access your account once you create one.

If you take a look at figure 6.1, you can see what my Google Drive storage space looks like. There is the main storage area labeled *My Drive*, and then you can have subfolders underneath that as I do. Think of My Drive as your C drive in Windows, and you can then create subfolders under that and then subfolders within subfolders.

Chapter 6 – Google Drive and Google Docs

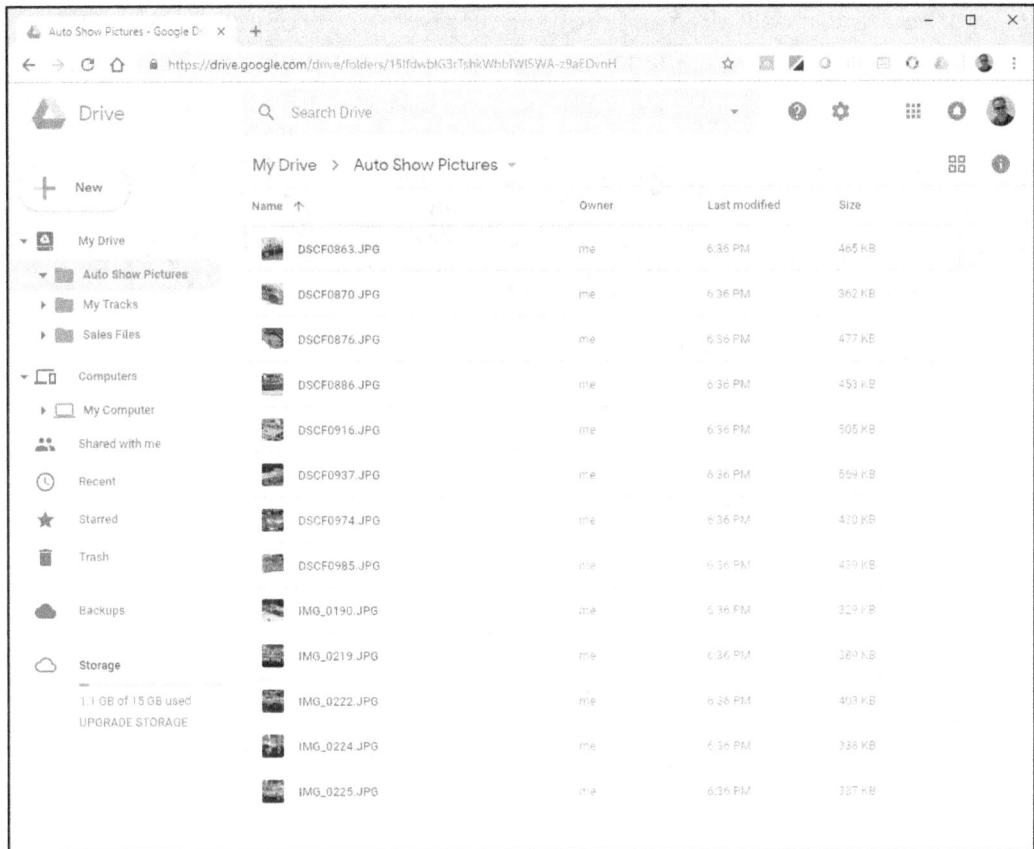

Figure 6.1

Also notice how there's a column for the owner of the files, as well as the date and\or time it was last modified, and the amount of space the files takes up on your drive. If it's a new file, it will just show the time, and older files will show the date. You can also sort by each one of these columns by clicking on the column header. In my example they are sorted by name, indicated by the up arrow next to the column heading that says Name.

Creating Folders and Uploading Files
It's very easy to create a new folder in Google Drive. All you need to do is click right on the location where you want to create your folder (such as My Drive), choose *New Folder*, and give it a name. Then you can go into that folder and upload some files. To do so, simply right click on a blank area and choose *Upload*

files, or you can actually drag and drop the files from your computer right into your web browser. When you upload files, you will see a status box for the upload, and when everything is complete, you will see a screen similar to figure 6.2.

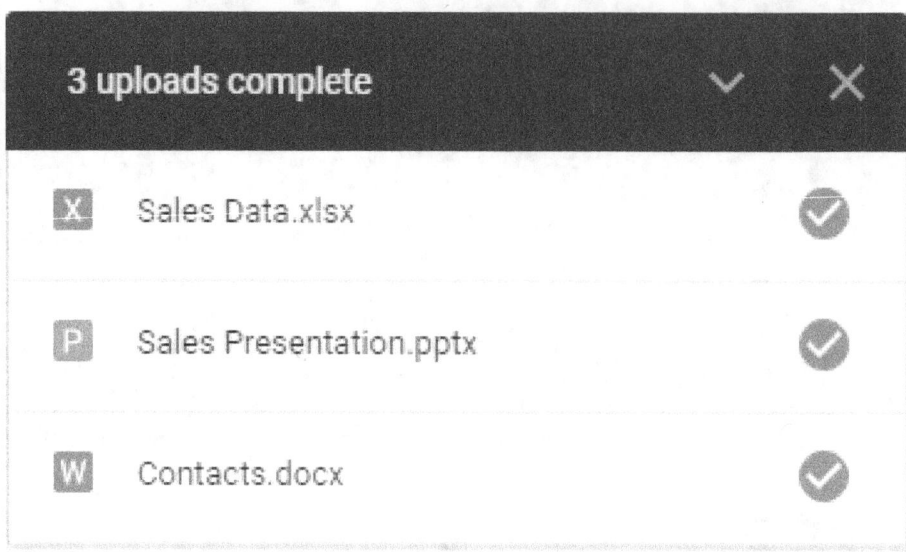

Figure 6.2

Then, when you are back at that folder, you will see your newly added files (as shown in figure 6.3).

Chapter 6 – Google Drive and Google Docs

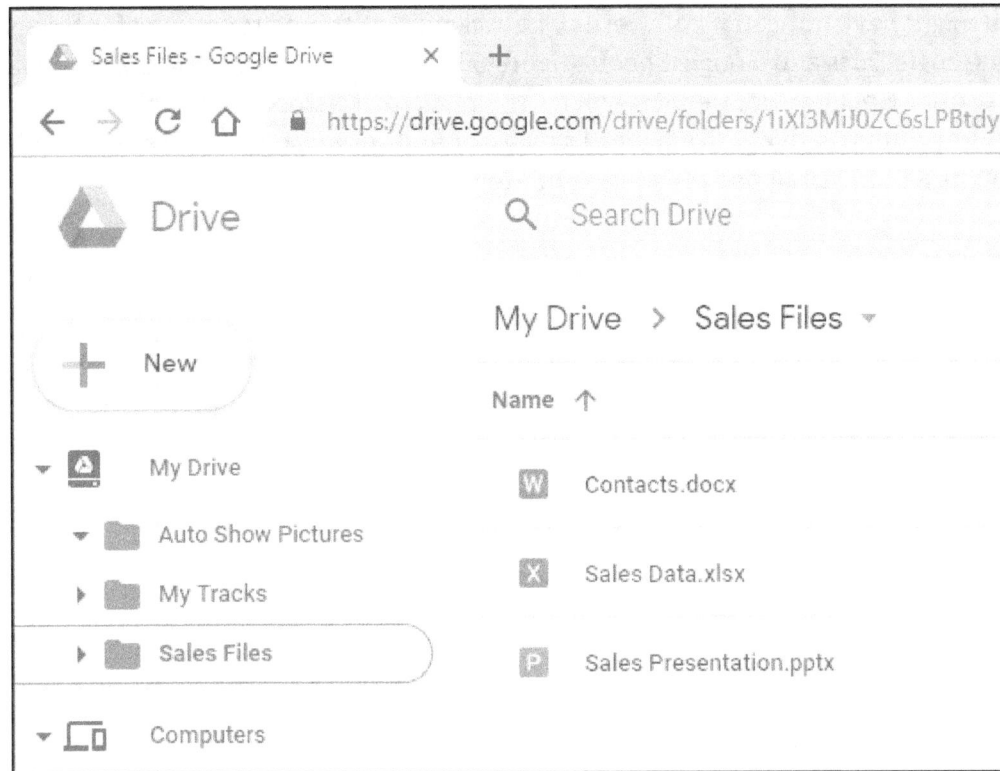

Figure 6.3

You can upload as many files as you have room for. You can also upload folders using the same methods that you can use for uploading files.

If you upload the same file to your drive, then you will have the option to overwrite the current file or keep the file you are uploading as a separate file and will get a notification as shown in figure 6.4. Also note the version number, which means I have uploaded this file three times.

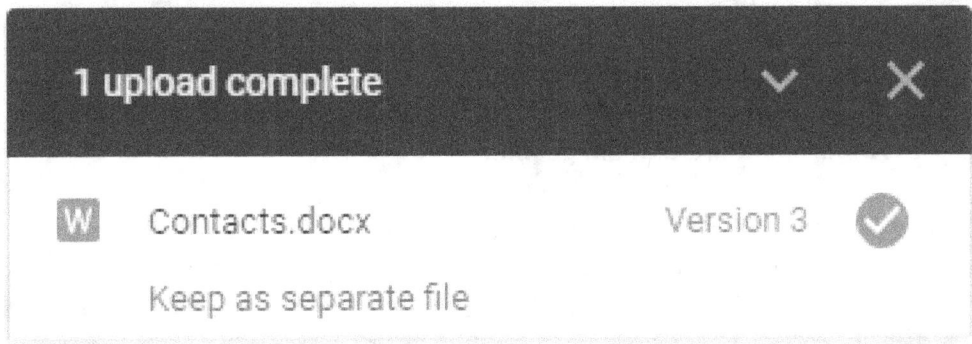

Figure 6.4

Chapter 6 – Google Drive and Google Docs

You might have noticed if you were right clicking that there are options for things like Google Docs and Google Sheets (figure 6.5). This is because Google wants you to use its Google Docs service, which is similar to Microsoft's Office 365, and allows you to use things like a word processor and spreadsheet app online rather than having to install one on your computer.

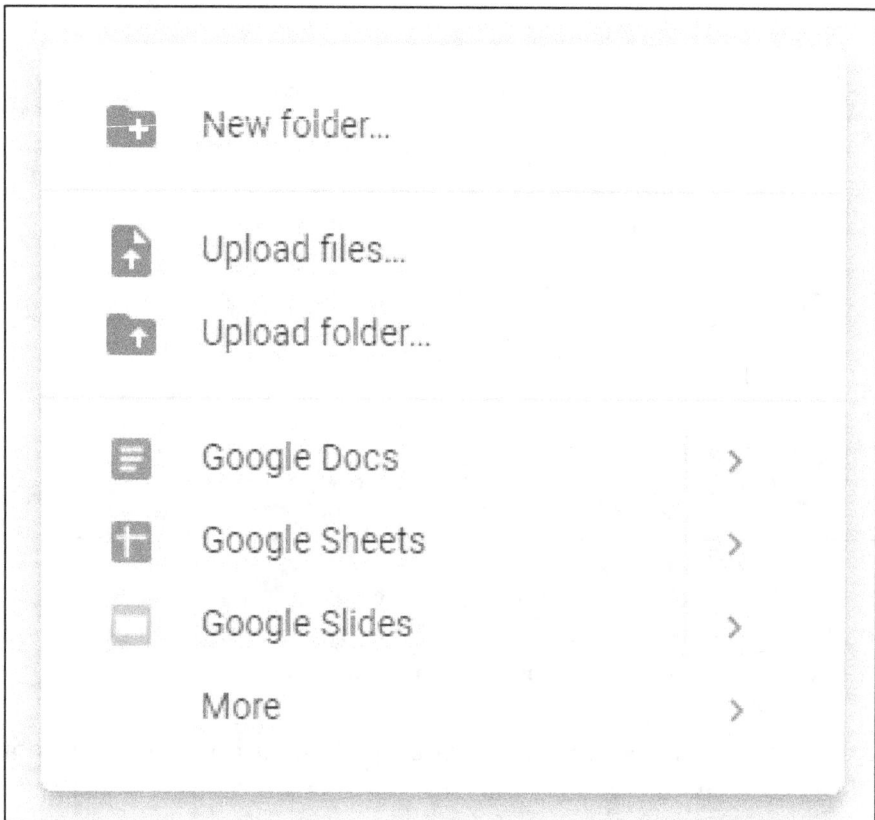

Figure 6.5

Managing Files and Folders
Once you get your folders created and files uploaded, you will need to know how to manage them, so you know where things are and so your storage doesn't turn into a mess of files that are unmanageable.

Going back to figure 6.3, let's say we need to move the file called Contacts.docx to a new folder for a user called Mary. The first thing to do is right click on a blank spot within the Sales Files folder and choose *New folder*. Then let's call it Mary's Files and click on *Create*.

Chapter 6 – Google Drive and Google Docs

Now, as you can see in figure 6.6, we have a folder called Mary's Files, and we just need to move the Contacts.docx file into that folder. There are a couple of ways we can this.

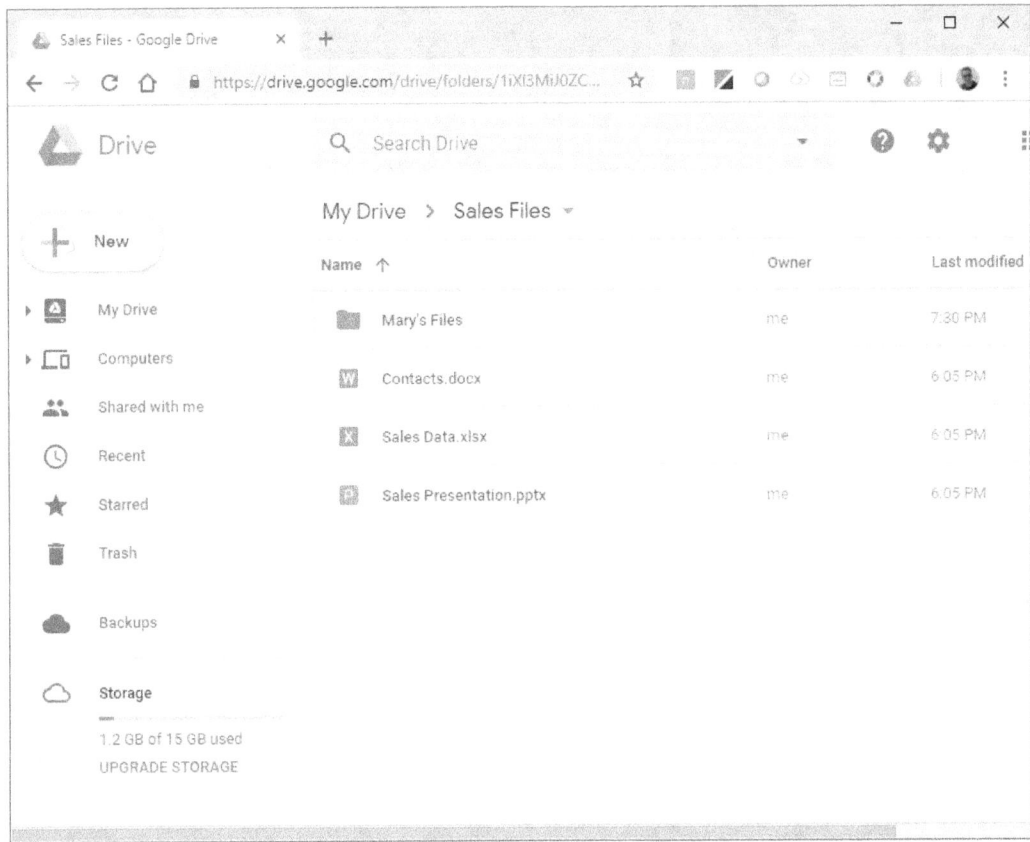

Figure 6.6

One way is to right click the Contacts.docx file, choose Move to, and then choose the Mary's Files folder (figure 6.7), which will get it moved into that folder.

Chapter 6 – Google Drive and Google Docs

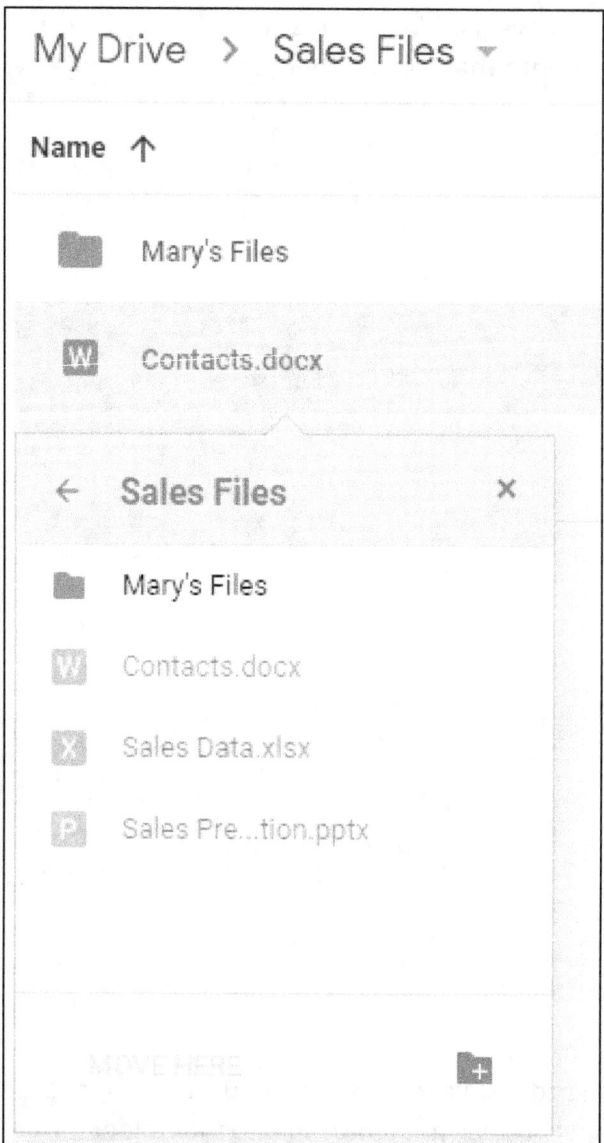

Figure 6.7

An easier way to do this is to just click on the Contacts.docx file and drag it into the Mary's Files folder. Either way, you will get a message similar to figure 6.8 telling you what happened.

Chapter 6 – Google Drive and Google Docs

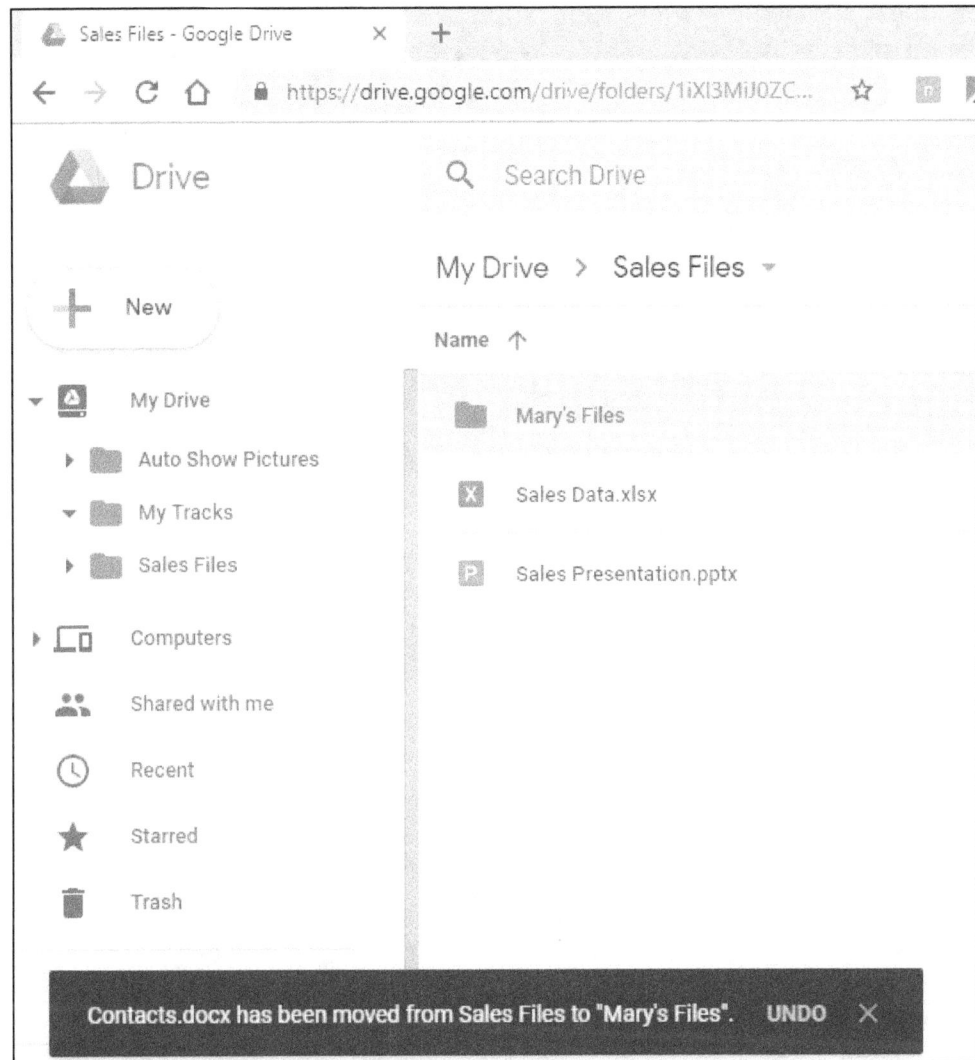

Figure 6.8

If you were then to go into the Mary's Files folder, you would find that the Contacts.docx file is now located in that folder.

Now I want to talk about the right click options that you have for files. When you right click a file, you will get a menu similar to figure 6.9, with many options to choose from.

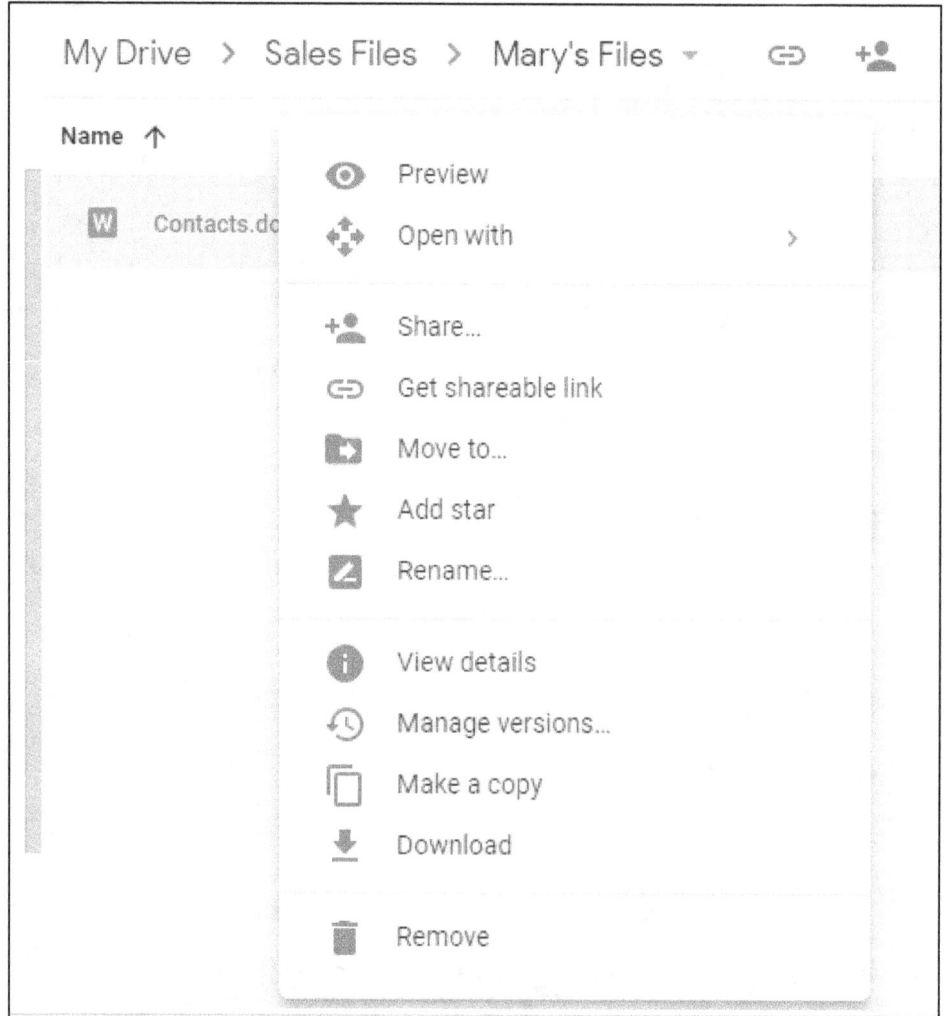

Figure 6.9

Here is what each of the right click options will do to your file:

- **Preview** – This option will allow you to preview your file right from your browser (assuming it's a supported file type). If you look at figure 6.10, I have opened the Contacts.docx file as a preview and can see the names and numbers in the file.

    Google Drive will also suggest other methods of opening your file based on the type of file it is. If you look at figure 6.10, you can see that it suggested opening the file using Word 2016, and if you click the dropdown arrow next to that, there will be other options such as WordPad and Google Docs, which you can try if the preview function doesn't work.

Chapter 6 – Google Drive and Google Docs

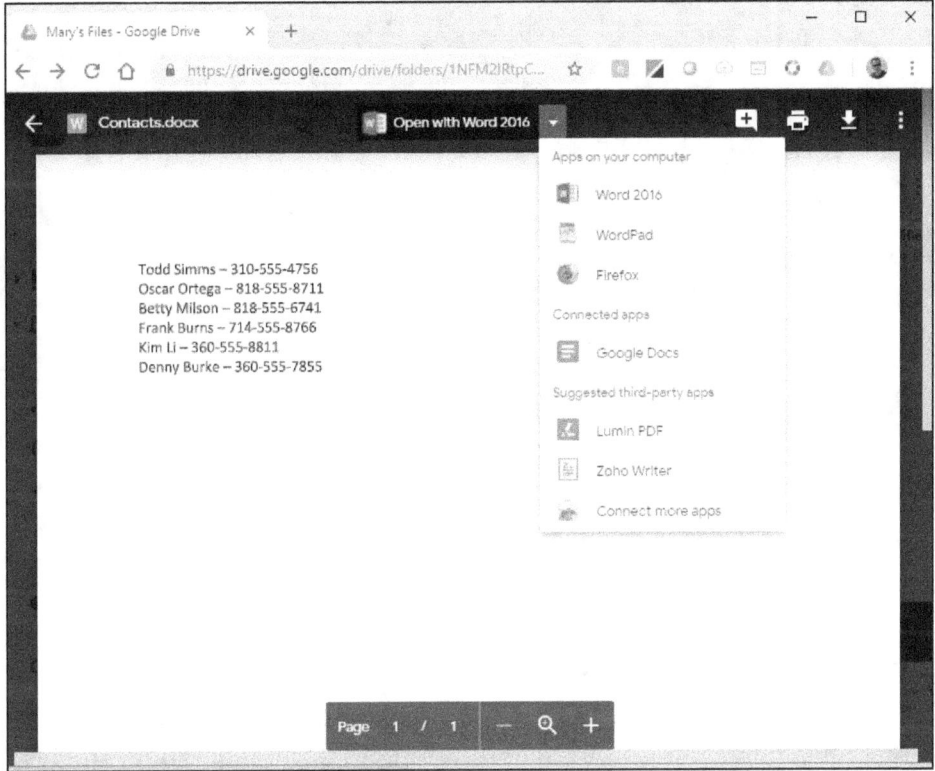

Figure 6.10

- **Open with** – This will give you choices of programs to open the file with (similar to the ones in figure 6.10).

- **Share** – This allows you to share your file with other people via a link or an email invite.

- **Get sharable link** – The same thing applies about sharing for this option, but what this does is create a link to your shared file that people can click on to have access to your file.

- **Move to** – I already discussed moving a file, but once again this will allow you to move a file from one folder to another.

- **Add star** – If you want a particular file to stand out, then you can add a star to it (figure 6.11), which will remind you that there is something special about it. There is also a Starred section in the main Drive area where you can view all of your starred files in one place.

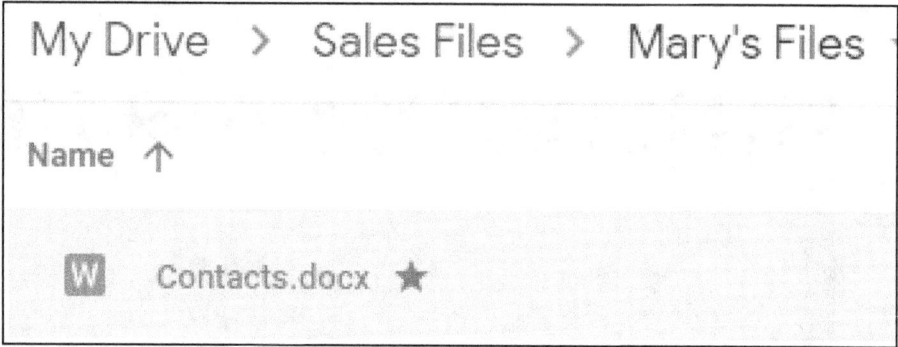

Figure 6.11

- **Rename** — This is pretty self-explanatory, but one thing you need to keep in mind is that if you change the file extension (in this case it's .docx) then you might not be able to open the file anymore since Windows (and Mac\Linux) use file extensions to tell the operating system what program it should open the file with.

- **View details** — Here you can view the details and activity of a certain file. As you can see in figure 6.12, there is a *Details* section and an *Activity* section, and each one shows different information about the file, such as its size, location, owner, as well as edit and move activity (etc.).

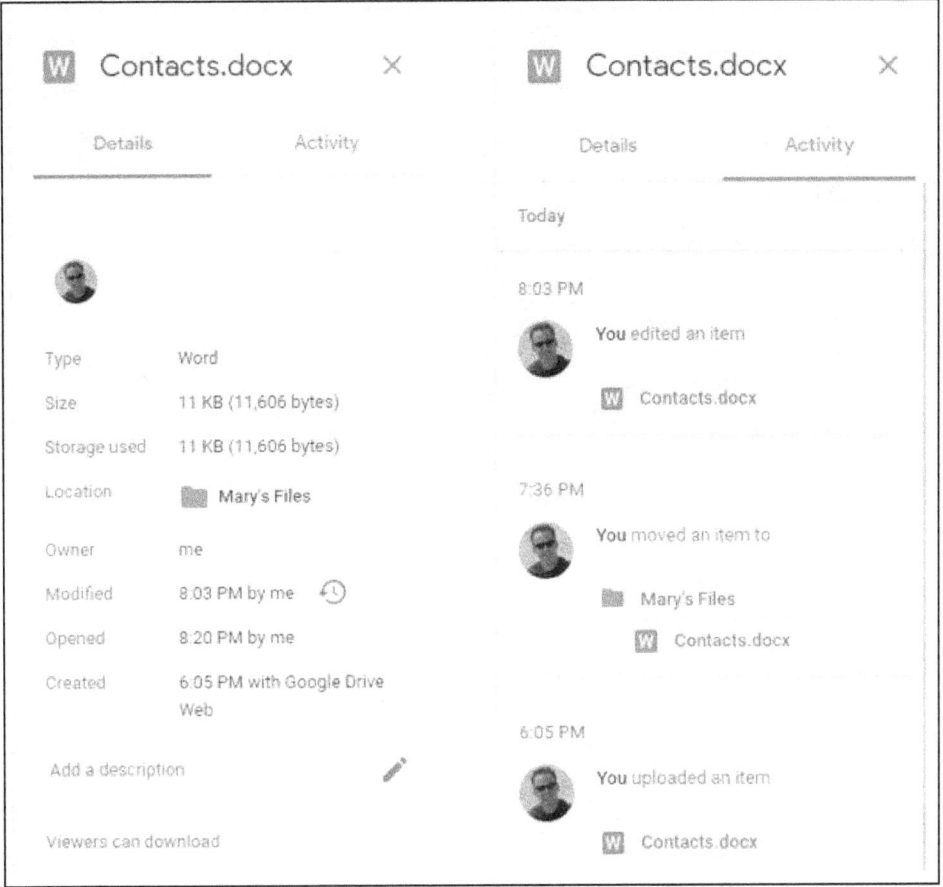

Figure 6.12

- **Manage versions** – If you have multiple versions of a file that you have either changed and saved or uploaded a new copy and overwritten the existing copy, then you will have some options as to what you can do with those various versions (figure 6.13). Google will keep your older versions for thirty days (or 100 versions) before removing them, so if you need to go back to an older version, you will be able to do so. Then you can click on the three dots menu to either download the file, delete the file, or have Google keep the file forever.

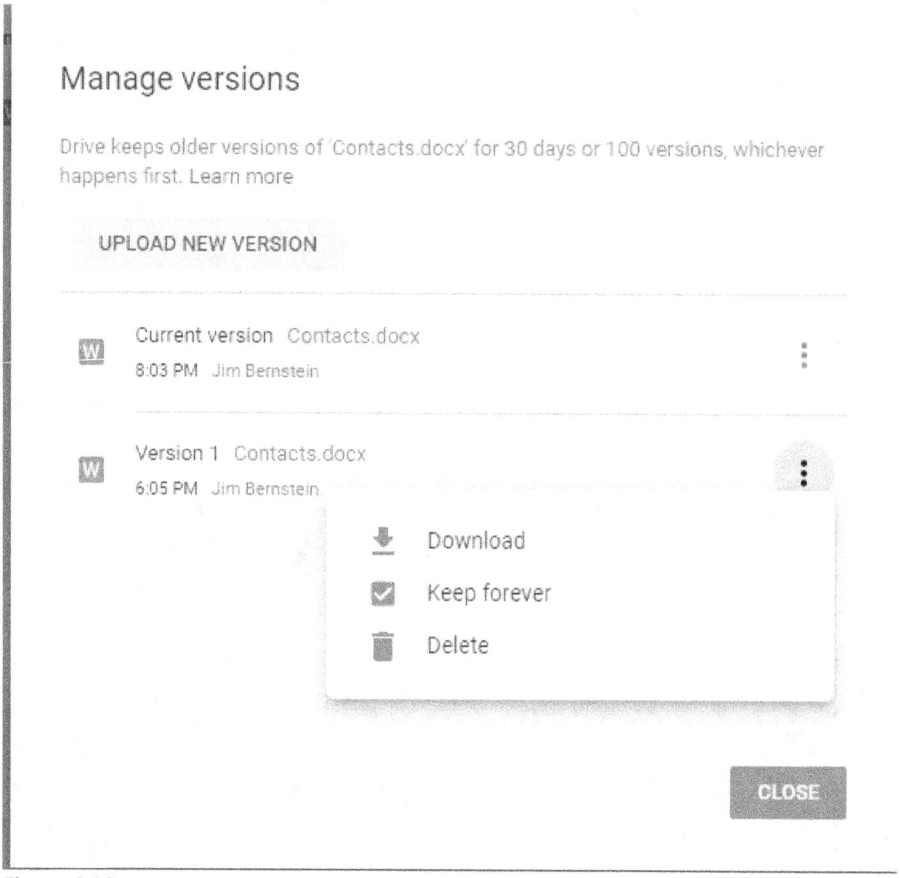

Chapter 6 – Google Drive and Google Docs

Figure 6.13

- **Make a copy** – This option will simply create a copy of the file and place it in the same folder with the same name, except it will say "Copy of" in front of it.

- **Download** – If you want to have a copy of this file on your local computer, then choose this option and select the folder on your hard drive where you want to download the file to.

- **Remove** – This option will remove the file from your Google Drive and place it in the Trash, where you can go and restore the file if needed. To do so, just right click the file in the Trash and choose *Restore*. Or you can choose *Delete forever* to permanently remove it.

These same options are available from the toolbar that appears when you click on a file (figure 6.14). The three vertical dots will give you additional options.

Chapter 6 – Google Drive and Google Docs

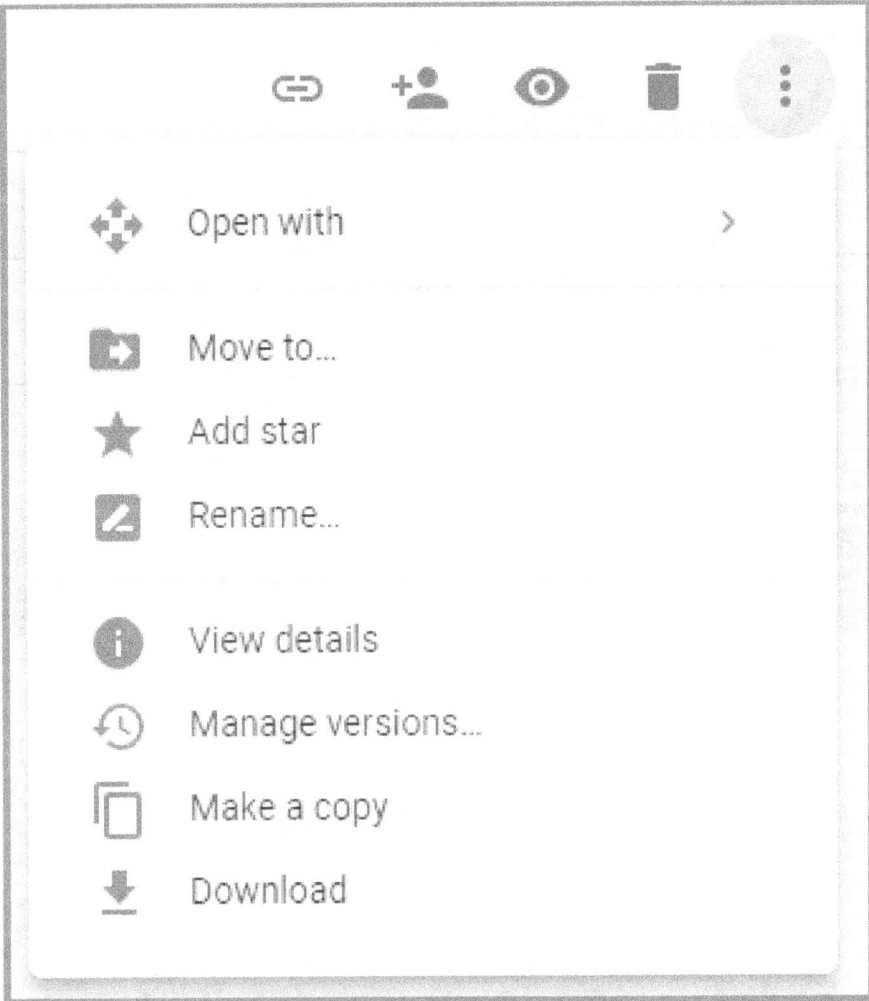

Figure 6.14

When you right click on a folder instead of a file, you get most of the same options, but there are a couple that are different (as highlighted in figure 6.15).

Chapter 6 – Google Drive and Google Docs

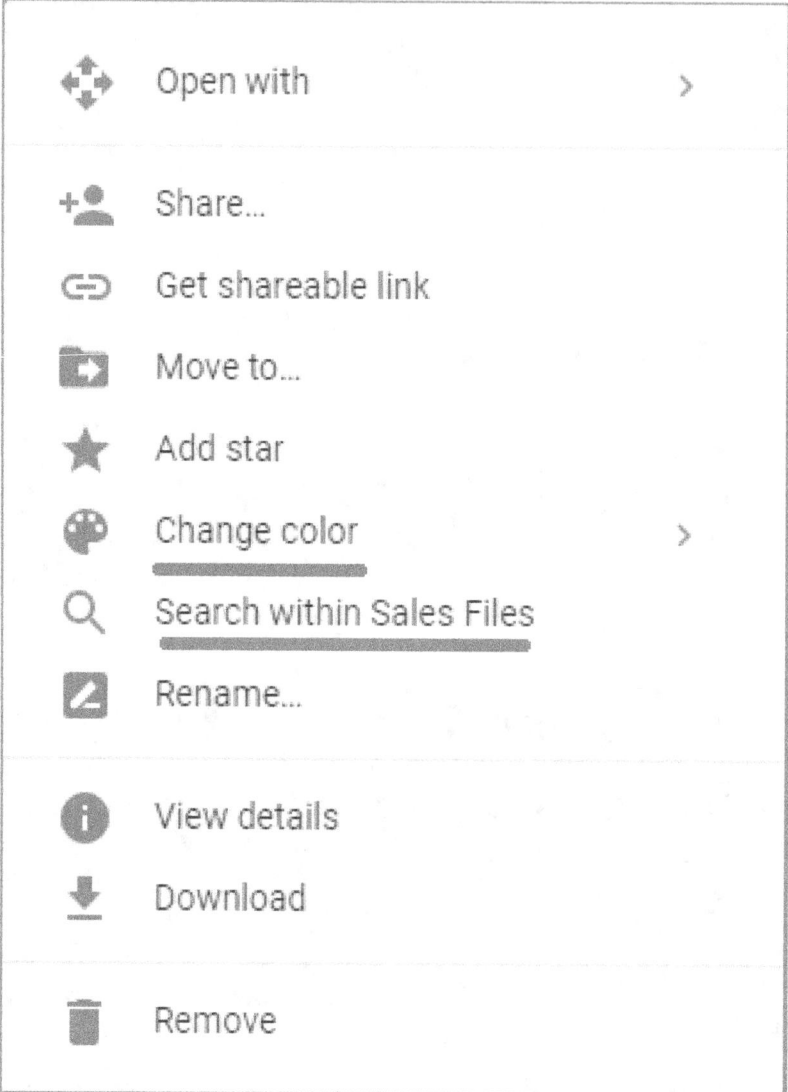

Figure 6.15

The *Change color* choice will change the color of the folder from the default grey to whatever color you like.

The *Search within* choice will let you search for files within the folder you right clicked on. You can search by name and also by file type.

One last thing I want to mention in this section is the *View* button. You can view your files in both list view and in grid view. Clicking on the button that looks like figure 6.16 will change the view of your files from just the file name to a thumbnail type view, which works well for pictures (figure 6.17). You can switch back and forth between these views in your folders.

Chapter 6 – Google Drive and Google Docs

Figure 6.16

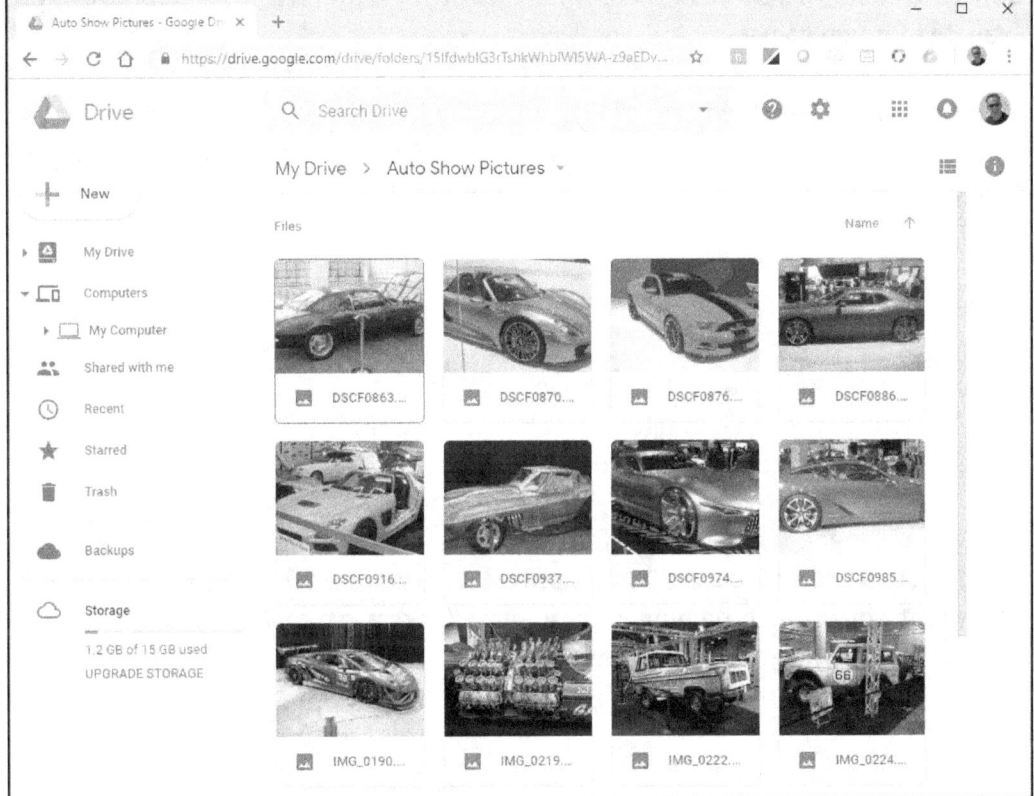

Figure 6.17

The View button is your friend, and it will make it a lot easier to manage your files because you can change the view based on the type of files you are looking at, so be sure to give it a try.

145

Chapter 6 – Google Drive and Google Docs

Google Docs

Many people refer to the suite of office apps provided by Google as Google Docs even though Google Docs itself is Google's word processing app that is similar to Microsoft Word. So if you hear the term Google Docs there is a good chance it is referring to more than just the word processing app. The Google office apps consist of Docs (word processor), Sheets (spreadsheet app), Slides (presentation app) and Forms and these are all free to use even if you are using a standard free Google account. If you have a G-suite account then there will be additional apps available for you to use.

Rather than go over each one of the apps individually I will just use Google Docs as an example and show you how it works and you can apply what you read here to the other apps since they all work in a similar fashion when it comes to their interface.

To access Google Docs all you need to do is go to the Google Docs website (https://docs.google.com/), or do a search for Google Docs and get to it that way. If you are already logged into your Google account, then it will take you to the Docs interface (as shown in figure 6.17). If you are not logged in, then you will be prompted to enter your Gmail address and password.

Since I have logged into Docs before, it shows me my recent documents on the bottom of the screen as well as an option to start a new blank document or a document from one of the built in templates. There are many templates to choose from, from resumes to letters to brochures and so on.

Templates are a great way to help to see what kind of things you can do in Google Docs. Try opening one up and playing around with it to see if you can figure out how it was put together.

Chapter 6 – Google Drive and Google Docs

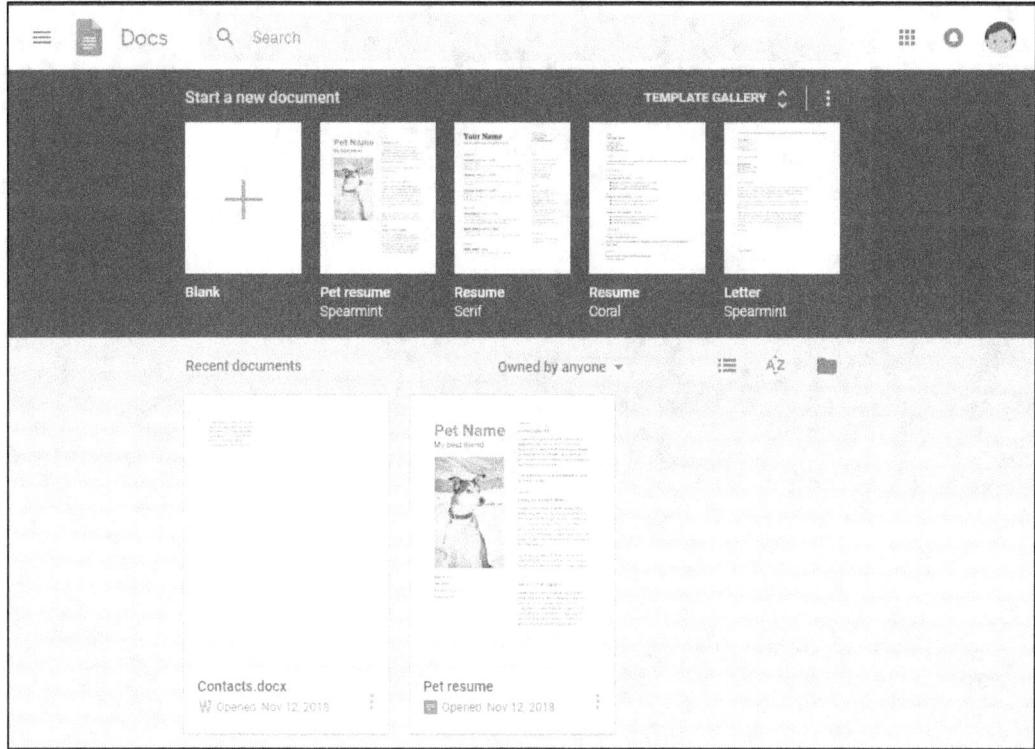

Figure 6.18

In order to start using Docs, I will either need to open a recent document, create a new blank document, or create a document from one of the templates. For my example, I will use a template called *Lesson Plan* from the template gallery (figure 6.18). Once I click on that template it will open up in Docs and be ready for me to start editing.

Chapter 6 – Google Drive and Google Docs

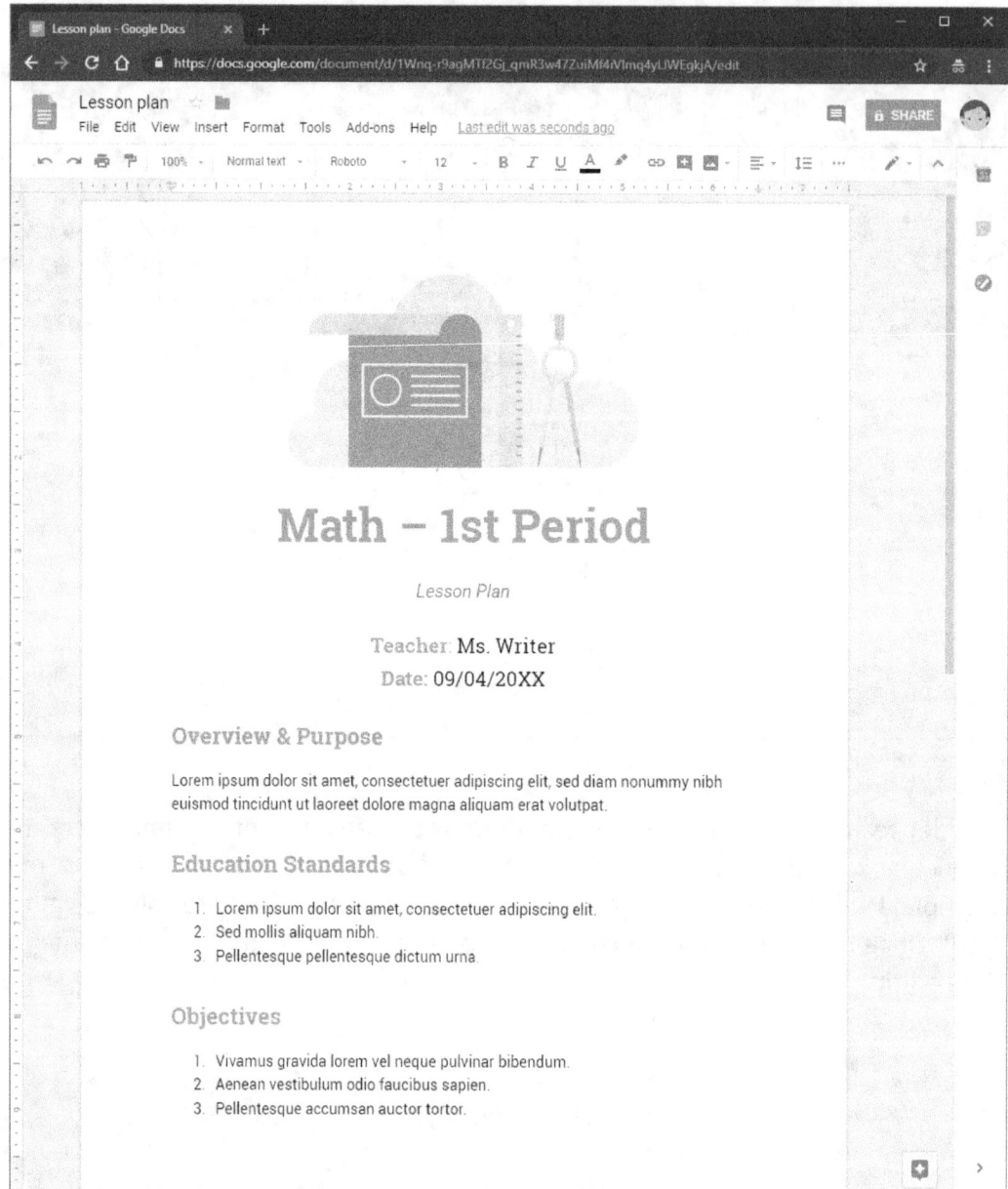

Figure 6.19

Now you can see the toolbars and menu items that you can use when working on your documents. The options are not quite as extensive as the ones with Microsoft Word, but there are plenty of tools to help you get the job done.

Many of the tool icons are obvious, such as the ones for changing the font type, size, and color. Plus there are buttons to do things like center and justify the text or insert images and hyperlinks. Plus, if you need to know what a button does, simply hold your mouse over the button and the tooltip will appear, telling you

Chapter 6 – Google Drive and Google Docs

what that button does and also give you the keyboard shortcut for that function. For example, in figure 6.20 you can see that the button allows you to insert a link in your document, and you can also press *Ctrl+K* on your keyboard to do the same thing.

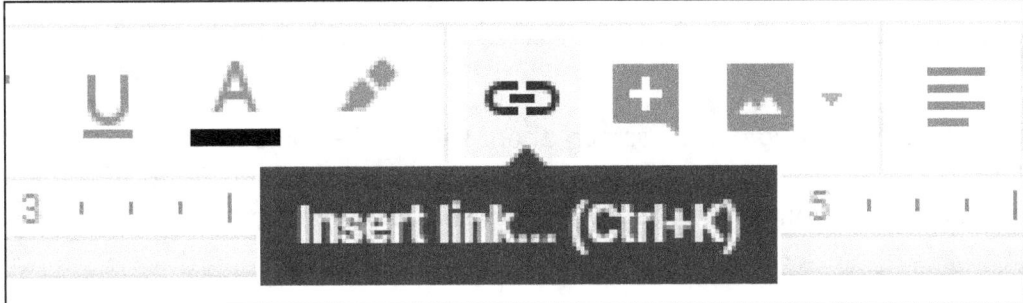

Figure 6.20

You will also notice next to the name of the document that there is an option to mark it with a star, which will mark it as starred in your Google Drive, and also allow you to access this particular document faster in the future.

Next to the star is a folder icon, which will allow you to move your document to a different folder within your Google Drive to help you keep things more organized. This is one of the reasons you should set up your Google Drive before getting too into the other Google apps, so things will make a little more sense.

Figure 6.21

At the upper right of the screen, you will see a message looking icon (figure 6.23), and this is where you can view or add any comments about this particular document. If it's shared with others, you can see their comments here as well. Speaking of shared, clicking on the *share* button will allow you to share the document with other people or groups. The icon to the right can be used to view your account settings or sign out of your account if needed.

Chapter 6 – Google Drive and Google Docs

Figure 6.22

On the right hand side of the screen, there will also be some icons that are used for quick access to your Google Calendar, Google Keep, and your Tasks. If you use these apps, this can come in handy, otherwise you can just ignore them.

Figure 6.23

Another thing I want to mention on the right side of the screen is the Editing Mode dropdown selection (figure 6.24).

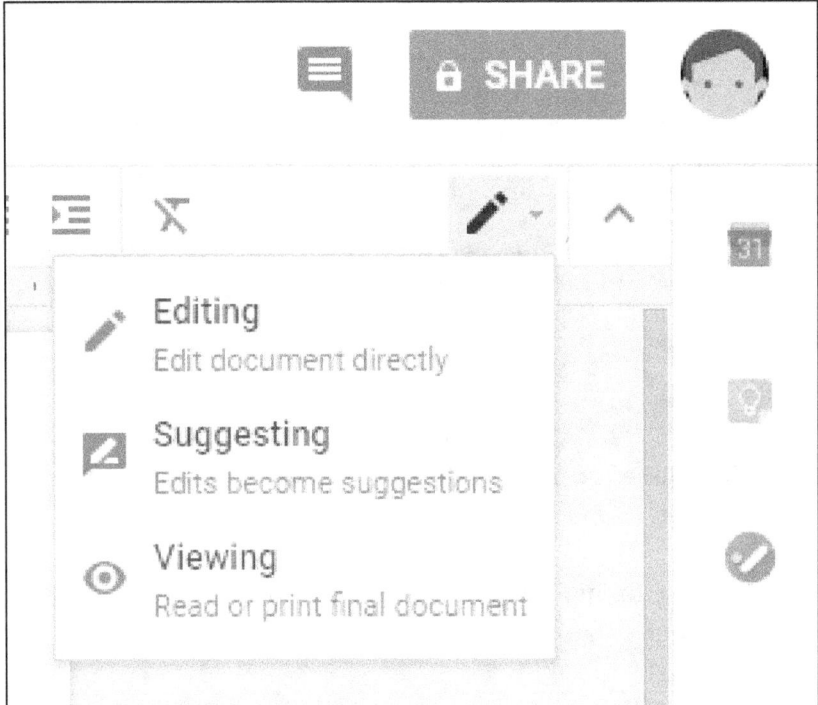

Figure 6.24

There are three different modes to choose from:

- **Editing** – *Editing* mode is what you will be using most of the time. This mode allows you to edit your document, meaning you can add text and images, change formatting, and so on.

- **Suggesting** – If you are sharing your document with others for collaboration purposes, the *Suggesting* mode can be used to make changes that are marked as suggested changes, and anyone with edit permissions on the document can accept or reject your suggestions. It's similar to the Track Changes feature in Microsoft Word. As you can see in figure 6.25, Todd Simms added the words *of this course,* which is marked with brackets above and below the text and also changed the text to red. Now there is an option to accept or reject the changes with the checkmark or the X.

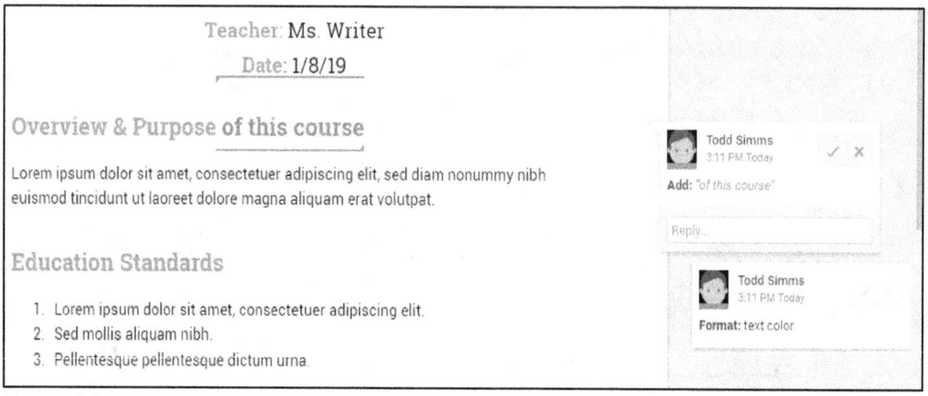

Chapter 6 – Google Drive and Google Docs

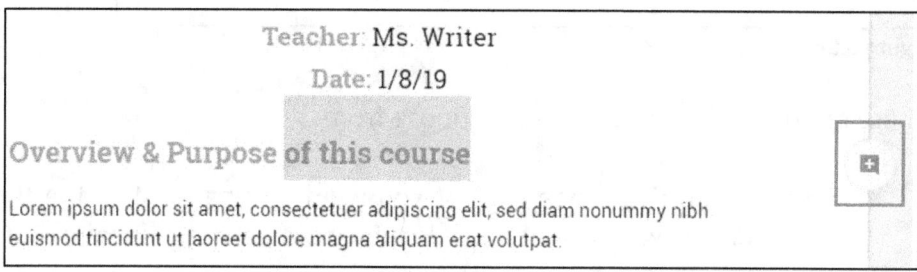

Figure 6.25

- **Viewing** – Viewing mode is used to put the document in a read-only mode where no changes can be made.

Clicking on an object or highlighting some text will bring up an insert comment button (figure 6.26).

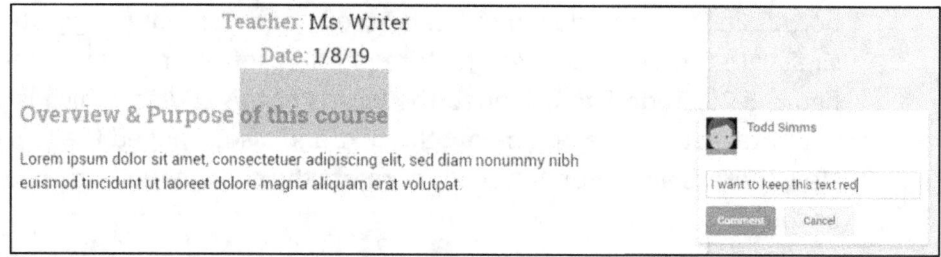

Figure 6.26

Clicking on that button will allow you to type in a comment for the particular item you selected, whether it be text or an image etc.

Figure 6.27

After you type in your comment, it will be shown to the right hand side of the page, and you will have some things you or others can do with that comment.

Chapter 6 – Google Drive and Google Docs

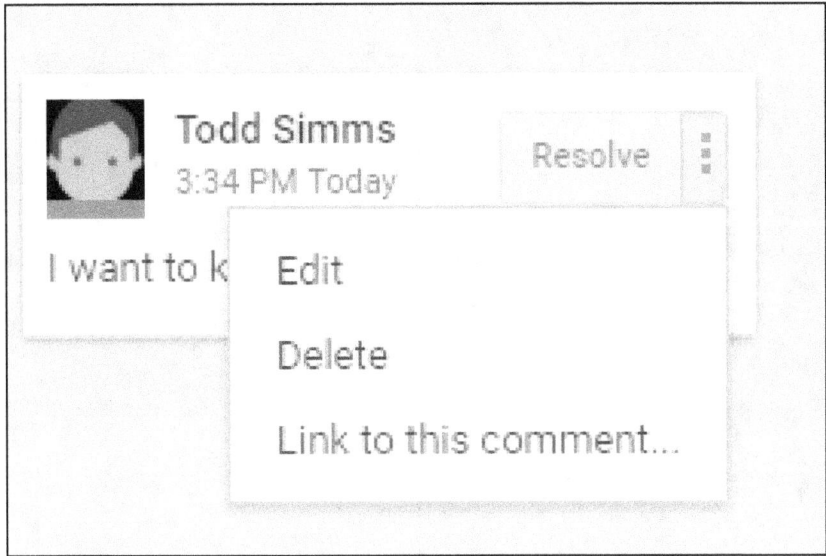

Figure 6.28

Clicking on *Resolve* will mark the comment as resolved and hide the discussion. Clicking on *Edit* or *Delete* are obvious, but when you click on *Link to this comment* you will be provided with a link that you can copy and paste into an email to send off to someone else so they can look over your comment. In order for that person to see your comment, they will need to have permission to access the document, otherwise they can request permission from the page the link brings them to.

Menu Items
Now I would like to go over the tools and functions that you can use from the menu items within Docs. Many of these are obvious, so I will go into more detail about the ones that might not be too obvious. Keep in mind that many of the items you will find under the various menus will be the same as what is available in the toolbars.

File Menu
The File menu is where you will find many of your administrative functions, such as opening a current document or creating a new one.

Chapter 6 – Google Drive and Google Docs

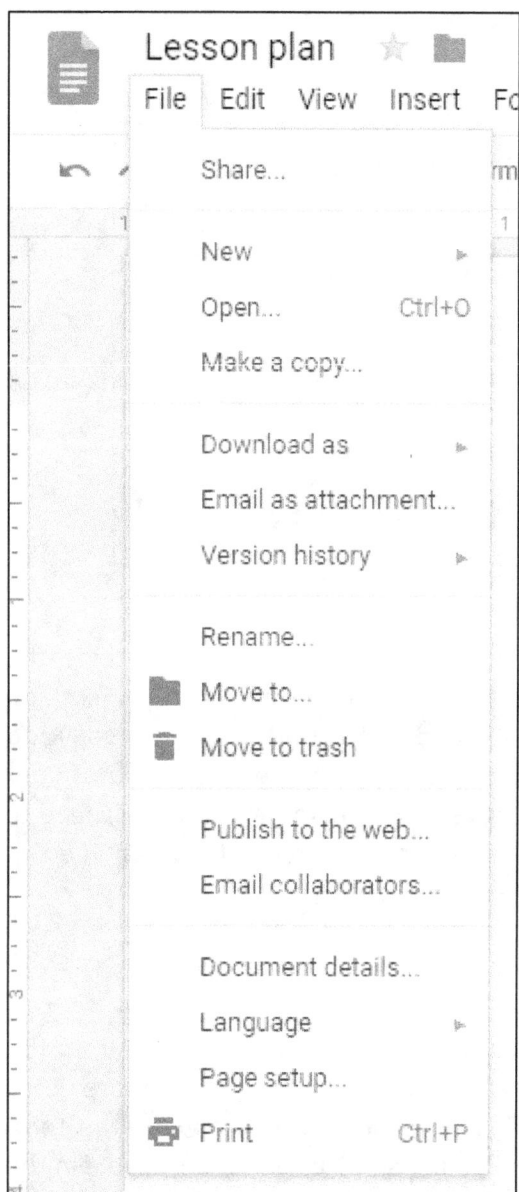

Figure 6.29

I will now briefly go over all of the items within the File menu:

- **Share** – I mentioned sharing your document earlier in the chapter, but if you decide to share your work with other people, you can use this option to send out invitations so that they can then view and\or edit your documents. All you need to do is type in their email address and choose if they can edit, comment, or view your document, and click on *Send*.

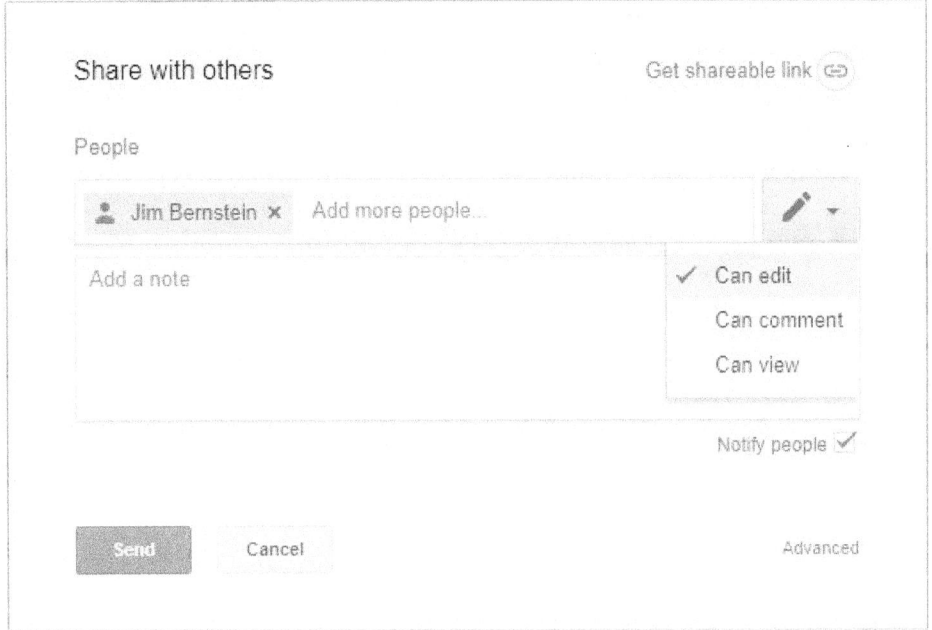

Figure 6.30

- **New** – The *New* option brings you back to where we were at the beginning of the chapter, where you can either choose to create a new blank document or create a new document from one of the included templates.

- **Open** – The Open option will let you open previously saved documents from your Google Drive, as well as documents that have been shared with you by others. If you want to upload a new document to work on you can do that from here as well.

- **Make a copy** – This option will make a copy of the existing document in the location of your choosing. You can name the copy anything you wish, otherwise it will be named **Copy of *document name***. There will also be checkbox options to share the copy with the same people as the original was shared with, and also an option to copy comments and suggestions.

- **Download as** – If you want to download a copy of the document to your local computer or other device, then you can do so using this option. You have several choices as to what type of document you want to save it as, such as a Word document, PDF, text file, and so on.

- **Email as attachment** – If you want to send your actual document to someone rather than inviting them to view it from your account, you can use the *Email as attachment option* (figure 6.31).

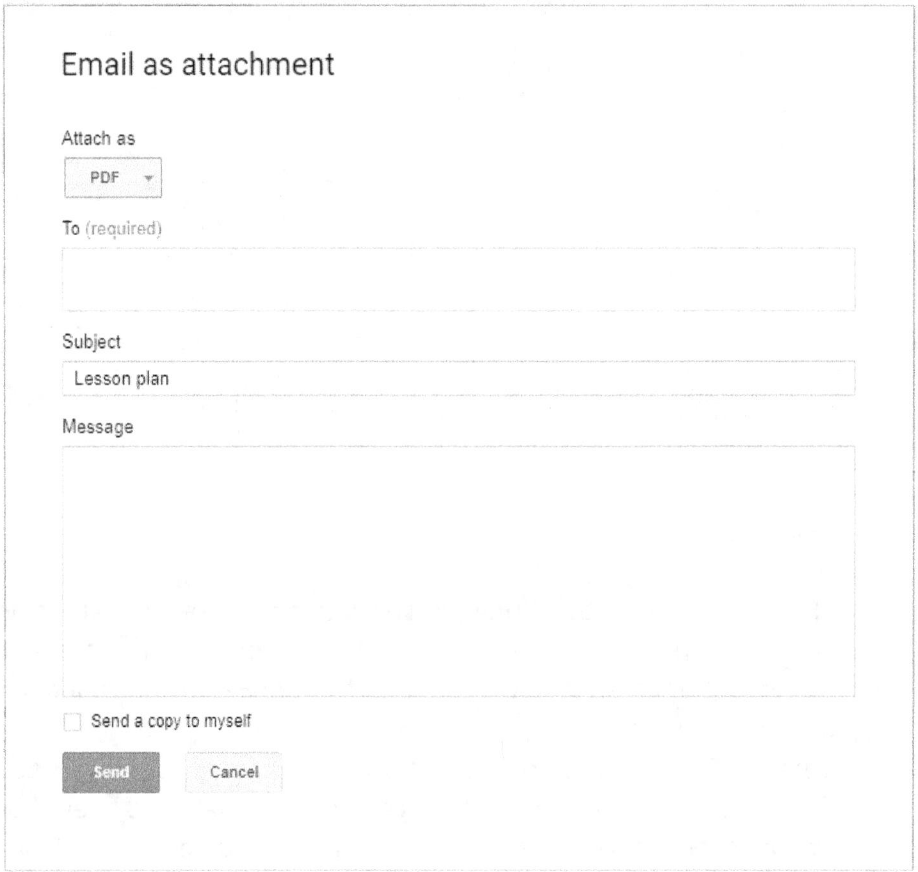

Figure 6.31

Here you can choose what type of file you can have your attachment sent as by clicking on the down arrow under *Attach as*. Or you can use the *Paste the item itself into the email* option if you want the document to be displayed in the body of the email.

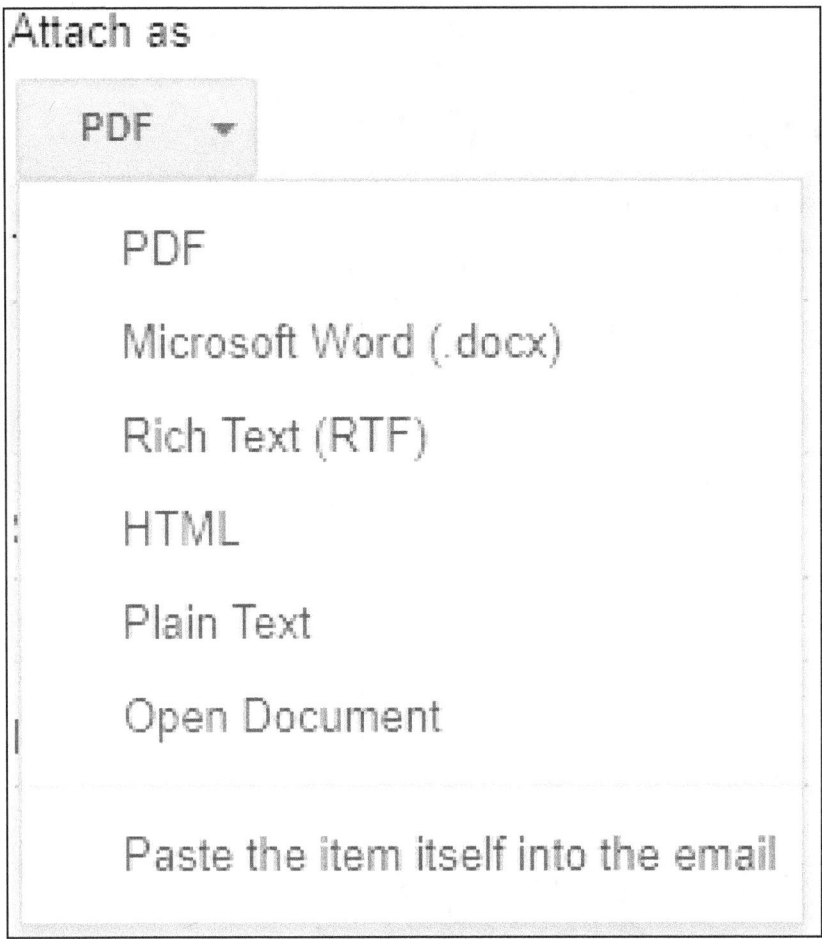
Figure 6.32

- **Version History** – As Google Docs saves your changes, it will keep various versions of the file in case you want to revert back to a different version, and maybe recover some changes as shown in figure 6.33. Clicking on the three vertical dots next to a version will allow you to copy that version or give that version a specific name (figure 6.34). You also have the option to have Docs only show named versions, so your version history only shows the versions you want to see.

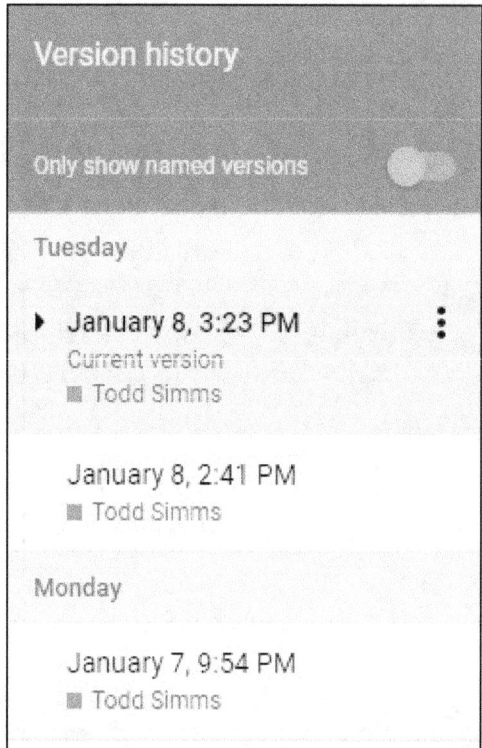

Figure 6.33

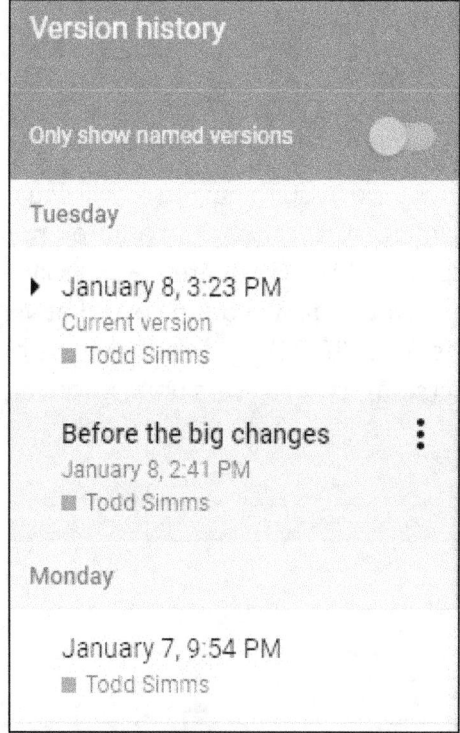

Figure 6.34

Chapter 6 – Google Drive and Google Docs

- **Rename** – The *Rename* option simply renames your document to a name of your choosing. As you can see in figure 6.35, when I clicked on *Rename,* it highlighted *Lesson plan,* allowing me to change it to something else if desired.

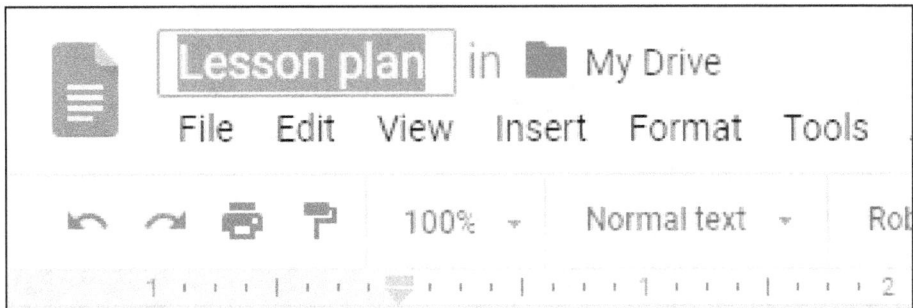
Figure 6.35

- **Move to** – Using this option does the same thing as clicking the folder icon next to the star and will allow you to move the file to a different location on your Google Drive or move it to your local computer.

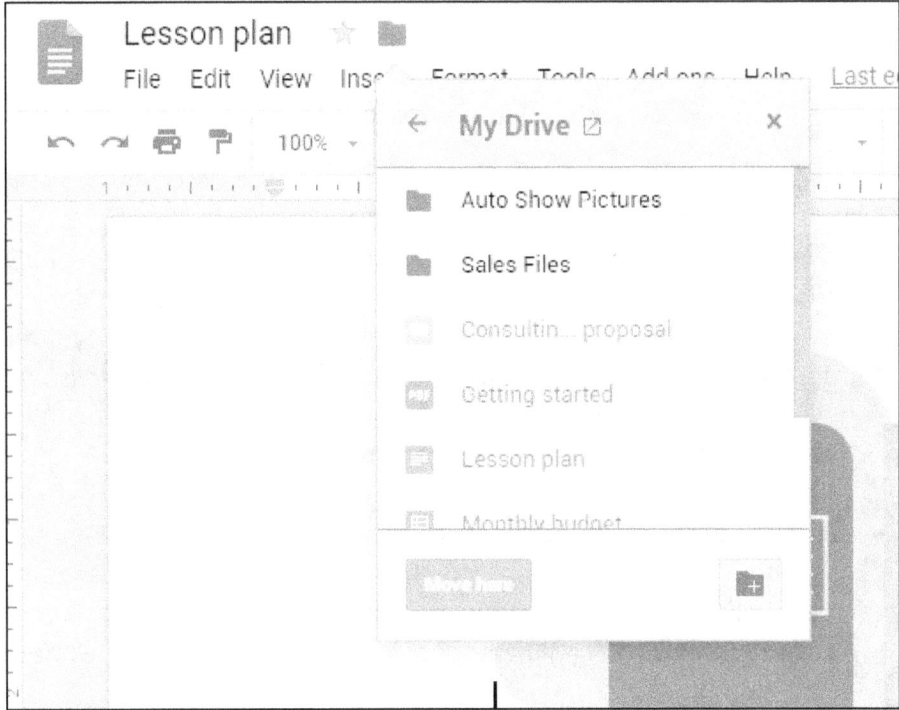
Figure 6.36

- **Move to trash** – If you want to delete your document, you can use this option. (You can recover it from your trash if you change your mind later.)

Chapter 6 – Google Drive and Google Docs

- **Publish to the web** – If you would like to share your document as a read only webpage version of the file, then this is where *Publish to the web* can come in handy. When you use this option, Docs will create a link when you click on *Publish* that you can copy and then send to other people so they can view your document within their web browser.

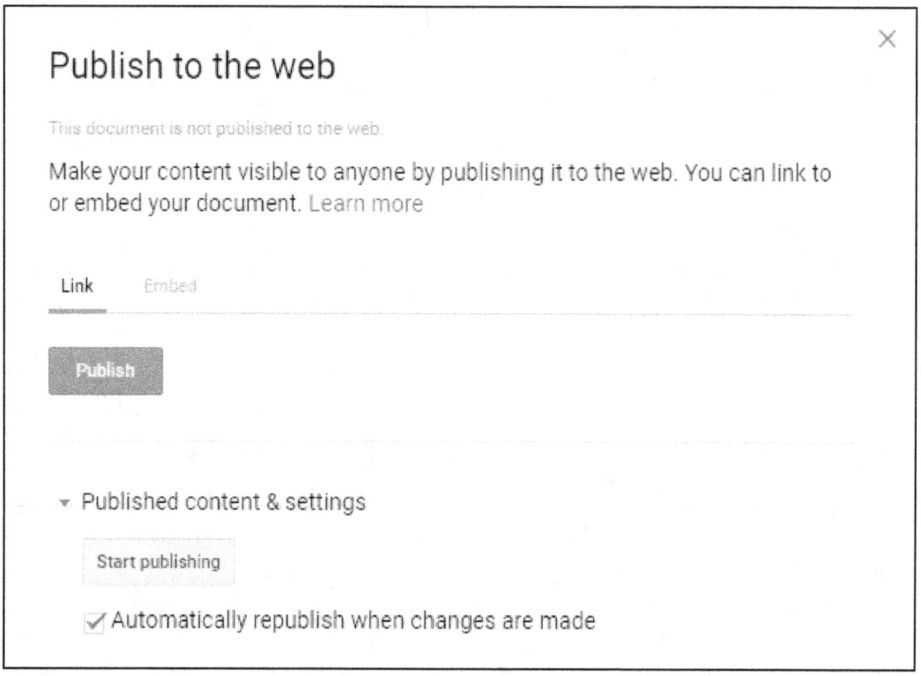

Figure 6.37

If you check the box at the bottom that says *Automatically republish when changes* are made, then when you make changes, the people with access to your shared link can refresh their browser and see your updated document. After you publish your document the *Start publishing* button will change to *Stop publishing* if you don't want your document to be available to people with the link anymore.

- **Email collaborators** – If you want to send a message to everyone who is a collaborator on this document, then use the *Email collaborators* option. Docs will automatically add everyone to the email who has access to the document, but you can uncheck any names that you don't want the email sent to.

- **Document details** – Choosing this option will give you basic information about the document you are working on such as its location, owner, modified date, and created date.

Chapter 6 – Google Drive and Google Docs

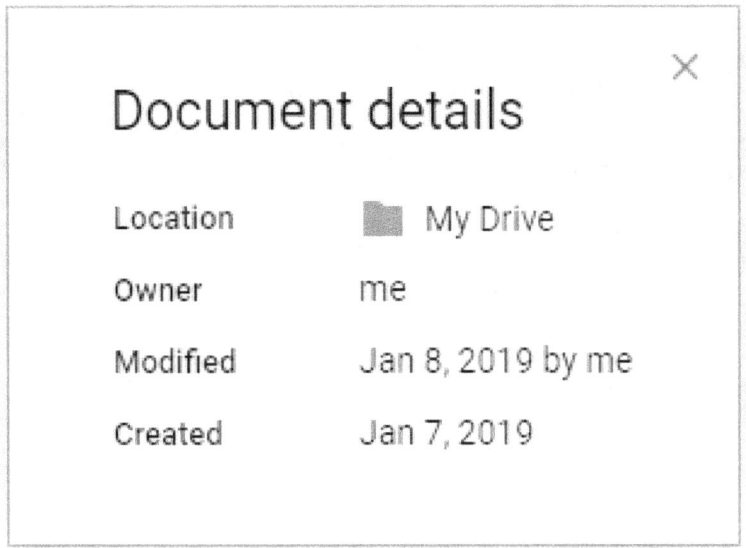

Figure 6.38

- **Language** – This is where you would change your typing language from its default.

- **Page setup** – *Page setup* allows you to change things such as the page orientation, margin sizes, paper size, and page color. You can also make your changes and then have Docs use them as the default for all new documents you create.

- **Print** – When it's time for you to print your document, you will do so from the *Print* option. Docs has its own print interface, but if you are used to the print interface that your computer normally uses for locally installed programs, you can click on the link that says *Print using system dialog*.

Edit Menu
There are not as many options on the Edit menu as there are on the File menu, but I still want to take a little time and go over them. Take a note of the shortcut key option to the right of each menu item. These can be used rather than clicking on the menu and then sub-menu item to do the same task.

Chapter 6 – Google Drive and Google Docs

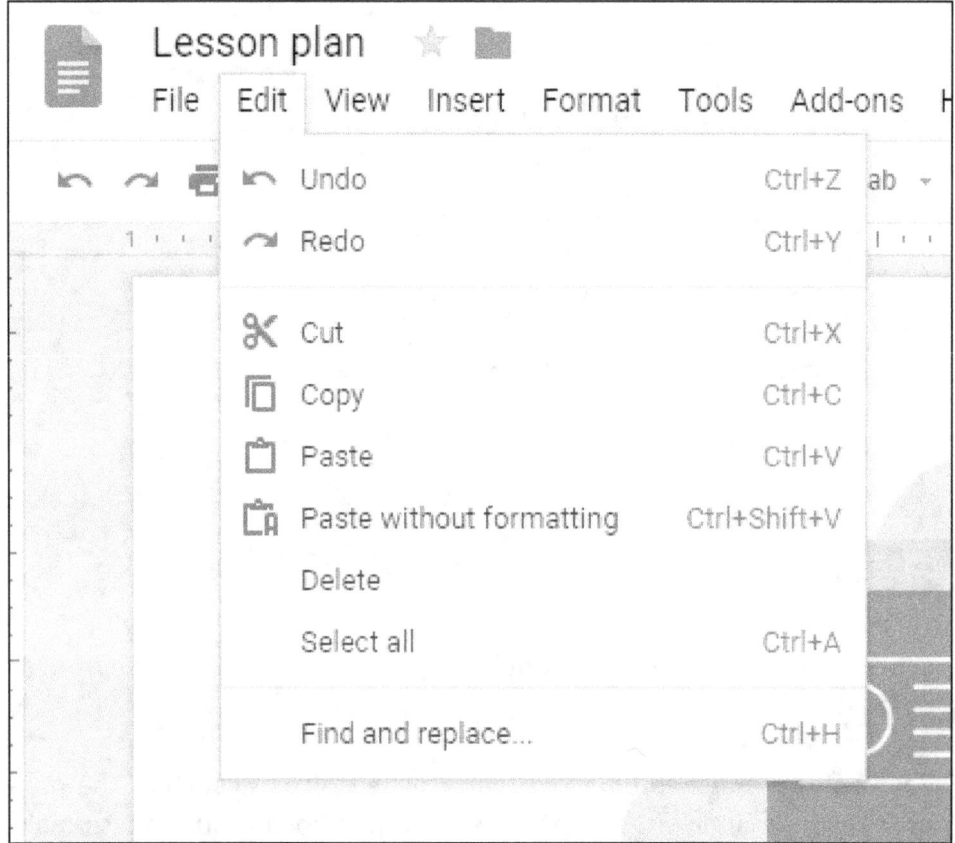

Figure 6.39

Here is what each of the items in the Edit menu does:

- **Undo** – If you make a change and want to revert back to the way it was before the change, you can use the *Undo* option. (This won't work if you have closed the document and then reopened it before using the Undo option.)

- **Redo** – If you undo a change and then decide you want it back after all, then you can use the *Redo* option. (This won't work if you have closed the document and then reopened it before using the Redo option.)

- **Cut** – When you want to remove some text or an image from a page or section and then place it in another page or section, you can highlight it and then choose *Cut*. Then you can paste it in where you would like it to be.

162

- **Copy** – When you want to make a copy of some text or an image and place it elsewhere, you will use Copy. This leaves the original text or image in place.

- **Paste** – After you cut or copy text or an image, you will use the *Paste* option to place that text or image within your document. Just be sure that your cursor is where you want the text or image to be before choosing Paste.

- **Paste without formatting** – Normally when you paste something into your document, Docs will keep the format of the text the same as the original text you cut or copied when you pasted it into your document. If you choose *Paste without formatting,* then it will paste the text in as the default text style that your version of Docs uses for new documents.

- **Delete** – *Delete* will simply remove any text or images you have selected. (Just remember you can use the *Undo* option to bring them back if needed.)

- **Select all** – If you want to highlight everything in your document all at once, simply choose the *Select all* option to do so. Then you can cut, copy, delete, or change the text and images you have highlighted.

- **Find and replace** – Many times you will want to replace a word with a different word within your document. For example, let's say you wanted to replace *John* with *Jon*. Rather than search for each instance of *John*, you can use the *Find and replace* option to have Docs do it for you. You can do this one instance at a time, or have Docs replace all of the text in one shot. If you look at figure 6.40, you will see that there are two instances of the name *John* in my document since it says 1 of 2.

Chapter 6 – Google Drive and Google Docs

![Find and replace dialog with Find: John, Replace with: Jon]

Figure 6.40

Find and replace can come in handy to make punctuation and capitalization changes as well. So, if you wanted to change : to ; or change Mcdonald to McDonald, you can use the find and replace option to do so.

View Menu

Docs allows you to customize your view so you can see only what you want to see on the screen, allowing for less clutter or viewing of more of the toolbars and so on.

Chapter 6 – Google Drive and Google Docs

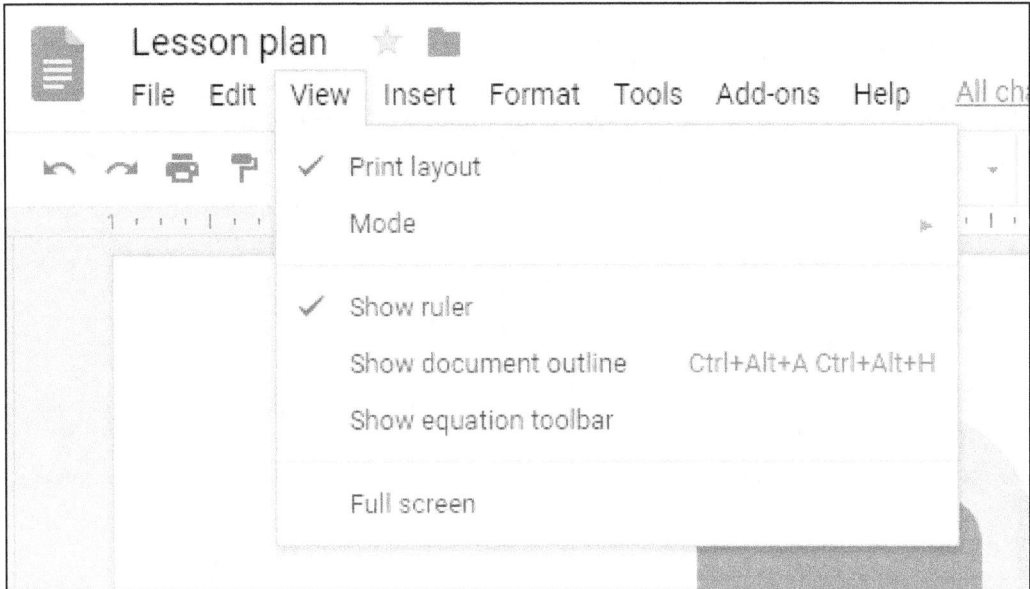

Figure 6.41

There are only a few options on this menu, and I will now go over what each one does:

- **Print layout** – The *Print layout* allows you to see your headers, footers, and margins between pages as if you have printed out the document.

- **Mode** – This will give you the same options I discussed earlier in the chapter when I went over the Editing, Suggesting, and Viewing modes.

- **Show ruler** – By default, Docs will show a ruler on the left hand side of the page, allowing you to measure things like images and other items to see what size they will take on the page. You can turn the ruler off if you don't need it, or don't want to see it.

- **Show document outline** – If your document is in an outlined format, you can use the *Show document outline* option to have it show each section. Then you can click on that section header to take you to that part of the document.

Chapter 6 – Google Drive and Google Docs

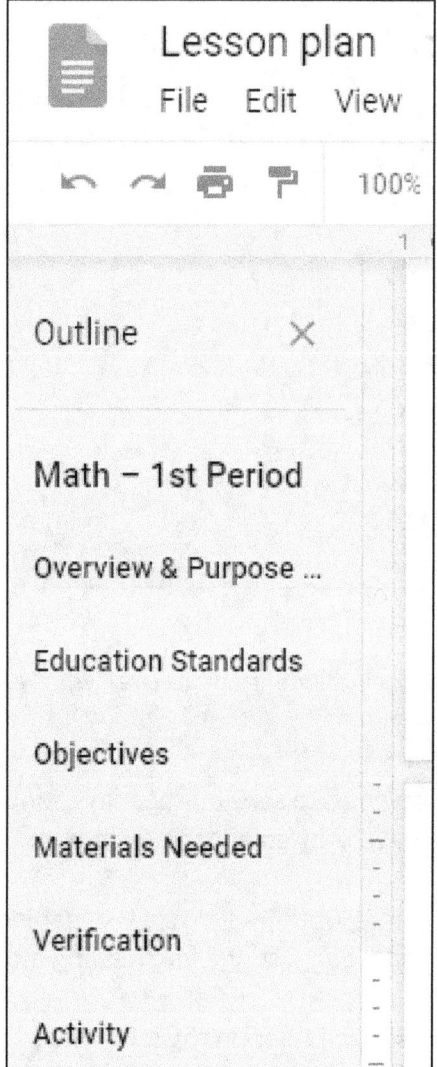

Figure 6.42

- **Show equation toolbar** – If for some rare reason you need to place a mathematical equation into your document, you can use the Equation Toolbar to do so, and selecting *Show equation toolbar* will make it available for use.

- **Full screen** – Choosing the *Full screen* option will hide the controls (toolbars), giving you more space to work. To bring the toolbars back simply press the Esc key on your keyboard.

Chapter 6 – Google Drive and Google Docs

Insert Menu

There are many items that you can insert into your document, and the Insert menu is where you will go for most of these types of tasks.

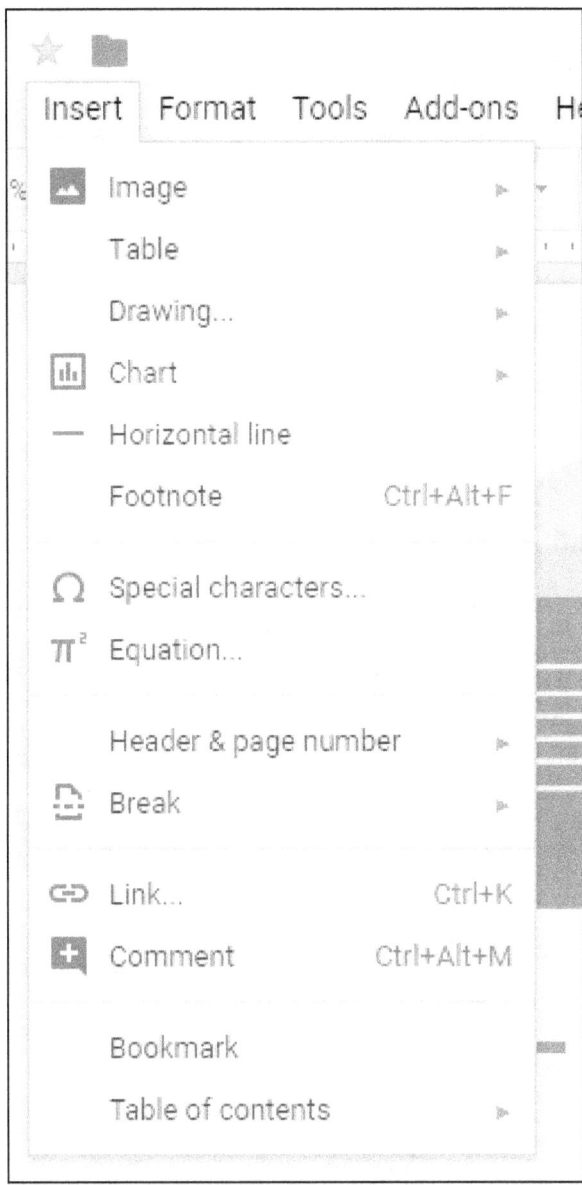

Figure 6.43

Now I would like to go over the items in the Insert menu:

- **Image** – Docs allows you to insert images\pictures into your document, and then you can place them where you want and resized them and so on. As you can see in figure 6.44, there are various locations you can insert an image from, such as your computer, Google Drive, a website location, and even your camera if you are working on your phone or tablet, etc.

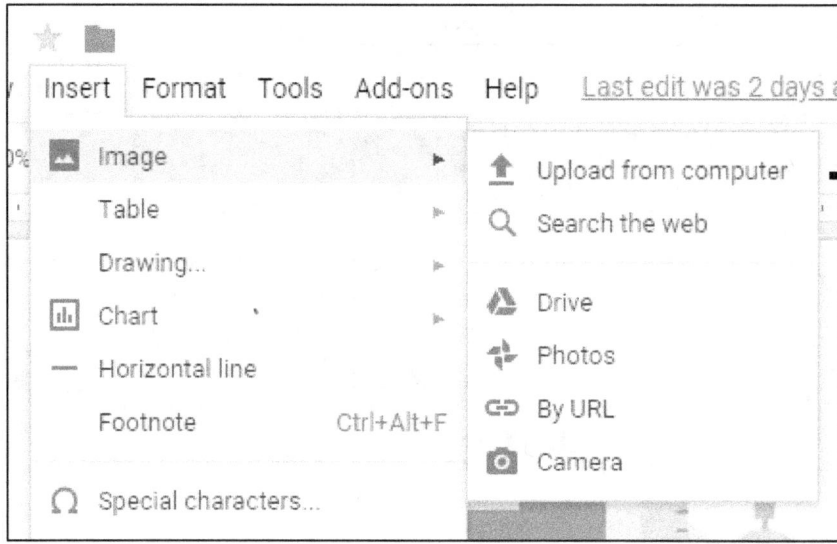

Figure 6.44

- **Table** – There may come a time where you want to make a listing of items in a table format. This is easy to do with Docs, and all you need to do is go to the Table option from the Insert menu, choose the size of the table you want, and then fill it in as desired.

Quantity	Size	Color	Availability
74	Large	Brown	4/19
62	Medium	Yellow	3/19
28	Small	Red	7/19

Figure 6.45

- **Drawing** – The *Drawing* option will bring up a drawing board where you can do things like add shapes, text, and even freehand draw if you like. Once you save your drawing it will be inserted into your document.

Figure 6.46

- **Chart** – Charts can be inserted into your document as well, and there are a couple of ways to do this. If you want to start from scratch, you can insert a new chart which can be a bar (figure 6.47), column, line, or pie chart. Or you can link to a Sheets spreadsheet and pull the information from there to create your chart.

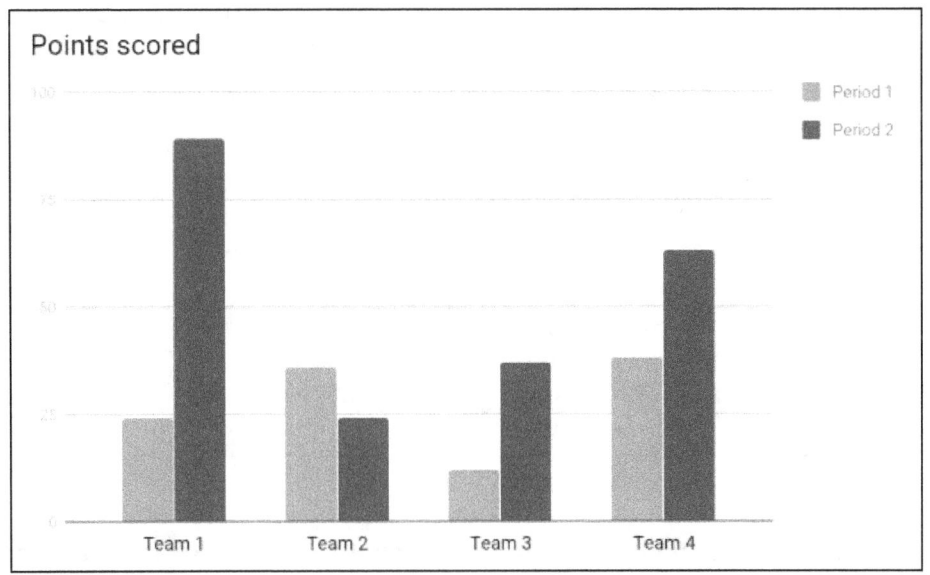

Figure 6.47

Chapter 6 – Google Drive and Google Docs

If you create a new one from within your document, you will have an option when you click on the chart to open the link to the source of the chart's data (figure 6.48). Clicking this will bring you to a Sheets file that will be created for you with some demonstration data that you can edit to fit your needs. After you make your changes in Sheets, simply go back to the chart in Docs and click on the Update button (figure 6.49) to have your data updated in your Docs chart.

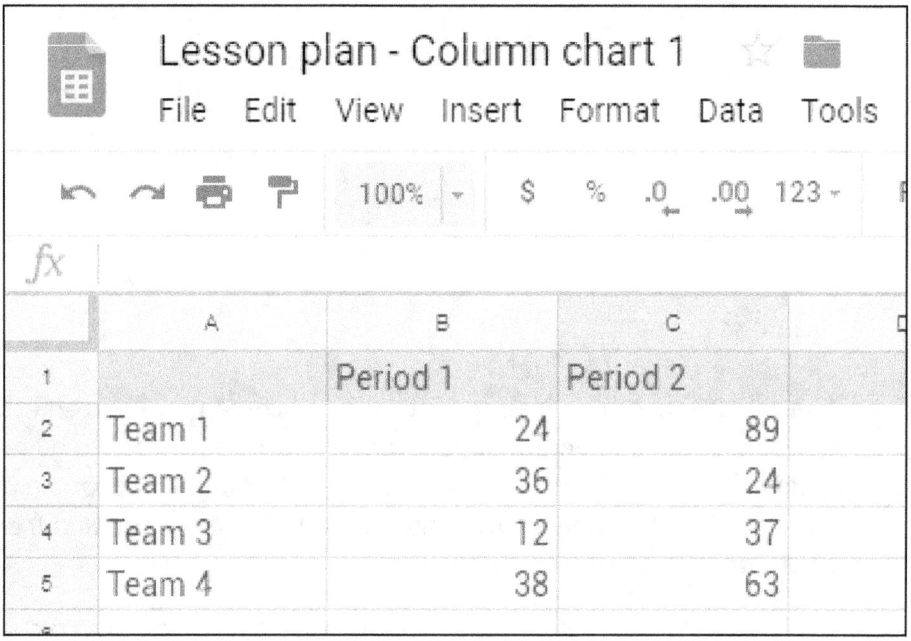

Figure 6.48

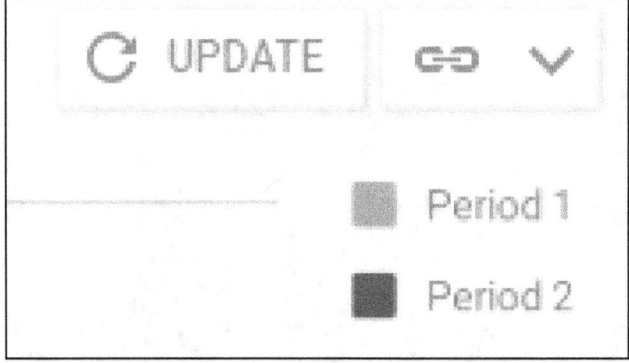

Figure 6.49

- **Horizontal line** – This option will simply insert a horizontal line across the page wherever you have the mouse cursor.

Chapter 6 – Google Drive and Google Docs

- **Footnote** – *Footnotes* are used to add information to the bottom part of the page outside of the margin. As you insert footnotes, they will be numbered, starting with the number 1.

- **Special characters** – Special characters are exactly what they sound like, characters that are different from your standard letters, numbers, and symbols (such as copy write symbols or emoji's and so on). If you look at the top left of figure 6.50, you will see that there are various categories to choose from, and you can even draw your own symbol and have Docs see if there is a match for it.

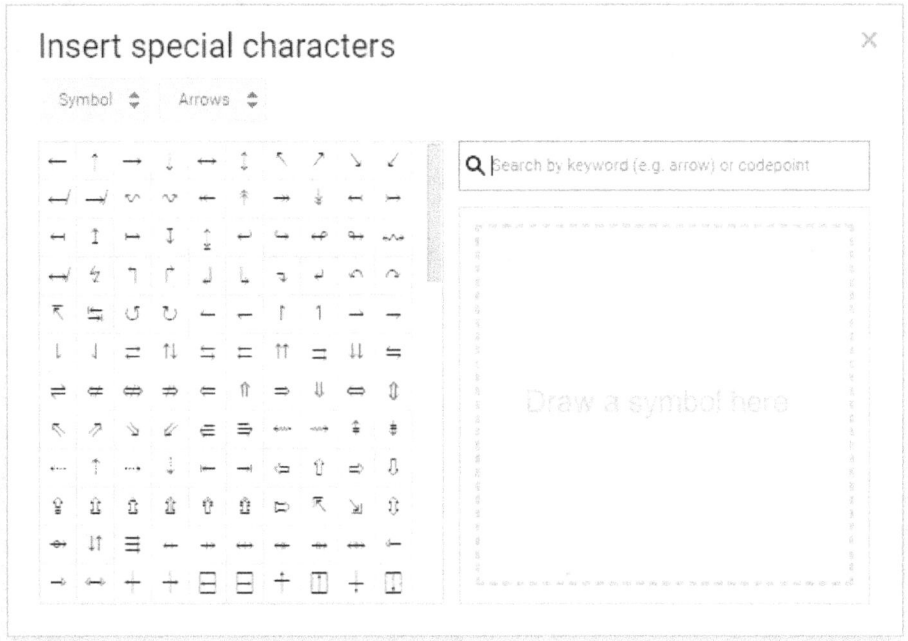

Figure 6.50

- **Equation** – This will bring up the Equation Toolbar as I discussed in the previous section.

- **Header & page number** – Headers and page numbers are commonly used in things like books or other documents that you might want to be numbered or to have a page title or header showing. You can also add footers from this option.

- **Break** – The *Break* option allows you to insert a page break to create a new page after the point where your mouse cursor is positioned. If you have

Chapter 6 – Google Drive and Google Docs

created any columns in your document, you can also insert a column break as well.

- **Link** – With everything being online these days, it's very common to see links to websites within documents. With the *Link* option, all you need to do is enter the website address you want to link to, and then the text that you want displayed in the document. Keep in mind that it's common to have the display text be the same as the link address.

    If your document has headings, then you can create a link that will take you back to a particular heading when clicked on.

- **Comment** – I mentioned comments earlier in the chapter, but once again they can be used to add a comment off to the side of the page that relates to a specific part of your document. Then other people that you are sharing the document with will be able to see that comment as well.

- **Bookmark** – *Bookmarks* are used to link within a document to a specific section or page. To create a bookmark, go to the location where you want to place that bookmark, and then choose *Insert > Bookmark* and give it a name (figure 6.51).

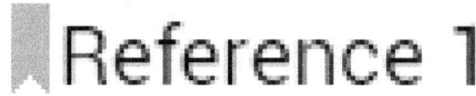

Figure 6.51

Next, you will go to the section of your document that you want to link to that bookmark and highlight it. Then go to *Insert > Link* and expand the Bookmarks section to find the bookmark you have created (figure 6.52). Finally, choose the bookmark that you created from the previous step and click *Apply*.

Chapter 6 – Google Drive and Google Docs

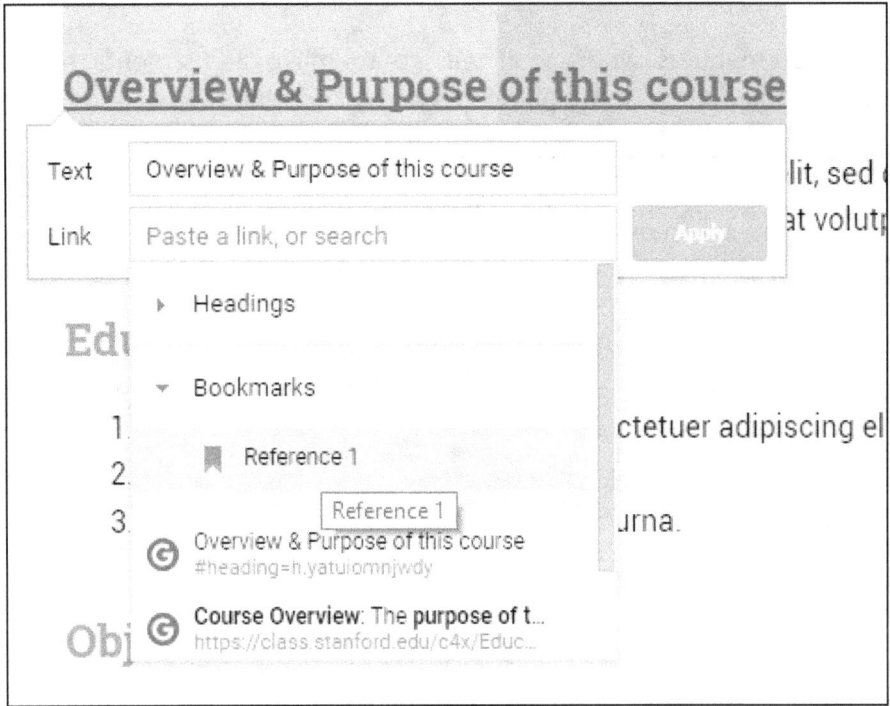

Figure 6.52

- **Table of contents** – If you are writing a book or manual (etc.), you will probably need a table of contents at the beginning if you want your readers to easily be able to find what they are looking for. If you are using headers in your document, then Docs can create a table of contents automatically for you and even add the proper page numbers after each section (I will go over heading text in the next section).

Overview & Purpose of this course	1
Education Standards	1
Objectives	1
Materials Needed	1
Verification	2
Activity	2

Figure 6.53

If you happen to make some changes to your document and the page numbers change, then all you need to do is right click on your table of contents and choose *Update table of contents*.

Format Menu

The Format menu is where you will go to make adjustments to how your document looks, such as changing fonts and formatting shapes, etc.

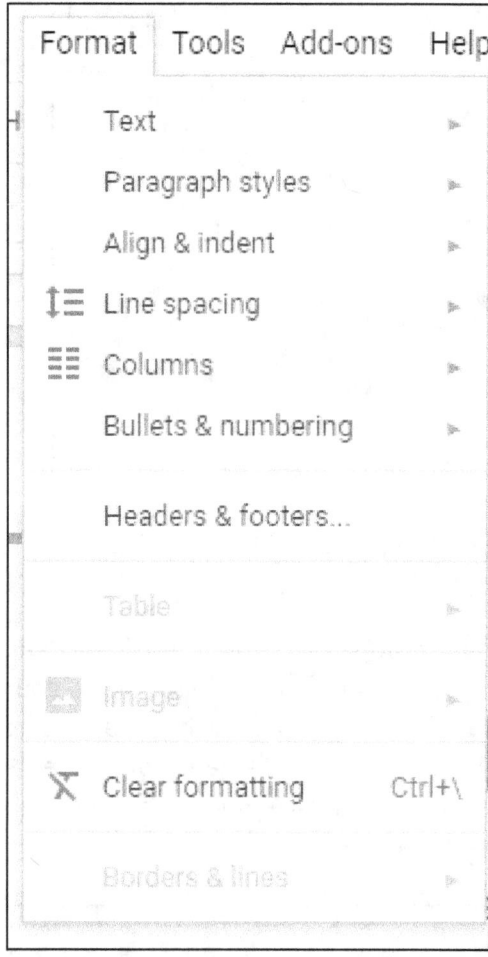

Figure 6.54

Since I will have a section on formatting your document later in this chapter, I will briefly go over the options from this menu.

- **Text** – This menu option allows you to change how your text looks in regards to things like bold, underline, text size, and capitalization.

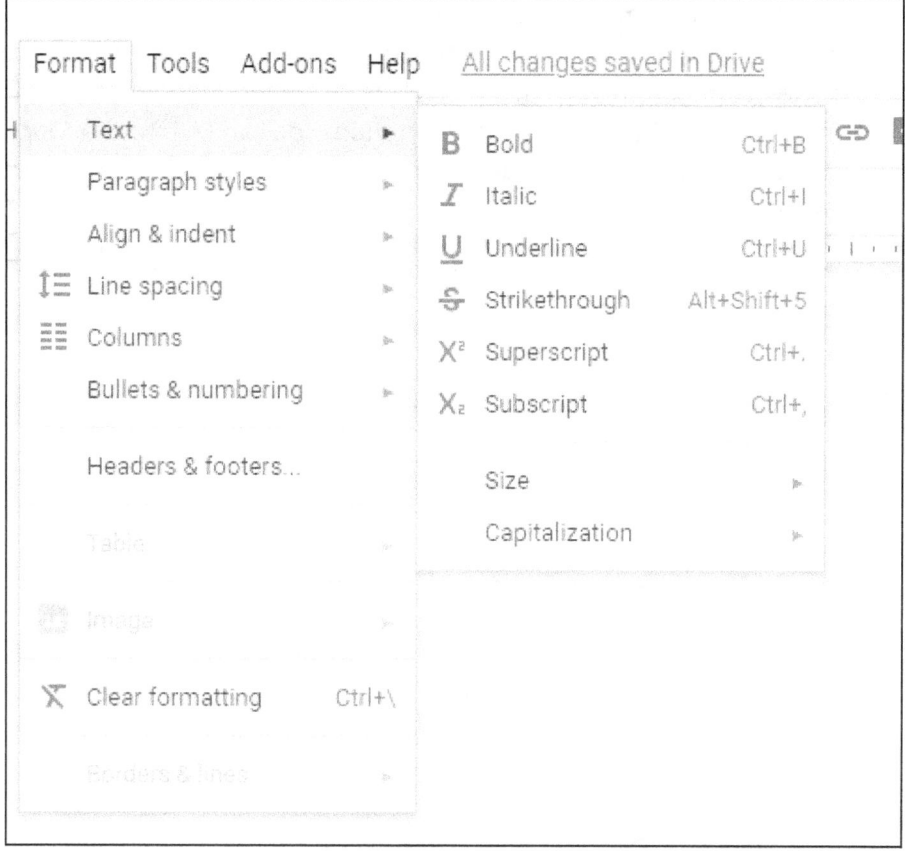

Figure 6.55

- **Paragraph styles** – *Paragraph styles* allow you to format an entire paragraph with various types of styles. For example, you can add a border with various types of line styles and shading. This is also where you can change text from normal text to a heading style text like I mentioned was required to create a table of contents.

- **Align & indent** – Many times you will need to set text alignment of a paragraph or entire document to be aligned to the left or right, centered or justified. Or you might need to indent a paragraph to make it stand out from the rest. If that's the case, then this is where you would do it from.

- **Line spacing** – *Line spacing* is just what it sounds like, the amount of space between the lines of text in your document. The default line spacing is 1.15, and you can also choose other spacing such as single, double, or even customize your own setting.

Chapter 6 – Google Drive and Google Docs

- **Columns** – Columns can be used to separate your text for things like lists and so on. In earlier versions of Google Docs, you would have to create tables with columns to get this done, but now you can do this from the Format menu if you want another option. You can go into the *More options* section to customize your columns and do things such as add lines between them.

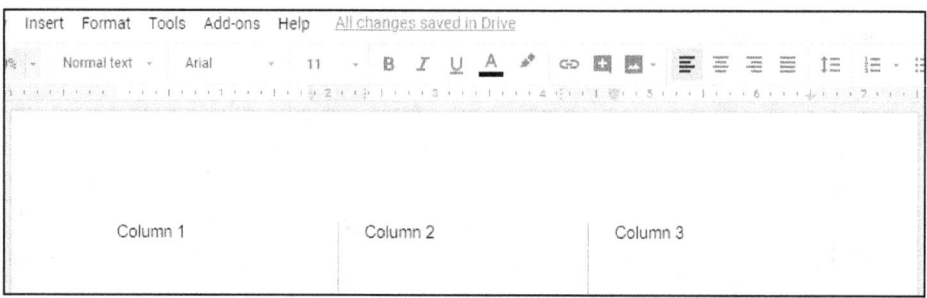

Figure 6.56

- **Bullets & numbering** – Bullets & numbering is used when you have created lists and want the items in the list to be separated with numbers and sub numbers, or a character like a bullet.

- Category 1
    - Sub category 1
- Category 2
    - Sub category 2
- Category 3
    - Sub category 3

1. Category 1
    a. Sub category 1
2. Category 2
    a. Sub category 2
3. Category 3
    a. Sub category 3

Figure 6.57

Once you create a bulleted or numbered list, then you can customize it by going to *Format > Bullets & numbering > List options*. (You will need to have the list highlighted to use this option.)

- **Headers & footers** – Headers are used to display information like chapter titles at the top of the page, while footers are used to display things like page numbers at the bottom of the page. This option will allow you to specify how many inches the header and footer are from the top and bottom of the page.

- **Table** – In order to use the *Table* option, you will need to have a table in your document, and also have the mouse cursor somewhere within that table. This option lets you do things such as insert and delete rows and columns, as well as merge and unmerge cells. The *Table properties* choice is used to configure things like borders, colors, alignment, and so on (figure 6.58).

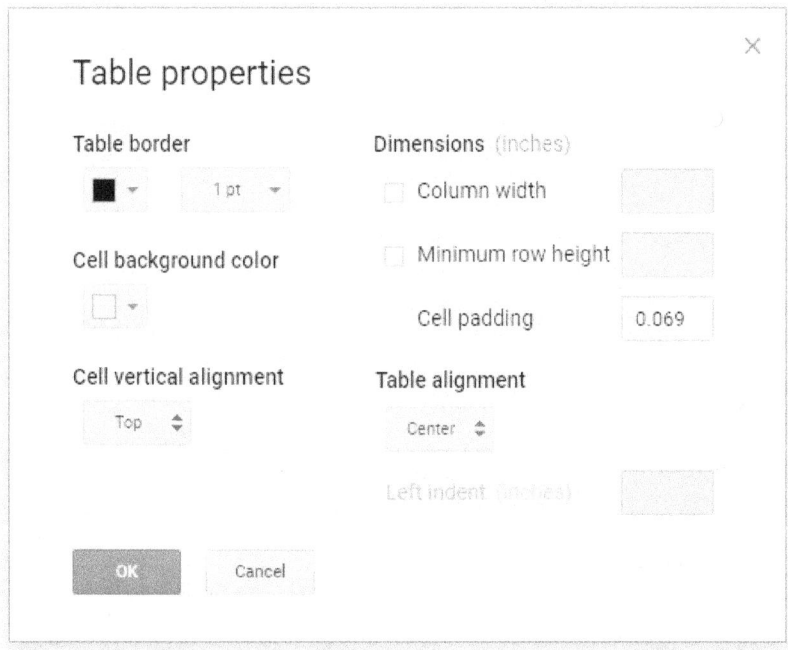

Figure 6.58

- **Image** – When you have images\pictures in your document, you can use the Image settings to do things such as crop the image or replace it with a different one. The *Image options* feature lets you do things like recolor the image and also adjust things like transparency, brightness, and contrast.

- **Clear formatting** – Most documents will have some kind of formatting, whether it be colored or underlined text (etc.), and many times you want to switch that text back to the default unformatted text. To do so, simply highlight the text and choose the *Clear formatting* feature to remove any formatting that was previously applied.

- **Borders & lines** – If you have any items that have a border around them or use a line above or below them, then you can use this option to change things such as the border weight (thickness) and dash type if any.

Tools Menu

The Tools menu is most likely not going to be used as often as some of the other menus but does have some helpful tools.

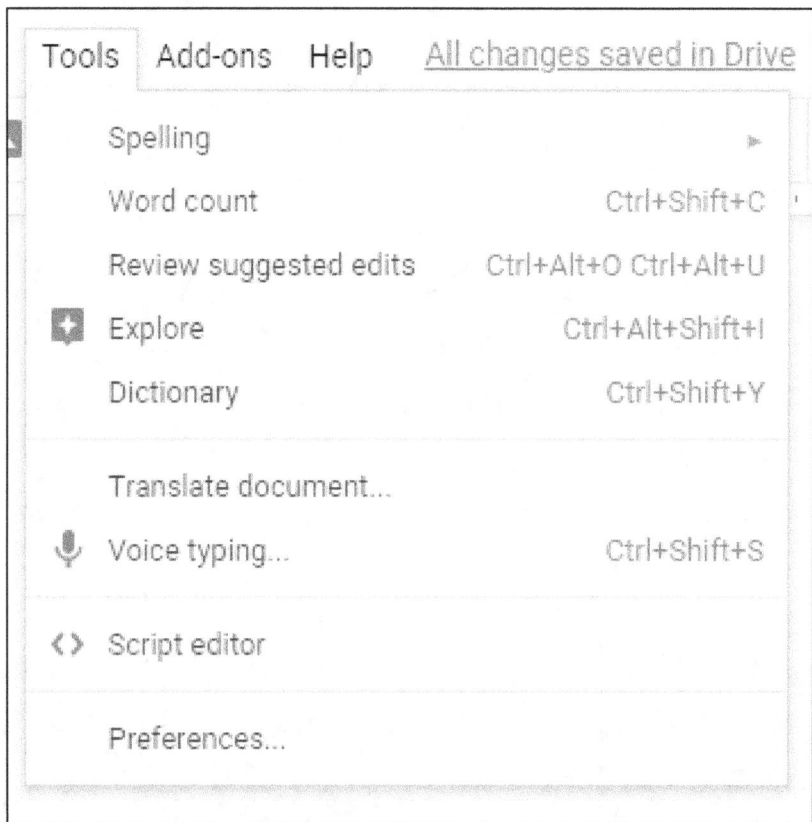

Figure 6.59

Even though you won't be using this menu as much as the others it's still a good idea to know what you can do from the items within it.

- **Spelling** – By default, Docs will underline spelling mistakes in red, but if you want to turn off that feature, then you can do so from here. You can also run a manual spell check if you want Docs to search over your entire document for errors. There is even a Personal dictionary option where you can add words that are not in the Docs dictionary, so it won't mark them as misspelled.

- **Word count** – Word count will not only tell you how many words you have in your document, but also how many pages, characters, and characters excluding spaces your document has.

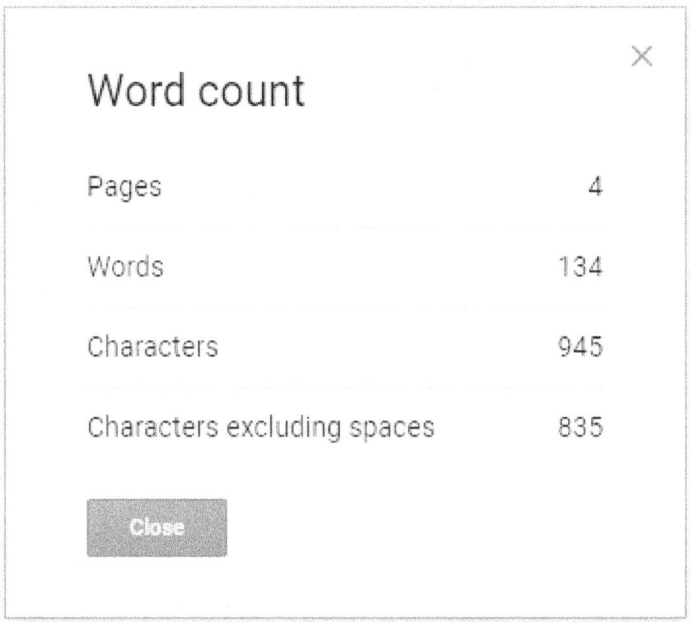

Figure 6.60

- **Review suggested edits** – As I mentioned earlier in the chapter, you can use Suggesting mode to suggest changes to a document that can then be viewed by others and either accepted or rejected. To see the suggested edits in your document, you would use this feature. You can also accept all or reject all from this setting and preview what the document would look like if you either accepted all of the edits or rejected all of the edits.

- **Explore** – The *Explore* feature is pretty neat because it will go through your document and pick out topics that you can then look up online to get more information on. It will also work for images that it finds. Plus, you can enter your own search terms if you want to look for something specific.

Chapter 6 – Google Drive and Google Docs

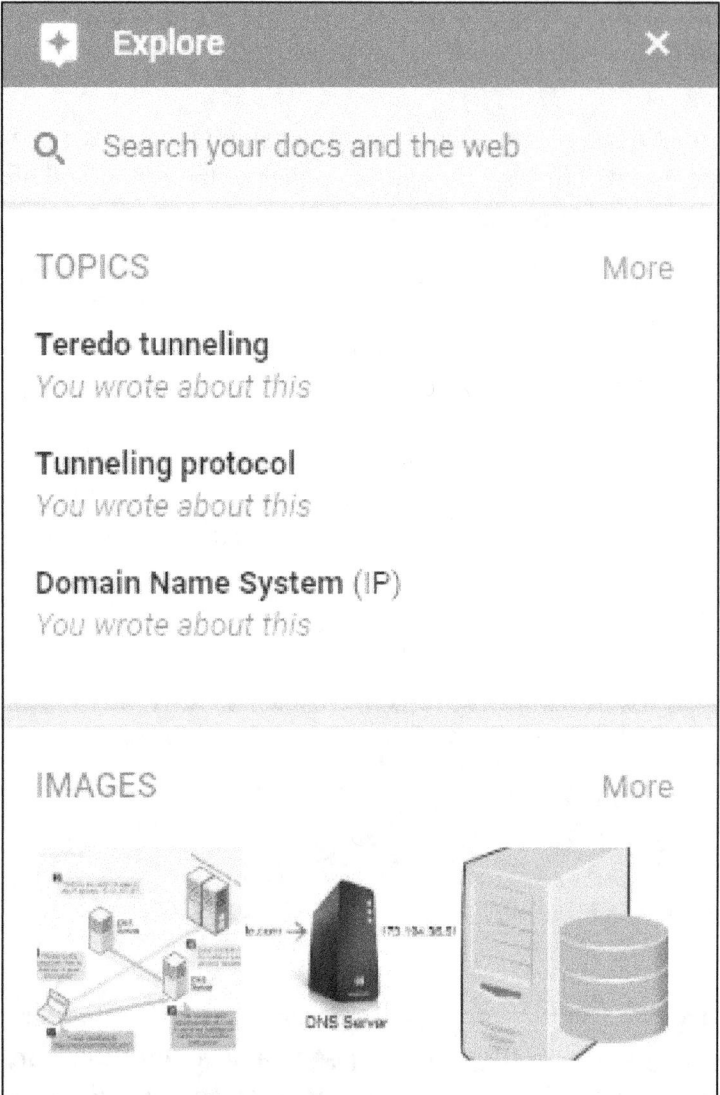

Figure 6.61

- **Dictionary** – The *Dictionary* option is another cool feature that you can use to get definitions of words in your document or others that you want to search for. Simply highlight the word you want to look up in your document and choose the Dictionary option, and it will go out on the Internet and then display its meaning.

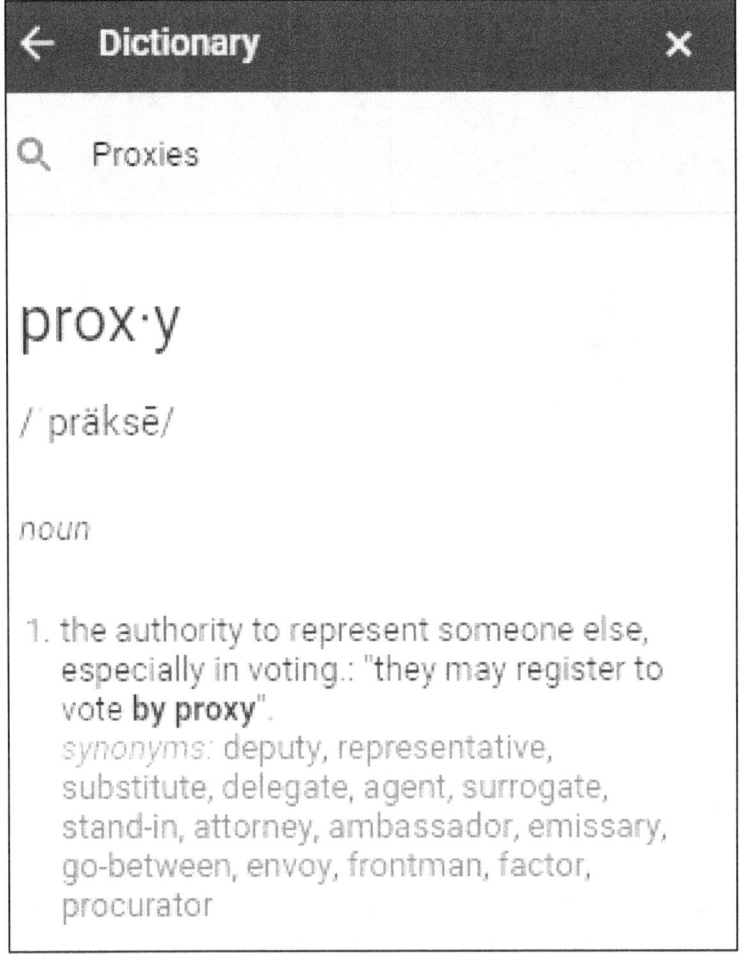
Figure 6.62

- **Translate Document** – This is a really neat feature as well because Docs can take your entire document and translate it into a language of your choosing. It will open the translated document in a new tab\page so you will still have access to the original.

- **Voice typing** – *Voice typing* works in a similar fashion to how you would use the voice to text feature on your smartphone. If you have a device that is capable of recording your voice, you can have Docs translate your voice to words in your document. You can even choose a different language if you speak more than one. For PC users, you can use this feature if you have a microphone attached to your computer.

Figure 6.63

- **Script editor** – Unless you are a JavaScript developer and want to write code for Google Apps, you will never use this feature.

- **Preferences** – This is where you can change the way Docs works when it comes to settings such as automatic capitalization, link detection, and substitution of characters. As you can see in figure 6.64, you can have Docs automatically substitute something you type with a properly formatted version, such as replacing the copyright symbol © when you type in (c).

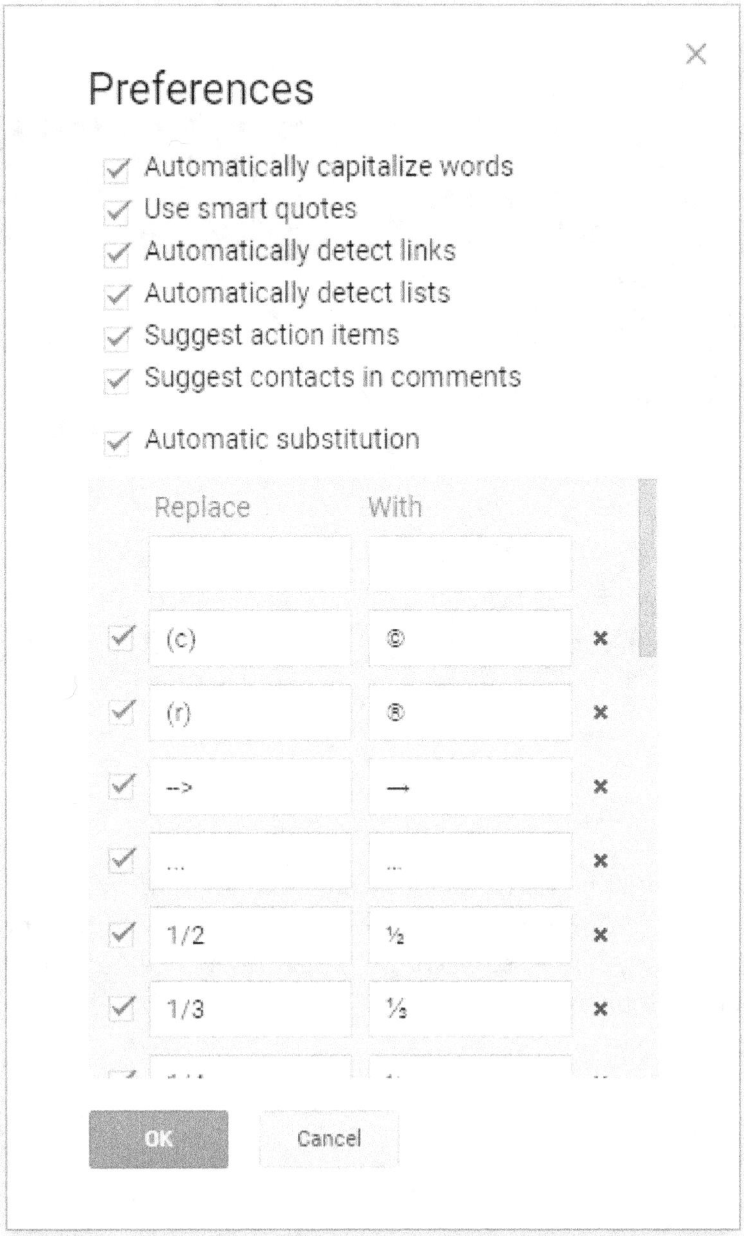

Figure 6.64

Add-ons Menu
Out of the box, Docs will not come with any add-ons, but there are many available that you can download and use with Docs to do things such as create labels, use additional fonts, or have access to clipart libraries. The top left of the Add-ons box (figure 6.65) will have a dropdown where you can select various categories such as business tools, education, productivity, and so on.

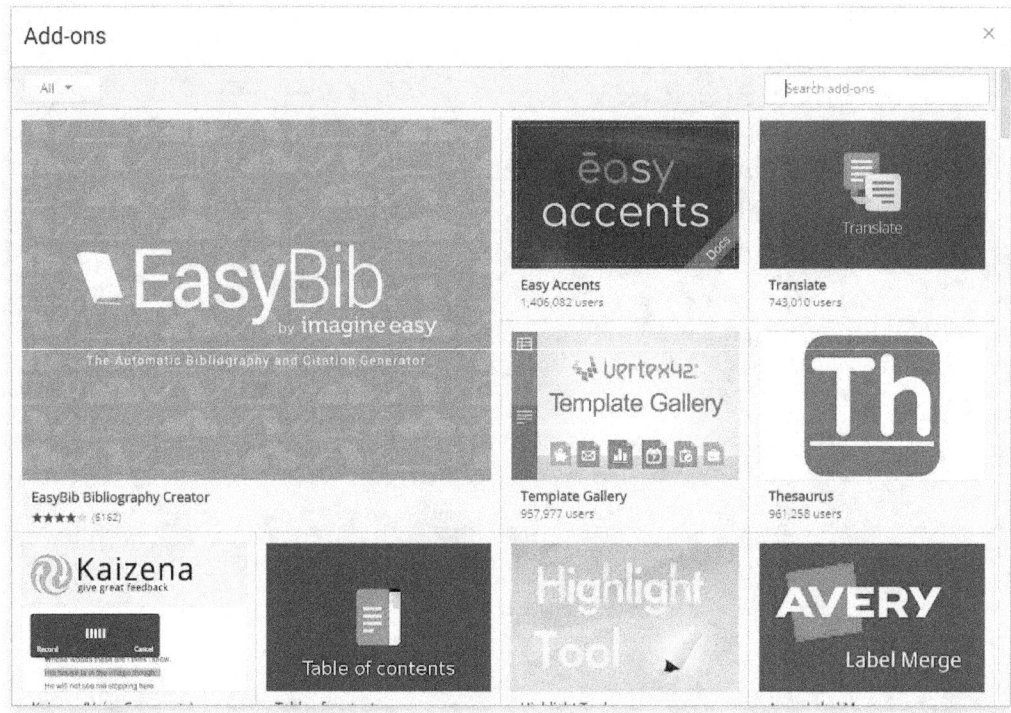
Figure 6.65

Help Menu
This menu option should be fairly obvious, but there are a few other things you can do from here as well. Besides clicking on the Docs Help item to bring up a listing of help topics, you can also search the help menu itself to hopefully find exactly what you are looking for.

Chapter 6 – Google Drive and Google Docs

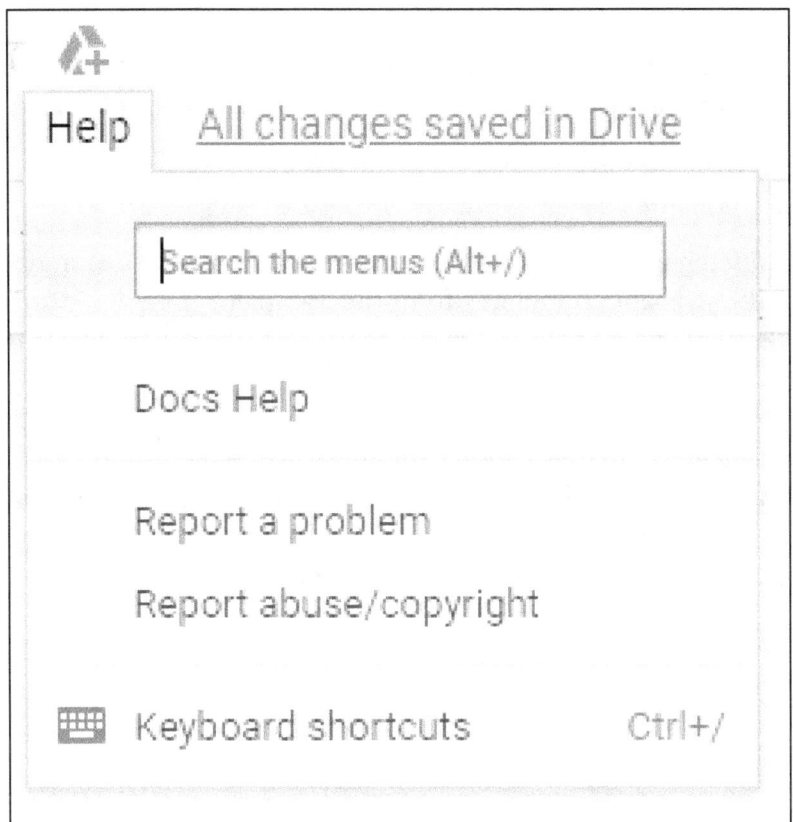

Figure 6.66

The *Report a problem* feature can be used to report any glitches you find in the software to Google so they can fix problems to make Docs work better. (I can't tell you for sure if anyone actually looks at it though!)

The *Report abuse\copyright* feature can be used to report a document to google that has illegal or plagiarized information in it. When you report the document, you can pick what category it falls under, such as spam, hate speech, illegal activity, copyright infringement, and so on.

Finally, the Keyboard shortcuts section will show you the available keyboard shortcuts that you can use within Docs. A keyboard shortcut is when you press a certain key combination that accomplishes the same task as one of the menu items does. For example, you can press Ctrl-b on your keyboard to make text bold rather than having to find it in the Format menu or on the toolbar.

Chapter 6 – Google Drive and Google Docs

Creating a Document
Now that you know what all the menu items do, it's time to create a new document and see how the process works. If you are used to using another word processing program like Microsoft Word, then you will find the process very familiar.

When you first open Docs, it will give you options to create a new blank document or start with one of the available templates from the Template Gallery. For my example I want to start with a blank document, so all I need to do is click on *Blank* under *Start a new document*.

The first thing you will want to do is give your document a name (unless you don't plan on keeping it, then you can just leave the default Untitled document name as is). To change the name, simply click on Untitled document, and it will become highlighted. Then you can then change it to whatever you like. I will change mine to *Notes*.

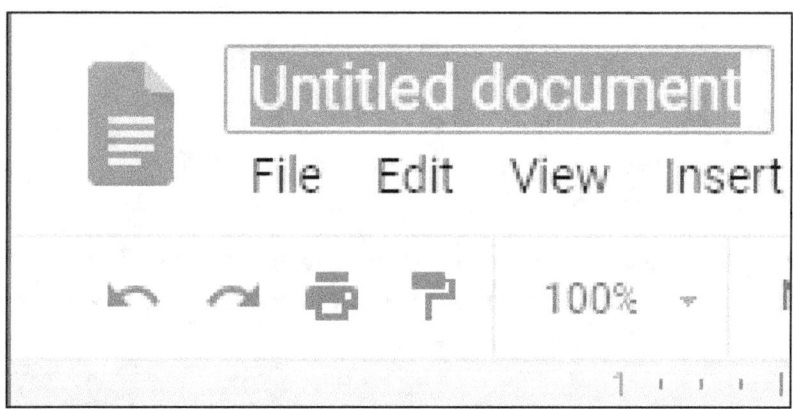

Figure 6.67

Now you can click within the blank page to get a cursor to start typing your text. Docs will automatically place the new text you type at the upper topmost section of the page, so if you want to start a few lines down, you can press the Enter key on your keyboard as many times as you need. (I am assuming you know how to type in text in a document, otherwise you might need to get some practice before even using Docs.) I am actually going to use the text from this chapter for my examples, so if it looks familiar, you will know why!

Chapter 6 – Google Drive and Google Docs

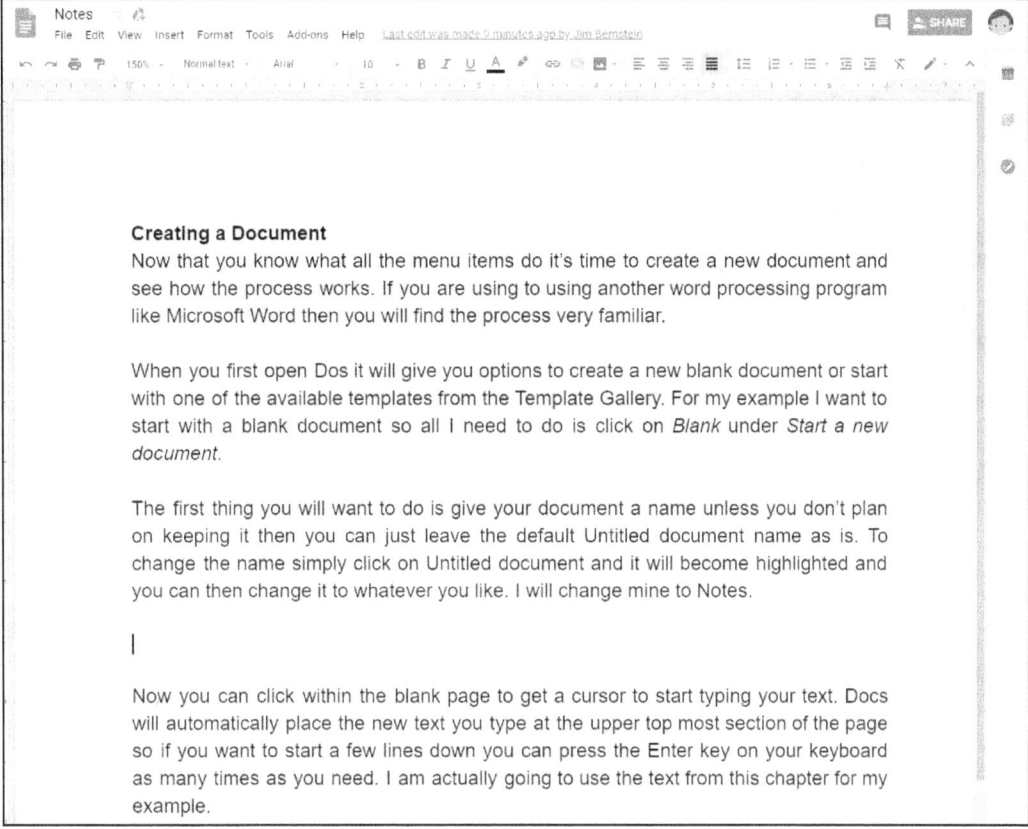

Figure 6.68

Now that I have some text in my document, I want to add an image between the third and last paragraph. To do so, I will put my cursor in between the paragraphs (as you can see in figure 6.68).

There are several ways to accomplish this task. I can copy and paste the image from this document over to my Notes document, but for this example I will insert an image from my local computer by browsing to its location from the *Insert > Image* menu (figure 6.69).

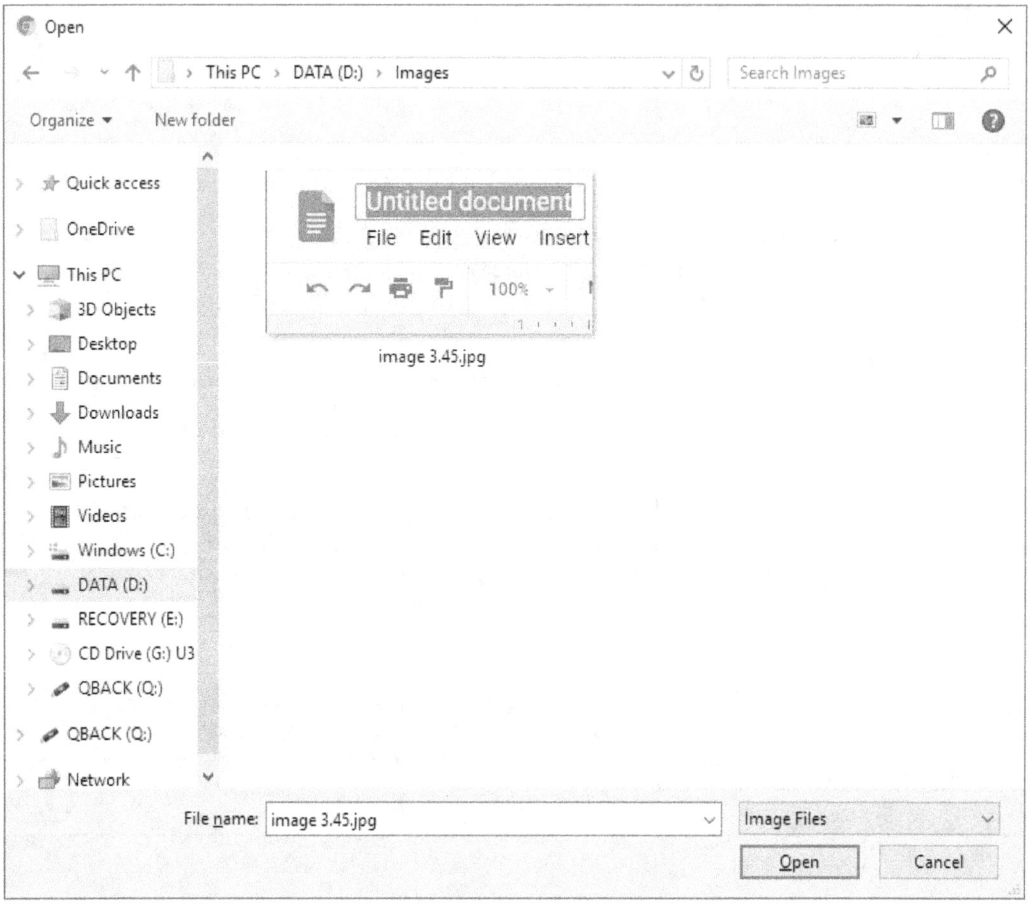

Chapter 6 – Google Drive and Google Docs

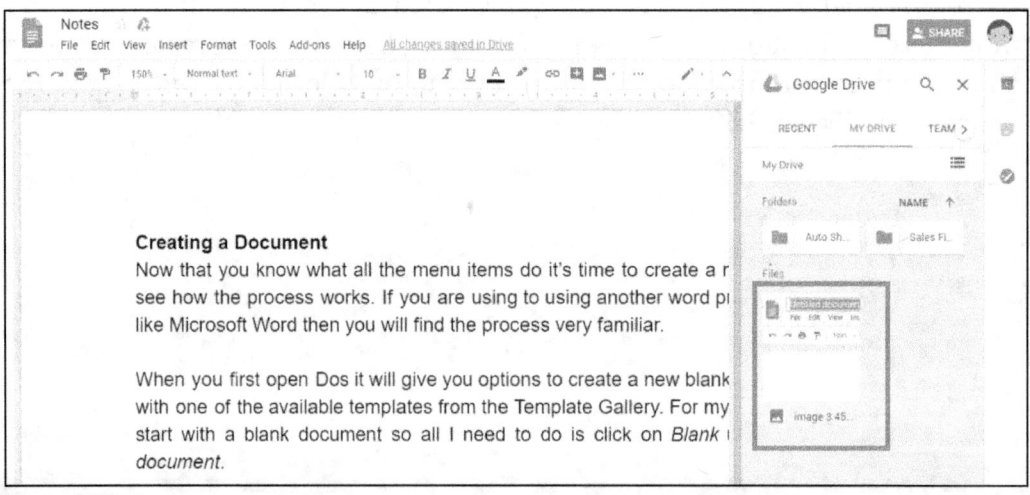

Figure 6.69

If I had the image on my Google Drive, I could have chosen that option and then browsed to it on my drive and inserted into my document from there.

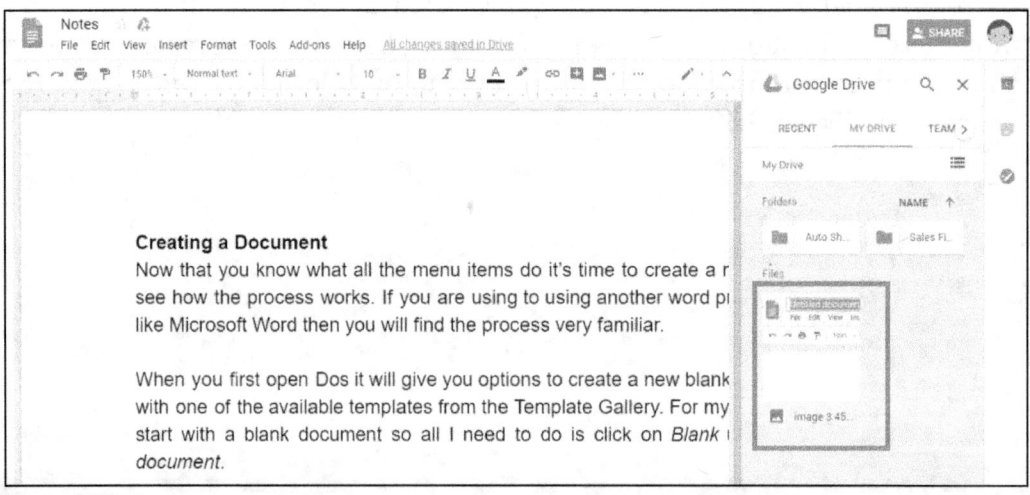

Figure 6.70

Chapter 6 – Google Drive and Google Docs

Regardless of my method, now I have my image within my document exactly where I wanted it.

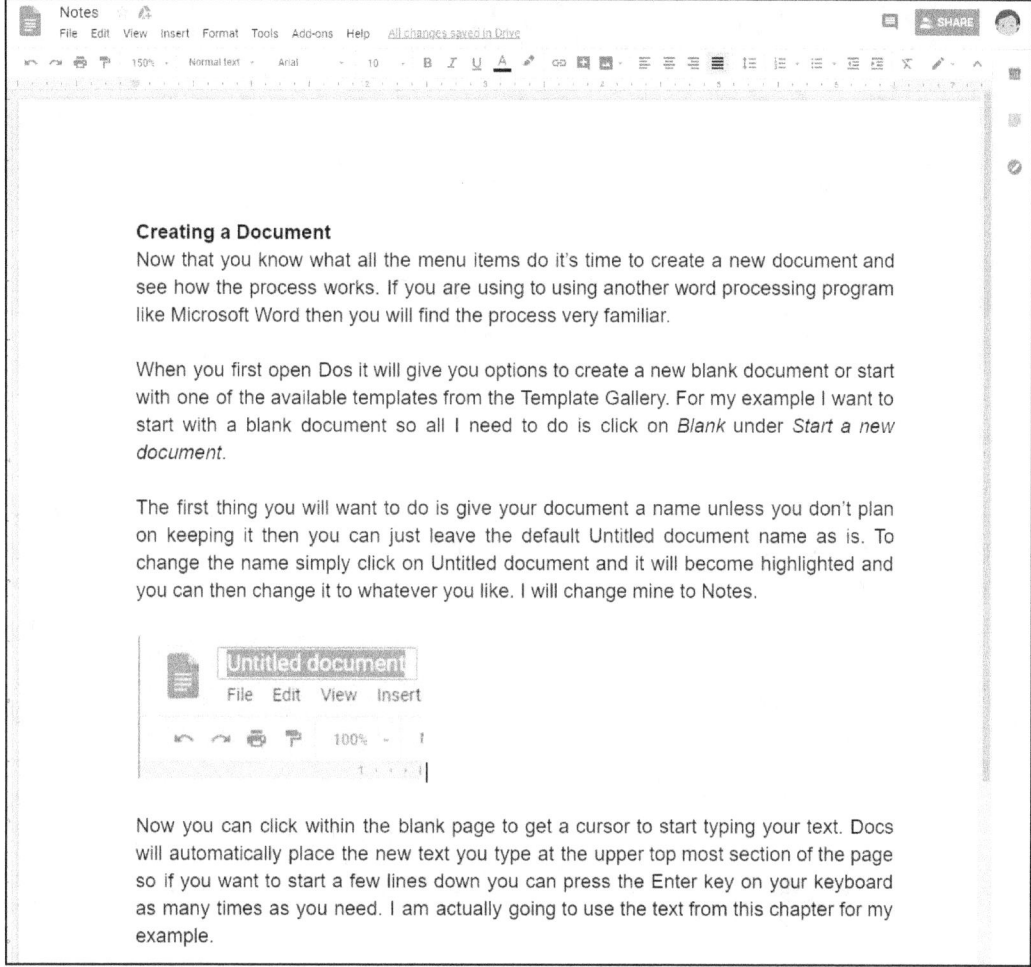

Figure 6.71

When you click on the image within your document, you will see that you have a couple of options as to how to position it (as shown in figure 6.72).

Chapter 6 – Google Drive and Google Docs

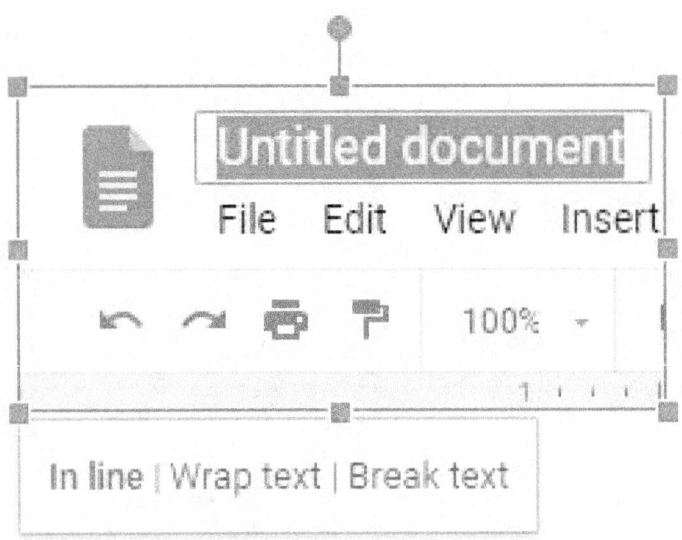

Figure 6.72

In line will be the default, which simply separates the text to be above and below the image like shown in figure 6.71. *Wrap text* will wrap the text around the image as shown in figure 6.73.

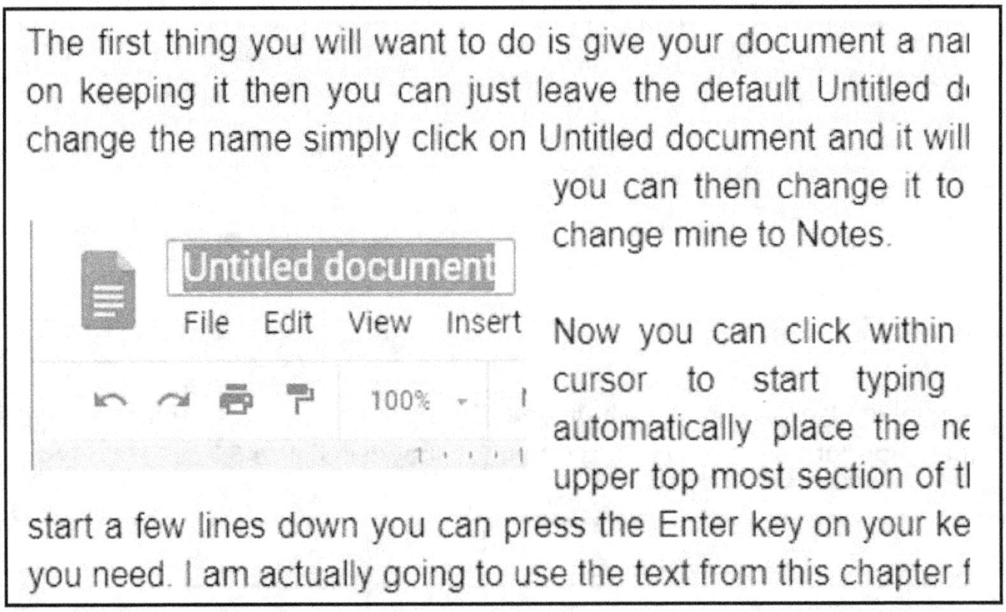

Figure 6.73

Break text is similar to the In line option, except you can decide how far you want the text to be away from the top and bottom of your image (such as ½ inch, ¼ inch, and so on).

To resize the image in your document, simply click on one of the small boxes in the corner of the image when it's highlighted (as shown in figure 6.72 above). When using a corner box, it will stretch the image and keep its proportions the same and just make it larger. If you use one of the top or side boxes to resize your image, it will get stretched out like in figure 6.74.

Figure 6.74

If you would like to copy the image and use it again in the same document or in a different document, all you need to is right click on it, choose *Copy,* and then right click where you want the copied image to go and choose *Paste.*

The same copy and paste procedure works for copying text from one area to another, or to another document, but you have a couple of different choices as to how you want to paste your text. You can either choose *Paste,* which will paste the text using the same formatting as the current text, or you can choose *Paste without formatting,* which will remove all the formatting such as bold and colors when pasting the text into your document.

Right Click Options
Speaking of right clicking on text and images, I would now like to take a moment to go over some of the right click menu items. Figure 6.75 shows the options when right clicking on some highlighted text.

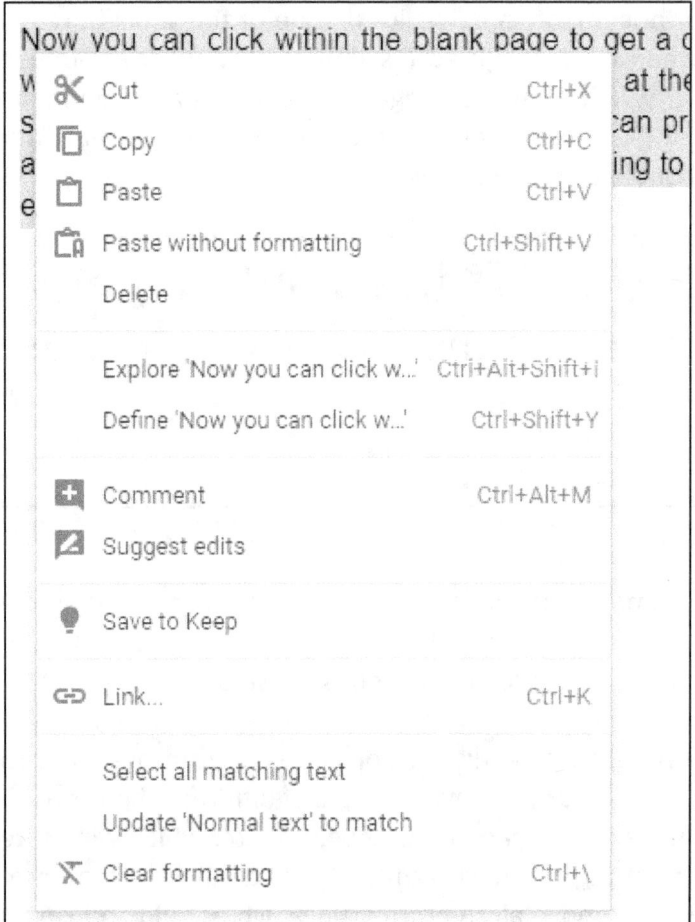

Figure 6.75

The first group of options are either obvious, or items that I have already gone over, and the *Explore* and *Define* items have been gone over already in this chapter, but basically they will either do web, image, and drive searches for that text if you choose Explore, and looked up in a dictionary if you use Define. When using *Define*, try to stick to just one word or a term to get the best results.

Here is what the other options do. There may be a little repetition from earlier in the chapter, but that never hurts! Plus, some of this information falls into the *formatting a document* section that is coming up next.

- **Comment** – This will let you make a comment about that text that will be visible to the other collaborators on the document.

- **Suggest Edits** – This will put the document into Suggesting Mode, where you can then add suggested changes to the text you have highlighted.

- **Save to Keep** – Google Keep is a note taking app that you might find useful, but using this option allows you to send the highlighted text to your Keep notebook. Keep can be accessed from within Docs, allowing you to see all of your notes.

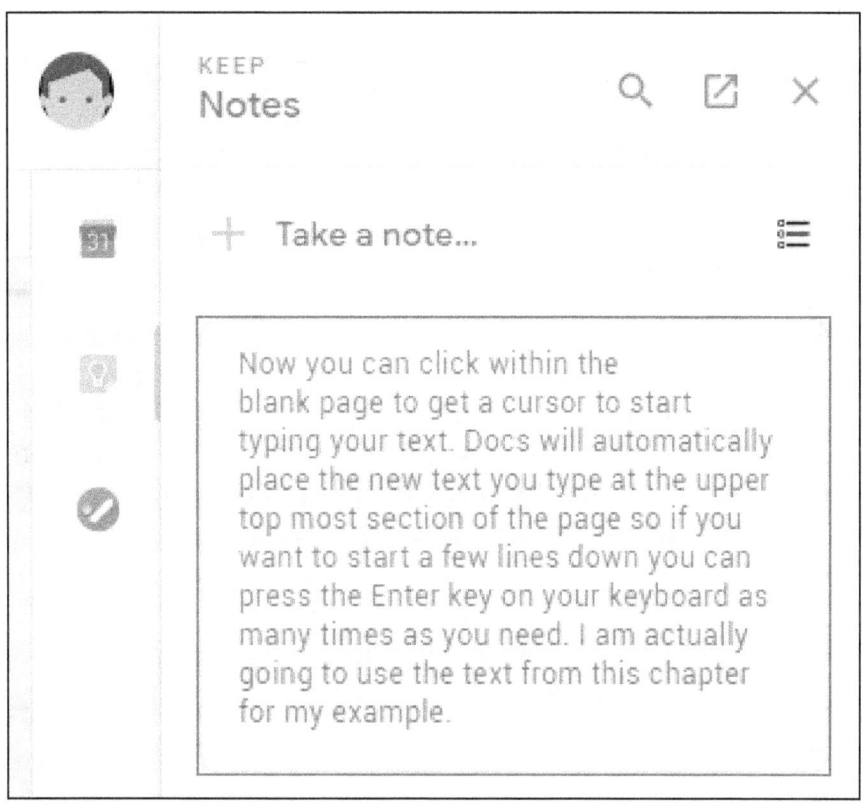

Figure 6.76

- **Link** – You can make a word or many words in your document into a link that can be clicked on to take you to a place such as a website by using the *Link* option. Once you choose *Link*, you will be prompted to enter the link address, and can also change the link text if you desire.

Chapter 6 – Google Drive and Google Docs

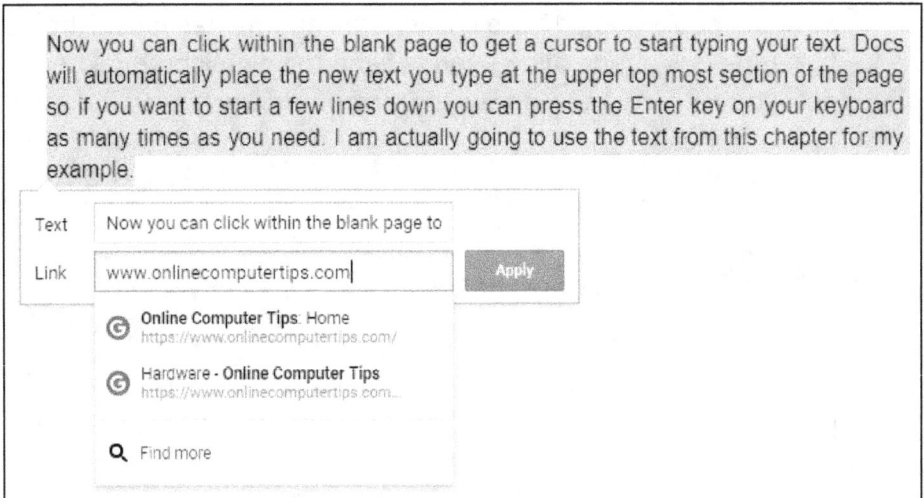

Figure 6.77

Once you make the link, the text will appear as a link with underlined text and clicking on the text will take you to the address that you entered in the Link box when creating the link. Normally you wouldn't make a link out of an entire paragraph, but I just did so for my example.

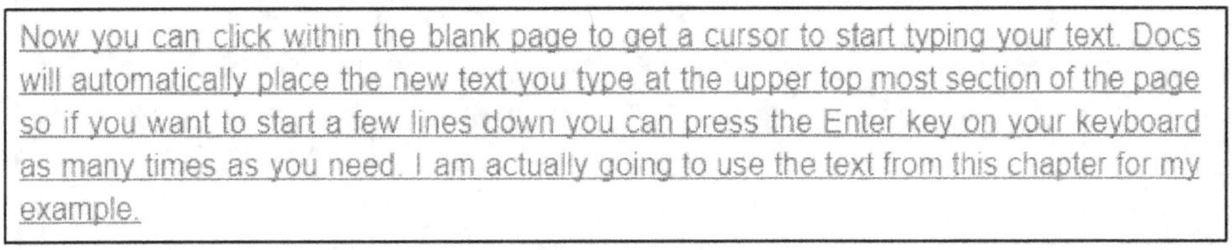

Figure 6.78

- **Select all matching text** – This is an interesting feature because it will allow you to highlight some text that is formatted a specific way and then find all of the other text that matches that same formatting. In figure 6.79, you can see the word **blank** was highlighted, and when the *Select all matching text* option was chosen, Docs highlighted all of the other text that was bolded like the word **blank** was.

Chapter 6 – Google Drive and Google Docs

> **Creating a Document**
> Now that you know what all the menu items do it's time to create a new document and see how the process works. If you are using to using another word processing program like **Microsoft Word** then you will find the process very familiar.
>
> When you first open Docs it will give you options to create a new blank document or start with one of the available templates from the **Template Gallery**. For my example I want to start with a blank document so all I need to do is click on Blank under Start a new document.
>
> The first thing you will want to do is give your document a name unless you don't plan on keeping it then you can just leave the default Untitled document name as is. To change the name simply click on Untitled document and it will become highlighted and
>
>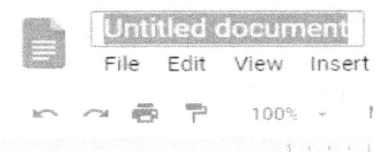
>
> you can then change it to whatever you like. I will change mine to Notes.
>
> Now you can click within the **blank** page to get a cursor to start typing your text. Docs will automatically place the new text you type at the upper top most section of the page so if you want to start a few lines down you can press the Enter key on your keyboard as many times as you need. I am actually going to use the text from this chapter for my example.

Figure 6.79

- **Update normal text to match** – This can be used to have Docs update the format of all of the text in your document to match the highlighted text. For example, let's say you highlighted a word that was bold and the color red, and chose *Update normal text to match*. Docs would then update the rest of your text in your document to be bold and red as well.

- **Clear formatting** – If you have formatted text that you want to reset to unformatted text, then you can use the *Clear formatting* option.

Inserting Headers, Footers, and Page Numbers
I mentioned headers, footers, and page numbers earlier in this chapter, but wanted to take a minute to go over how to use them in Docs. All of these can be put into your document from the *Insert* menu within Docs.

Chapter 6 – Google Drive and Google Docs

If you choose *Headers*, it will allow you to enter header information at the top of the page, while *Footers* will do the same thing at the bottom of the page. Once you type in your text for your header or footer, you can click on *Options* to determine how far you want the header or footer to be from the top. Then this text will be added to every page of your document and every new page you add after that. To remove a header or footer simply delete one of them on any page and it will delete the rest on all of the other pages.

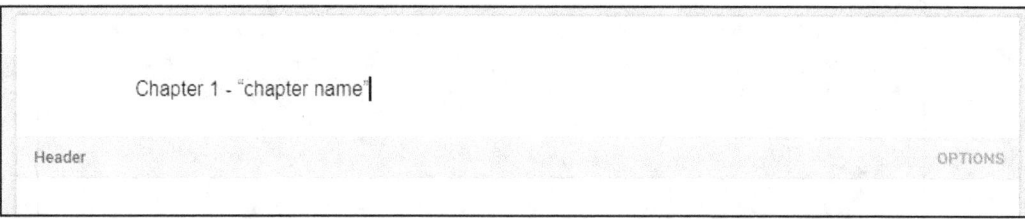

Figure 6.80

Page numbers work the same way, and you have a few choices as to where the numbers are placed on the page and if you want the first page to not be numbered at all. As you add pages, they will be automatically numbered for you.

Figure 6.81

Chapter 6 – Google Drive and Google Docs

Importing Charts From Sheets

Sheets is Google's version of Microsoft's Excel spreadsheet program. If you have any charts that you have created in Sheets, then you can import them into your document as well as link them so when changes are made, your document will be updated as well.

To insert a Sheets chart go to the *Insert* menu, choose *Chart,* and then *From Sheets*. You will be prompted to choose one of your existing Sheets files to import into Docs.

Figure 6.82

Once you choose one don't forget to decide if you want the data in your document to be updated whenever your spreadsheet is updated. If so, then leave the box for *Link to spreadsheet* checked, and if not, uncheck it.

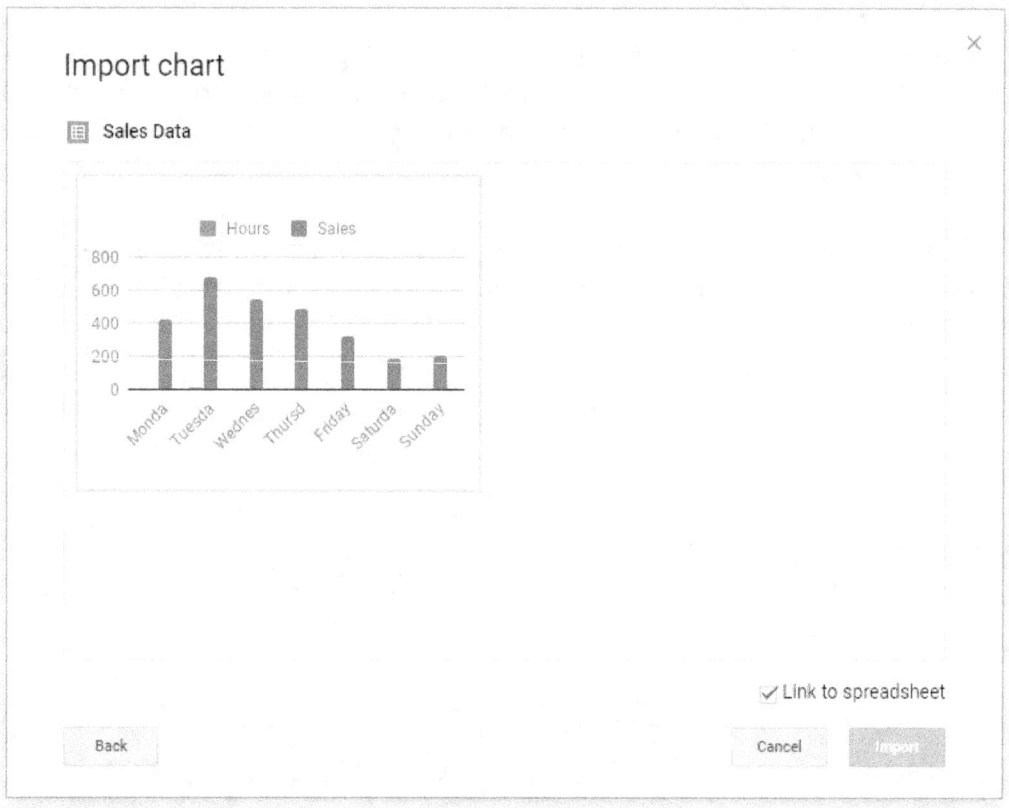

Figure 6.83

Formatting a Document
Now that I have some text and images in our document it's time to format it to make it look a little more presentable and professional. There are many upon many ways to format your document to suit your tastes, but for this section I will be going over the most common formatting procedures that you will most likely be using.

Editing Text
Let's begin by adding a title to the document and have that title text use the Title style for the document. I decided to call my document *My Exciting Document*. After I type in the title, I will highlight it (as shown in figure 6.84).

Figure 6.84

Then from either the *Format > Paragraph* styles menu item or the Styles toolbar option, I will choose *Title* as the style and have Docs apply the style to my highlighted text.

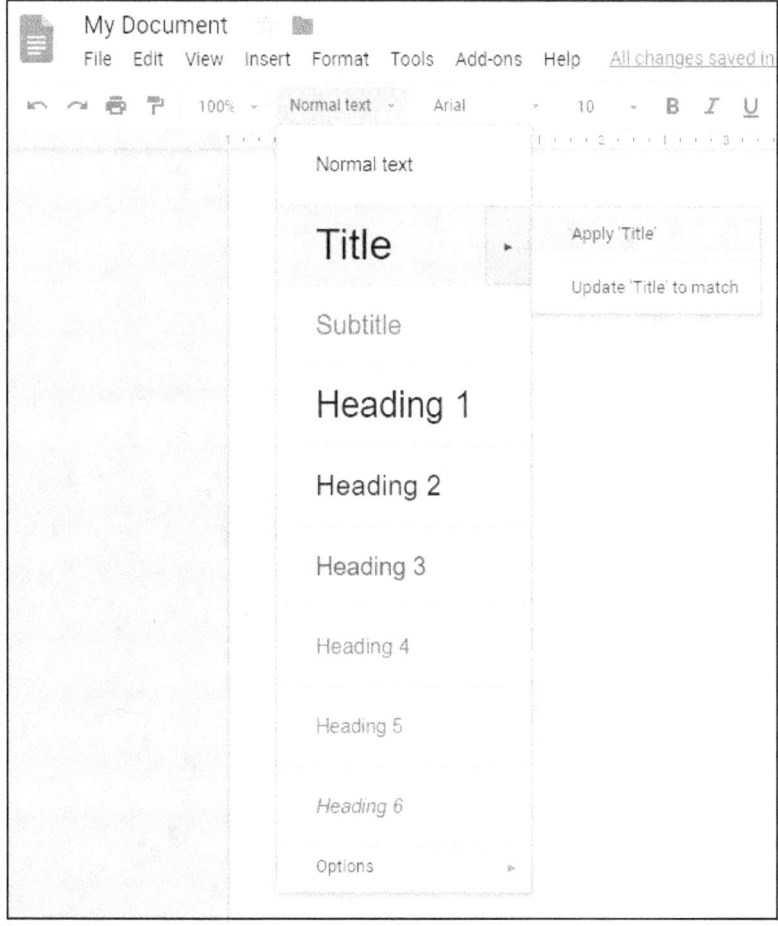

Figure 6.85

Chapter 6 – Google Drive and Google Docs

Now you can see my title is in *Title* style format, and now can also be used if I want to make a table of contents.

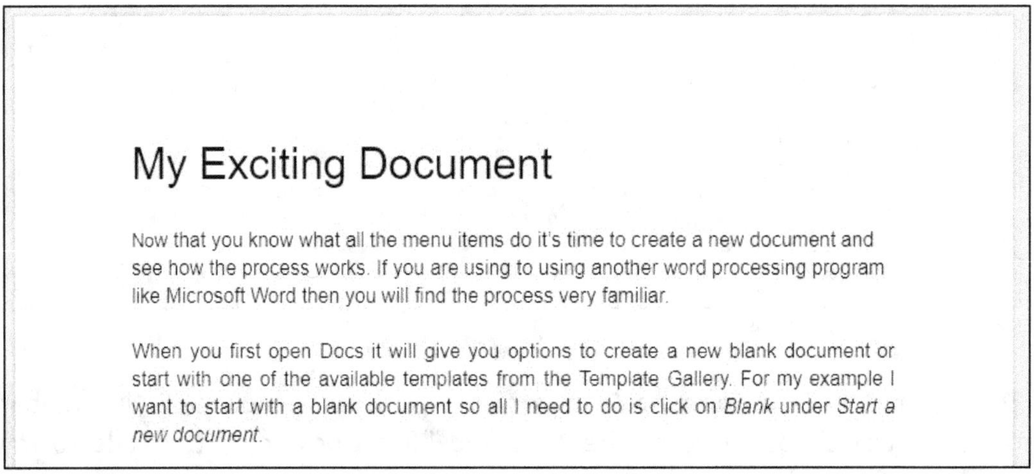

Figure 6.86

I will now make some section headings called Section 1 and Section 2 and apply the Heading 2 style to the text, which can also apply to the table of contents if I add one later.

Chapter 6 – Google Drive and Google Docs

> ## My Exciting Document
>
> Now that you know what all the menu items do it's time to create a new document and see how the process works. If you are using to using another word processing program like Microsoft Word then you will find the process very familiar.
>
> ### Section 1
>
> When you first open Docs it will give you options to create a new blank document or start with one of the available templates from the Template Gallery. For my example I want to start with a blank document so all I need to do is click on *Blank* under *Start a new document*.
>
> The first thing you will want to do is give your document a name unless you don't plan on keeping it then you can just leave the default Untitled document name as is. To change the name simply click on Untitled document and it will become highlighted and you can then change it to whatever you like. I will change mine to Notes.
>
>
>
> ### Section 2
>
> Now you can click within the blank page to get a cursor to start typing your text. Docs will automatically place the new text you type at the upper top most section of the page so if you want to start a few lines down you can press the Enter key on your keyboard as many times as you need. I am assuming know how to type in text in a document otherwise you might need to get some practice before even using Docs. I am actually going to use the text from this chapter for my examples so if it looks familiar you will know why!

Figure 6.87

Now I will apply some basic text formatting to the title and section names to make them stand out a little better. I will first make the title bold and underlined so it stands out. To do so, I will simply highlight the text from the title and then click on the B in the toolbar (for bold) and then click the U in the toolbar (for underlined) and I will be all set. I can also go to the *Format > Text* menu and do the same thing from there.

Chapter 6 – Google Drive and Google Docs

Then I will make the section headings red by highlighting the Section 1 and Section 2 text, click on the underlined A in the toolbar (for text color), and choose red from the color choices. You can see the results from these changes in figure 6.88.

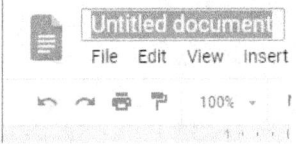

Figure 6.88

Next (for some reason) I want to have the first paragraph have all the words capitalized, but don't want to retype the whole thing. Once again, I will highlight the text I want to change, then go to the Format menu and then *Text > Capitalization > UPPERCASE*. (You might have noticed by now that I am using the Format menu a lot on this section on formatting!)

Chapter 6 – Google Drive and Google Docs

> ### My Exciting Document
>
> NOW THAT YOU KNOW WHAT ALL THE MENU ITEMS DO IT'S TIME TO CREATE A NEW DOCUMENT AND SEE HOW THE PROCESS WORKS. IF YOU ARE USING TO USING ANOTHER WORD PROCESSING PROGRAM LIKE MICROSOFT WORD THEN YOU WILL FIND THE PROCESS VERY FAMILIAR.
>
> Section 1
>
> When you first open Docs it will give you options to create a new blank document or start with one of the available templates from the Template Gallery. For my example I want to start with a blank document so all I need to do is click on *Blank* under *Start a new document*.

Figure 6.89

Text Alignment

Next, I want to center the title in the document and change the text alignment to left aligned rather than justified like it is currently. To do so, I will once again highlight the title text, and then either go to the align section on the toolbar or go to *Align & indent* on the Format menu and choose the align center option (figure 6.90).

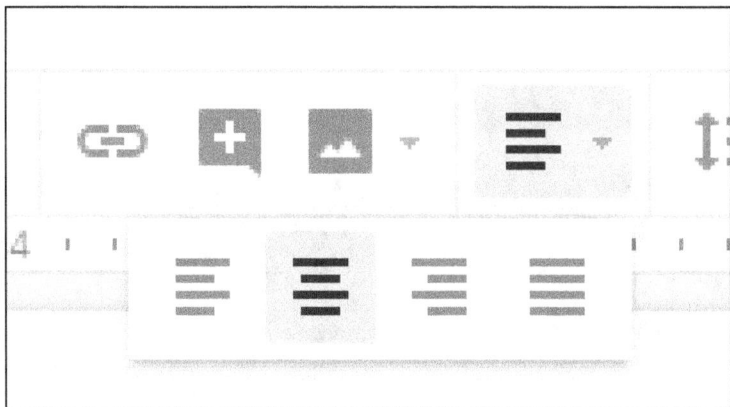

Figure 6.90

Now to change the alignment of the main document from justified to aligned left, I will highlight the text I want to change and do the same process, but this time I will choose *align left* rather than *centered*. When doing this you might have to do it in sections if there is other text you don't want changed in between the text you do want to change. You can see the results in figure 6.90. I will say I prefer justified over aligning the text to the left, and you might have noticed that's the format I used for this book!

Figure 6.91

Line Spacing

Docs uses a default line spacing of 1.15, which is a little wider than single spacing and is fine for most people. But sometimes you might want to change that to increase or decrease the amount of space between each line of text. Figure 6.92 shows the difference between single and double spacing.

> **Single Spacing**
>
> Now you can click within the blank page to get a cursor to start typing your text. Docs will automatically place the new text you type at the upper top most section of the page so if you want to start a few lines down you can press the Enter key on your keyboard as many times as you need. I am assuming know how to type in text in a document otherwise you might need to get some practice before even using Docs.
>
> **Double Spacing**
>
> Now you can click within the blank page to get a cursor to start typing your text. Docs
>
> will automatically place the new text you type at the upper top most section of the page
>
> so if you want to start a few lines down you can press the Enter key on your keyboard
>
> as many times as you need. I am assuming know how to type in text in a document
>
> otherwise you might need to get some practice before even using Docs.

Figure 6.92

If neither single nor double spacing works for you, then you can choose a custom spacing of your own to fine tune how your text looks. To set the spacing, highlight the text you want to change, go to the Format menu, then to Line spacing, and configure it the way you want.

There is also an option to add a space before or after the paragraph if you just need more or less space in between paragraphs rather than all of the lines of text. You can customize the paragraph space as well if the default doesn't work for you.

Numbered and Bulleted Lists
I went over numbered and bulleted lists when discussing the format menu but want to spend a little time going into them in a little more detail since there are different ways to use this type of formatting in your document.

When creating a list in Docs, you can use this feature to have them be automatically numbered or marked with bullets or other characters, so you don't have to do it manually. Your lists will also be easier to read and they'll look more organized.

For example, take a look at the *Sales Teams* list in figure 6.93. It gets the job done but looks rather boring and not too organized. Now take a look at figure 6.94

Chapter 6 – Google Drive and Google Docs

where I added a little formatting to the text and made a bulleted list out of the teams. It's much easier to see the three teams and their members and is easier on the eyes as well.

```
Sales Teams

Team 1
Sue
Dan
Johnny
Molly

Team 2
Ronald
Tisha
Kim
Beth

Team 3
Sal
Murr
Joe
Brian
```

Figure 6.93

Sales Teams

- Team 1
    - Sue
    - Dan
    - Johnny
    - Molly

- Team 2
    - Ronald
    - Tisha
    - Kim
    - Beth

- Team 3
    - Sal
    - Murr
    - Joe
    - Brian

Figure 6.94

If I don't like the style I used, I can simply highlight my list and go back to *Format > Bullets & numbering,* choose a new style, and it will be updated automatically.

Sales Teams

- Team 1
  - Sue
  - Dan
  - Johnny
  - Molly

- Team 2
  - Ronald
  - Tisha
  - Kim
  - Beth

- Team 3
  - Sal
  - Murr
  - Joe
  - Brian

Figure 6.95

Now let's say I want a numbered list rather than a bulleted list. All I need to do is highlight the list again and go back to *Format > Bullets & numbering*, choose one of the numbered lists, and once again it will be updated automatically.

Chapter 6 – Google Drive and Google Docs

```
Sales Teams

  1. Team 1
       a. Sue
       b. Dan
       c. Johnny
       d. Molly

  2. Team 2
       a. Ronald
       b. Tisha
       c. Kim
       d. Beth

  3. Team 3
       a. Sal
       b. Murr
       c. Joe
       d. Brian
```

Figure 6.96

Page Setup
Page setup is where you can change things such as margins and paper size, and for many people, the default settings will work just fine. But if you plan on printing your document, you should check these settings before doing so in case you need to make changes so everything looks correct when printed.

The default Docs settings are 1 inch margins, portrait layout (tall), 8.5 x 11 inch paper size, and a white background.

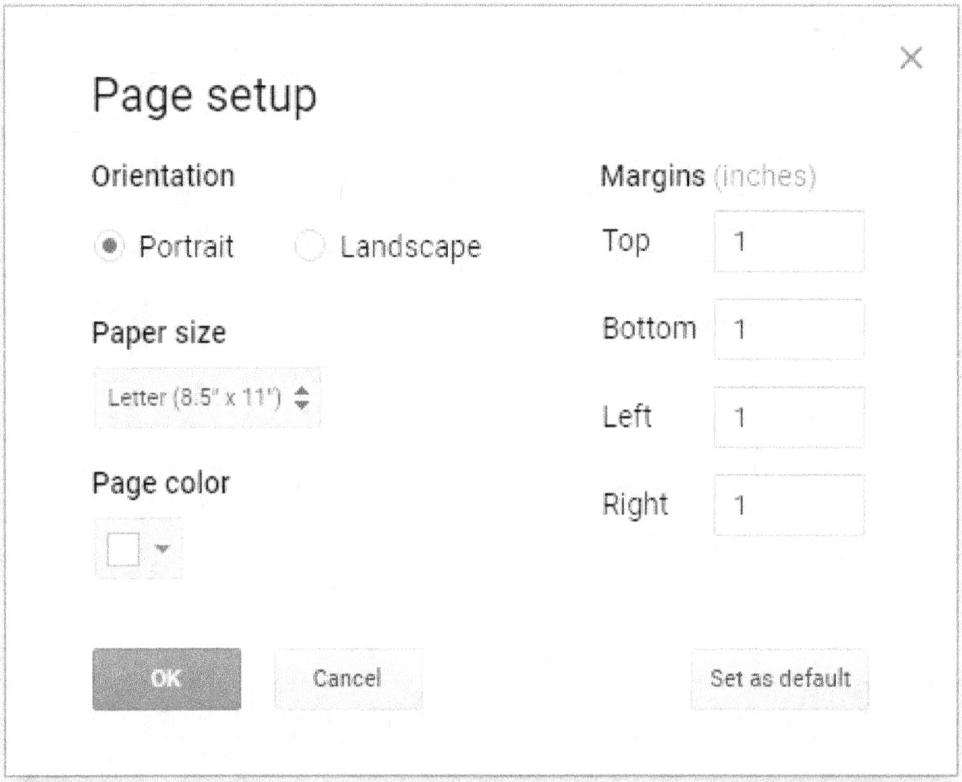

Chapter 6 – Google Drive and Google Docs

Figure 6.97

Most people print their documents on 8.5 x 11 paper, which is also known as letter size, but this can be changed if needed. Unfortunately, there is no custom size option in Docs like there is in Microsoft Word. You *can* enter a custom setting when printing your document though (discussed next).

If you change the margins to make them smaller, be sure that your printer can print that close to the edge of the paper without cutting off some text. It's always a good idea to print just one page to see how it looks before wasting paper and ink printing the entire document just to print it all over again.

I don't recommend changing the page color to anything else but white unless you like using a lot of ink, and after all is said and done it might not look as good on paper as it does on the screen after you print it.

If you change the settings of your document and want to use those exact same settings for future documents, then you can click the button that says *Set as default* to have it apply to new documents as you create them.

Chapter 6 – Google Drive and Google Docs

Keep in mind that over formatting a document can sometimes be worse than under formatting it. If you use too many fonts, colors, text sizes, and so on, your document can lose its consistency and look too "busy".

Printing and Publishing a Document
Now that you have your document completed and formatted the way you like, it's time to print it out on some paper, or maybe even publish it online so others can view your work for themselves.

To print your document, go to the *File* menu and then to *Print,* and you will be shown a preview of how your document will print, and also have some choices to make before actually printing your document. As you can see in figure 6.98, my document will require six sheets of paper, meaning it's six pages long.

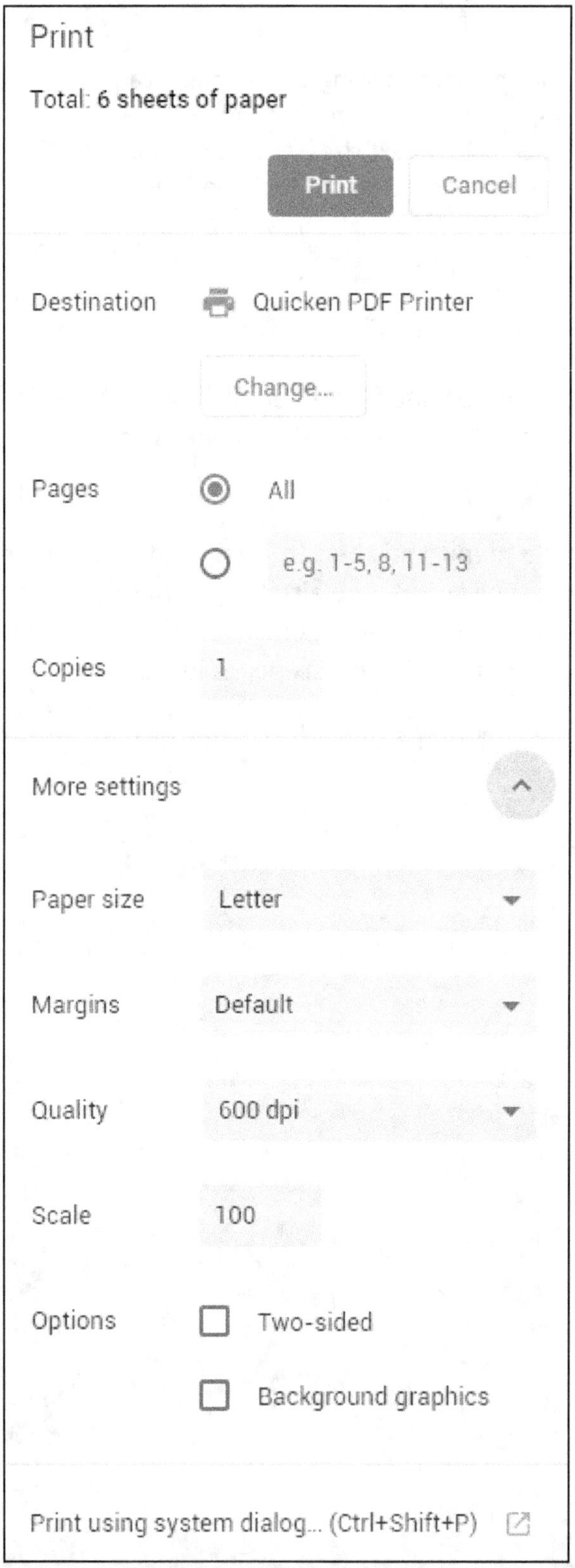

Print

Total: **6 sheets of paper**

[Print] [Cancel]

Destination Quicken PDF Printer

Change...

Pages ● All
       ○ e.g. 1-5, 8, 11-13

Copies 1

More settings ^

Paper size Letter

Margins Default

Quality 600 dpi

Scale 100

Options ☐ Two-sided
         ☐ Background graphics

Print using system dialog... (Ctrl+Shift+P)

Figure 6.98

Chapter 6 – Google Drive and Google Docs

The *Destination* shows what printer the document will be sent to for printing, so if you need to change that to another printer or even a PDF printer, you can click on the *Change* button. As you can see in figure 6.98, I have many other options to choose from for printing. Also notice that it is showing destinations for the tsimms account, and if you have other Google accounts, you can choose one of them for things such as sending to a different Google Drive.

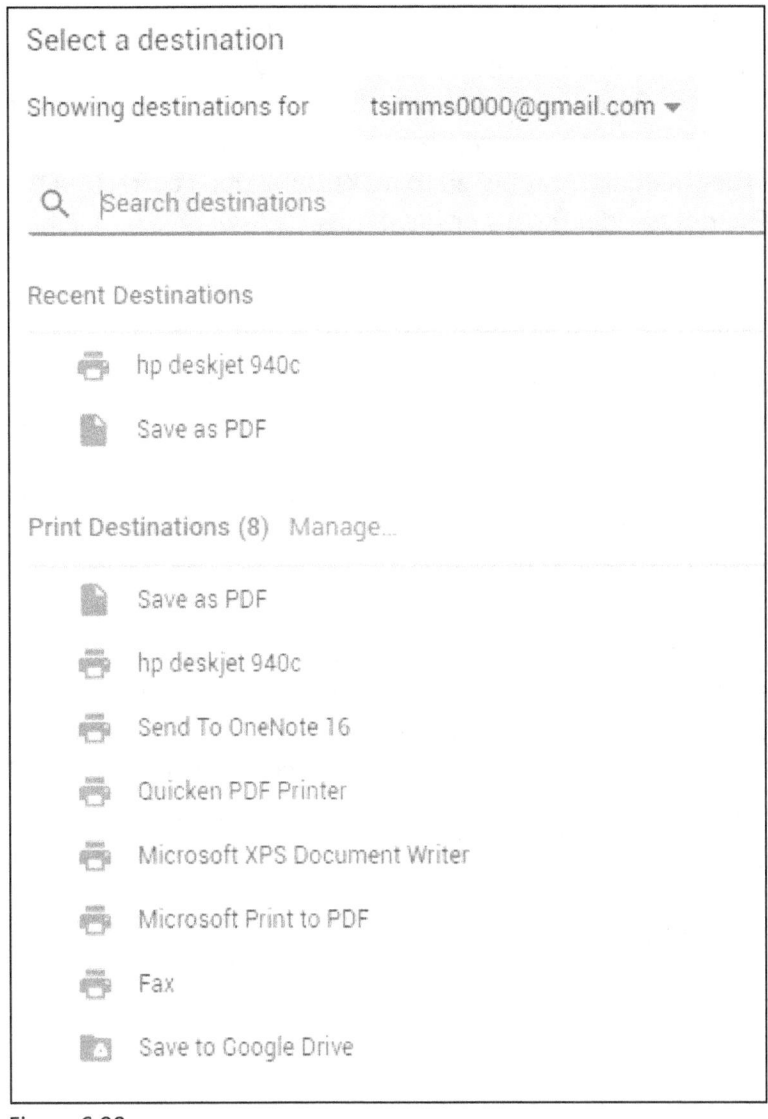

Figure 6.99

By default, Docs will want to print the entire document, but you can change that by clicking the radio button under *Pages* to the second one and adding the pages you want to print. So, if you wanted to only print pages 1 through 3, you would enter *1-3* in the box. If you wanted to print pages 1,3, and 5, you would enter *1,3,5* in the box.

If you need multiple copies printed then change the *Copies* section from the default of 1 to however many copies you need. Just be sure things are the way you want before printing a bunch of copies, so you don't have to do it again!

Under *More settings,* which can be accessed by clicking the down arrow next to it, there will be some additional formatting options that you can apply to your document before printing it. Here you can change the *paper size* to one of the included sizes, as well as enter in a custom page size of your own. You can also change the *margins* if they need to be adjusted to make things look correct on the page when printed. The default dpi (dots per inch) next to *Quality* is 600, which should be plenty for most print jobs (unless you are printing super high resolution pictures and your printer can actually *do* so). If things are a little too big for the paper you are printing on, you can *scale* them down from the default 100%, or even make them larger if needed. (Keep in mind that increasing the size might affect the quality of how images print out.) If your printer supports printing on both sides of the paper, you can choose the *Two-sided* option to save paper. Finally, if you have graphics\images in the background of your document, you can have those printed as well by checking the box next to *Background graphics*.

At the bottom of the print dialog window is a setting for *Print using system* dialog. If you click on this, Docs will open the print management interface that your operating system uses to print rather than use the web based one from Google Docs. If you take a look at figure 6.100, you can see that when I click on *Print* using system dialog, it brings up the Windows print interface (since I am using Microsoft Windows for my operating system). Using this method will give you more choices for fine tuning printer settings before printing.

Chapter 6 – Google Drive and Google Docs

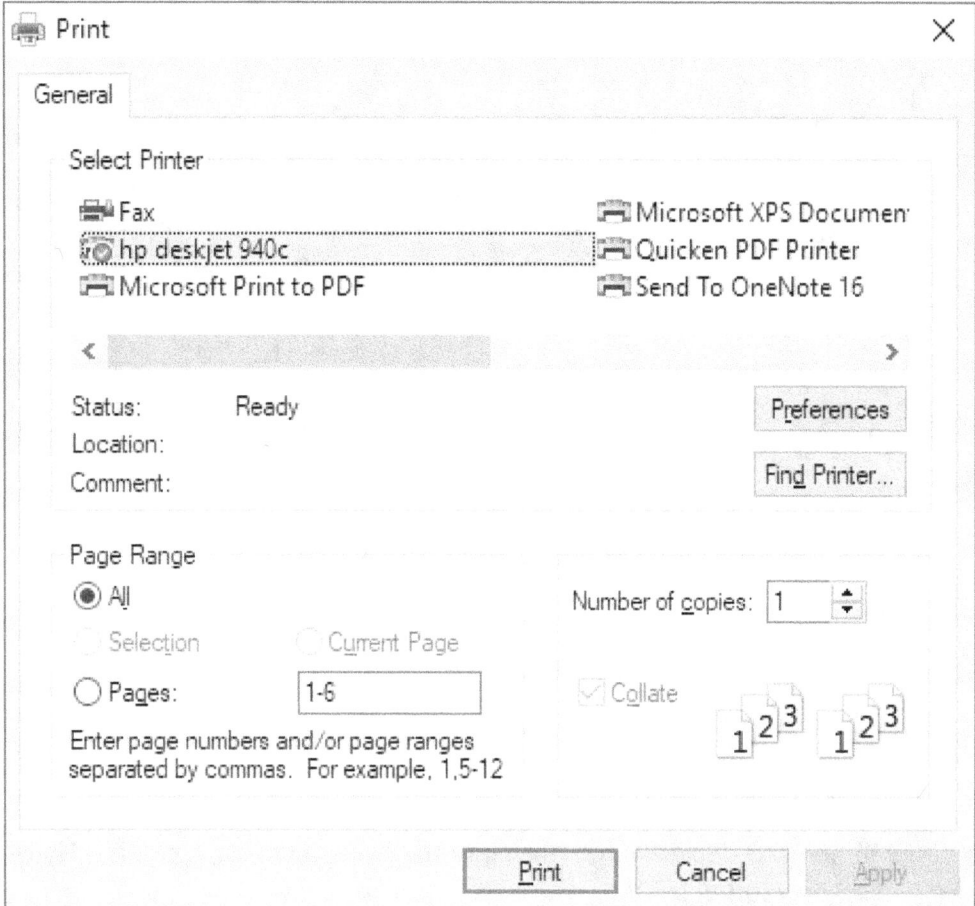

Figure 6.100

Publishing a Document
I mentioned publishing a document earlier in this chapter but wanted to go through the process in a little more detail in case this is something you wish to do with your document.

To publish your document to the Internet you will go to the *File* menu and then choose *Publish to the web*.

Chapter 6 – Google Drive and Google Docs

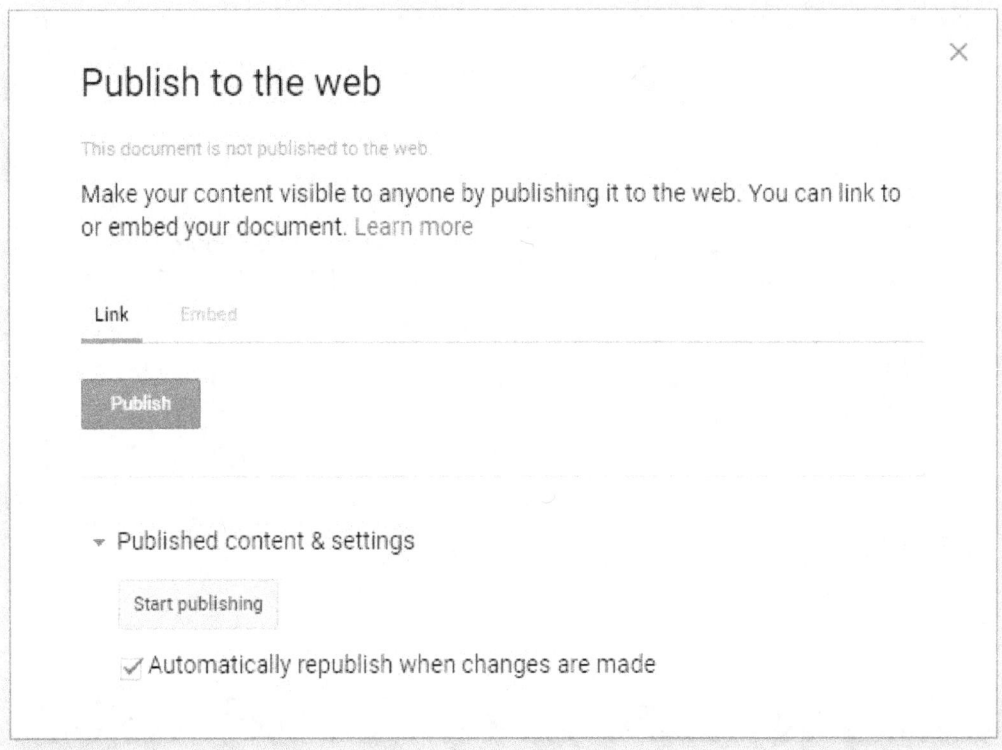

Figure 6.101

Then you will need to decide if you are going to make a link or get some HTML code to embed on your website.

- **Link** – Using this option will publish your document to the Internet, where others with the link will be able to view it. They will not be able to edit it or do anything else with it except print it. Once you click on *Publish* (as seen in figure 6.101) it will publish your document and give you a link (as shown in figure 6.102).

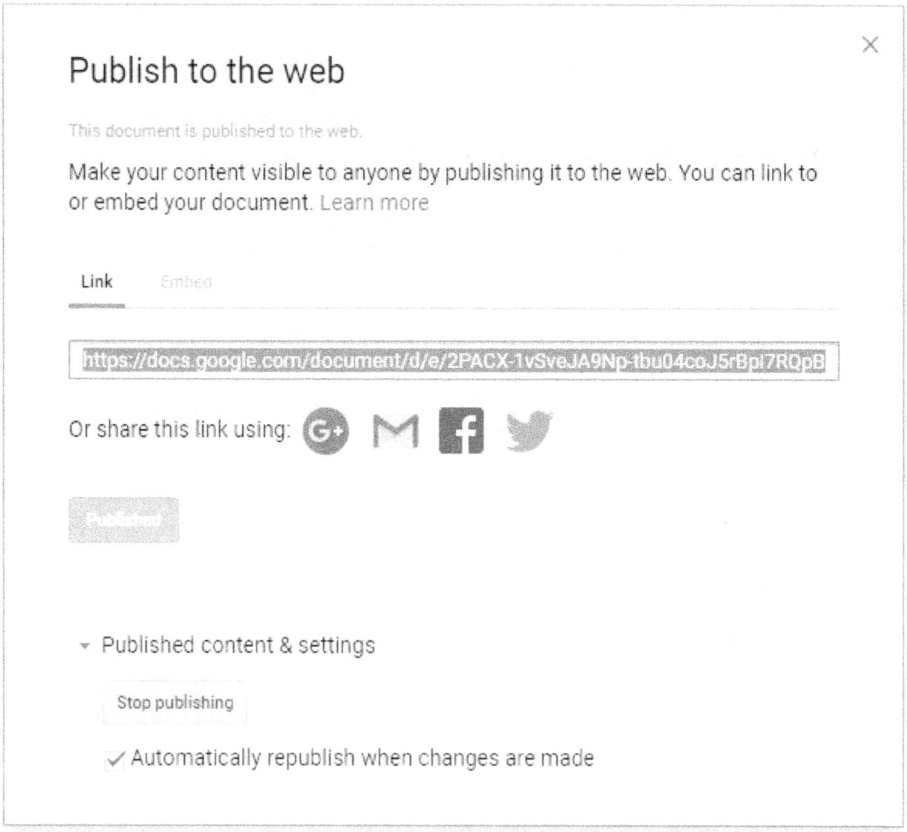

Chapter 6 – Google Drive and Google Docs

Figure 6.102

Then you can share that link via services such as Google+, Gmail, Facebook, and Twitter, or copy the link and email it to someone else so they can view your document. Figure 6.103 shows what my document looks like formatted as a web page when I paste the address into my web browser.

Chapter 6 – Google Drive and Google Docs

Figure 6.103

- **Embed** – Choosing this option will get you HTML code that you can use to embed your document into an existing webpage. By "embed" I mean place the actual document within the webpage, so it looks like it's part of that page. A common example of embedding code is when someone places someone else's YouTube video on their website. This is done by embedding the code linked to that video.

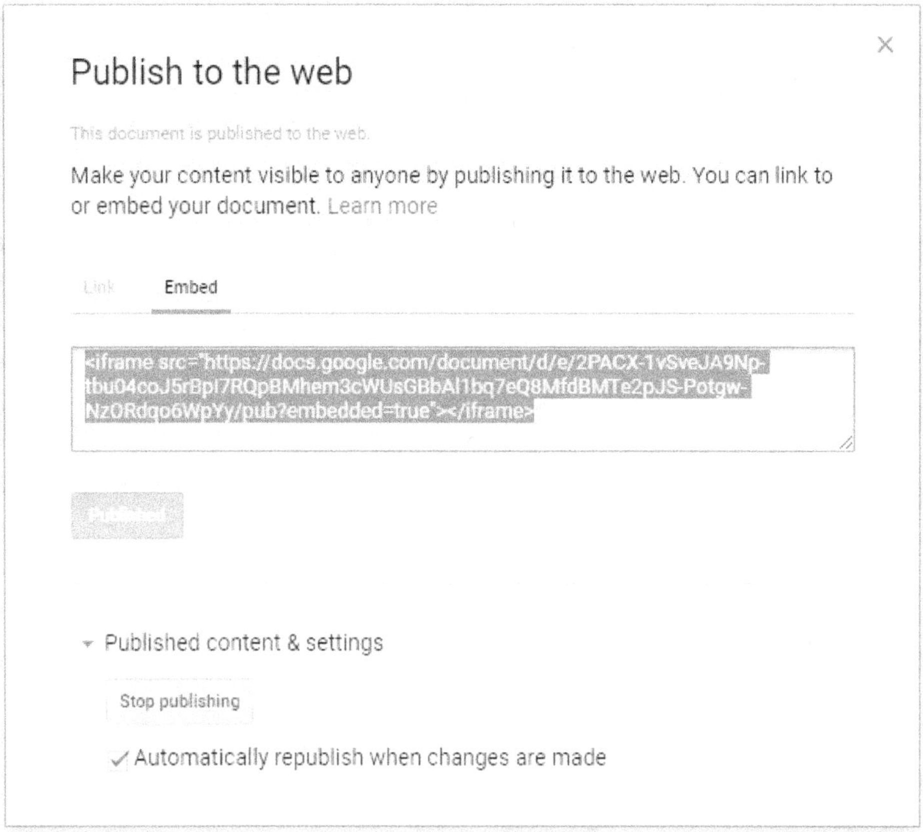

Figure 6.104

Once you click on *Start publishing*, you will be presented with the HTML code required to embed your document onto your website.

If you don't want your document published anymore, all you need to do is click on the *Stop publishing* button. If you want your published document to be updated online whenever you update the document itself, then you can check the box that says *Automatically republish when changes are made* (which should be checked by default).

Sharing a Document
Sharing a document is similar to publishing a document with the main difference being that it's actually opened with Google Docs, and you can give other people the right to edit your document. The sharing process works the same for other Google apps like Sheets and Slides, so I will only be going over the process in this chapter.

Chapter 6 – Google Drive and Google Docs

You can share your document by clicking the *Share* button next to your profile picture on the top right of the screen. Figure 6.105 shows the Share settings window after you click on *Advanced,* which gives you additional sharing options.

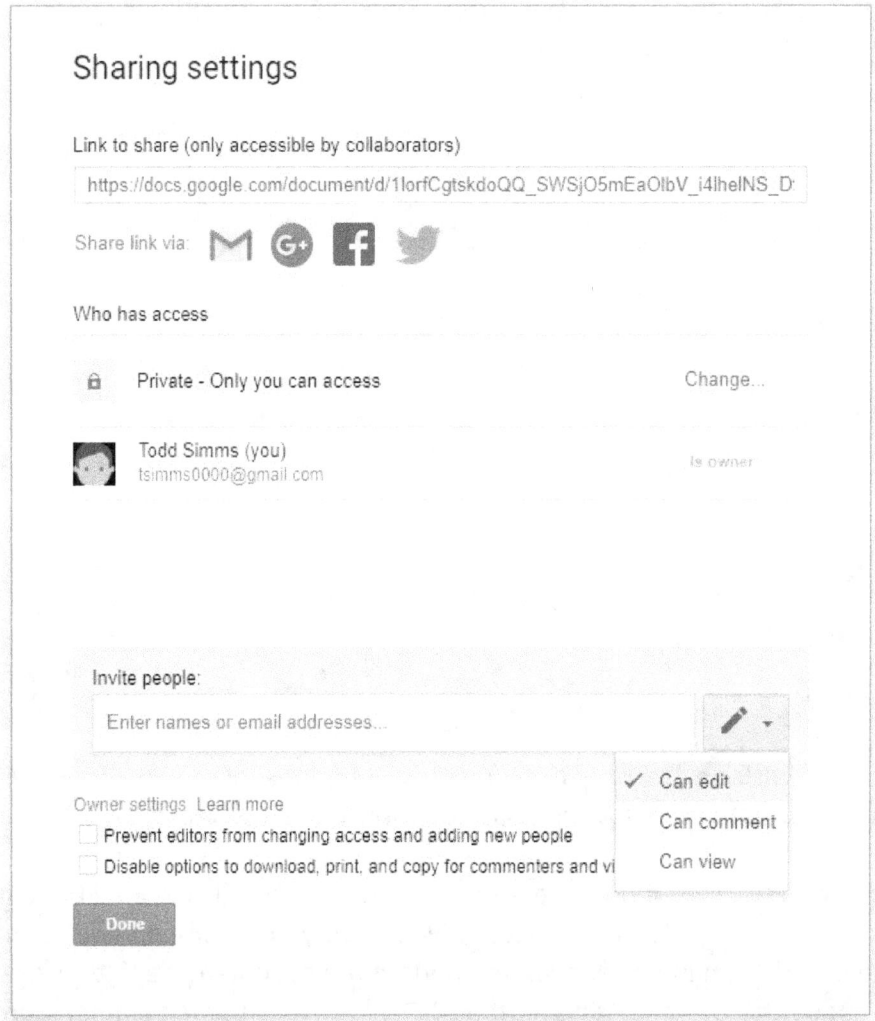

Figure 6.105

By default, your document is set to private so only you can access it, but it's easy to give others permission to view and even edit your document by clicking on *Change*.

There are three options you can set for link sharing:

- **On (public on the web)** – This will make your document public on the Internet and allow anyone to find it by searching for items contained in it.

If you choose this option you can set the permissions to be view only, comment, or edit.

- **On (anyone with the link)** – This option publishes your document on the web, but the only people who will be able to view it are ones who have the actual link that you create when sharing the document. You can still choose the view only, comment, or edit settings for your document.

- **Off (specific people)** – The Off option disables sharing of your document, but you can still publish it to the web for yourself if desired.

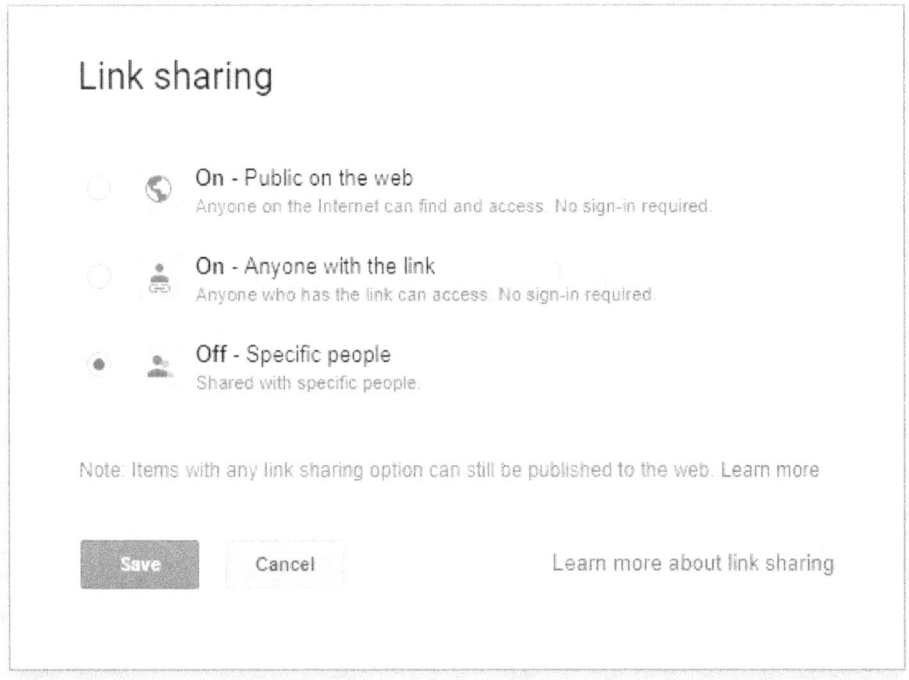

Figure 6.106

If you had your document shared with others, they would show up in the list of who has access, so now I am going to invite someone to access my document by putting their email address in the *Invite people* box (figure 6.105), and then give them the edit permission.

When you invite a person who doesn't have a Google account you will need to make a choice between *Send an invitation* or *Send the link* (as shown in figure 6.107). If the person you are sending the invitation to will need to edit the document, then they will need to sign in with a Google account. If they just need

Chapter 6 – Google Drive and Google Docs

to view the document, then they can do so by clicking on the link they receive in the email that will be sent to them.

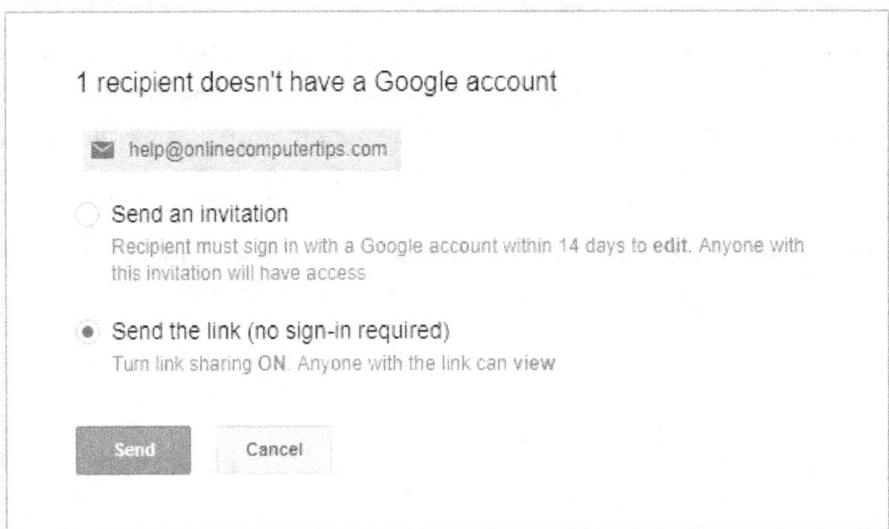

Figure 6.107

Figure 6.108 shows what the email they receive will look like. It has the document name and a button that they can click to open the document in Google Docs.

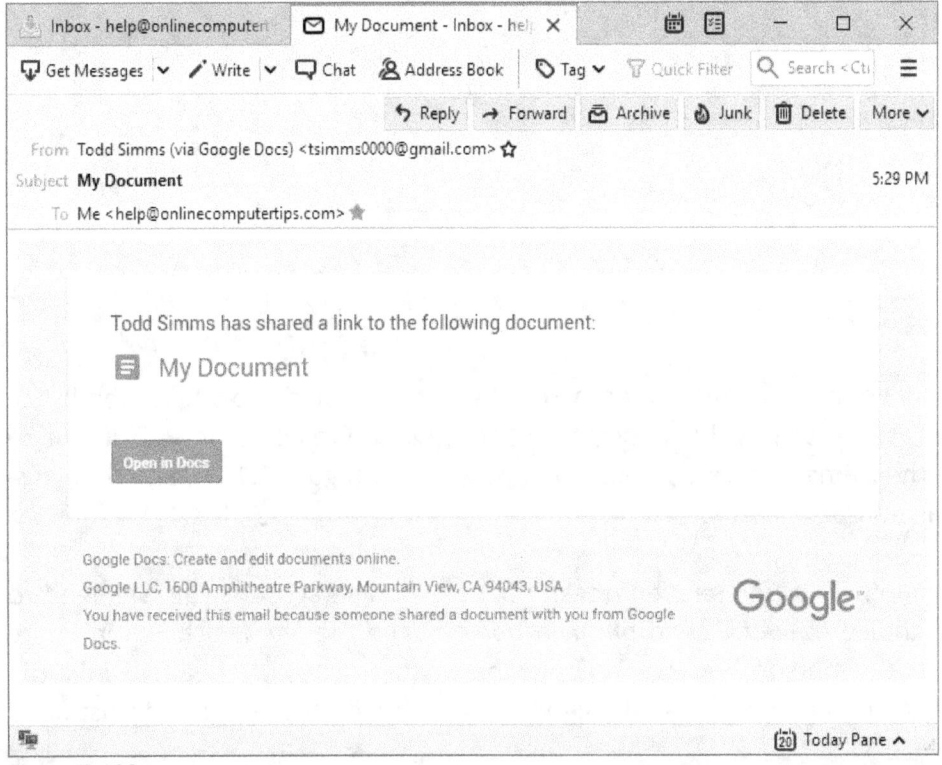

Figure 6.108

Chapter 6 – Google Drive and Google Docs

Once you share your document with a non-Google user, you should see a new icon on your toolbar next to the Share button. (It's usually some random animal showing you that there is an anonymous user accessing your document.)

Figure 6.109

Now I shared the same document with my Google account, and as you can see in figure 6.110, my name appears in the list of who has access, but the non-Google account does not.

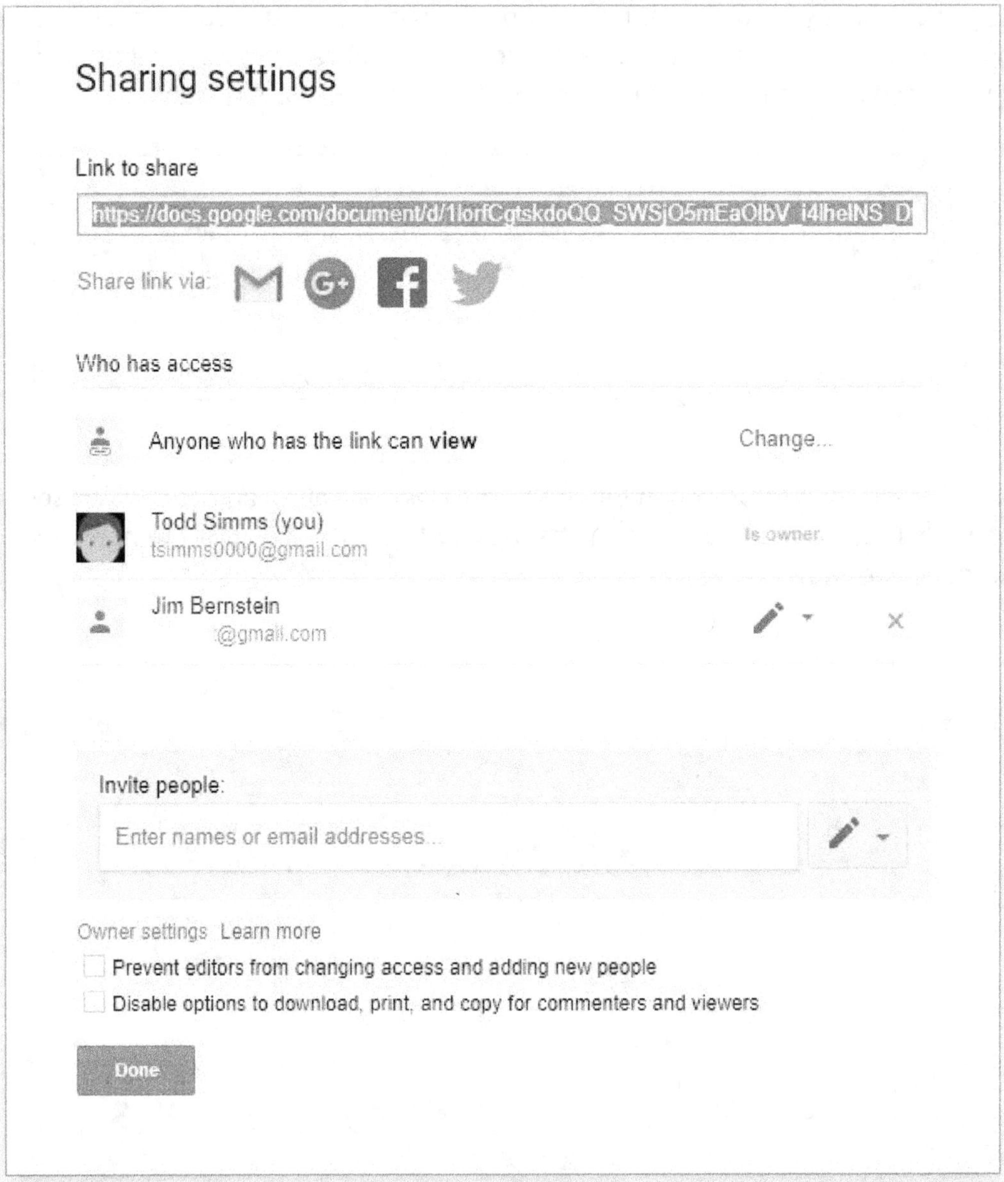

Chapter 6 – Google Drive and Google Docs

Sharing settings

Link to share

https://docs.google.com/document/d/1lorfCgtskdoQQ_SWSjO5mEaOlbV_i4lheINS_D

Share link via: M G+ f 🐦

Who has access

Anyone who has the link can **view**   Change...

Todd Simms (you)
tsimms0000@gmail.com   Is owner.

Jim Bernstein
@gmail.com

Invite people:

Enter names or email addresses...

Owner settings Learn more
☐ Prevent editors from changing access and adding new people
☐ Disable options to download, print, and copy for commenters and viewers

Done

Figure 6.110

Now when I open Todd's document with my Google account, you can see that the document shows that I have access to it by showing my Google profile picture on the toolbar next to the Share button.

Figure 6.111

The last section of the Sharing settings I want to discuss is the *Owner* settings that you can see in figure 6.110 at the bottom of the window.

If you don't want anyone that you have assigned the editor right to change your sharing access or add other people without your permission, then you can check the box that says *Prevent editors from changing access and adding new people*.

The box that says *Disable options to download, print, and copy for commenters and viewers* will disable those features for other users. This comes in handy when you have sensitive information that you don't want shared or leaked. This option is also available for files stored in your Google Drive.

Chapter 7 – Additional Features

Now that you have an overall idea of how Google Classroom works (I hope), I figured I would take some extra time to go over some of the additional features of Classroom that might not be used so much by the majority of teachers. Of course this doesn't mean that these features are not helpful or important!

I will also be going over a third party addon that you can use with Classroom to enhance its functionality to show you how these work. There are always others who try to make these types of applications better and I have a couple of these that I would like to share in case they are something you would like to use in your environment.

Classroom Calendars
We all know how important our calendars are since they help us keep track of things we need to do as well remind us about our upcoming meetings and appointments and so on.

Each classroom that you create will have its own calendar that you and your students can use to keep track of upcoming assignments etc. to make sure that you don't miss something important or turn in something late. There are a couple of ways to see your class calendar within Classroom.

From the three horizontal bars menu at the top left you can click on *Calendar* and you will be shown a weekly calendar view as seen in figure 7.2. You can also get to the Calendar link from your main classroom page (figure 7.1).

Chapter 7 – Additional Features

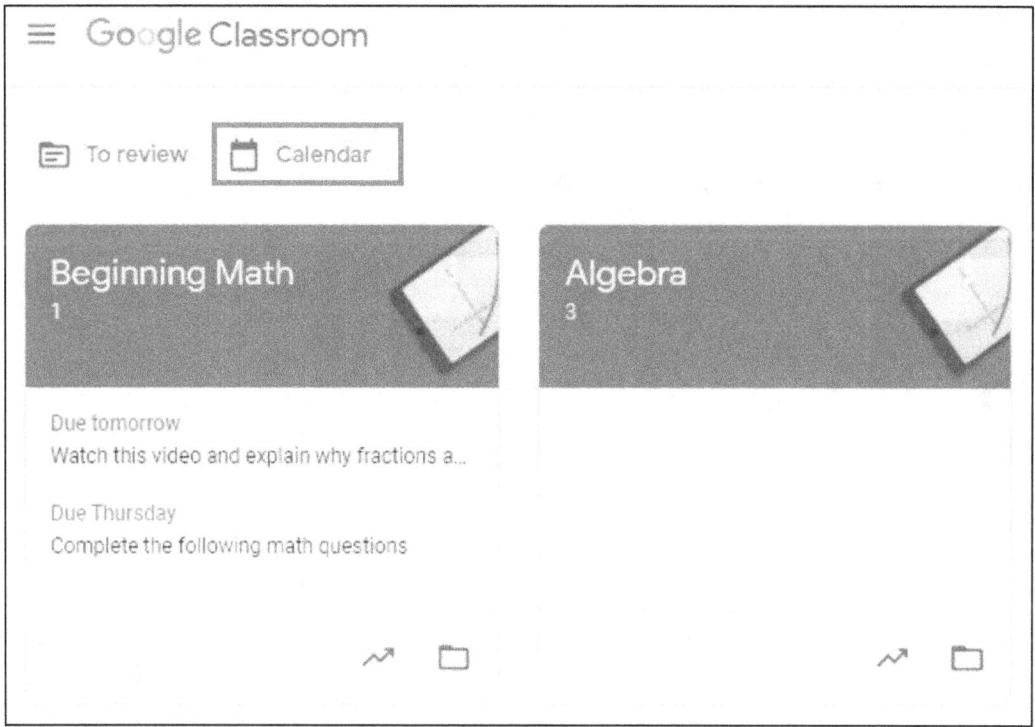

Figure 7.1

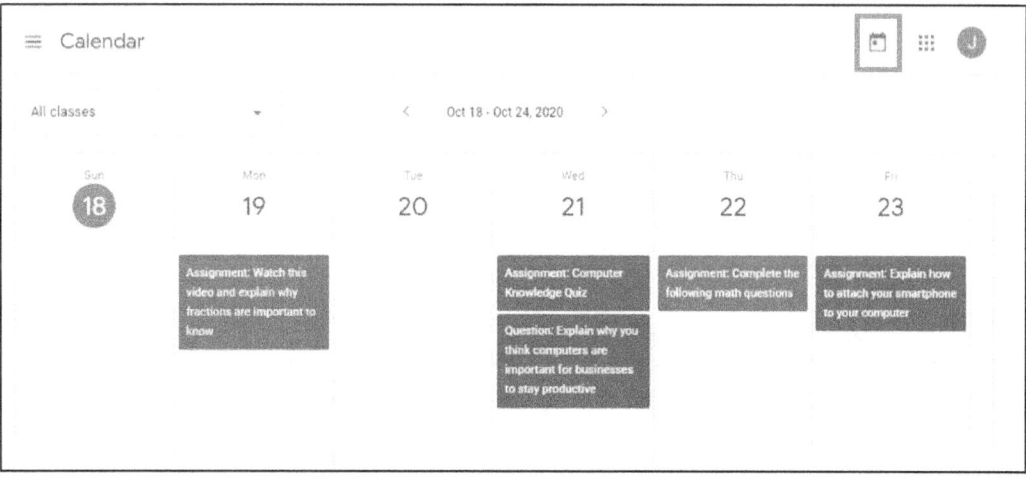

Figure 7.2

From here you can see what assignments and quizzes you have coming up for all of your classes or you can also choose to show upcoming items for one particular class by selecting it from the dropdown menu at the upper left.

If you wish to be brought back to the current day you can click on the calendar icon that is highlighted in figure 7.2.

Chapter 7 – Additional Features

If you click on any item within the calendar you will be taken to that item in your classroom so you can then review or grade the assignment or quiz.

Another way to get to your class calendar is to click on the *Google Calendar* link from the Classwork tab within any one of your classrooms.

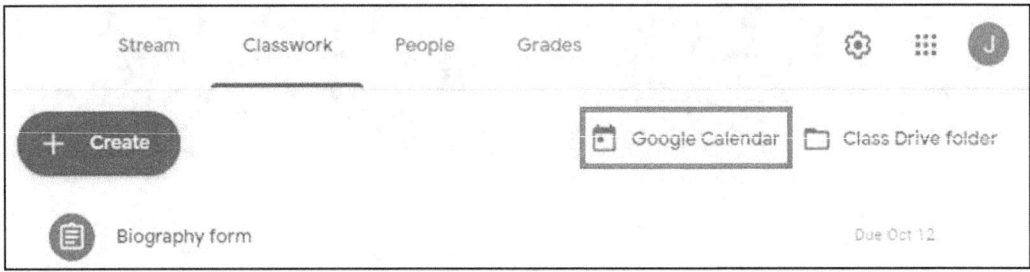
Figure 7.3

When you access your calendar this way you will see additional information such as any personal appointments or holidays as shown in figure 7.4. You can check and uncheck any of the boxes on the left to fine tune what is shown on your calendar.

You can also change the view to daily, weekly, monthly and so on as seen in figure 7.5 to get a better overall view of what you have going on. When your students click on their calendars they will see all of their classes and related assignments and can also fine tune what they see on their calendar.

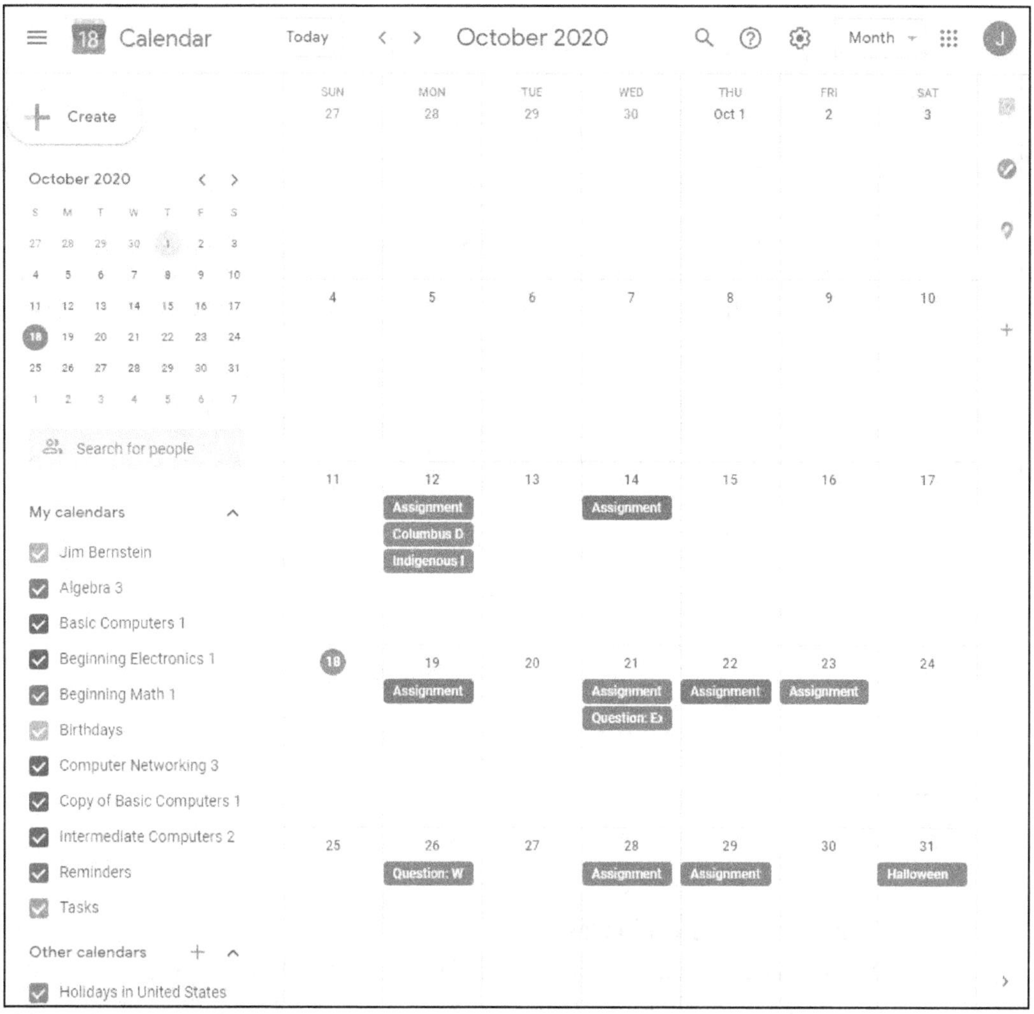

Chapter 7 – Additional Features

Figure 7.4

Chapter 7 – Additional Features

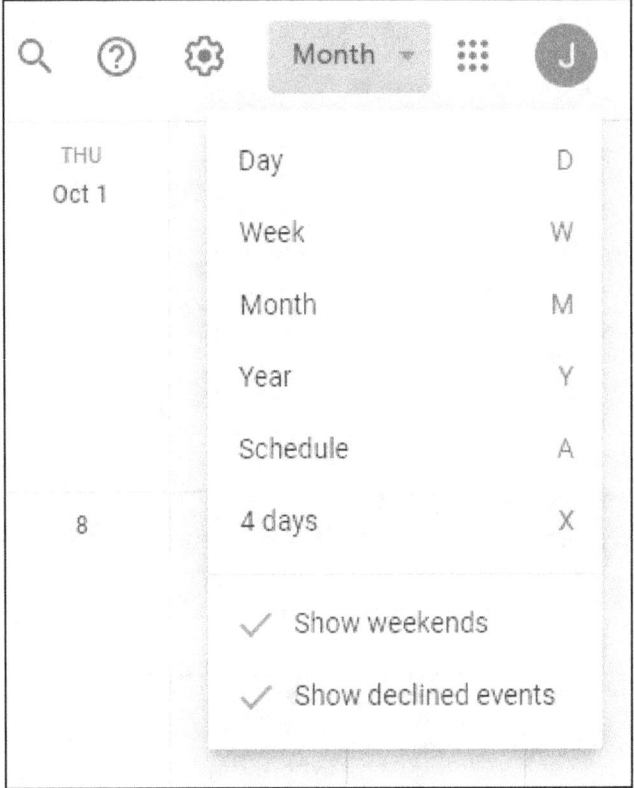

Figure 7.5

Using Google Meet For Your Classes
If you are not familiar with Google Meet then I will tell you that it is Google's online meeting and video conferencing software that is now free to use by anyone who wishes to take advantage of it. It is Google's answer to the very popular Zoom application that many schools are using to teach their classes.

 If you are interested in learning about how to use the popular Zoom software for your online meetings and video calls then check out my book titled Zoom Made Easy.
https://www.amazon.com/dp/B088B96YNK

In order to integrate Meet with your classes, you will need to be using a G-suite educational account so you can have your Meet links incorporated into your classrooms. This doesn't mean that you can't use Meet with your classrooms, and you can always create Meet meetings and share the join links with your students.

Chapter 7 – Additional Features

If you do have a G-suite account you will need to enable the Meet link for your classes from the settings for each class as seen in figure 7.6.

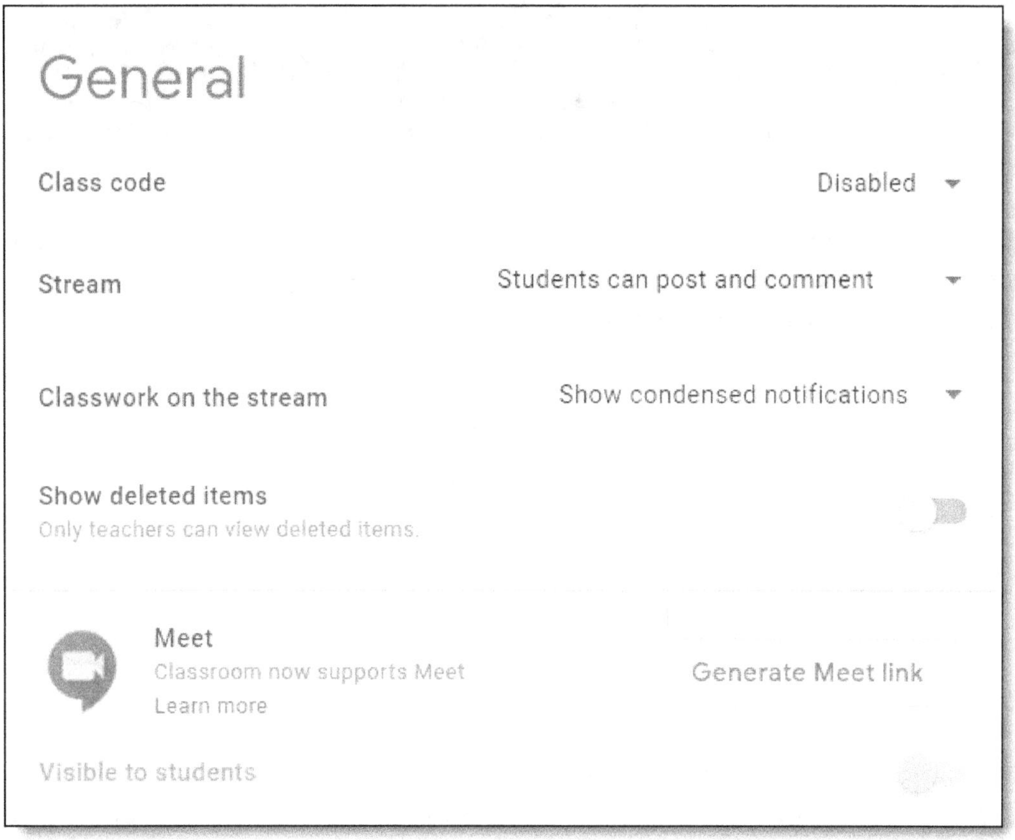

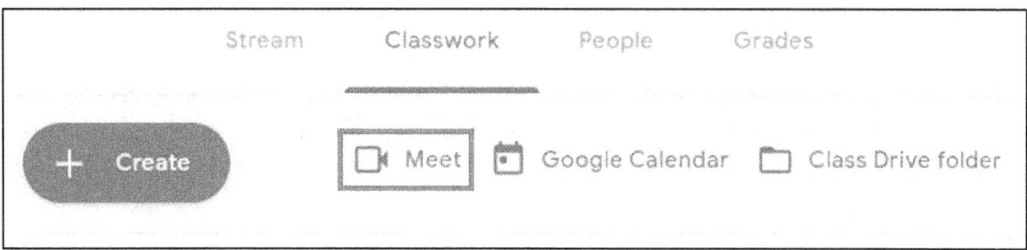

Figure 7.6

Once you do that you will see a Meet link on your Classwork tab as well as on your main class page.

Figure 7.7

Chapter 7 – Additional Features

Figure 7.8

When your students click the link they will be taken into that meeting where you can then do things such as share your screen and interact with your students via your computer's camera and microphone.

If you are interested in learning about how to use the Google Meet for your classes and other meetings then check out my book titled **Google Meet Made Easy**.
https://www.amazon.com/dp/B08DFQPSD7

Transferring Ownership of a Classroom
If you happen to have co-teachers in your classroom and need one of them to take over your class for you then you can easily transfer ownership of that class to them making them the primary teacher for that class.

When you transfer ownership of a classroom to a new teacher then that person will become the owner of the class Google Drive folder, materials in the class templates folder and any student work that has been turned in.

To transfer class ownership, go to the People tab for that particular class and find the co-teacher you wish to transfer ownership to. From there, click on the three vertical dots by their name and then choose *Make class owner* (figure 7.9).

Chapter 7 – Additional Features

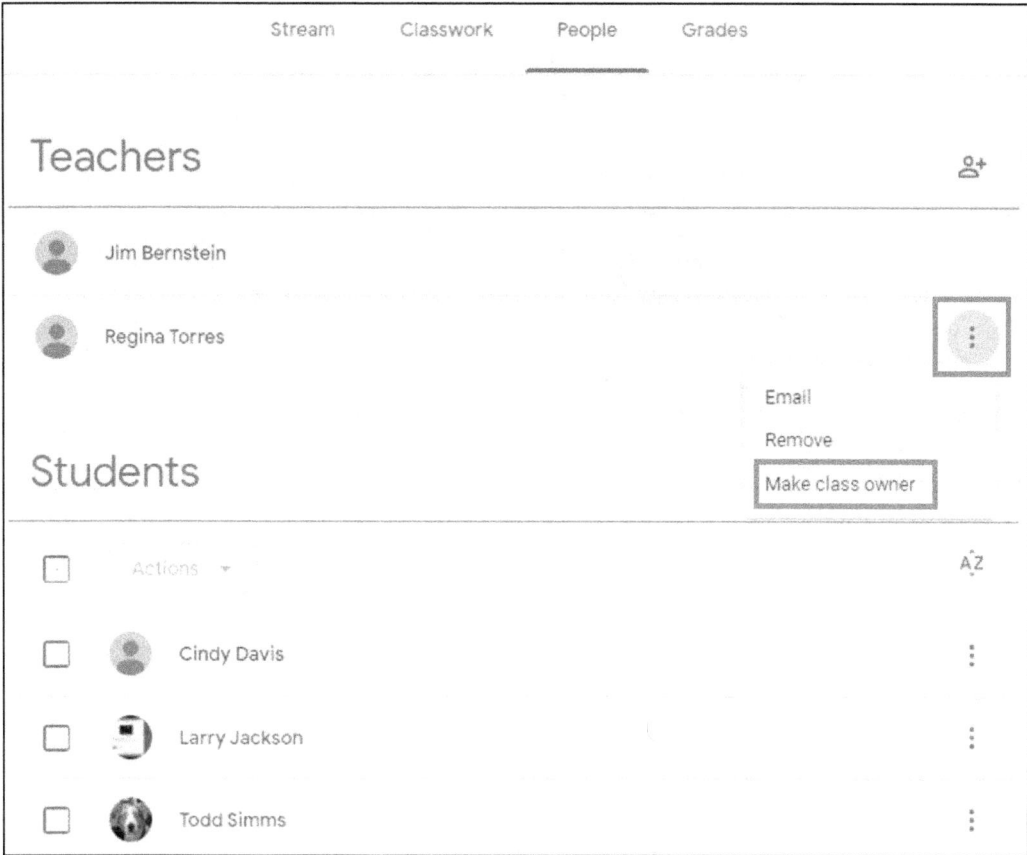

Figure 7.9

You will then get a notification popup telling you that you will remain the class owner until the co-teacher accepts your invitation. From there, click on *Invite* to start the transfer process.

Chapter 7 – Additional Features

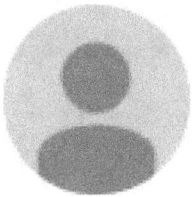

Figure 7.10

The co-teacher will get an invitation in their email that looks similar to figure 7.11. When they click the Respond button they can then become the new class owner by clicking on accept as seen in figure 7.12.

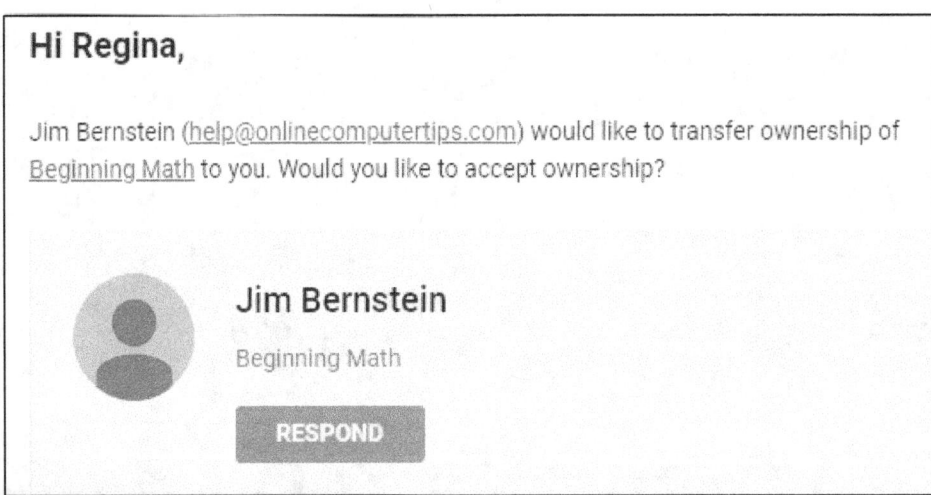

Figure 7.11

Chapter 7 – Additional Features

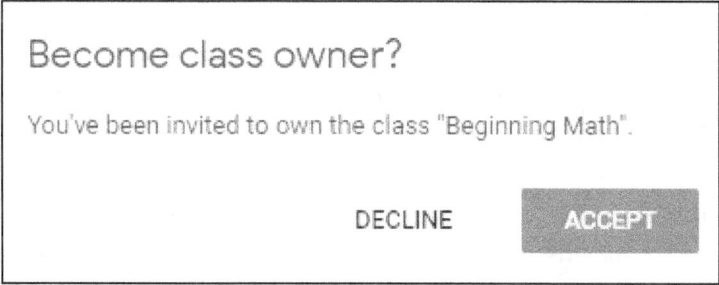

Figure 7.12

Now they appear as the class owner at the top of the list with the original class owner below them. They now have the option to make the original class owner the owner of the class again if necessary.

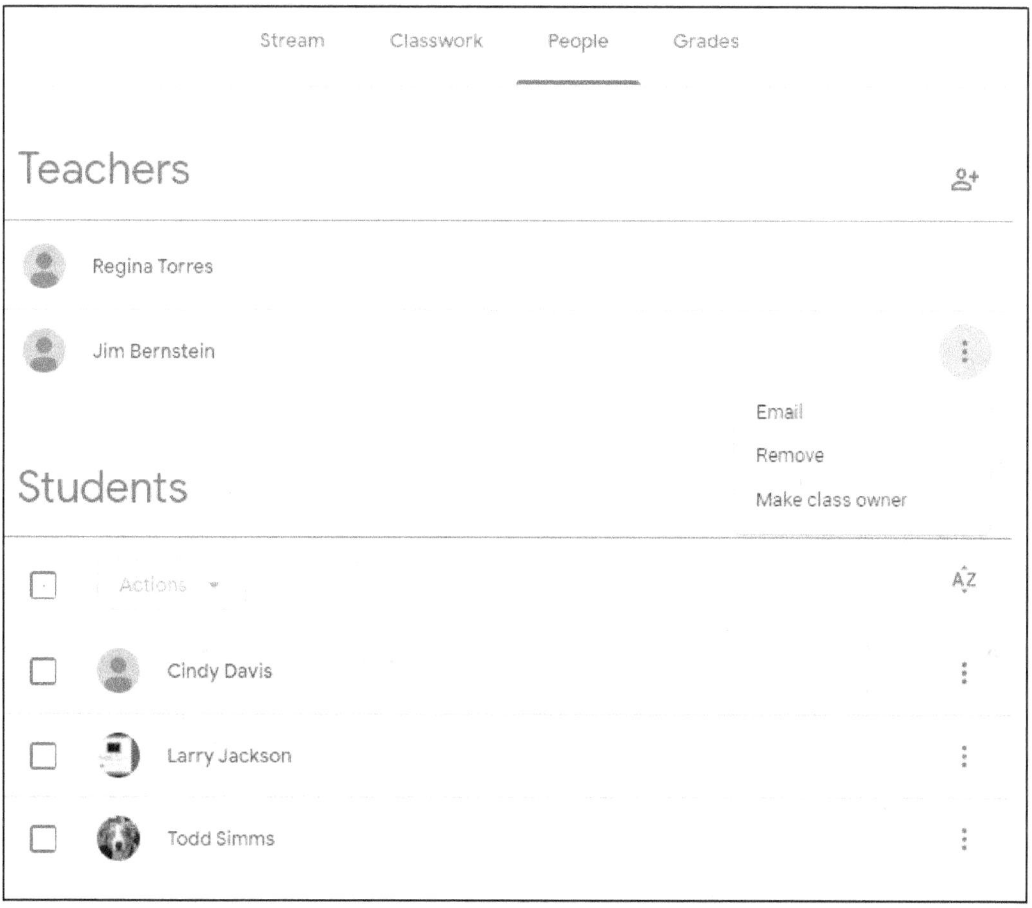

Figure 7.13

Chapter 7 – Additional Features

Reusing Assignments and Posts
If you are like most teachers then you probably use many of the same assignments for more than one of your classes and it can be a lot of work recreating identical assignments and quizzes for each class.

Fortunately, there is an option which allows you to reuse assignments and other posts that you have already created so you don't have to keep doing the same work over and over.

To use this feature you can go to your *Classwork* tab, click on the *Create* button and then choose *Reuse post*.

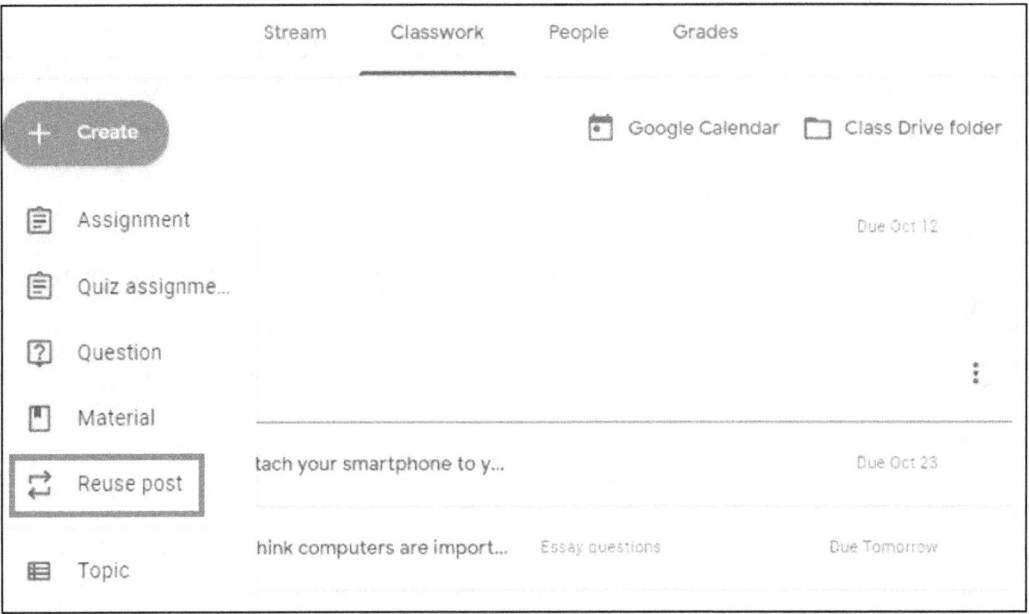

Figure 7.14

Next you will need to choose the class that contains the assignment or post that you wish to reuse (figure 7.15).

Chapter 7 – Additional Features

Figure 7.15

Once you select the appropriate class you can then choose the assignment or post you want to reuse from the list. If you would like to have new copies of any attachments you have created for the class be made then you can check the box that says *Create new copies of all attachments*. I will be reusing my biography assignment for this example. Once everything looks good simply click on the *Reuse* button to start the process.

Chapter 7 – Additional Features

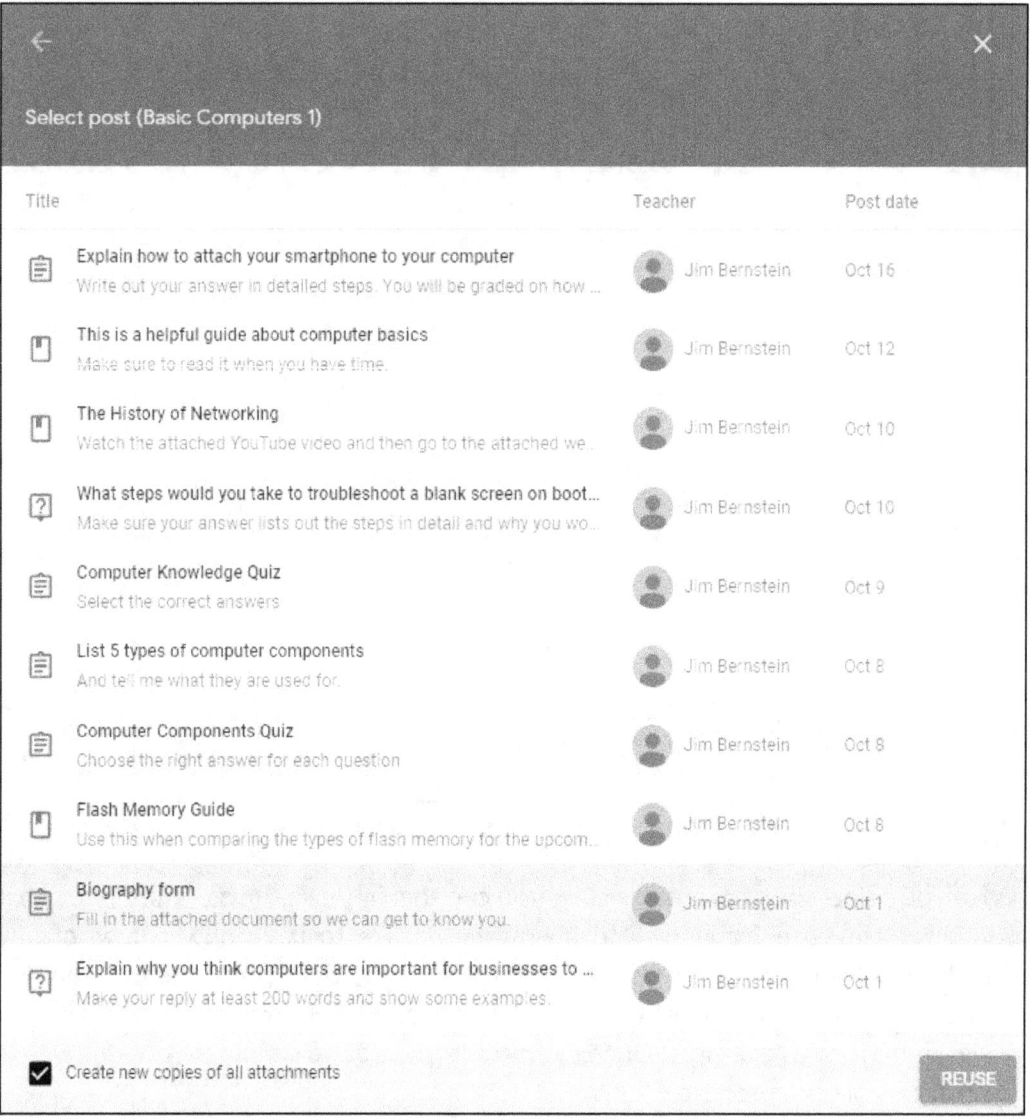

Figure 7.16

Once my duplicate assignment has been created, I can then make any needed adjustments to its contents, due date, points and so on. When I am ready to assign this work to my students, all I need to do is click on the *Assign* button.

Chapter 7 – Additional Features

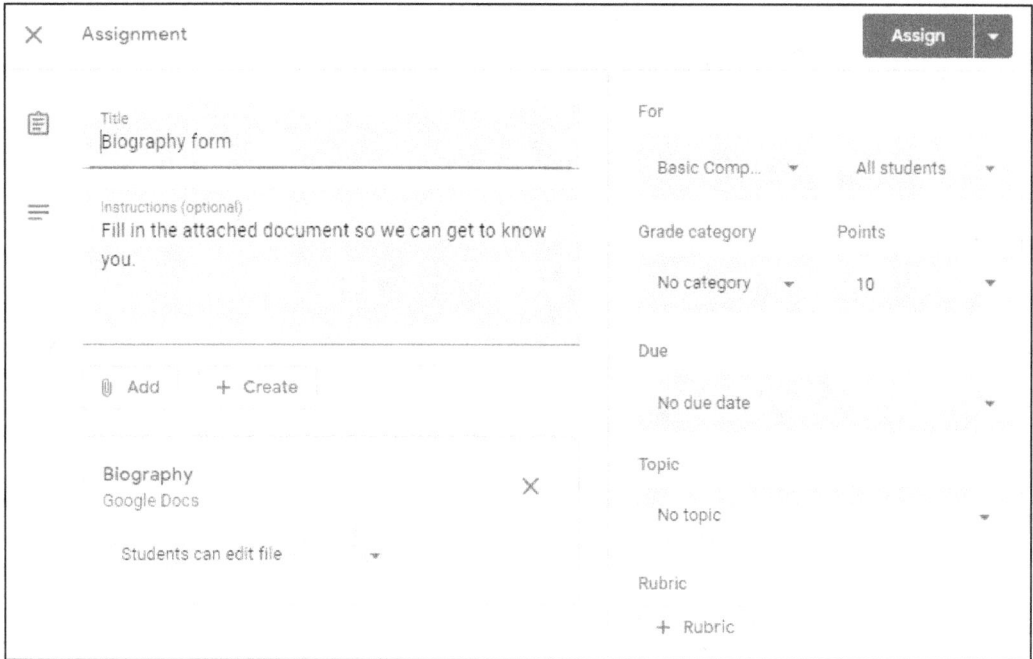

Figure 7.17

 One thing you might notice when reusing posts for different classes is that Classroom will have the original class selected by default and will not let you uncheck it. So you can reuse the post\assignment with additional classes, but it will be reused with the original class as well.

Using Google Classroom on Your Mobile Devices
If you are the type who prefers to work from your smartphone or tablet or maybe even the type who likes to be able to work outside the office then you can install Google Classroom on your mobile device so you can manage your classes from anywhere you happen to be.

The mobile version of Classroom works in a very similar way to the desktop version and once you install it and login you will see how similar it looks. Obviously, it will be a little harder to navigate the mobile version since you will be working with a smaller screen, especially on a smartphone. Figure 7.18 shows how your list of classes will look and figure 7.18 shows the Classroom tab for a class.

Chapter 7 – Additional Features

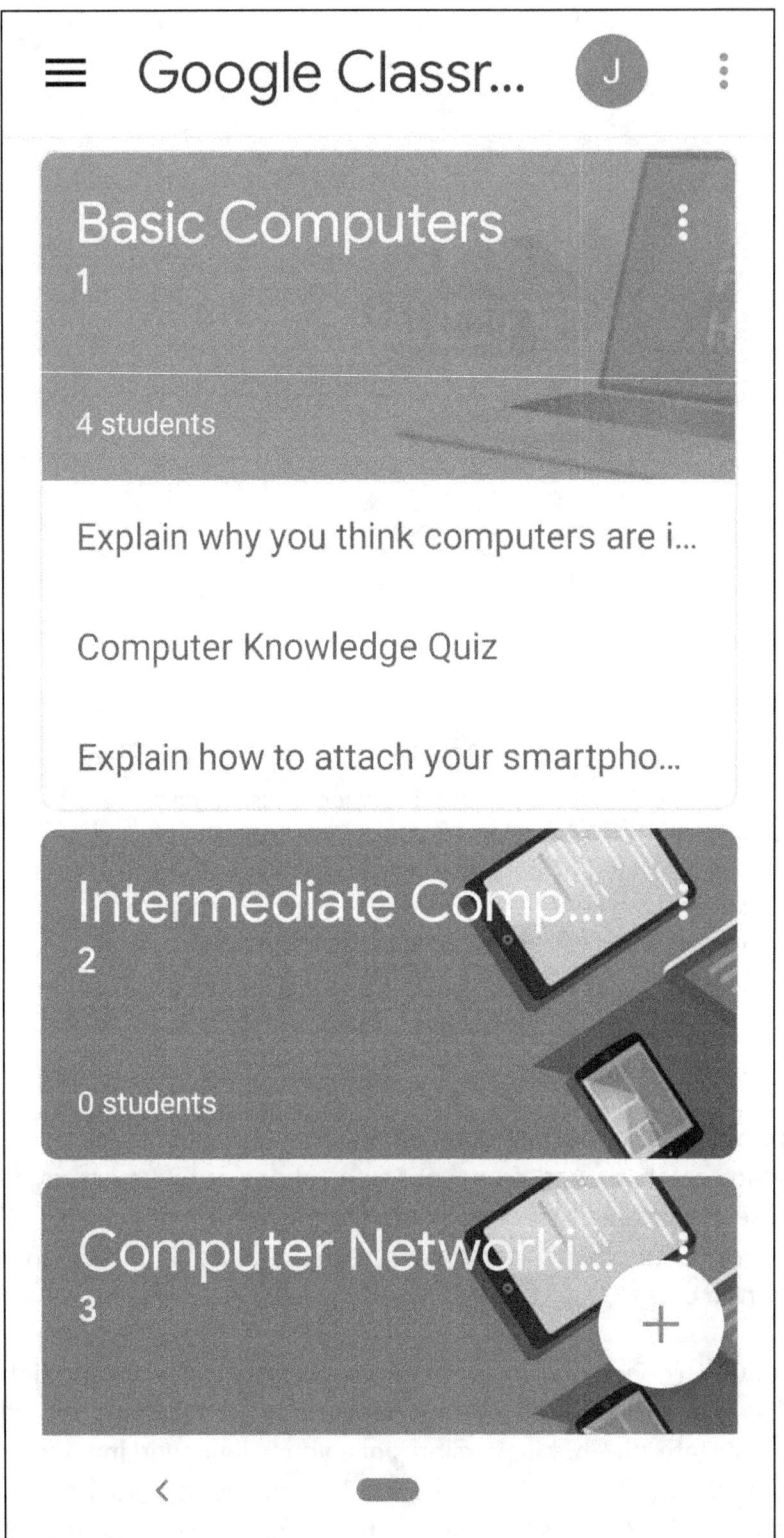

Figure 7.18

Chapter 7 – Additional Features

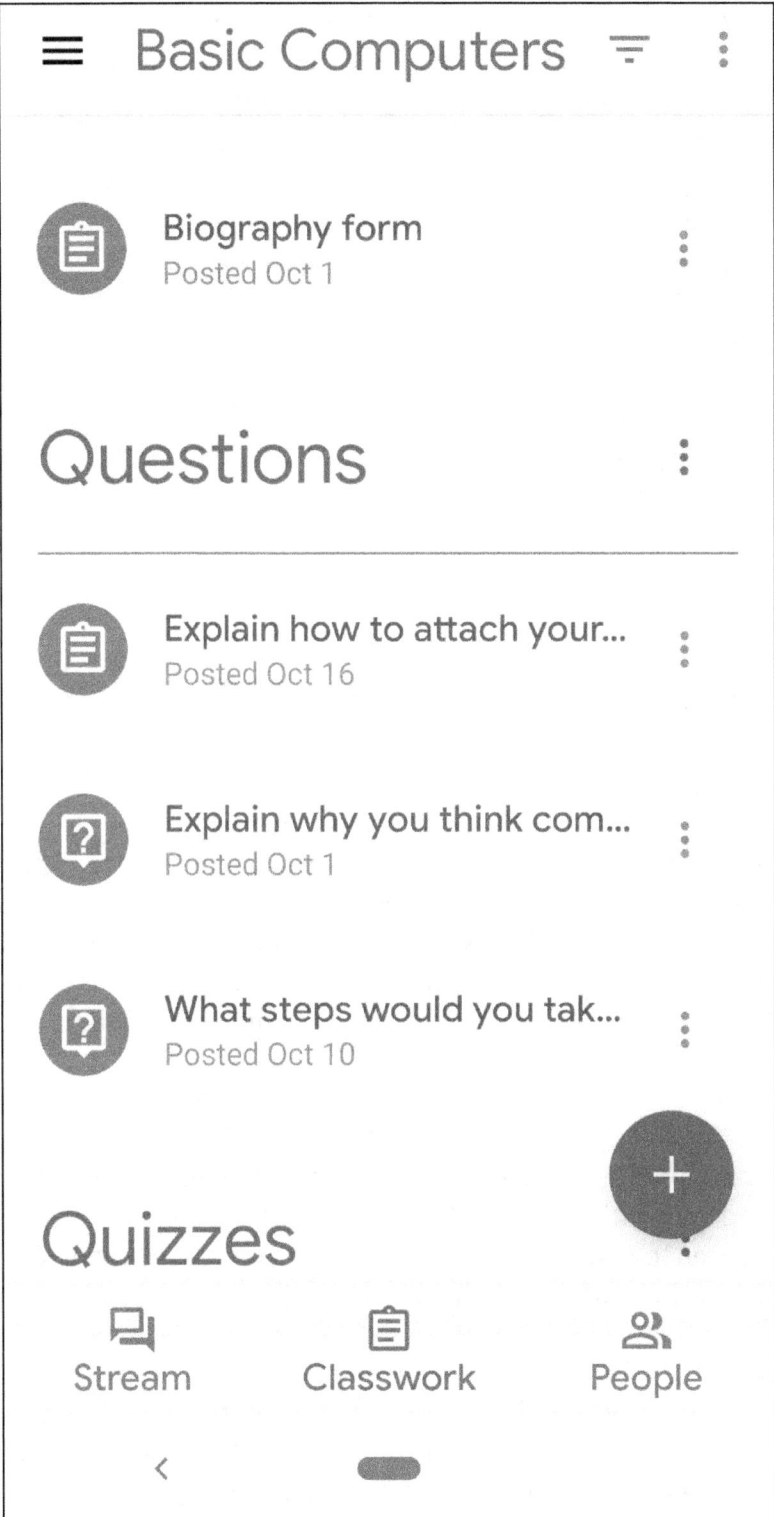

Figure 7.19

Chapter 7 – Additional Features

You can do perform many of the same tasks on the mobile version of Classroom as you can on the desktop version but not everything. Here is a basic rundown of what you can and can't do with the mobile version of Classroom.

What you can do
- Create or join a class
- Edit a class
- Edit and delete assignments
- Turn in assignments
- Email students
- Invite students to classes
- Access your files in Google Drive
- Reset or disable your class code

What you can't do
- Create new assignments
- Edit assignments
- Modify class settings
- Create a quiz assignment
- Copy assignment links

To install Google Classroom on your mobile device simply go to the Play Store (Android devices) or the App Store (Apple devices) and do a search for Google Classroom and download\install the app just like you would with any other app. Just be sure you are getting the official app from Google and not some other third party app that might be trying to trick you to install it by using a similar name.

Notification Settings
I have gone over the settings that are specific to classrooms but wanted to take a little time to go over the notification settings that are related to Google Classroom itself. Notifications are used to notify you of specific events such as when someone turns in some work or makes a comment in your class and you can turn these on and off as needed.

When you click on the three horizontal bars like you have done many times by now you will see an option for *Settings* at the bottom of the list that appears. This is where you can go to change options for your class notifications.

Chapter 7 – Additional Features

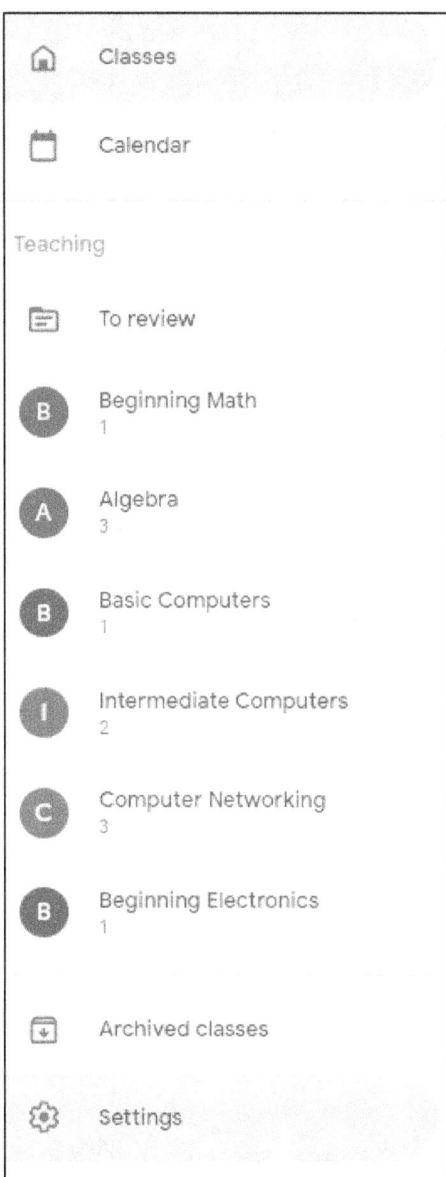

Figure 7.20

As you can see in figure 7.21, the notification options are split up into categories for email, comments, classes you teach and class notifications. There is also a Profile setting which I will get to in a bit.

The *Email* notification option is pretty self-explanatory, and it allows you to either enable or disable notifications that are sent to you via email for everything so if you turn this off then all of the other notification options will be disabled as well.

Chapter 7 – Additional Features

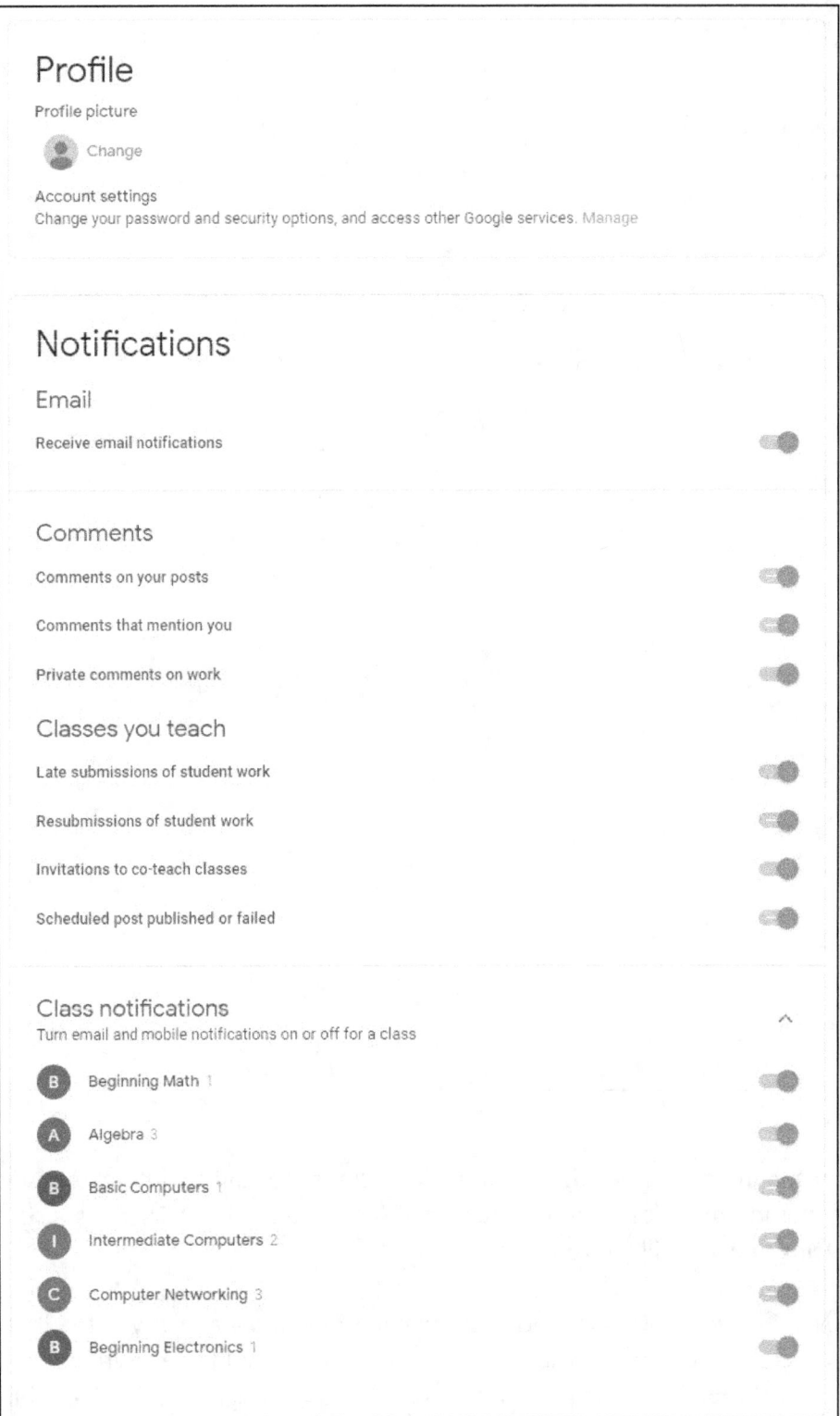

Figure 7.21

Chapter 7 – Additional Features

If you don't like being bombarded with a notification every time someone leaves a comment in your stream or on an assignment then you can disable these notifications from the *Comments* section.

When students do things such as turn in their work etc. you will also be notified so you might want to keep the *Class notifications* enabled so you know when work has been turned in or is late.

Finally there is the *Class notification* settings and from here you can enable or disable notifications for specific classes. For example, if you don't need to see notifications about your math class you can disable them just for that class.

The *Profile* area is where you can go to change your profile picture from your initial to an actual picture. You can use a picture from your Google Drive or upload one from your computer. After you choose your picture, you will be able to crop it as needed so it fits in the circular area.

The *Account settings* area will take you to your Google account details and will let you view and change your personal details, review security settings, manage your Google Drive storage options and so on. What you see here will vary based on the kind Google account you are using.

Originality Reports
Since it's so easy to get information online about almost any subject, it makes it difficult to know if your students are doing their own work or just copying and pasting it from a website that they just happened to find on the topic their assignment covers.

Originality reports are used to help you to check your student's work against content that is posted on the internet such as web pages and books to see if they are using other people's work and passing it off as their own. Plus your school admin can add additional content that you can use to search against. In order to use this feature you will need to be using Classroom with a G-suite account.

To use the originality reports you will need to enable it for your assignments by checking the *Check plagiarism (originality) box* when creating an assignment.

Chapter 7 – Additional Features

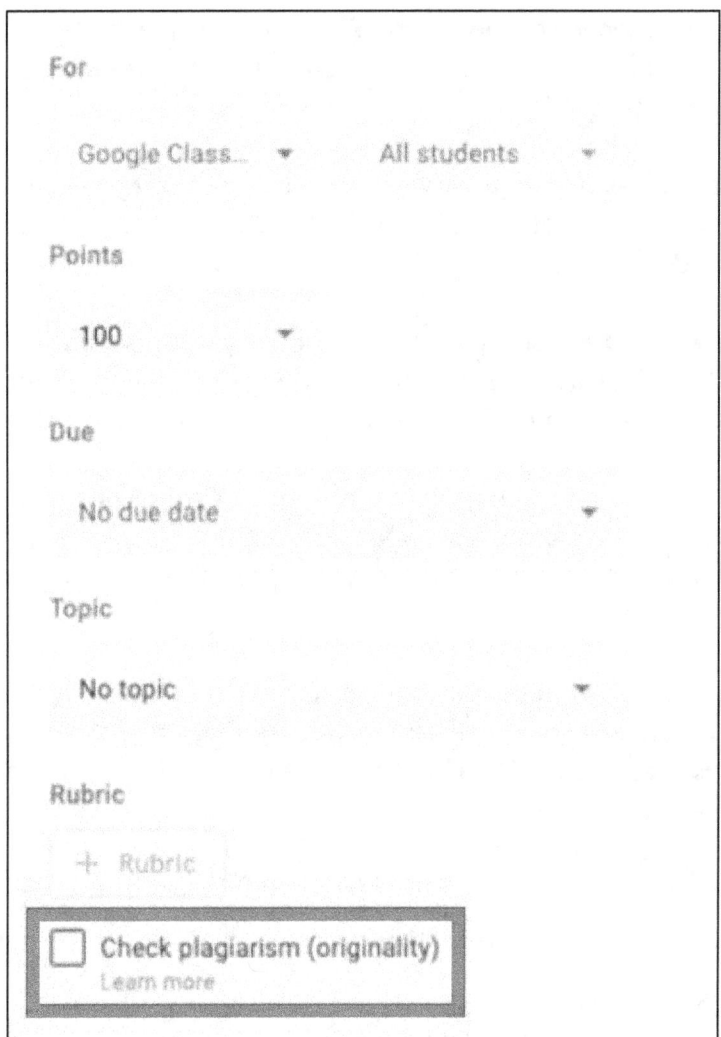

Figure 7.22

To check a students work for originality you will need to go back to the assignment and click on *flagged passages* to have Classroom check for copied content. Then you will be able to see if they have done all of their own work or not.

Chapter 7 – Additional Features

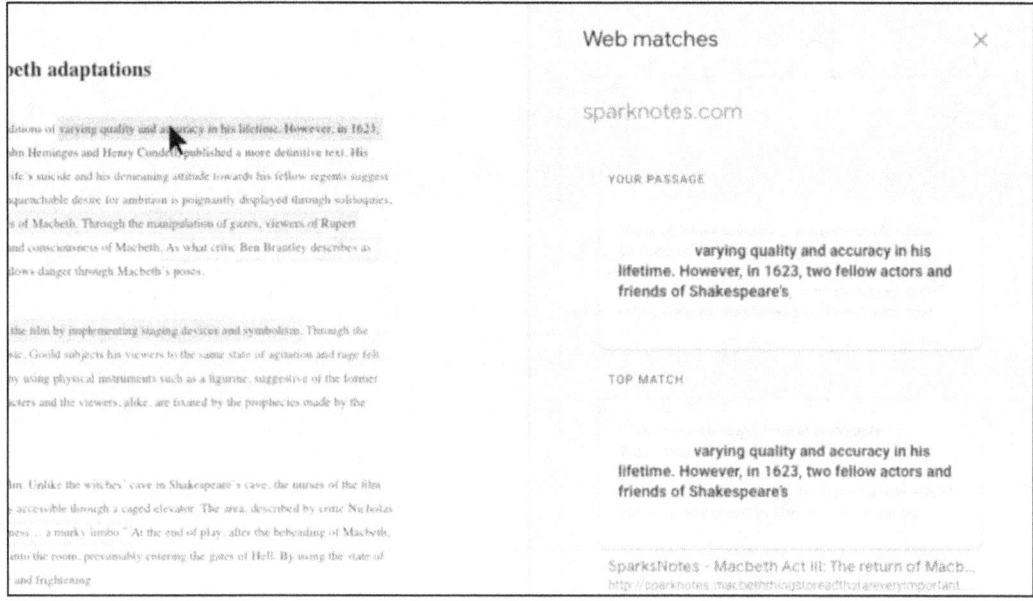

Figure 7.23

Comment Bank

Back in Chapter 5 I showed you how to make comments directly on your student's Google documents so they can see exactly which part of their work you are referring to.

If this is something you do often and you find yourself typing in the same comments over and over then you can use the Comment bank to store commonly used comments to quickly insert them into your student's documents.

What the Comment bank does is store any comments that you need to use on a regular basis. Then any time you wish to use one of these stored comments you can quickly insert it by clicking on it or by typing the hashtag symbol # and the first letter or so of that comment.

When I go to an assignment and click on the Comment bank icon (figure 7.24) the first time it will tell me that my comment bank is empty and then I can click the *Add to bank* link to start adding my comments.

Chapter 7 – Additional Features

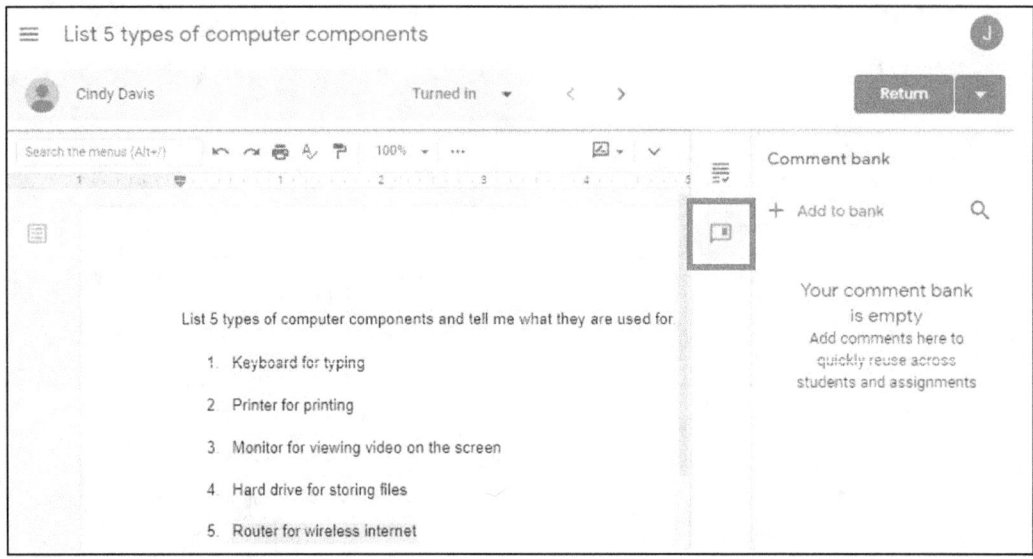

Figure 7.24

I can add one comment at a time or add a bunch of them all at once by typing them in the *Add comment* box and clicking the *Add* button.

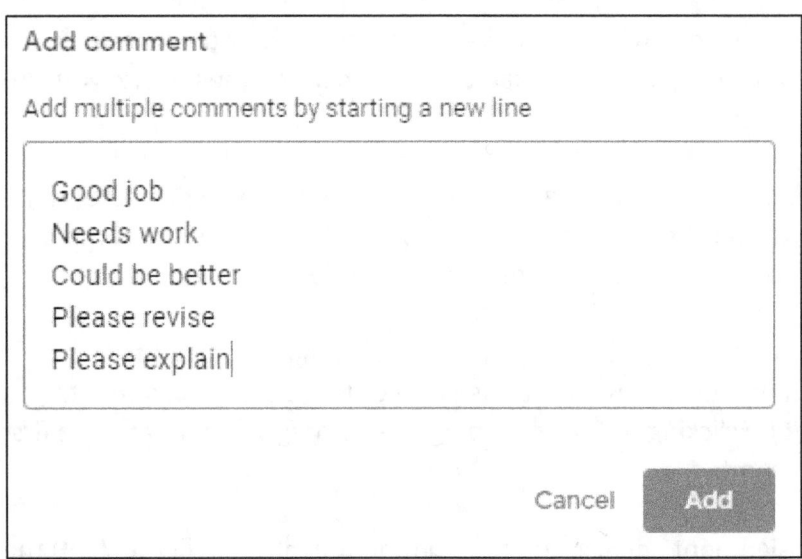

Figure 7.25

Then I can see that my new saved comments are listed in the Comment back section and I can click on one of them at any time to copy, edit or delete them.

Chapter 7 – Additional Features

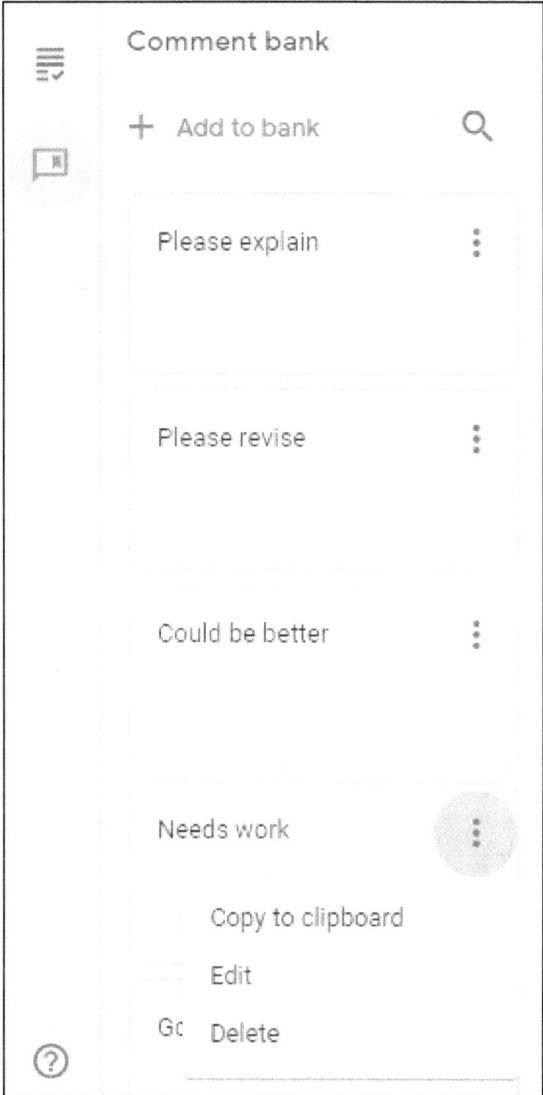

Figure 7.26

To use one of my saved comments I simply need to highlight the area of the document I want to comment on and click on the **+** icon just like I did before. The key here is to type # and then the comment so if I type **#p** it will bring up any stored comments that start with the letter P (figure 7.27) and I can just click on the one I wish to use.

249

Chapter 7 – Additional Features

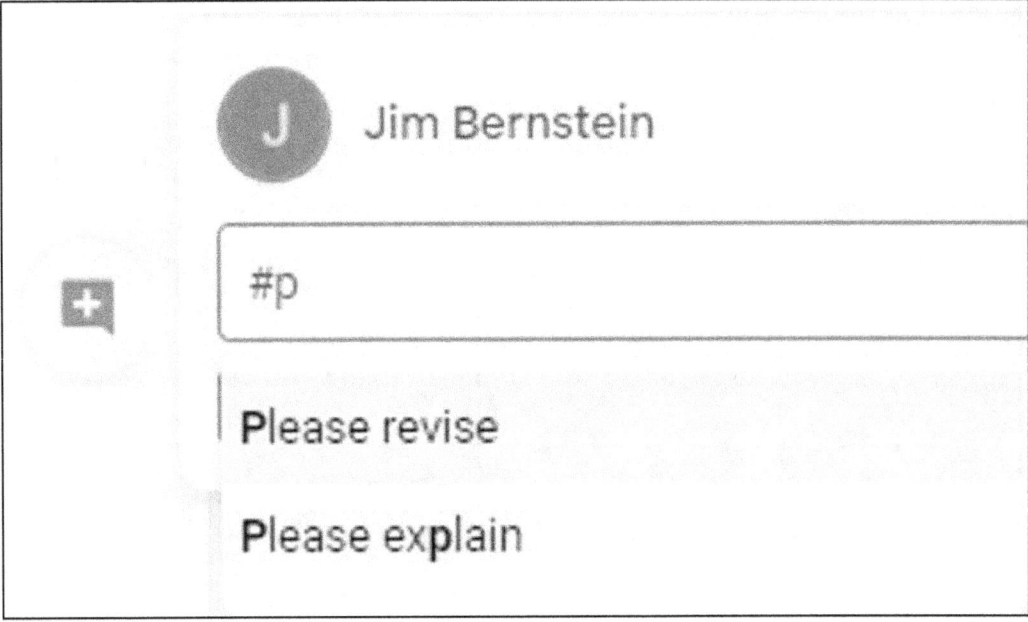

Figure 7.27

If you find a comment that you have already typed previously and want to add it to your Comment bank then all you need to is click on the three vertical dots and choose the *Add to comment bank* option.

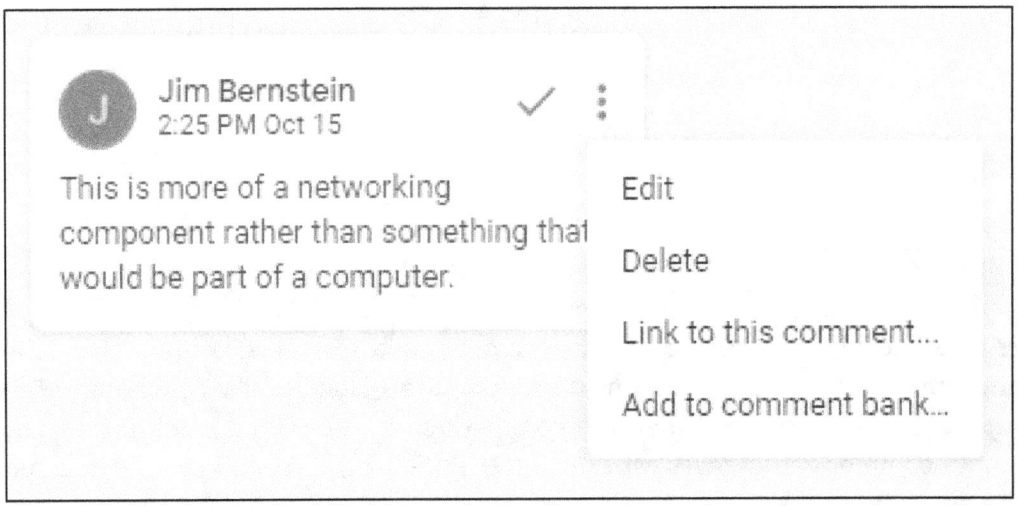

Figure 7.28

Mote Google Chrome Web Browser Extension
One of the best things about the Google Chrome web browser is all the available extensions that can be installed into it in order to increase its functionality. If you

Chapter 7 – Additional Features

go to the Chrome Web Store you can see what's available and even search for any addons you might find useful.

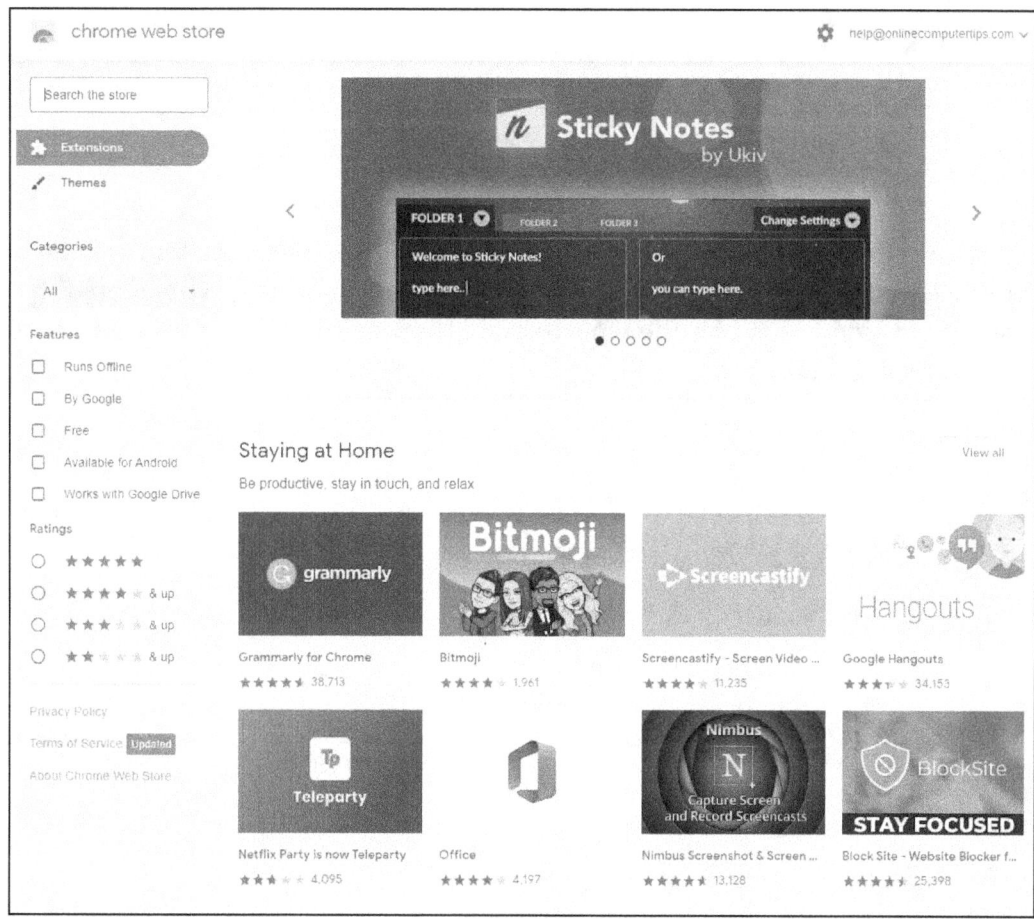

Figure 7.29

One very useful Chrome extension is called **Mote** and what it does is allow you to record and post voice comments within Google Classroom and also within your Google documents, so you don't have to type out long winded comments but rather speak them. Then your students can listen to your voice recording when they click on the play button within the comment section.

Once you find the Mote extension in the Chrome Web Store (*chrome.google.com*) simply click on the *Add to Chrome* button to have it installed. You will then need to sign in and can use your Google account to do so.

Chapter 7 – Additional Features

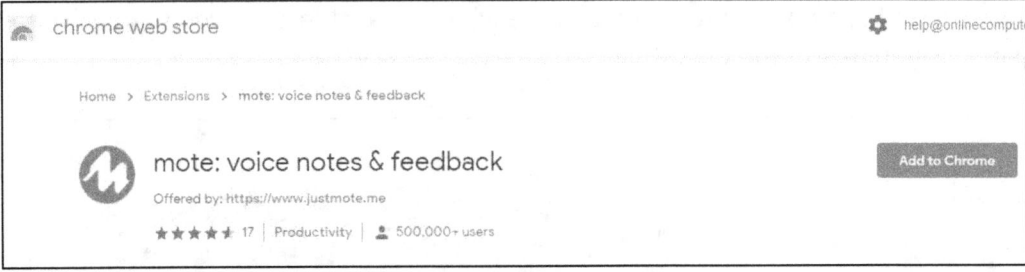

Figure 7.30

Once the Mote extension is installed and you refresh your page you will see a purple M icon in your comment box where you would normally type. From there you would simply click on the icon to start the recording and speak into your microphone. When you are finished recording click on *Done*.

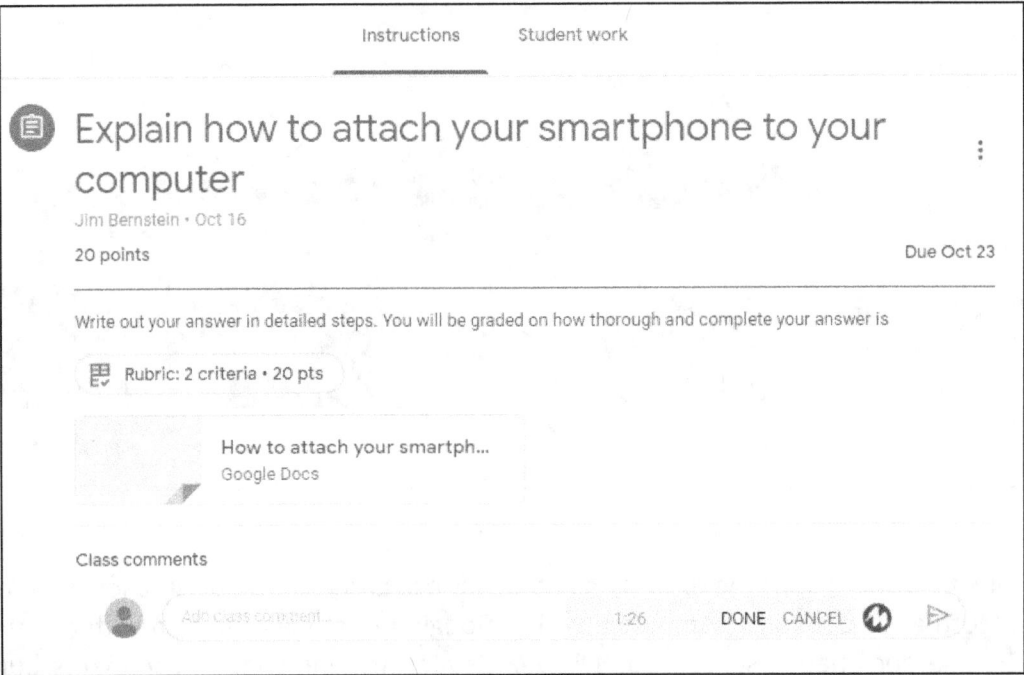

Figure 7.31

Once your recording is complete you would send the message like you would a text based message.

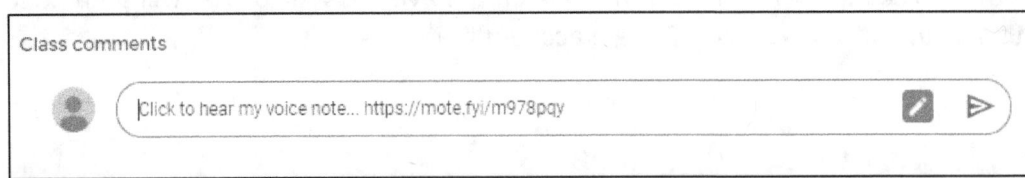

Figure 7.32

Chapter 7 – Additional Features

When the student opens the assignment they will see the voice note that they can click on to play **assuming they have the Mote extension installed in their browser**.

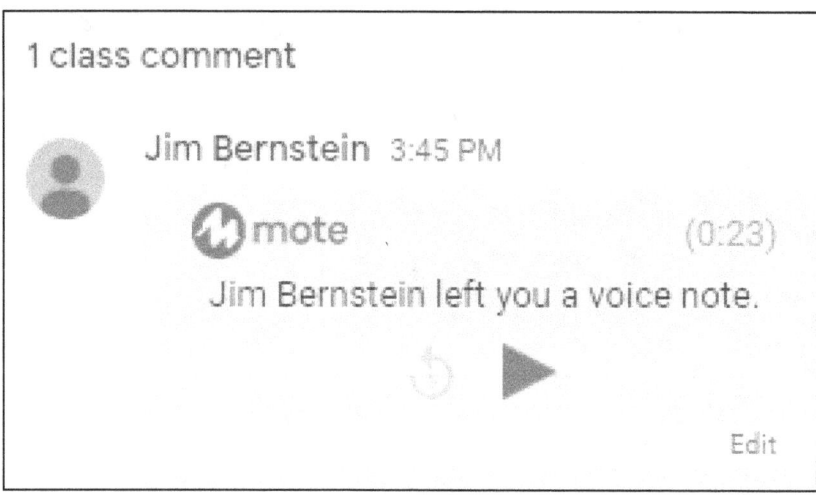

Figure 7.33

If they don't have the extension installed they will see a link to the recording as seen in figure 7.34.

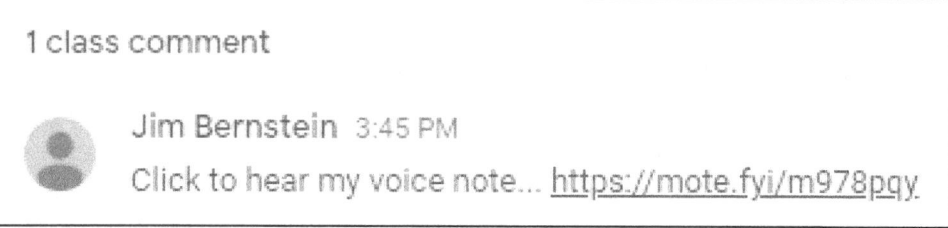

Figure 7.34

Then when they click the link they will be able to play the voice recording and also be given the option to add the Mote extension to their Chrome browser.

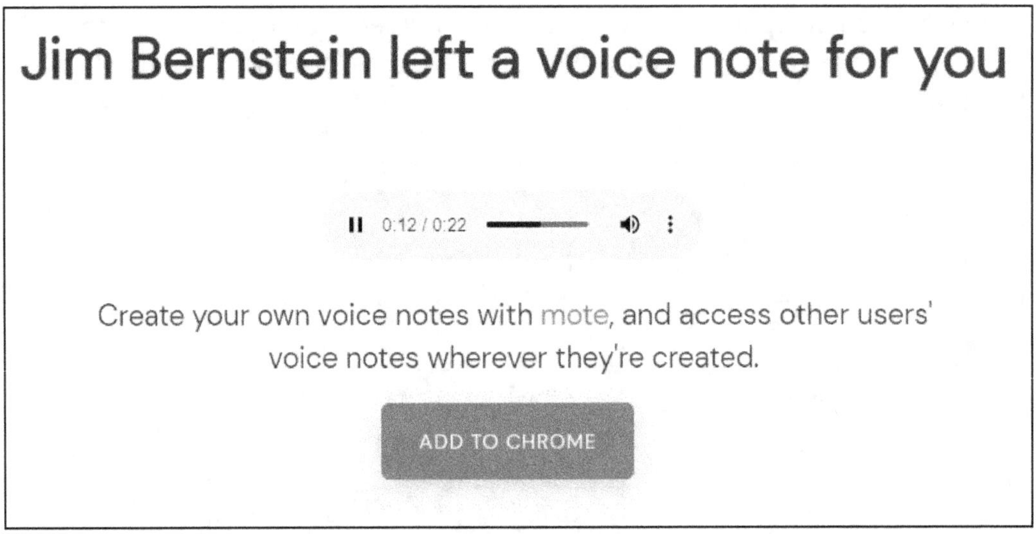

Chapter 7 – Additional Features

Figure 7.35

Mote can also be used within your Google documents to add voice comments where you would normally add text comments.

There are other useful extensions that can help you out with your teaching duty so check out the Web Store to see what's available but just make sure to read the reviews on these extensions to make sure you don't end up with a headache rather than help!

What's Next?

Now that you have read through this book and learned how Google Classroom works and what you can do with the application, you might be wondering what you should do next. Well, that depends on where you want to go. Are you happy with what you have learned, or do you want to further your knowledge of Classroom and its more advanced features or even take the next step and become a certified Google Trainer?

If you do want to expand your knowledge and computers in general, then you can look for some more advanced books on basic computers or focus on a specific technology such as Windows, Google Apps or Microsoft Office, if that's the path you choose to follow. Focus on mastering the basics, and then apply what you have learned when going to more advanced material.

There are many great video resources as well, such as Pluralsight or CBT Nuggets, which offer online subscriptions to training videos of every type imaginable. YouTube is also a great source for instructional videos if you know what to search for.

If you are content in being a proficient Classroom user that knows more than your fellow teachers, then just keep on practicing what you have learned. Don't be afraid to poke around with some of the settings and tools that you normally don't use and see if you can figure out what they do without having to research it since learning by doing is the most effective method to gain new skills.

Thanks for reading **Google Classroom Made Easy**. You can also check out the other books in the Made Easy series for additional computer related information and training. You can get more information on my other books on my Computers Made Easy Book Series website.

https://www.madeeasybookseries.com/

What's Next?

You should also check out my computer tips website, as well as follow it on Facebook to find more information on all kinds of computer topics.

www.onlinecomputertips.com
https://www.facebook.com/OnlineComputerTips/

About the Author

James Bernstein has been working with various companies in the IT field for over 20 years, managing technologies such as SAN and NAS storage, VMware, backups, Windows Servers, Active Directory, DNS, DHCP, Networking, Microsoft Office, Photoshop, Premiere, Exchange, and more.

He has obtained certifications from Microsoft, VMware, CompTIA, ShoreTel, and SNIA, and continues to strive to learn new technologies to further his knowledge on a variety of subjects.

He is also the founder of the website onlinecomputertips.com, which offers its readers valuable information on topics such as Windows, networking, hardware, software, and troubleshooting. James writes much of the content himself and adds new content on a regular basis. The site was started in 2005 and is still going strong today.

www.ingramcontent.com/pod-product-compliance
Lightning Source LLC
Chambersburg PA
CBHW081424220526
45466CB00008B/2267